Also by Samuel G. Freedman

Upon This Rock: The Miracles of a Black Church
Small Victories:
The Real World of a Teacher, Her Students, and Their High School

The Inheritance

How Three Families and the

American Political Majority Moved

from Left to Right

Samuel G. Freedman

A TOUCHSTONE BOOK
Published by Simon & Schuster

TOUCHSTONE
ROCKEFELLER CENTER
1230 AVENUE OF THE AMERICAS
NEW YORK, NY 10020

FIRST TOUCHSTONE EDITION 1998

TOUCHSTONE AND COLOPHON ARE REGISTERED TRADEMARKS
OF SIMON & SCHUSTER INC.
DESIGNED BY LEVAVI & LEVAVI
MANUFACTURED IN THE UNITED STATES OF AMERICA

1   3   5   7   9   10   8   6   4   2

LIBRARY OF CONGRESS CATALOGING-IN-PUBLICATION DATA
FREEDMAN, SAMUEL G.
THE INHERITANCE : HOW THREE FAMILIES AND THE AMERICAN POLITICAL MAJORITY
MOVED FROM LEFT TO RIGHT / SAMUEL G. FREEDMAN.
P.   CM.
INCLUDES BIBLIOGRAPHICAL REFERENCES AND INDEX.
1. WORKING CLASS—UNITED STATES—POLITICAL ACTIVITY—HISTORY—20TH
CENTURY.   2. WORKING CLASS FAMILIES—UNITED STATES—HISTORY—20TH CENTURY—
CASE STUDIES.   3. PARTY AFFILIATION—UNITED STATES—HISTORY—20TH
CENTURY.   4. UNITED STATES—POLITICS AND GOVERNMENT—
20TH CENTURY.   I. TITLE.
HD8076.F69   1996
320.973—DC20   96-21814
CIP
ISBN 0-684-81116-2
0-684-83536-3 (PBK)

Photo Credits

6: U.S. Army; 7: photo by Anthony Vitulli for Westchester County; 16: Sigma Alpha Epsilon, Bucknell University; 18: Chi Sigma Theta, State University at Albany; 19: photo by Anna Lisa Raya.

All other photos courtesy of the families.

Grateful acknowledgment is made for permission to reprint the following:

"(There'll Be Bluebirds Over) The White Cliffs of Dover," words by Nat Burton, music by Walter Kent. Copyright © 1941 Shapiro, Bernstein & Co., Inc., New York and Walter Kent Music, California. Copyright renewed. All Rights outside the United States Controlled by Shapiro, Bernstein & Co., Inc., New York. International Copyright Secured. All Rights Reserved.

To Aaron and Sarah,
Joy in the morning,
And to Barney Karpfinger,
Strength in a real dark night of the soul

Contents

Part Three • Counterrevolution

The Families

Martin Burigo, *emigrated from Italy to New York in 1890, committed suicide in 1910*

SILVIO BURIGO, *his son, a plumber and union officer*

Concelia "Delia" Burigo, *Silvio's wife*

LORRAINE BURIGO, *their daughter, a switchboard operator*

FRANK TROTTA SR., *Lorraine's husband, a janitor in a public housing project*

FRANK TROTTA JR., *their son, a Republican election lawyer*

Mary Elizabeth Sanford, *widow, emigrated from Liverpool to New York City in 1906*

LIZZIE SANFORD GARRETT, *her daughter, a domestic*

Edward Garrett, *Lizzie's husband, a gravedigger*

RICHIE GARRETT, *their son, a gravedigger*

EDITH GARRETT CAREY, *their daughter, a waitress*

CHARLES CAREY, *Edith's husband, a butcher*

TIM CAREY, *Charles and Edith's son, a Republican campaign strategist*

Aleksander Obrycki, *emigrated from Poland to Baltimore in 1895*

JOSEPH OBRYCKI, *his son, a gambler and ward heeler*

Lillian Obrycki, *Joseph's wife*

VILMA OBRYCKI MAEBY, *their daughter, a housewife*

JACK MAEBY, *Vilma's husband, a warehouse manager*

LESLIE MAEBY, *their daughter, a Republican Party staffer*

The
Families

Edward and Lizzie Garrett on an outing at Coney Island in about 1918.

Lizzie Garrett in the 1960s.

Richie Garrett *(right)* in 1972, receiving a check from the U.S. government for turning in a corporate polluter.

Edith Garrett Carey and
daughter Cathy, 1949.

4

5

Charlie Carey, a fireman at seventeen.

6

Tim Carey, basic
training, 1966.

7

Tim Carey being sworn in as a Westchester County
legislator by Peekskill Mayor George Pataki, 1984.

Silvio and Delia Burigo, wedding day, 1924.

Silvio Burigo *(standing, left)* and his plumbers' bowling team.

Frank and Paulie Trotta on Birch Street during World War II.

11

Frank and Lorraine Trotta in front of their home at 33 Birch Street.

12

Frank Jr. with Lorraine and his mentor, State Senator Joseph Pisani.

Frank Jr. and Frank Sr. dressed for work at the Hartley Houses.

13

VOTE FOR

JOSEPH OBRYCKI

Democratic Organization Candidate

FOR CITY COUNCIL

First Councilmanic District

Primary Election

Wednesday, April 12th, 1939

Joe Obrycki's palm card for his 1939
city council campaign.

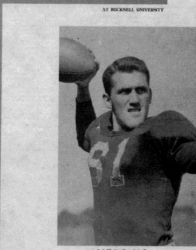

Jack Maeby, starting quaterback
at Bucknell, 1950

RUSH WEEK

AT BUCKNELL UNIVERSITY

Jack Maeby, One of the Boys

PUBLISHED BY SIGMA ALPHA EPSILON

Vilma and Jack Maeby at their
daughter Colleen's wedding, 1976.

Leslie Maeby, as one of the
cheerleaders who became the
Field Girls.

17

18

Leslie Maeby in Chi Sigma Theta
at SUNY, 1973.

Frank Trotta, Leslie Maeby, and Tim Carey on May 18, 1996, at the Crystal
Bay Restaurant in Peekskill.

Foreword

Three generations passed between the morning in March 1933 when Franklin Roosevelt was sworn in as president of the United States and the evening in November 1994 when the Republican Party swept into control of Congress. These events demark the New Deal dynasty, the age of Democratic leadership and liberal dominance. And in its rise and fall alike, that dynasty defines the American Century.

This book is the saga of three families and their journey across those three generations. It is the chronicle of how they made and unmade the Democratic majority and so wrought history. It starts with a plumber, a domestic, and a ward heeler, all the children of immigrants and all ardent Democrats. It ends with their grandchildren, college friends turned political comrades, each one a Republican.

These families are not famous and yet they are emblematic. For in their migration from the party of Roosevelt and Truman to the party of Reagan and Gingrich, in their estrangement from the welfare state that once had sustained them, they represent voters by the millions—the vast shifting middle of American politics.

The center is filled with former Democrats and the wavering faithful. Some are southern evangelicals, gone from their dirt farms and mill towns to the valleys of California. Some are working-class

Jews, drifting from their liberal cousins in the suburbs. And many, perhaps most, are blue-collar Catholics, the backbone of auto factories, construction crews, and police departments. It was they who wrested citizenship from a nativist nation, rose from privation into the middle class, and swung the pendulum of ideology from left to right.

For all their importance, few groups of voters have been so stripped of depth and complexity, even by the politicians who court their support. They have been ridiculed in the form of Archie Bunker, the bigoted blowhard of television fame. They have been labeled Middle America, The Silent Majority, Joe Six-Pack, and Reagan Democrats. They have been reduced to digits in opinion polls, answers in focus groups, and buzzwords in campaign commercials.

Four years ago I set about searching for the names, faces, and lives behind the facile phrases. I believed there was more to voting than mere reflex, the twitch of muscle. I believed that politics was not a soliloquy but a conversation, a dialogue between candidate and citizen, theory and experience. And in the experience of three families, I was convinced, I could comprehend the realignment of a nation.

My search eventually led to a group of students who gathered in an attic in Albany, New York, in the early 1970s. They belonged to the College Republicans and called themselves the State Street Gang in honor of their headquarters. They were Italian and Polish, Norwegian and Jewish, Irish and German. They were the children of a butcher, a janitor, a carpenter, a warehouse manager, a scrap-metal dealer, and a farmer who doubled driving a school bus—of parents, in most instances, of unshakable Democratic loyalty.

Three members of the State Street Gang emerged in particular, for their families had not simply voted Democratic but had acted on those beliefs in direct ways. Frank Trotta was the grandson of a plumber, Silvio Burigo, a union man of such devotion that a labor hall just outside New York City bore his name. Tim Carey was the grandson of a domestic, Lizzie Garrett, the vocal leader of a shanty-Irish enclave in a factory town along the Hudson. Leslie Maeby was the granddaughter of a ward heeler, Joseph Obrycki, who bought and bartered whatever votes the Democratic Party needed in his corner of Baltimore.

The Democratic coalition rested on the very pillars those grandparents represented—organized labor, class identity, and big-city bossism. And yet, two generations later, the grandchildren were Republicans toiling the conservative counterrevolution—Tim Carey as a campaign manager, Frank Trotta as an election lawyer, and Leslie Maeby as a fund-raiser.

The annals of politics and power rarely record such names. History remembers presidents and not the voters who elected them. Yet America bears their imprint of obscure hands, the hands even of three families. In their story lies the essence of a century.

Part One

Forged in Fire

Chapter One

Orphan in the New World
(Silvio Burigo)

IN THE WANING DAYS OF JANUARY 1918, SILVIO BURIGO carried an autograph book to his classroom at Public School 85 in the Italian slum of East Harlem. He was fifteen years old, halfway through the ninth grade, and about to conclude his formal education. Silvio had excelled in school, perfecting his spelling and penmanship in particular and aspiring to become a court reporter. But he was an orphan who had spent the last seven years with relatives who were already raising four children of their own. They lived in a fifth-floor walk-up and stored their heating coal in a bathtub, filling it in the summer when Silvio's uncle worked steadily in construction, rationing every lump through the winter when the jobs disappeared. Now it was time for Silvio to make his own way.

During those final afternoons at school, Silvio opened the autograph book for his classmates, who signed their names and occasionally added a doggerel verse. He saved the first page for his teacher, Romeo J. Perretti. "Life is what you make it," Mr. Perretti wrote. "So is success a thing of your making. All that is essential for success in life is ambition and the will power to strive earnestly. For, 'where there's a will, there's a way.' Then strive and you'll succeed."

Silvio literally clung to those words, saving the autograph book as its pages yellowed and its binding cracked. Even at fifteen he understood he would require ambition and will to subsist, much less to succeed. Already, he knew much of calamity and dislocation; already, he had seen his own birthright vanish in disaster.

Silvio grew up the second of five children of an immigrant who had done more than well. Within a decade of reaching America in 1890, his father, Martin, owned his own construction company and a home in the New York suburb of New Rochelle. He could afford to dress his children in coats of supple leather to sit for formal portraits. But in 1907, Martin's wife fell ill with tuberculosis. Then his youngest son died at age three, drowning in a rain-filled gutter. Finally, his business faltered. Martin exhausted his savings and lost his house to the bank, but still could not meet his payroll or settle his bills. The only people willing to loan him money were some acquaintances from his hometown of Longarone, who exacted a price in both interest and humiliation. On March 19, 1910, normally the day when Italian Catholics feast to honor St. Joseph, Martin Burigo instead went to his idled construction site, looped a rope over a beam, and hanged himself.

Burdened even in death by the sin of suicide, Martin was buried in unconsecrated ground at the far edge of a Catholic cemetery, the headstone turned to face an adjoining graveyard for Protestants. His widow scattered the older children among relations and then, taking the baby girl of the family with her, returned to Italy to die. Silvio never spoke of the circumstances of his father's death; years later his children overheard a conversation among neighbors about the secret. So when it came time for Silvio to start working, he chose a field in which the risks seemed more physical than fiduciary.

A plumber in the Bronx had consented to take him on as a helper. As it was usually practiced, the arrangement hovered between apprenticeship and indentured servitude, but at its end waited a trade and self-sufficiency. Like any novice, Silvio was expected to carry his superior's tools, haul lengths of pipe, batter holes into walls. In return, he could learn how to cut cast iron with a hammer and chisel, wield a hand stock to thread pipes, and pour lead to make "collars" at the joints, with only a handkerchief wound over his fingers for protection. The careless paid dearly, losing an eye to a flying chip of cast iron or searing a limb with molten lead. Silvio absorbed the lessons so well that years later he would become the most demanding instructor of apprentices in his union.

By the early 1920s, he earned the title of mechanic, as a trained plumber was known, and moved just beyond New York City to New Rochelle, where his family had lived in the comfortable years. He took a room with his aunt Virginia in the West End, the burgeoning Italian neighborhood. Coming after East Harlem, with its gasworks, garbage dumps, and contagions, the West End must have seemed a paradise. Wrapped in burlap to survive the American winters, fig trees flourished. Garden plots overflowed with corn and escarole, tomatoes and fava beans. Backyard trellises provided shade all summer and the grapes for homemade wine. The main shopping street, Union Avenue, wide and lined with frame storefronts, masqueraded as a frontier town when a local film studio shot westerns.

A trolley line linked the West End to the downtown district, but most of the Italians rode it only for Christmas shopping and other exceptional occasions. In their own half-mile-square enclave stood a public school named for Christopher Columbus, a Catholic church dedicated to St. Joseph, and mutual-aid societies serving immigrants from several separate regions. Every manner of shop operated within walking distance from home—Marciano's bakery, DiNapoli's stationery, Uzzi's tavern, hardware and dry goods, blacksmiths and butchers, soda fountains and funeral parlors, even Zito the druggist with his patent medicines and leeches.

Of course, the gentry regarded the West End and its inhabitants with rather less affection. Their New Rochelle claimed descent from the Huguenots of La Rochelle, France, and counted among its early residents Thomas Paine. It stretched lazily northward from nine miles of shore along Long Island Sound, sending its executives and salarymen to Manhattan by way of the New Haven Railroad and the Boston & Westchester, more colloquially known as "the millionaires' line." Indeed, by the 1920s, the decade when Silvio arrived, New Rochelle boasted the highest per capita income in New York State and the third highest in the nation. That money could be measured in yacht clubs, golf courses, bridle trails, and associations for art, music, history, and gardening—all in a city of only 46,000. *Scientific American* devoted a cover article to the architecture of New Rochelle, printing the floor plans for a three-bedroom home with library, parlor, and Tiffany-brick fireplace, which the magazine called a "cottage." Compared to the villas in Tudor and Tuscan styles, the Beaux Arts edifices downtown, and the thirty-nine-room American Gothic mansion named Sans Souci, it actually did qualify as modest. As a critic for the *Architectural Record* opined in 1909, "There is thus every natural and hereditary reason why New Rochelle should be a thoroughly charming suburb, a place to which the commuter should repair with particular alacrity after his day's work was done . . . and to which he should hie for his weekend with glad relief."

The conditional "should" had to do with immigrants; the author decried the presence of a "Ghetto" near the train station, alluding to an area of Italian and Jewish shops, and berated one bank for not maintaining "more dignity and self-respect . . . than can be exacted [sic] of a hustling Yiddish store keeper." In 1905, with the foreign-born population approaching one-third of New Rochelle's total, the city council found it necessary to pass an ordinance regulating tenements. Two years later the Italian community held its first Columbus Day parade, a public declaration of growth and permanence.

The first Italians had arrived in New Rochelle thirty years earlier as itinerants, intending to earn dollars laying railroad track, digging trenches, and quarrying stone and then return to families left behind in the Mezzogiorno. A few hundred stayed, settling in shanties beside the rail lines in the hills west of downtown. It was there that New Rochelle's Little Italy developed, filling with tradesmen and plain laborers alike, fitting three or four generations of one family into a single flat, and exciting no small anxiety among the Protestant elite. The status of Italians in the affluent suburbs ringing New York had been ranked and quantified in the 1890s, when the contractor then building the second Croton Reservoir compiled a list of daily wages:

Intelligent labor	$1.50 to 1.60
Common labor, white	1.30 to 1.50
Common labor, colored	1.25 to 1.40
Common labor, Italian	1.15 to 1.25

In New Rochelle, the wealthy chose the "colored" to work inside their homes, while restricting Italians to the perimeter. Italians cleaned the stables and dug the earth, hauled garbage from estates by horse-drawn wagon, and rowed into the Sound to collect rubbish from pleasure boats. The vegetable gardens Italians tended after work represented less a hobby than a means of survival. So, too, did their livestock—chickens, goats, cows, and so many swine that one street became known as Pig Shit Alley. More than a few parents sent their children of Silvio's generation down to the rail yard to collect chunks of coal that had tumbled from freight cars.

There were abundant jobs in construction that paid decent wages. During the most bustling months of the Roaring Twenties, as much as $1.5 million worth of construction proceeded in New Rochelle. The local newspaper, the *Standard-Star,* reported in 1927 that New Rochelle ranked fifth among American cities in per capita spending on construction. But for an Italian immigrant, however skilled, a reliable paycheck required demeaning compromises.

Well into the 1920s the Irish so dominated the building-trades unions around New Rochelle that few Italians even applied for entrance. Those who did found the price of admission their identity. The plumber Carlo Tomasino gained his union card as Carl Thomas; one carpenter went from Millenardi to Miller. Even after the Italians wedged themselves into the locals—as plumbers, laborers, hod carriers, masons, carpenters, electricians, and tile setters—they had to pay political tribute to obtain the most lucrative work. Those jobs, which were on large public projects like schools, flowed through a municipal government dominated by Republicans.

The precinct captains in the West End were Republicans of German extraction, holdovers from the days when the neighborhood was known as Dutch Hill, and so were many of the largest contractors. Often, a foreman doubled as a ward heeler, the better to ensure compliance from his underlings on Election Day. Few of the Italian immigrants had yet become fluent in English, so they were taught to look on their ballot for the Republican insignia, an eagle. *"Votare a gallina,"* a complicit countryman would say, explaining the logo in more familiar terms. "Vote the chicken."

Such allegiance was hardly limited to New Rochelle's West End. At the presidential level, urban America had voted steadily for Republicans from 1896 through 1924. As the party of Yankees and bankers, the GOP did not exactly court the immigrant, ethnic constituency. But the Democratic Party was too paralyzed by an internal split to afford an alternative. At the local level, Catholic and Jewish immigrants sustained urban Democratic machines. Yet the national party, under the leadership of William Jennings Bryan, actively abhorred such voters. As an agrarian populist and fundamentalist Protestant, Bryan doubly alienated the cities' masses. In practical terms, he stood between them and political power. During the 1924 Democratic convention the Bryan forces not only denied the presidential nomination to Al Smith, an Irish Catholic, but also defeated a resolution condemning the Ku Klux Klan. And when the spectators at New York's Madison Square later booed the Great Commoner in mid-oration, he retorted, "You do not represent the future of our country."

• • •

Into the West End's nearly feudal society, a new world that in disquieting ways resembled the old one of peasants and padroni, strode Silvio Burigo, a man not inclined toward obeisance. Barely into his twenties, he made a dramatic physical impression. He was lean through the torso, muscular across the shoulders, and possessed of an especially intense face—widow's peak, cleft chin, crystal blue eyes gleaming from dark, deep sockets. Already a master of much of his trade, he impressed other plumbers with his exactitude, his mechanical skills, and the dexterity under pressure they called "good hands." When he was initiated into Local 86 of the United Association of Journeymen Plumbers and Steam Fitters on February 28, 1924, receiving card number 228915, he counted among its first handful of Italian members. Only four years later he earned the position of plumbing foreman on a vast, year-long job, the construction of a junior high school so ambitious in design that the *Standard-Star* hailed it as "a modern castle for gallant knights searching for knowledge." Even on the baseball field, in the Yankee-style pinstripes of the Union Social and Athletic Club's nine, Silvio both played and managed.

His charisma served him well on the dance floor, too, and Silvio enjoyed some choice in young ladies. But he discovered his future wife on a different sort of floor entirely. One afternoon in early 1924, Silvio went to the home of Martinetti the butcher, perhaps to install a fixture. As he entered the front hall he came upon a young woman down on all fours, taking scrub brush to hardwood. The angle afforded Silvio a long, favorable gaze at her bust. Her name, he soon learned, was Concelia Girone, and friends called her Delia, and she was boarding with the Martinettis, her relatives. Delia had creamy skin, warm eyes, a flapper's insouciant style, and, perhaps most important, a background as turbulent as her suitor's own. She had lost her mother in childbirth and spent her youth being shuffled from orphanage to foster home to extended family. In Silvio, friends said, she responded even more to security than to love. But there must have been much love as well, for the two were in such a hurry to wed that they stealthily arranged a civil ceremony on April 9, 1924, fully three months before a priest married them in St. Joseph's and they could actually begin living together.

The couple held their reception nearby in the North Italy Society hall. The Workingman's Mutual Aid Society of Northern Italy, as it was formally known, was one of the key institutions in Silvio's public life, one of the arenas for his idealism. The society traced its history to an earlier agency that Martin Burigo had helped found to assist immigrants from the vicinity of Belluno, a city located about halfway between Venice and the Austrian border. For the first nineteen years after its creation in 1909, the North Italy Society occupied a converted barn on the northern fringe of the West End. Then its members began building a home more commensurate with their commitment. The effort consumed every weekend for nearly three years and progressed in spite of the onset of the Great Depression. Some in overalls and caps, others in suit coats and fedoras, several dozen volunteers posed on the site for a group portrait. An inscription announced: "Through sacrifice and forebearance [sic], and with the untiring leadership of the committee, we have completed our new desired clubhouse."

The structure was made of stone, steel, and brick, all fitted into a two-story shell as sturdy as an armory's. From room to room each group of tradesmen tried to outdo the others with its contribution. The iron-workers fashioned six chandeliers, each two feet in diameter, for the main ballroom. The plasterers shaped molding in geometric patterns and decorated the stage's proscenium with bas-relief roses. The plumbers and tile setters collaborated on a shower room, which may well have been the most appreciated donation of all. In a neighborhood with limited indoor plumbing, a neighborhood whose men trudged home from work covered with mud, dust, oil, and grease, a shower rated as a luxury. Clad in filthy khakis, carrying clean underwear and a fresh shirt in a paper sack, the men who were bound for the shower room often joked, "I'm goin' to church."

Over the decades Silvio served the North Italy Society as treasurer, secretary, cook, and part-time bartender. As the latter roles attest, the society largely operated as a social club. It offered a place to play bocce, sip grappa, eat a plate of polenta and shredded rabbit, and down the herbal extract called *fernet* for good health. The society also mediated between generations and between continents. The favorite card game gradually shifted from *briscola* to gin rummy. A dance usually featured two bands, one playing the tarantella and mazurka on accordion and mandolin, the other fox trots. The commemorative program for such affairs contained not only the predictable advertisements from neighborhood merchants, many written in Italian, but also appeals from political candidates, especially Republicans. So great remained the fear of retribution that anyone who placed an ad for the Democratic slate signed it simply "A Friend."

What the North Italy Society and its like in cities across America (from the Czech *sokol* to the Jewish *landsmanshaftn*) brought to politics was the very notion of mutual assistance, available not only during times of tragedy but as a hedge against them. Implicitly, these efforts assailed relief as it was then practiced, whether in the person of a condescending "Lady Bountiful" from a private charity or a suspicious inspector from city hall. Few phrases stirred such dread among the West End's Italians as "going to see Jim Canty," the Canty in question being New Rochelle's welfare director.

For a few cents a week the North Italy Society sold its members burial insurance. These policies banished the fears of so many immigrants that they would be interred like paupers in a potter's field or that the cost of a decent funeral would leave their survivors destitute. Since seasonal layoffs and severe injuries often afflicted construction workers, the society developed its own system of financial support, a sort of precursor to unemployment insurance and workmen's compensation. It was called *La Festa Della Raccòlta,* the Harvest Celebration. For the occasion, wire was strung high above the ballroom floor. From the wire dangled hams, sausages, and candies solicited from local shopkeepers, and vegetables and fruits grown in family gardens. As a couple danced, the man would lift his partner to snatch an item. In well-scripted fashion, the pair would always be caught, sent to a corner of the room cordoned by chicken wire and called "jail," and forced to pay a "fine" to get out and keep the food. A nickel Hershey bar, for instance, might fetch a fifty-cent price. The evening's take, which amounted to hundreds of dollars, would be spread among the community's needy, free of stigma.

Through most of the 1920s, the years Silvio Burigo built both a career and a family, he never needed such assistance himself. He was a union man. He carried his card. He paid his dues. Every Tuesday evening he drove to the Labor Hall in Mount Vernon, an adjoining city, for the regular meeting of Local 86. On foul nights Delia would follow him from the kitchen table to the front door, saying, "You're crazy, you're crazy. You'll be the only one there." To which Silvio always replied, "I want to go. It's my union."

What small luxuries Silvio had accumulated—his radio, his used car, his bowler and spats—he attributed to the union. In the boom year of 1927, when more than 1,200 homes went up in New Rochelle, Local 86 won a wage of $1.50 per hour and a forty-four-hour week. The national union offered sickness, death, and strike benefits, almost boastfully listing the recipients in each issue of its monthly magazine. The individual amounts remained moderate, rarely rising above $65 per month for the ill and a lump sum of $500 for the bereaved, but these measures anticipated elements of the New Deal's social compact. The United Association even created a lexicon of its own, meant to instill dignity and worth, in which every member was addressed as "Dear Sir and Brother." Here, indeed, was an orphan's family.

Protection mattered perhaps more than money. As part of a union, Silvio did not need to grovel for a job, bribing contractors with a cut of his pay or Republican leaders with his vote. It seemed no accident that the nascent Democratic movement in the West End arose from organized labor. One of the movement's leaders was Salvatore Tocci, ultimately the president of a local representing construction laborers and at this time the captain of the baseball team Silvio managed. As a Catholic from immigrant stock, as well as a unionist, Tocci typified the new breed of Democrat. From such humble bases as the West End and Local 86 and the North Italy Society, these insurgents were seizing power from the nativists who had dominated their party since the late 1800s.

Their ascent was less a function of strategy than of numbers. Some twenty-five million immigrants reached America between 1880 and 1924, the preponderance of them Jewish and Catholic. As early as 1910 the bulk of schoolchildren in thirty-seven different cities had foreign-born fathers. Petitions for naturalization, and with it the right to vote, rose from about 55,000 per year as the century began to 130,000 in the 1910s to 180,000 in the 1920s. By the end of that period, cities accounted for the majority of America's population for the first time ever. And in nominating Al Smith for president in 1928, the Democratic Party decisively turned its vision from the farms to the tenements.

Silvio made a point of never registering for either party. "You don't owe your allegiance to anyone," he later instructed his children. But in the privacy of the voting booth he passed over the chicken for the Democratic star.

• • •

Proud and assertive, yet ultimately moderate, the United Association's personality reflected Silvio's own. The union emerged from an era of strife and violence. It was founded in 1889, three years after the Haymarket bombing in Chicago and three years before the massacre of striking steelworkers by Pinkerton's in Homestead, Pennsylvania. Nearly half of the delegates at the union's first convention hailed from the radical Knights of Labor. But from the very outset the United Association steered wide of socialism, anarchism, and class struggle, arguing instead for the same goal as the New Deal and much postwar liberalism later would— a fairer version of capitalism. "Recognizing the right of the employer or capitalist to control his capital," the union declared in its preamble, "we also claim, and will exercise, the right to control our labor, and be consulted in determining the price paid for it." The objective, then, was not to upheave the industrial order but to more fully share in its bounty, to "secure . . . for ourselves and our children, a steady demand and fair compensation for our toil, and a position in society to which as wealth-producers and citizens we are justly entitled."

The union realized its power rested, paradoxically, in simultaneously building membership and restricting it. The control valve was the system of admitting apprentices and training them to become journeymen. As the United Association's president, P. J. Quinlan, put it in a speech to the union's second convention: "The number of apprentices should be limited, and it is a well-known fact that in many of the cities the boys outnumber the men. In case of [strike] trouble, the bosses, with the assistance of these boys could get along comfortably well, even if there was not the polish and finish on it [the work] that it would receive from the journeyman; hence the necessity of controlling this matter."

The apprenticeship system grew into an educational program replete with schools, courses of study, and standardized tests. Silvio himself would spend years teaching in Local 86's training program and judging national competitions between student plumbers. Apprenticeship, he believed, guaranteed quality control.

And it all but guaranteed an insular quality to the United Association's locals. Fathers brought in sons; uncles brought in nephews; brothers brought in brothers. Gradually a local might evolve from being the bastion of one ethnic group to another, just as Local 86 had shifted over the generations from German to Irish dominance, and during Silvio's lifetime would assume an Italian character. The men Silvio worked alongside in the union were his card partners in the North Italy Society and his neighbors in the West End. All this homogeneity never struck them as being anything but logical. Why shouldn't a son want to follow his father? Why shouldn't a father help him out?

The outside world, after all, bristled with hostility. Herbert Hoover buried Al Smith, one of organized labor's greatest allies, in the 1928 election. Although Local 86 grew during the 1920s, union membership nationally plummeted throughout the decade, as both government and industry abandoned the informal détente they had maintained with labor during World War I. Congress refused to extend federal protection to collective bargaining. Private business attacked unions with weapons as subtle as "The American Plan," a suave public relations campaign, and as blunt as spies, strikebreakers, and armed industrial detectives. While the bloodiest labor wars occurred in the mining regions of West Virginia and Idaho, the specter of personal dispossession haunted the plumbers of Local 86. They told and retold the story of the hatters who had struck in Danbury, Connecticut, in 1908. A judge had ruled that their homes could be seized to satisfy a judgment against the union; seven years later, pressing a boycott against a manufacturer, members were ordered to pay $252,000 in damages.

When the Great Depression descended, that particular fear was rendered irrelevant. To go on strike, you needed to have a job. In a growing city like New Rochelle, its economy driven by construction, the jobs disappeared. The money spent annually in the building trades dropped from $11.2 million in 1927 to $757,000 in 1932. Put another way, for every dollar that poured into salaries or materials in 1927, less than seven cents trickled through in 1932.

This drought, as real as the one that was turning wheat fields into the Dust Bowl, struck households, stores, local government, and New Rochelle's very aura of self-congratulatory affluence. By the time Franklin Roosevelt was running against Herbert Hoover, nearly 15 percent of the eight hundred stores in town were sitting vacant and an identical proportion of the municipal budget was being directed into relief— $793,000 compared to $25,000 less than a decade earlier. The city carried out mass layoffs in May 1932 and defaulted on $1 million in short-term notes that had been sold the previous winter to pay teachers, police officers, firefighters, and other public employees.

Around the West End, the most fortunate men, relatively speaking, found manual labor at a fraction of their former wages. Silvio's younger brother Jimmy, for instance, went from being an electrician to a gardener. Others stood in line for soup at St. Gabriel's, the Irish church, or took dry food from the Woman's Club. Their children shined shoes, peddled papers, or combed through the city dump for deposit bottles. With so many of its members already jobless, the North Italy Society began to constrain its generosity. When an unemployed tile setter who was blind in one eye applied for membership, he was rejected as a drag on the society's finances. Only begrudgingly did the society later admit him.

Those who turned to the city and its Republican officials for welfare had to accept with it punishing indignities. Relief often took the form of vouchers for clothing, and every recipient got the same stock items from the same one or two stores, making each ward as visible as a newly released convict in a prison-issue suit. Caseworkers turned home visits into little inquisitions. A friend of the Burigos had an inspector rummage through her groceries, making sure none were lavish, and then pointed a finger at the family radio, saying, "You're wasting electricity running that." Finally, learning the client had relatives who were working, the woman asked, "Why can't they help you out?"

For union members like Silvio, the Great Depression became a test of faith. Nationally, the United Association saw its membership plummet from 60,000 to 26,000 in the four years after the stock market crash. The union did not even bother to hold a convention from 1929 until 1938. Paying out about $300,000 per year in benefits while income from dues fell because of resignations and prolonged unemployment, the United Association itself started to worry about going broke.

In the West End, as elsewhere, many tradesmen betrayed their unions by taking off-the-books work. There was always a crowd of masons, carpenters, and others milling around Edwards Grocery in the morning, waiting for a builder to drive up and make an offer. "My kids are not gonna starve," they would say. Silvio went instead to the union hall in Mount Vernon, joining in pinochle and poker until noon came and hope left. On the rare occasions when a contractor did appear, the plumbers would "shape up," stand in ranks for inspection. Whatever the weather, certain men wore fedoras, and from the hatband peeked out the red, sulfurous head of a matchstick. That bit of rakish fashion promised a kickback.

Silvio knew as much temptation to break ranks as anyone else. He and Delia already had two children—Silvio Jr., known as Seely, born in 1925, and Lorraine, born in 1928 and later to become Frank Trotta's mother. They were letting an apartment from Delia's relatives, the Martinettis, so it was a matter of familial obligation to make the rent. As Martin Burigo's son, Silvio understood the consequences of failing to meet one's obligations.

Every time Local 86 shaped up, however, Silvio went hatless. Offered plumbing jobs outside the union, he refused, and for the rest of his life railed against the traitors who accepted. But neither did Silvio consider relief. "I'm not gonna take bread from the government," he insisted. "I'm not that desperate." He endured the early years of the Depression, the Herbert Hoover years, by working as a night watchman on a construction site. It was a job, he told Delia, "nobody else wanted." And with the skills that would later serve him as treasurer of Local 86 and bookkeeper for the North Italy Society, Silvio accounted for every cent of his paltry pay.

The household ran on $10 a week. Two sets of clothes had to last each child a year. Christmas presents came from the Salvation Army. A splurge was a bottle of root beer on a Sunday afternoon. Silvio's children were never reduced to scavenging coal from the freight yard or bottles from the dump, but if they wanted an ice-cream bar they had to search the gutters for a Good Humor stick that was part of a two-for-one promotion.

The strain of financial struggle showed most clearly in Silvio's marriage. It was not simply frugality that made him lord of the family purse; he was the sort of man who opposed the creation of a women's auxiliary to the North Italy Society. He believed in routine, in dinner on the table the same time every night. Delia was a rebel, an iconoclast. Instead of cooking, she read tea leaves and told fortunes in the apartment, dispensing common sense as a kind of placebo. In case Silvio intruded, she set deep pots of water to boil on the stove, hoping the coils of steam would fool him into thinking a meal was imminent.

He was not so easily gulled. "You got your own house," he would scream at Delia's clients. "Get the hell home." Then the real arguing would begin. Silvio and Delia had grown up to embody polar responses to childhoods of family tragedy and borderline poverty. He craved stability; she lived for the moment. They could, and did, literally fight over pennies—the coins Delia would lift from Silvio's bureau as he slept, realizing too late that he counted his change before and after retiring.

One summer evening in 1931 or 1932, Silvio walked into the apartment house. At the second-floor landing, he found his children sitting beneath the single hallway light.

"Why?" he asked.

"It's dark inside," they replied. "The lights are out."

Opening the door, Silvio screamed at Delia, "You gotta learn how to save something."

But blaming his wife was too simple. In the Burigo family Silvio took the responsibility for paying the bills. He surely would have known how much he owed the electric company and for how long he had owed it. However ashamed he felt at that moment, Silvio never spoke of it, just as he never spoke of his father's suicide. As skillful and self-possessed as he was, determined as only an orphan could be not to depend upon others who might fail him, Silvio Burigo had just made the same discovery as had tens of millions of Americans. He could not survive the Great Depression without help, help larger than any Local 86 or the North Italy Society could possibly muster, help as large as the president's.

Chapter Two

Liverpool on the Hudson
(Lizzie Sanford Garrett)

As summer yielded to autumn in 1905, Mary Elizabeth Sanford confronted her choices. Her husband, John, a merchant seaman, had just died, leaving her with three children younger than twelve. She was poor, Irish, and Catholic, all conditions that in the English port city of Liverpool guaranteed scorn. With John Sanford's income, the family had managed to rent an apartment in a tenement, placing it above the most indigent Irish, who crammed a dozen to a room in the lodging houses. It had been Mary Elizabeth's vanity to scrub the stoop every morning.

Now, widowed and without means at the age of thirty-six, she could receive assistance only by presenting herself and her sorrows to the relief administrator known as a vestryman. His title deliberately evoked church rather than state, for he evaluated his petitioners less by the criterion of need than of sin. And since Liverpool at the turn of the century felt itself beset by impoverished Irish, there was also the matter of cost to be considered.

Those the vestryman judged to be "deserving" would obtain "outdoor relief," the dole. Those categorized as "undeserving" got "indoor relief," a euphemism for the poorhouse. In all likelihood a jobless mother and three young children would have appeared too expensive to be kept together. Sundering a family was nothing new in Liverpool. There was a separate poorhouse for children.

Even with the most favorable outcome, with her family intact and buoyed by public aid, Mary Elizabeth would have been surrounded by bigotry and violence. When a plague of fungus ruined several successive potato crops in the late 1840s, Irish by the thousands began crossing the water to Liverpool, with Mary Elizabeth's father, Thomas O'Brien, very likely part of the exodus. The London *Times* called the influx "a fetid mass of famine, nakedness and dirt and fever." Deaths by cholera, typhus, and starvation mounted, and so did the English perception of the Irish as drunks, criminals, professional beggars, and drains on the public coffers. It seemed only appropriate that the booking agents for the companies shipping Irish immigrants to America maintained their offices on the Gorée Piazza; the street carried the name of a prison island off the coast of Senegal and had served as the epicenter of England's trade in slaves until abolition.

The years leading up to John Sanford's death had proven especially hostile. From the Protestant districts of Liverpool rose campaigns against what one slogan termed "Romanism, Ritualism, and Infidelity." Led by their trademark fife-and-drum corps, Orange clubs marched to Catholic churches, decrying the "idolatry" of confession, belief in purgatory, and devotion to saints and the Virgin Mother. The Irish responded by calling praises to the pope, singing nationalist anthems, and joining in an escalating series of street battles. Through the first years of the new century, Liverpool convulsed with sectarian warfare.

So Mary Elizabeth had her choices. She could stay in Liverpool and risk the poorhouse, the loss of her children, prejudice, and bloodshed; or she could book steerage for the 3,043 miles to New York. A ticket cost $10, and she had enough money for just one. Her eldest child, Susan, used it to reach New York on October 25, 1905, and moved in immediately with an aunt and uncle. Several months later they sent Mary Elizabeth the fare for herself and the other children—Tommy, the youngest; and eight-year-old Mary Elizabeth, who, like her namesake, went by the nickname of Lizzie. On March 29, 1906, aboard the White Star Line's *Teutonic,* they arrived at Ellis Island.

Reunited, the Sanfords stayed first with their relatives in an area of Manhattan's West Side known as San Juan Hill. Soon after, Mary Elizabeth rented a railroad flat nearby on a treeless block of tenements populated by butchers, dressmakers, and streetcar conductors. With her nearly military passion for spit and polish, Mary Elizabeth scrubbed the light fixtures and emptied the cupboard once each month, washing every last dish. She found work as a chambermaid in a series of hotels while her daughters in turn left school and took a first job at fourteen.

San Juan Hill abounded in such struggles. While it mercifully lacked the notoriety of the Irish slum just to the south, Hell's Kitchen, then in the midst of a savage contest between criminal gangs and railroad police, it was certainly no more prosperous. The Interborough Rapid Transit powerhouse at the far end of West Fifty-ninth Street anchored the neighborhood. At one point, the plant generated more electricity than any other such facility in the world, and the exertions of its turbines and engines could be heard for blocks. Freight tracks ran along the surface of Eleventh Avenue, occasioning the nickname Death Avenue, and the Ninth Avenue El cloaked the street in shadows. So poor was the populace and so threatened by disease that in 1906 the city erected a public bathhouse on Sixty-second Street large enough to accommodate four thousand people each day.

Labor was often brutal. As one newspaper observed: "There are several sorts of power working at the fabric of this Republic—water power, steam power and Irish power. The last works hardest of all." Some of the neighborhood men made their way into Hell's Kitchen to the wharves and slaughterhouses. As New York thrust its elevated trains underground in the early decades of the century, many Irish burrowed beneath rivers as sandhogs or blasted through the stubborn Manhattan schist as rock tunnelers. The IRT powerhouse hired scores of San Juan Hill men to stoke the boilers, unload coal from docked freighters, and oil the massive corpus of machinery. In an atmosphere of oppressive heat and air thick with coal dust, they toiled twelve hours a day, seven days a week, earning one day off every seven weeks. IRT, the revealing joke had it, stood for "Irish Rapid Transit."

As for the women, Mary Elizabeth proved typical. Nearly two-thirds of the Irish women who held jobs, the 1900 census found, worked as domestic servants or laundresses. One newspaper in Ireland warned its female readers that life in America consisted of "slave and scrub and stifle." A Protestant minister, writing in an instructional book for "our Catholic servant girls," suggested they follow the scriptural admonition "Servants, obey in all things your masters." It was one of the verses used a century earlier to concoct a theological defense of black slavery.

The consequences of such an existence could be calibrated precisely. Of the Irish students in New York's public schools in the mid-1910s, one-tenth of one percent graduated from high school. Irish immigrants died of tuberculosis, the signature disease of urban poverty, at a rate greater than that of almost any other national group, a federal analysis of the 1930 census showed. So common was early death that, as one truism put it, you never saw a gray-haired Irishman.

The Sanford family knew all this only too intimately. Mary Elizabeth died of uterine cancer on January 18, 1915, at the age of forty-five. Susan, the eldest daughter, perished with her baby in childbirth only three and a half years later. That left Lizzie, all of twenty-one years old, to preside over a household that had dwindled to herself, her younger brother, and Susan's pet poodle.

Already, though, Lizzie Sanford had shown herself to be a survivor, the heir to her mother's pluck as well as her name. For the three years before Mary Elizabeth's death, Lizzie had worked in a candy factory, putting her pay into the family till. Then, when Lizzie was orphaned, an aunt, known in the extended family as Nanna Walsh, helped her find a position as a maid on Long Island, assuring the girl of bed and board during the week. Somehow, neither drudgery nor obligation hardened Lizzie's spirit. She still had enough of the schoolgirl in her to dash to the El with her bootlaces untied. With the money she saved, Lizzie treated herself to dresses at Wanamaker's, even a squirrel cape. A photograph taken when she was nineteen shows her clad in satin, crowned by a velvet hat with marabou. She was, people said, "a pip."

The young men of the neighborhood noticed. Lizzie, the jest went, had "one boyfriend in the parlor and one in the kitchen." Mary Elizabeth herself had once warned, "Someday you're gonna get killed." For a time Lizzie kept company with a Jewish fellow named Irving, no small show of independence. And years later, after Irving owned three laundries and installed his wife on Riverside Drive, Lizzie would tease her husband, "I should've married *him.*"

The man she did wed, Edward Garrett, was the best friend of yet another of Lizzie's beaus. He was tall, ruddy, and lean, with big hands and a shock of bristly black hair. Around San Juan Hill, he stuck out as one of the first men with a driver's license, delivering fruit by truck and later, during World War I, serving as a colonel's chauffeur. Beside garrulous Lizzie, Edward was quiet, at times even melancholy. His father had died so young that Edward could not remember him. There was a joke in his family that six brothers had to share one suit, and whoever could afford to pay the dry cleaner got to wear it.

Edward donned what was probably the first new suit of his twenty-six years on November 9, 1918, when he and Lizzie uttered their wedding vows. With the armistice signed two days later, they moved into a tenement flat of their own on West Sixty-second Street. Sixteen months later Lizzie gave birth to a daughter, Edith, who would become Tim Carey's mother. A son, Jack, followed in November 1922.

Those children arrived at a historical moment of financial comfort and political possibility, if only by comparison with the cataclysmic first years of the Depression. Edward Garrett worked steadily through the 1920s for a contractor named Kenney, whose business, in all probability, depended on amicable relations with the Tammany Hall Democratic machine. Lizzie moved through a series of jobs—"opening up" a town-house for a rich family returning from winter in Florida and summer in Maine, delivering babies as a practical nurse, and waitressing for the original Oscar at the Waldorf. From one banquet there, apparently for the Democratic Party, she brought home a pin in the shape of a donkey. Another time Jimmy Walker, the flamboyant and felonious mayor, tipped her a hundred dollars.

At home Lizzie instilled values of grit and compassion in her children. Maternal as she looked in her flowered apron and wire-rim glasses, hair drawn up in a bun, she refused to respect gender as a boundary. "If he can do it," went one of her mottoes, "*I* can do it." Others held, "Own up to what you did" and "Tell the truth and shame the devil." Lizzie herself wielded truth as a blunt object. When a neighbor visited with the delicious gossip of a local girl's unwed pregnancy, Lizzie declared, "She isn't the first and she won't be the last. Leave her alone." Another time Edith ran home upset that an elderly woman had hollered at her for wearing shorts she deemed too revealing. Lizzie, who forbade her own children to curse, thundered, "You go out there and tell that old bitch to mind her goddamn business."

For Edith, San Juan Hill was an entrancing and cosmopolitan place. Beneath the El thrived the stores working people could afford—Mandell's Waists and Corsets, Maisel Drugs, Kaskel and Sons Pawn Shop—and a few blocks up Broadway stood Woolworth's, where Lizzie took Edith Christmas shopping. On the sidewalks a German oompah band might play for spare change, or a Jewish vendor peddle rosaries from a pushcart, or a portable carousel offer rides for five cents. Yard to yard went the tinker, chanting, "Sharp knives, fix pots." And, of course, there was the "candy store" to which Lizzie sent Edith with a nickel and her number, as well as a penny for a sweet, gummy "green leaf" so the girl wouldn't tell her father.

Poor as it was, San Juan Hill was no isolated slum. Some of the grandest apartments in Manhattan lined Central Park, two blocks from the Garretts' tenement. The German-Jewish aristocracy built its kingdom just to the north, where "Death Avenue" changed its name to West End. San Juan Hill took its title from the exploits of black soldiers in the Spanish-American War and had been home to a black community since the 1840s. Within three blocks of each other sat a Roman Catholic church staffed by the Paulist Fathers, known for their urban ministry, and Father Divine's Peace Mission.

Edith and Jack found themselves captivated by the sight of black children dancing and singing for the strollers on Broadway, and earning a shower of coins. One night, praying their parents wouldn't happen down the block, they did the same. Not that the Irish kids lacked pleasures. Spring brought the "May Parties" and summer the "June Walks," days of costumes, games, and sweets on the Sheep Meadow in Central Park, run as fund-raisers by various Irish social clubs. Every fall, in loose celebration of a traditional festival called Samhain, they paraded as "ragamuffins." Burnt cork on her face, Edith would waddle through the streets in her mother's old clothes; Edward dressed Jack in his World War I uniform and handed him a bottle filled with tea to look like whiskey.

● ● ●

More than a neighborhood was evolving around the Garretts. So was a political culture, affected by events both proximate and distant. Across the ocean, Ireland wrested its freedom from the detested British, and the surge of nationalism rippled all the way to San Juan Hill, especially to a fraternal lodge on West Sixty-fifth Street. Tara Hall served as the headquarters of Clan na Gael, a secret society founded in 1867 to unify American Fenians. For many of the intervening decades, Clan na Gael devoted itself to supplying guns and money to the Irish Republican Army. But by the mid-1920s it was turning to immigrant causes, most notably organizing what would ultimately become the Transport Workers Union. For a supposedly clandestine group, Clan na Gael assumed a decidedly visible role, publishing its own newspaper and sponsoring the weekly dances known as *ceilidh*. These were the pageants of a hyphenated population, with one floor of Tara Hall spinning to reels and jigs and another shimmying through the Black Bottom.

Day by day, the Irish of San Juan still relied on the Democratic machine. Tammany Hall operated a virtual social-service bureaucracy, endowing the poor with shoes, coal, summer outings, Christmas dinners, and leverage with the landlord and beat cop alike. The machine also pioneered a crude version of that staple of Keynesian economics, deficit spending for public employment. At the turn of the century, Tammany controlled 60,000 municipal jobs with a collective annual payroll of $90 million, most of it kept within the ethnic family. A song of somewhat later vintage described the system thusly:

You go down to see Gilhooley
Gilhooley will see Dooley
Dooley will go down to see O'Shea.

O'Shea will see Regan
Regan will see Keegan
Keegan will go down to see O'Day.

O'Day will see Sweeney
Sweeney will see Feeney
Tomorrow night at Clancy's meetin' hall.

And he'll go see the corker,
The mayor, Jimmy Walker,
And everything will be OK.
You're on the police force,
Everything will be OK.

Tammany Hall exacted its price in more than votes. It expected latitude for graft, fraud, patronage, inefficiency, and such varieties of sin as gambling, prostitution, and opium-smoking. Predictably, good-government reformers inveighed against the machine. More important, Tammany's excesses cost it the obedience of the Jewish immigrants who began streaming into New York in the late 1800s. The Socialist Party drew as much as 30 percent of the Lower East Side's Jewish vote in congressional elections.

Wiser heads, however, recognized the machine's interest in attracting and accommodating the burgeoning Jewish vote. Through the early decades of the 1900s, Tammany diminished its role in vice crime and enacted both antidiscrimination laws and labor reforms that appealed to Jewish voters. The machine cultivated Jewish precinct captains fluent in Yiddish and instructed the Irish holdovers in tolerance. The contemporary ward heeler "eats corned beef and kosher meat with equal nonchalance," George Washington Plunkitt boasted, "and it's all the same to him whether he takes off his hat in church or pulls it over his ears in synagogue."

More than anyone else, Alfred E. Smith personified the historic alliance of the Tammany Hall machine and the Progressive movement, the body and soul of an emergent Democratic coalition. Smith grew up in the very bosom of the machine, the Irish slums along Manhattan's East River docks. Elected to the state legislature in 1903, he demonstrated diligence and rectitude but not great independence. When Tammany fought "the interests," Smith voted with reformers to regulate industries and control utility rates. When Tammany protected its own interests, Smith voted against the reformers who sought female suffrage and primary elections. From the machine's perspective, fighting against a robber baron or a bluestocking satisfied the same venerable formula of Us versus Them.

Then, on the first Saturday of spring in 1911, the Triangle Shirtwaist factory on the Lower East Side caught fire. Some 146 people perished, girls and women mostly, earning wages for their families in the Jewish and Italian slums. Some were burned to death at their sewing machines, others plummeted from a fire escape that collapsed, and still others leaped from the ninth-story ledge in vain hope of survival. What transformed catastrophe to scandal was the revelation that the Triangle's owners had locked the door to a stairway, allegedly to stop workers from pilfering goods. Just two years earlier the company had borne and broken a strike rather than recognize a union.

In the aftermath, Smith chaired a state commission that investigated factory conditions. The panel brought him into direct partnership with the union leader Samuel Gompers and under the influence of social workers such as Frances Perkins, later to become secretary of labor in the Roosevelt cabinet. Within three years, the commission pushed through thirty-six laws governing factory practices from sanitation to child labor to fire prevention. Smith's rhetoric acquired an edge rarely heard from Tammany Hall as he attacked unchecked capitalism as "the caveman's law, the law of the sharpest tooth, the angriest brow, and the greediest maw."

Endorsed by reformers and machine bosses alike, Smith won election as governor in 1918, and held office for eight of the next ten years. During his tenure he relied increasingly for advice on Jews with origins in the Progressive movement, most notably Belle Moskowitz. With her ideas and his political instincts, their alliance produced a bounty of liberal legislation. New York enacted a minimum wage and an eight-hour day for women and children. It raised school aid nearly tenfold and placed waterpower under the control of a public authority. It greatly expanded the system of state parks and put forward bond issues for public works and fire safety in hospitals.

A half century after the Triangle Shirtwaist fire, Frances Perkins would trace the New Deal to the political alliances and social causes it forged. And in the years before Franklin Roosevelt's election, the historian Oscar Handlin writes, it was Al Smith who stood as the "symbol of the capacity of government for progressive action." When he ran for president in 1928, he became the symbol of Lizzie and Edward Garrett, too.

• • •

In the kitchen and the parlor, over dinner and after church, the Garretts talked about Al Smith. He was Irish and Catholic and Democratic; they were Irish and Catholic and Democratic. His arrival would be their arrival. Even eight-year-old Edith, wearing her Smith button and listening to the grown-ups, understood the equation: All those things went together. In fact, she would not encounter an Irish Catholic who voted Republican until 1947. The Garretts had practical reasons, too, to support Smith. Mr. Kenney, Edward's boss at the construction company, had put all his savings into the campaign, and, if the nation operated like the city, his generosity would surely be remembered with some business from the president.

Yet there was always a wary edge to the conversations Edith overheard. For just as Al Smith embodied the most extravagant dreams of people like Edward and Lizzie, he also represented their waking fear of marginality. The Garretts could hardly speak of his candidacy without speaking, too, of the avalanche of opposition that was seeking to crush it. Much of the criticism purported to center on Smith's association with Tammany Hall and his "wet" stand on Prohibition, but neither Lizzie nor Edward doubted the true source. "They'll never let him get elected," they would say with a mixture of disgust and certainty, "because he's Catholic."

Within one week of Smith's nomination, ten million pieces of anti-Catholic literature appeared, under such titles as "Popery in the Public Schools," "Convent Life Unveiled," and "Crimes of the Pope." The Imperial Wizard of the Ku Klux Klan declared Smith must be defeated for "America to remain Protestant" and "the Nordic stock . . . to finish its destiny." Such bias reached into the topmost echelons of American society. A prominent Manhattan attorney, writing an open letter in *The Atlantic Monthly,* cited papal encyclicals to cast doubt on Smith's loyalties. Even as respected a commentator as William Allen White termed Smith's race a challenge to "the whole Puritan civilization, which has built a sturdy, orderly nation."

The attacks against Smith resembled nothing so much as one of Liverpool's "anti-Romanism" campaigns. In the eyes of New York's Irish, Smith was doing battle against all enemies, past and present, at home and abroad. The *Irish World,* the community's newspaper of record, presented Herbert Hoover as the candidate of both the Ku Klux Klan and the British monarchy. One editorial cartoon depicted Hoover as John Bull, replete with a Union Jack vest. Another featured a Klansman smearing mud over the Statue of Liberty, an image that implicitly linked

Irish fortunes to those of other immigrants. In these same editions, the *Irish World* reported admiringly on Mohandas Gandhi's crusade against British rule in India and noted with distress instances of anti-Semitism in America and abroad. With Smith's campaign, it seemed, the Irish-American identity had reached a liberal apogee.

San Juan Hill throbbed with the excitement of Smith's campaign. Two of his largest events took place within minutes of the Garretts' apartment, one a rally at Madison Square Garden and the other a motorcade up Broadway, ending in Central Park. Dispatching its finest orators and most reliable minions, the local Tammany Hall clubhouse pitched as many as twenty or thirty street-corner rallies in a day. The neighborhood literally echoed with Smith's theme song, the Irish immigrant anthem "The Sidewalks of New York."

When it was over, Smith had carried the Fifth Assembly District, which covered San Juan Hill and Hell's Kitchen, by 13,950 to 4,077. His majority, 77 percent, far exceeded the 55 percent he drew citywide in a record turnout. Nationally, however, Smith lost by a staggering margin, partly for the reason that Edward and Lizzie had grimly predicted. Riding the twin crests of prosperity and nativism, Herbert Hoover won forty states to Smith's eight, 444 electoral votes to Smith's 87.

Few landslides, though, ever proved so deceptive, for in defeat Al Smith created what Samuel Lubell would later call a "revolution." Decades of Republican dominance in urban America collapsed in the face of Smith's magnetism for Catholic and Jewish immigrants. The nation's twelve largest cities, which the Democrats had lost by a collective 1.2 million votes in 1924, gave Smith a 38,000-vote margin. In such industrial states as Massachusetts and Michigan, he increased Democratic turnout by roughly 50 percent from the 1924 level for the Democratic and Progressive tickets *combined*. The ultimate beneficiary of Smith's achievements would be Franklin Delano Roosevelt.

The Garretts could hardly foresee such a future. If anything, they felt Smith's defeat even more personally than did most Irish Catholics. Mr. Kenney had emptied his bank account into the campaign and now, without a president to repay favors, his construction company went bankrupt, taking with it Edward's job. Edward had neither a pension nor unemployment insurance to absorb the blow. For several months in 1929, the Garretts actually left the city for an unheated bungalow on the outskirts of Ossining, thirty miles up the Hudson. With winter descending and Lizzie homesick for neighbors and card games, the family returned to San Juan Hill. The stock market had crashed just a few weeks earlier, but the Garretts paid no particular attention. For them, the Depression had been under way for a year, since the day Al Smith lost.

Their latest tenement sat not on a residential cross street but along congested Amsterdam Avenue, and the only windows in their rear apartment looked downhill to the IRT powerhouse. Edward sold his Dodge to pay for groceries, coal, and rent, and, with that money gone, took to bootlegging. Using a flat a few blocks up Amsterdam, trading off day and night shifts with his brother John, he cooked barley and rye purchased legally at a "malt store" into whiskey that sold for twenty-five cents a pint. Sometimes Lizzie sent Edith there with Edward's dinner, and she would knock on the door in code, earning a dime for her daring.

It seemed to Edith that every tenement had its resident bootlegger; if you saw a ceramic swan appear in a particular window you knew someone was open for business. Whatever the proliferation said about Prohibition as a law or the Irish inclination toward liquor, it also suggested just how little legitimate work was available. Along Ninth Avenue young Edith shuddered at scenes that would endure as the classic images of America during the Great Depression—dispossessed families sobbing on the sidewalk beside their piled furniture; men with wise eyes or laborer's muscles reduced to selling apples, each within eyesight of his competition.

By the early 1930s, there were 6,000 such peddlers in New York City and eighty-two breadlines. Scores died of starvation. In Central Park, where Edith had frolicked through May Parties, a shantytown called Hoover Valley now sprawled. Vast public construction projects like the Triborough Bridge halted, and one-third of the city's private manufacturers shut down. Some 1.6 million New Yorkers were taking some form of relief, pushing the city itself toward default. So far had Gotham fallen that several natives of Cameroon sent a donation of $3.77.

And Jimmy Walker, lavish tipper though he was, proved as unequal to the moment as Herbert Hoover. While constituents went hungry, Walker frequented casinos in the company of showgirls, gliding through hard times on a million-dollar slush fund. Only when an investigative committee revealed the secret account, and Walker's removal by Governor Franklin Delano Roosevelt appeared imminent, did he resign. Tammany Hall tumbled from power along with Walker, surrendering the mayoralty in 1933 to a Republican reformer, Fiorello La Guardia, who would hold office for a dozen years.

With the Depression deepening, Edward Garrett scrambled yet again to support his family. Although he no longer owned a car, he remained a skillful driver, and he talked himself into a job chauffeuring the family's landlord. But Lizzie, usually the source of a second income, could not help. She gave birth to a daughter, Helen, in March 1931, and only eight months later became pregnant again, this time with a son, Eddie. By the time Roosevelt was campaigning against Hoover, Edward Garrett had four children younger than thirteen and, with a drop in his landlord's income, no more work as a driver.

Whatever anger or despair Edward felt, he refused to express. The clue to his thoughts came at three o'clock on Sunday afternoons. Lizzie would be in the kitchen cooking dinner by then, and Edward would order quiet from the older children, Edith and Jack. Then he would switch on the Philco radio, light a Camel, and settle into his morris recliner, the one he had inherited from his mother. Father Charles Coughlin was on the air, and dinner would wait until the sermon had ended.

Later in his career Coughlin would evolve into an anti-Semite and an enemy of Franklin Roosevelt. Before turning rightward, however, he had lent his voice and his national radio network to a progressive agenda, born both of scholarship and personal experience. As a seminarian, Coughlin had steeped himself in the Catholic teachings on social justice, from St. Thomas Aquinas's writings on community through Pope Leo XIII's 1891 encyclical advocating industrial reforms; as a young priest, Coughlin had endured a cross-burning from the Ku Klux Klan and pastored a parish filled with jobless autoworkers.

During the early 1930s, the years Edward listened most faithfully to him, Coughlin was expanding his range from the standard denunciations of the Klan and Prohibition to a more thoroughgoing critique of high finance and big industry. He echoed the class politics of populism but, as an urban Catholic himself, shed its nativism and hatred of cities. And when Coughlin assailed the gold standard, a favorite topic, he chose words that seemed designed to stir the Irish communal memory, to conflate the Great Hunger with the Great Depression. America was suffering, he said in one typical broadcast, from a "cursed *famine* of currency money which *blights* our progress and which multiplies *starvation.*" [Italics mine.]

It hardly mattered to Edward or millions of other listeners, the majority of them Irish Catholics, that Coughlin officially maintained neutrality in the 1932 election. They heard all they needed to hear in the priest's maledictions on Hoover. Once Roosevelt took office, Coughlin broke cover. "The New Deal is Christ's Deal!" went one of his slogans. Another declared, "Roosevelt or Ruin!"

But the Garretts had Roosevelt and ruin. By June 1933, Edward had not worked in a year and could not see even the prospect of a job. There was rent to pay and food to buy, and no money for either. So he got hold of a truck and packed what furniture fit, leaving behind an entire living-room set. Lizzie gathered the children and her few little treasures, a collection of cut glass and a matching silver mirror and comb. Then, like East Coast Okies, they drove to a place where they could live for virtually nothing and grow their own food. It was called Crotonville.

• • •

Lizzie Garrett had first made the trip thirty miles north a decade earlier, in the summer of 1923, and in a spirit of joy rather than desperation. Then she was taking her children to the country, to a bungalow her aunt, Nanna Walsh, rented on the Hudson River just within the town border of Ossining. It was a weathered shack without heat, electricity, insulation, or running water, but it sat along a beach known as Mother's Lap, with a view of the Hudson Highlands.

More than 150 similar cabins studded the peninsula, Croton Point, and almost all housed Irish Catholics from New York. There were stevedores and sandhogs, cops and construction workers, people so thoroughly citified that one could give his home address as "double nickels and minute street," and have the rest instantly understand it as the corner of Tenth and Sixty-second. To achieve this paradise, all anyone needed was $75 to lease a plot for the summer and brawn enough to hammer together a hut and dig a hole for the privy. The seasonal migration had begun in about 1910 and, by now, a dance hall, carousel, and hot dog stand had sprung up among the willows.

As Irish Catholics and city dwellers, the summer residents were barely tolerated in Ossining, but there was nothing the town fathers could do. The rentals were legal and the landlord was a large developer. Then late in the summer of 1923 a consortium of black investors from Harlem contracted to buy the 300-acre site and create on the unoccupied portion a bungalow colony for their people.

Within days the Westchester County Park Commission stepped forward with its own proposal. For the same property that the blacks had agreed to pay $500,000, the county offered $360,000. The low bid won. In the next few years the park commission would present its purchase as a victory for recreation, hygiene, regional planning, and any number of other virtues. At the time a local newspaper struck closer at the truth with this headline:

COUNTY BUYS CROTON LAND FOR A PARK
FOILS NEGROES

In the process, the county seized the opportunity to oust the Irish as well. It halted seasonal rentals after the summer of 1925, razing 168 bungalows. In their place the park commission installed a youth camp, which charged as much for one child as entire families had been accustomed to paying, and a tent city with showers and a general store. Each tent, though, could be taken for just a week and only by certain sort of people. "The Park Commission aims to eliminate 'undesirable groups,' " the Ossining *Citizen Sentinel* reported, "and for the present 'only residents of Westchester County should be permitted to rent sites.' "

So the Irish left Croton Point, but they did not leave Ossining. A local speculator named Samstag owned land on a steep hillside rising from the Croton River gorge, about two miles closer to the center of town from the Point. Trappers and traders had first settled the area back in the 1600s, and, more recently, Germans had formed their own ethnic enclave there. Now Samstag, seeing in the displaced Irish a ready clientele, carved up his acreage into pieces forty feet wide by a hundred deep, and offered them for as little as $300. For good measure, he purchased the old hot dog stand from Croton Point, hauled it uphill, and sold it as a bungalow.

Ever the matriarch, Nanna Walsh bought three lots, one for herself and one each for her two daughters. Lizzie, who accompanied her that day in 1925, put $5 down on a $500 plot. At the time, with Edward working steadily in construction, the couple planned to build a summer cottage, a refuge from the heat and racket of New York's streets.

Being a conservative man in matters of money, Edward decreed they would start building only after paying off Samstag. Within a year they did so. Even then, the Garretts would construct only what they had cash on hand to afford and would perform most of the work themselves, down to nailing together ladders from scrap wood. Over time Edward felled the locusts and hemlocks, sparing one apple tree for the future front yard. He wrenched so many chunks of granite and gneiss out of the soil that folks nicknamed him Eddie Rock. When the Kenney company took a long-term job on a nearby bridge Edward earned enough to buy wood for the floor and frame, and canvas tarp for the roof. By the summer of 1927, the Garretts had four rooms and a porch, all lit by oil lamps. They had neighbors from the Point and San Juan Hill, Ennis and Bale, Reynolds and Doyle, Thomas and Truss. Eventually, six hundred people settled on the slope, and Crotonville was born.

The county park on Croton Point was open by then, and it was a glorious place, with bathhouses, concession stands, and a cleanly swept, curving beach. Nearly 300,000 people flocked to the park that summer, but not the Irish Catholics of Crotonville. They kept to their own beach, along the Croton River instead of the Hudson, at the foot of Samstag's hill. They knew where they were hated and by whom. "Hell's Kitchen," the well-to-do of Ossining called Crotonville. The summer Irish were *"those* people" or, in direct conversation, "you people from the hills." Well into the 1990s, an Ossining matron could say without hesitation, "They're so . . . so . . . so *inbred."*

These class antagonisms, which would figure so importantly in Ossining during the Great Depression and beyond, had been gestating for nearly a century. Ossining may have imagined itself as prosperous and refined, like its Westchester cousins Bronxville and New Rochelle, but it was really a factory town with pretensions of grandeur. It sat beside a river port on a major railroad line, doubly bound to New York City, and its terrain of hills and ravines hardly allowed for sprawling estates.

Ossining developed instead into what one lifelong resident diplomatically termed a "sectional town." Down by the river, near the Sing Sing penitentiary, gathered the blacks. The Italians occupied the slopes of a nearby hollow. Although many of their families had come to Ossining as far back as the 1830s to build the first Croton Dam, they were still regarded as aliens, their neighborhood derided as "Guinea Gulch." Just north of there began the original Irish quarter, supplying labor for the quarries, the railroad, and the prison.

Above them all, topographically and otherwise, perched the elite of a district called Chilmark. They were not notably rich, certainly not by Westchester standards, but they affected the manner. Instead of public parks and public schools, they favored the Ivy Club with its swimming pool and four private academies. They mounted operettas downtown at the Victoria Theater and sponsored white-glove dances on Fridays for their young people. To gain entrance to Chilmark one needed more than money; by covenant, residence was restricted to "Caucasian Christians."

The local government, long controlled by Republicans, held a similar goal. In 1930, Ossining adopted a long-range "master plan," which within its arid, technical tone largely concerned itself with keeping out the lower classes. It opposed apartment houses and "outside speculators," perhaps meaning Samstag himself, and placed regulations on lot size, subdivision dimensions, and street length and width. All those provisions raised the price of building or buying a home.

But Crotonville and its Irish Catholics were already here, so the master plan simply chose to ignore them. Elsewhere in Ossining, streets were to be paved and widened, new schools erected. In Crotonville, the dirt roads would stay dirt and the one-room schoolhouse would just have to suffice, even as its enrollment in the 1930s approached fifty. The sole fire station in the area was earmarked for closing. And for a Crotonville park, the plan recommended a one-acre gulley that, never improved, wound up serving as a dump.

The sectarian warfare Ossining practiced was of a subtle, indirect sort. For spectacle, a master plan or a restrictive covenant hardly compared to the Orange laying siege to a Catholic church. The physical battles in Ossining would always be left for the bottom-dwellers to pursue among themselves.

But in this town of only 16,000, along the Hudson instead of the Mersey, there existed no small amount of Liverpool, Liverpool not as a geographical place but a condition of being. And in the spring of 1933, Lizzie Garrett and her family had nowhere else to go. Like her ancestors escaping the Potato Famine, she was landing in a harbor that did not want her, that saw her as a burden and a shame.

One day several months after arriving in Crotonville, having detected the first sting of winter in the air, Lizzie put on the coat she normally saved for church and teetered down the hillside to catch the ten-cent bus downtown. There she presented herself at the municipal building to apply for relief. Her family had owned property in Ossining for seven years by then, and had been paying taxes all that time. But the clerk at the desk told Lizzie, "No, you haven't lived here long enough."

Nearly thirty years earlier, Lizzie's mother, left with three children and no way to support them, had come to a comparable juncture. From Liverpool, though, the liners steamed almost daily to America and new prospects. Ossining's trains only ran back to New York and the life the Garretts had already been forced to abandon. What they had in the world was the shell of a house in a place as disparaged as Crotonville. There was no choice but to stay and try to survive.

Chapter Three

The Dreamer and His Son
(Joseph Obrycki)

TWO OR THREE TIMES EACH WEEK, AS THE LATEST STEAMSHIP reached Baltimore from the German port of Bremen, disgorging its cargo of Polish immigrants for a return load of tobacco, Aleksander Obrycki sprang into his personal ritual of welcome. In this, the year 1907, he had just become a citizen of the United States of America, and he had appointed himself to instruct the newest arrivals in the glories of democracy. So he donned a dark suit and fixed his necktie with a stickpin. He brushed his mustache and oiled his hair, sweeping it symmetrically back from forehead to temples. Then he crowned it with a derby and set out for the docks. As he had acknowledged in his citizenship papers, Aleksander was a common laborer, but he still envisioned himself as he had been in Cracow—a member of the nobility, the *szlachta;* an intellectual; a nationalist whose moral obligation was to bring education and political awareness to the peasantry.

Sometimes Aleksander went to Pier Nine at Locust Point, where the transatlantic liners moored, and waited just outside the immigration station for the new arrivals to sort themselves. Those who had purchased a "dual ticket" climbed directly onto B&O trains bound for Cleveland, Detroit, or Chicago. Others, not yet ready to journey farther, paid seventy-five cents for a night's stay at Mrs. Koether's lodging house.

A good number of the rest dragged their children and belongings onto the ferry *Samuel H. Tagart* for the half-hour ride across the harbor to Fell's Point, Baltimore's largest Polish neighborhood, its Polonia.

The ferry docked at the foot of Broadway, just a few blocks from Aleksander's bakery, and he often waited there, a gentleman in formal attire set improbably among the stevedores, saloon keepers, and push-cart vendors. Twelve years earlier he had very much resembled the immigrants he now anticipated. Like them he had escaped from the Russian sector of partitioned Poland to Germany, a passage made most often beneath a wagonload of vegetables or chickens. Almost every Pole, however poor or wealthy, traveled light—a pillow, a change of clothes, a pair of spatterdashes, and, for the roiling seas, a jar of the anodyne called Hoffman's Drops.

Only in his immediate reasons for leaving had Aleksander differed. He grew up in a monied family, aspiring to write verse, but also re-sponding to the nationalist fervor left behind by the failed revolution of 1863. For Aleksander, yet in his teens, these ideals took the form of surreptitiously teaching Polish at a time the czarist regime sought to eradicate the language. Then an informant reported him and a sentence in Siberia loomed. The night before he was to be arrested, friends spir-ited him away and ultimately onto the steamship *Ohio*. Fugitive, exile, refugee, he was but seventeen.

The peasants now thronging into Baltimore were known as *za chlebem* immigrants, those who had come "for bread." They had been oppressed not only by Poland's occupiers but also by a system of tenant farming known as *odrodek,* which was markedly similar to the share-cropping then driving blacks from the rural South into such cities as Baltimore. In America, with its mines, mills, and packinghouses, an unskilled worker could earn eight times the wages available in Poland.

And in America, Aleksander wanted the newcomers to know, there was not just bread but liberty. Just as he had taught Polish in Cracow, he now taught English in Fell's Point, sometimes in his home and some-times in a night school. For those illiterate in both languages, Aleksander wrote letters. He lent immigrants books to study for the citizenship examination and accompanied them to court for their swearing-in. Be-fore long, Aleksander had delivered so many candidates that a judge ordered him to desist.

"Mr. Obrycki," he said, "you cannot vouch for all these people."

Aleksander lifted his right arm, opened his palm, and said, "I do."

The moment a Pole had been naturalized Aleksander walked him straight to the local political club to register as a Democrat. The ward boss, in turn, hired Aleksander to escort all his charges to the polling place on Election Day and to ensure that each marked the correct X on the ballot. For each day's service, Aleksander earned the generous sum of $10.

Nobody believed Aleksander did it for the money. Nor did he trade in favors. He wanted only respect and admiration, confirmation that his idealism had been well spent. To most of the community, Aleksander stood as a kind of statesman, a mainstay in the cultural and athletic organizations, a benevolent association, a political club, and a building-and-loan society. It was he whom Fell's Point selected to lay a wreath on President Harding's grave, to greet such visiting dignitaries as the piano virtuoso and ardent nationalist Jan Paderewski, and to host Madame Curie in his own home. Aleksander, in turn, enlisted his daughter Marie to present the renowned scientist with a bouquet as cameras flashed.

From within the Obrycki household, Aleksander cut quite a different figure than he did in the surrounding Polonia. As a provider, he was a *dupa jas,* a "blockhead." None of the seven children suffered more acutely than the firstborn, Joseph, who from his earliest years was cleaning up his father's messes. There were enough to quickly bend the dreamer's son toward pragmatism.

Twice in Joe's youth, for instance, the family lost its home. The first residence was the finest the Obryckis would ever occupy, a three-story brick townhouse on a hill rising gracefully from the harbor, with a state senator and a future city councilman as neighbors. Finished with the indignities of manual labor, searching for a way to make money without sweating, Aleksander joined in a real-estate partnership. When it collapsed in about 1910, the townhouse went to his debtors, and Aleksander stooped to a job selling burial insurance. There was little enough income to be extracted from weekly premiums of a nickel or dime, but worse, Aleksander insisted on paying for the clients who could not afford these installments.

He eventually managed to buy a second house on a noisier street closer to the docks, cobbling together the mortgage by taking in boarders at $8 a month and managing a bakery on the ground floor. Aleksander, unfortunately, knew nothing of dough and ovens and considered it beneath himself to learn. The only work he did, one of his daughters observed, was changing the paper in a pet parakeet's cage. "His hands," she remembered, "were always soft." The same could not be said of his wife, Barbara. She rose well before daybreak to cook breakfast and pack lunch for the boarders. Then she handled the bakery's counter. When the morning's business subsided, she started her twelve-hour shift in a can factory. On Sunday, her only day free from the assembly line, she scrubbed and dressed her eight children and led them to worship at Holy Rosary Church.

Aleksander showed interest in his children only when it suited a larger narcissism. He bestowed on all four of his boys the middle name Aleksander. Around the dinner table he demonstrated the refined way to wield cutlery and pronounce the word "aunt." Unlike other youngsters in Fell's Point, he boasted to friends, his never needed to take day labor on the outlying farms. What Aleksander neglected to add was that, while he busied himself training future citizens and serving the community, he readily dispatched the children to peddle bread in the Broadway market, using a cigar box as a cash register. As the eldest child, Joe dropped out of school after the fifth grade to work.

Even at that, the bakery sank toward bankruptcy. Aleksander sold both it and the house to several employees and led his family down the social ladder into rented rooms. Perturbed by the apartment's bare fireplace, which Barbara dismissed as "a hole in the wall," he covered it with an armoire. While he was attending a political gathering one evening, the accumulated creosote in the chimney somehow caught a spark and combusted. Jewelry, clothing, and keepsakes were all incinerated.

By this time, just as World War I was ending, Aleksander had embarked on yet another venture, running a tavern. "If a man has a nickel in his pocket on the way home from work and passes a saloon," he maintained in a rare moment of practicality, "you can be sure he'll buy a beer." But even in hard-drinking Fell's Point, where a grandmother in bedroom slippers might pad down the block to get her growler filled, Aleksander struggled. Joe had been conscripted for the dirty chores, strewing fresh sawdust across the floor, washing out the brass spittoons, and rolling barrels of National Bohemian down the ramp from street to cellar. Then, at last, Aleksander discovered an effortless means to profit, as well as an enduring vocation for his son. For a fee, he let the local numbers boss operate from the bar. And Joe, at the age of fifteen, started working as a runner.

• • •

The neighborhood that young Joe plied was a thousand-acre peninsula named after a shipbuilder who ultimately became commissioner of the colonial Baltimore Town. Fell's Point bespoke English origins from its very stones. Brick row houses fitted with dormers and side chimneys lined streets named Shakespeare and Thames and Fleet. For more than a century the population had hailed mostly from the British Isles and northern Europe. Then, in the 1870s, Poles began arriving by the hundreds, some of them the gentry but most peasants.

The initial attraction was as simple as work. Fell's Point drew to its point at a deep harbor lined with piers, barges, warehouses, and a rail terminal. The raw materials that such facilities handled in turn nourished an array of manufacturers inside or close by the neighborhood, from shipyards to canneries, packinghouses to breweries, garment factories to steel mills. The surrounding districts, too, swelled with immigrants— Little Italy to the west, Jewtown to the north, and Canton with its Czechs to the east. The same paychecks had attracted them all.

In the classic pattern of Polish immigrants, Baltimore's built their world around the fundamental institutions of church and mutual-aid society. The first fraternal group formed in 1875; only five years later it organized a Roman Catholic church with a Polish priest. Within a generation two similar parishes and one National Catholic offshoot arose. Some twenty building-and-loan societies were operating on the eve of the Great Depression, holding $15 million in assets.

With 50,000 Poles now in Baltimore, the greatest concentration of them in Fell's Point, the beachhead of a half century earlier had grown into a miniature metropolis. There were a Polish library, a Polish newspaper, a Polish theater, a Polish gymnastics club, and a Polish drill team. From the stalls of the Broadway market drifted the aromas of another continent, freshly grated horseradish and the duck's blood soup called *czarnina*. Twice each year the community paused for Polish remembrance. On May 3, Fell's Point danced to commemorate the issuance of Poland's liberal constitution of 1791. A somber Mass on November 29 marked the anniversary of the 1830 uprising, although at the reception afterward the mourners raised enough vodka toasts to the souls of the martyrs to turn the mood boisterous.

These people had grounds for celebration. They were not living any longer in Poland, bereft and divided Poland. They were in *Ameryki*. The ode written by a local Polish-language journalist spoke for them all:

> A rich wondrous land
> With abundance of everything
> A true Paradise

Paradise, though, had its problems. A population newly removed from virtual vassalage in rural Poland now wrestled with an alien, industrial society. Neither the Catholic Church nor the familial patriarchs could possibly exert the overarching authority they had abroad. The predictable rhythms of subsistence on the tenant farms had given way to the factory's spasms of boom and bust, double shift and layoff. "If there is work in America, then it is good," one immigrant wrote to relatives still in Poland. "But if there is no work, then there is no greater misery than there is here."

The Baltimore dispatches of *Dziennik Chicagoski,* a newspaper with national circulation, amounted to a portrait of jarring dislocation. A grappling line breaks and a huge sack of flour plummets onto a dock, crushing a longshoreman. Despondent because he has developed tuberculosis, a man of thirty-eight hangs himself, leaving behind a widow and five children younger than ten. A group of jobless men, promised a day's farmwork, are locked in a railroad car and delivered to a forest, where they are ordered at gunpoint to start chopping trees. Wife-beating, drunken murders, runaway teenagers, abandoned infants—all were reported with a matter-of-fact tone. Calamities were understood to be part of life in Polonia.

During this period of agonizing flux, such a community needed diplomats, mediators, and interlocutors. For all the richness of its culture, Fell's Point remained a clannish place whose most potent institutions faced inward. When it came to politics, the traditional immigrant route to employment and influence, the neighborhood sputtered with infamous futility. In 1889, a full generation after massive Polish immigration had begun, the members of the local Democratic club formally petitioned the mayor for a sole janitor's job. As of 1913, not a single officer in the central police station could speak Polish. Blacks, Jews, Italians, and Bohemians all sent one of their own to the city council before the Poles, in 1923, elected a grocer, Edward Novak, Aleksander Obrycki's onetime neighbor.

This lackluster record occasioned much hand-wringing and numerous explanations. The Polish community, it was true, had never fully healed from a bitter split in the late 1800s between Catholics content to exist under an Irish-dominated archdiocese and those demanding an independent, self-supporting church. In the years after World War I, the plight of the revived Polish nation animated Fell's Point far more than any domestic issue. Politics, it seemed, called only a few. But, before long, Joseph Obrycki would be one of them.

• • •

Nearly every day in the years immediately after World War I, Joe made the rounds of Fell's Point, up Broadway and down Fleet, along Eastern Avenue, and into the Polish Home, Siemek's grocery, and Simon the florist. He was collecting nickel bets on the number, all to be presented to his boss at the saloon. The number was based on the winning horses of three ever-changing races from three ever-changing tracks, and while those races were being run Joe had time to linger around the gambling operation. He studied the games of craps and poker, the system of bookmaking. He learned his trade. And he supported the family with his pay.

As the surrogate father, Joe enjoyed the deference that Aleksander, in his fecklessness, had forfeited. When one of his sisters needed shoes, he took her to the store and ordered a pair several sizes too small. She objected; he insisted; young ladies, Joe believed, should have dainty feet. Begged by another sister for a toy, Joe handed her a game of chance called a punchboard and told her to start selling turns. "Now be honest and pay off," he explained paternally, "and you'll always keep your customers."

Around his own customers, Joe was building a reputation. He charmed, he complimented, he impressed. Reading three newspapers a day, and employing Aleksander's lessons on manners and elocution, he reinvented himself from fifth-grade dropout and low-level criminal to man of the world. Or so it could seem within the confines of Fell's Point.

A certain vanity went with the pose. Joe favored a daily manicure and preferred his underwear ironed. Maddened to stand only five feet nine, he wore both lifts and Cuban heels. Some years later he would throw open a closet door and announce to his daughter that he owned seventeen summer suits, one for every week of the season.

On most weekends Joe competed as a "party dancer," testing his fox trot from speakeasy to political club to an excursion boat dubbed the Dreamland. At one of the competitions he met a young woman from outside the neighborhood, a twenty-year-old garment worker named Lillian Lubawski. It is not difficult to imagine how much this preening peacock must have thrilled her. A year later, on February 9, 1926, they were wed.

At about the same time Joe entered business for himself. His father had just purchased another home and opened a candy store on the ground floor. Joe commandeered it. What could provide better cover for gambling, after all, than a sweetshop run by that pillar of the community, Aleksander Obrycki. Joe hired one sister to take bets at the counter, paid several other siblings to act as lookouts, and oversaw both numbers and bookmaking from a phone bank installed in the parlor. Sometimes, to break up the routine, he went to the races, offering better odds than the track itself did.

Not yet twenty-five, Joe Obrycki appeared positively rich. When Lillian delivered the couple's first child, Corinne, he paid for a private room in the hospital. By the time a sister, Vilma, followed in 1929, he had moved the family out of Fell's Point altogether, to a neighborhood so newly hewn from farmland that a stray cow would occasionally amble onto somebody's lawn. The Obryckis' home, a modern version of the venerable row house, featured full electricity and plumbing, a garage and front porch, and two yards. The place cost $3,500, and Joe paid cash.

When the Depression arrived it barely ruffled him. Hard times, if anything, drove more people to play the numbers, most other ways of making a dollar having disappeared. While the family did eat mashed potatoes and cabbage more often than before and relied on Lillian to sew clothes, when Corinne needed orthopedic shoes that cost $20, Joe simply counted out the bills. He had money enough for family dinners of chicken pot pie at the Horn & Horn cafeteria and for weekend jaunts to a buddy's cottage on Chesapeake Bay, where everyone feasted on steamed crabs and beer.

The source of the money was no secret to Joe's family. Lillian herself enjoyed playing poker for stakes reaching into the hundreds of dollars. Corinne accompanied her father to the track and all-night card games. Often she fell asleep to the sounds of voices wagering in Polish and ice cubes clinking in highballs. Hours later she would awaken on the rumble seat of the family Studebaker as her parents argued about who had lost all the money or had had too much to drink. Gambling seemed so mundane, it never struck her that it might be illegal.

One day in grade school a teacher asked Corinne, "What does your father do?"

"He's a bookmaker," came her sprightly reply.

A classmate, turning to her, asked, "What kind of books does he make?"

• • •

In any other city Joe Obrycki's credentials would have seemed dubious indeed for a career in public service. Baltimore, however, subscribed to a set of standards wholly its own. Criminal behavior, up to and including murder, was tolerated in the interest of electoral success. Rarely did the ruling Democrats make the concessions to honesty, efficiency, or large-scale public works that other big-city machines found expedient for remaining in power. Reformers snuck into office only when the party's two factions were preoccupied by their own feud.

The Baltimore machine developed in the late 1800s and made its converts among the immigrants then thronging into the city. In a city with very southern ideas about race, these newcomers represented a counterweight to the substantial black population, which supported Republicans in homage to Lincoln. And with the organization's connivance, the immigrants could vote several times apiece.

In return for obedience, the machine offered the usual rewards. There were jobs as a lamplighter or street sweeper, a police officer or firefighter, a bailiff or garbage collector. There was Election Day employment for a total of 3,600 clerks and judges in the city's 600 precincts. And for those among the 40,000 foot soldiers without any sinecure there was influence with the bureaucrats who had already been installed. To people like the Poles of Fell's Point, separated by language and culture from the larger society, government seemed distant and intimidating. But the precinct captain or ward executive was someone familiar, and it was he who smoothed out trouble with the judge or the foreman or the health inspector.

While virtually every machine practiced patronage, Baltimore's reveled in a particularly brazen sort. Early every fall the mayor appeared before the city council carrying a green corduroy satchel from which he produced a list of political appointees. In the sort of typeface used for baseball box scores, the next day's *Sun* duly recorded the names and salaries of those loyalists made purchasing agent or chief engineer, court clerk or city surveyor, member of the smoke-control bureau or the public-bath commission. During election season every last one would be expected to tithe one percent of his salary to the campaign chest.

These kickbacks formed the bulk of "walk-around money," the bribes used to buy votes. The machine spent about $70,000 on each election in the 1920s and 1930s, doling it out to ward executives in a windowless room of the Rennert Hotel. From the ward executive the money went to the precinct captain, and from the precinct captain to the runner, and from the runner to the voter, a dollar at a time. The cash always came with a sample ballot, showing where to mark the X; even better, the runner would weasel into the booth as an "interpreter" and cast the vote himself.

From time to time the organization lent its methods to a candidate with a higher purpose, but never did it produce a leader the caliber of Al Smith. Absent such a figure, the machine never transcended the barter of favor for vote to embrace any larger causes. Rather than building a coalition based on class, it fomented rivalries along ethnic lines. Even by the standards of Tammany Hall, then, the Baltimore machine spent an inordinate amount of its energies on immediate and often illicit gain.

A number of mayors and ward executives grew wealthy operating insurance companies, selling political influence as an unwritten rider to each policy. So deeply was the machine enmeshed in Baltimore's red-light district that a civil court judge was discovered in 1924 to be part owner of a brothel. Then there was Jack Pollack, a boxer turned bootlegger turned ward boss. He had an arrest record sixty charges long, including one, mysteriously dropped, for murder. None of it stopped him from becoming the city's most dominant, albeit unelected, politician for decades after World War II.

The true Election Day fell not on the first Tuesday in November, when the enfeebled Republicans were dispatched, but in the preceding spring, when the factions of the Democratic Party clashed in a primary. One group, led during the 1920s and 1930s by the mayor, Howard Jackson, centered its power in the city government; the other, headed by an attorney, William Curran, had its base in the state administration. Each group sought absolute power, and the two leaders sincerely detested each other. The rift had apparently begun in 1927, when Curran refused to support Jackson for reelection, partly because of the incumbent's habit of passing out drunk at public affairs. Ousted for a term, Jackson regained his power in 1931 with a measure of sobriety and a grudge like a tumor.

As a divided city—governed by Jackson but flush with state jobs that Curran controlled—Baltimore provided the principal battleground for a civil war that stretched from the Roaring Twenties into the atomic age. Any given primary involved two sets of clubhouses, two sets of ward executives, two sets of precinct captains, two sets of runners, and two sets of walk-around money. But there would always be the same one issue: who got his hands on the green bag.

• • •

By nine o'clock on most mornings of the early 1930s, Joe Obrycki stepped out of his front door clad in a starched shirt and hand-tailored suit, and drove the four miles from his actual home to his official one. So far as any unit of government knew, he resided in the Second Ward at 1718 Fleet Street, the site of his father's home and his own gambling business. This specious address formed the cornerstone of his burgeoning career in politics.

In the ethnic equation of Baltimore, the Twenty-sixth Ward, where Joe really lived, remained a German stronghold. Worse for Joe, it already had a local boss of rare power, a man named Hofferbert who held the patronage plum of serving as the Internal Revenue Service commissioner for Baltimore. Here was someone neither an aspiring politician nor a professional criminal would want to antagonize, and Joe was both of those things. Instead, he returned to the Second Ward, Fell's Point, a neighborhood often described as "one thousand percent Polish" and given to almost perpetual political disarray.

There was, to begin with, a local aspect to the citywide fissure in the

Democratic Party. Mayor Jackson watched the ward through Dick Bonnet, a city council member who dispensed favors from an office in the Polish National Home. But as a German among Poles, Bonnet had his limits, so when another council seat became vacant, the mayor instated the editor of *Jednosc Polonia,* the weekly newspaper. He appeared in its pages as *Nasz* Mayor Jackson, *Our* Mayor Jackson.

On the streets, however, it was William Curran many Poles saluted as their leader. Unlike Jackson, he was a Catholic, and one canny enough to appoint seminarians to patronage jobs in the court system every summer. To Joe Obrycki, in particular, Curran loomed as the ultimate model. Born into poverty and fatherless from early childhood, Curran had transformed himself from "Barefoot Billy" the newsboy into a college graduate, renowned lawyer, and congressman's son-in-law. Even the traits that had hobbled Curran as a candidate—the pince-nez, the Latin aphorisms—resembled some of Joe's own affectations.

In the late 1920s, Joe had first insinuated himself into Curran's neighborhood outpost, the Polish-American Democratic Club of the Second Ward. The club occupied the top two floors of a storefront, and it sponsored poker nights, a basketball team, and the seafood feast inexplicably called an oyster roast, since the bivalves were actually stewed or shucked. For all the fellowship, the club proved to be a fractious place, encompassing a half-dozen Jackson supporters and even a stray Republican or two. Once during Prohibition, some members planned a party with beer and liquor while others threatened to alert Treasury agents.

Joe steered through the thicket carefully enough to be chosen club treasurer by his thirtieth birthday and ward executive a few years later. True, he had no job, at least within the law. True, he had little formal education. But he had a résumé of practical talents. As a professional gambler, going back to a childhood spent running numbers, he knew hundreds of prospective voters by name. Bookmaking had taught him to maintain scrupulous records. In a political club that kept its minutes in crude peasant Polish until 1946, Joe spoke unaccented English. And from his father's idealistic efforts to train immigrants for citizenship, he had learned that most essential of skills for the urban ward heeler— how to turn a greenhorn into a Democrat, fast.

Every day the people of Fell's Point beseeched him for jobs, loans, and bail money, and he smiled his brilliant smile and reached for his wallet. To them he seemed courtly and fair, hardly the household tyrant his family knew, cursing and screaming, "Christ kill me!" To his petitioners he said only, "You're gonna see me election time."

As much as Joe showed the public face of the machine, he functioned more precisely as a middleman, an errand boy, a cog. He had eight precinct captains below him, one of the six district leaders above him, and a sinecure that lasted only as long as he delivered votes in profusion. The machine ran like the military, through layers of command, and just as walk-around money flowed down, bids for favors flowed up.

If someone needed a job in sanitation or public works, Joe could not produce it. If someone wanted a liquor license or the forgiveness of an electric bill, Joe could not make it happen. The Curran machine, to be sure, had all the necessary connections; its very strength, in fact, lay in such state bodies as the courts, the Public Service Commission, and the Board of Liquor License Commissioners. But Joe could not approach Curran on every trifling matter. At best he could see a district leader who could see the appropriate commissioner or elected official, who understood he owed his position to Curran.

The one arena in which Joe enjoyed autonomy was the magistrate's court in East Baltimore, established to hear misdemeanors and lesser felonies. The judge, a man named Janetzke, was not even a lawyer, although he led a political club known for its crab feasts. Not infrequently a drunkard would wobble into court from the street, demanding of Janetzke, *"Daj mie para dulaty,"* "Give me two dollars."

But for anyone charged with waking the neighbors or smacking his wife, otherwise known as disturbing the peace and assault, magistrate's court seemed more than serious enough. Back in Poland, such disputes had rarely landed with civil authorities, being mediated within the extended family. Here there awaited public trial, punishment, and shame. And it required one arm of the machine to stay another. So the accused climbed the stairs of the Second Ward club to entreat Joe Obrycki. Sometimes Joe sent them to an attorney with the proper organization pedigree. Other times he appeared in court himself as a "character witness." Either way, jurisprudence followed the same script.

"Tso ty wrobi zedras?" Janetzke asked. "What did you do?"

The defendant explained and the judge forgave.

"I don't wanna see you again," Janetzke characteristically concluded. Then he indicated a metal box on a counter across the room, purportedly for donations to two nearby churches. "You put fifty cents in and get outta here."

Such was Joe's version of a lesson in democracy. Some ward executives loved to walk the streets, slapping backs, cracking jokes, and tugging sleeves. Joe always preferred to sit upstairs in the club, waiting to be solicited. The tribute he coveted was not money, not exactly power, but the illusion that he, Joe Obrycki, was the boss.

• • •

Several hours after midnight on January 30, 1934, Aleksander Obrycki died of heart disease. True to his nature, he had spent his last evening attending a meeting of a building-and-loan society. Typically, too, the society was sliding into insolvency.

The Obryckis hung a black wreath of mourning on the front door of their home and laid the body in an open casket in the dining room. In the days that followed, Aleksander's friends and admirers paid for four obituaries, eight masses, and twenty-six floral arrangements. They remembered him from Society 1065 of the Polish Roman Catholic Union, Group 21 of the Polish National Alliance, and Nest 16 of the Polish Falcons. They remembered him fronting a nickel or dime for their burial insurance. And those whom he had guided through the naturalization process remembered him teaching about the Bill of Rights, the three branches of government, and all the other things you needed to know to become a citizen.

On the morning of Aleksander's funeral, the cortege filed six blocks from the Fleet Street house to Holy Rosary Church, as a bell tolled one time for each of his fifty-six years. After the Mass the worshipers sang the Polish national anthem. *"Jeszcze Polska nie zginela, kiedy my zyjemy,"* it promised, "Poland has not perished, as long as we still live." Then the handful with cars drove fifteen minutes to the parish cemetery, interring Aleksander in what was then the sylvan fringe of the city.

Through it all, the numbers and bookmaking proceeded. The phones rang; the runners came and went; business was brisk. Joe Obrycki had placed two of his brothers-in-law in charge. It was only right, after all, that he take these days off, to honor his father, God rest his soul.

Chapter Four

The Sewing Room
(Lizzie Garrett)

ON NEW YEAR'S EVE OF 1933, THE FIRST ONE LIZZIE AND Edward Garrett spent in Crotonville, they celebrated with a newly ingrained sense of caution. Back in New York, before the Depression, they would have caroused with their friends, downing beer by the crock, devouring platters of sandwiches, and nearly weeping with sweet heartache when Edward sang "Galway Bay." In Crotonville it was just the two of them and the older children, Edith and Jack, gathered around a potbelly stove that was the only source of heat in a bungalow never meant to withstand winter. They allowed themselves just one drink, a midnight toast, and then stepped onto their porch to greet 1934 by ringing a cowbell and clanging pots and pans. The hillside fell away darkly before the Garretts, and the only other sound issued from a neighbor, Mr. Colby, firing his shotgun.

Christmas had been no better. In search of presents she could afford, Lizzie had traveled on Christmas Eve all the way to Manhattan. There she lingered outside the display windows of stores, hoping that one still glutted with gifts would panic and lower the prices. Late that evening she returned home, not with the dolls and carriage Edith craved but with a couple of board games and a lunchbox handed down by an older cousin.

Ossining was supposed to have given the Garretts a better chance of survival, but these days it resembled San Juan Hill in Manhattan. War veterans peddling apples and pencils, one of them a legless man on a rolling wooden platform, haunted the street corners. Hobos drifted through the center of town. Instead of new shoes, the 5&10 sold glue-on soles to sustain old ones. Cars sat abandoned by owners who could not pay for repairs. Every afternoon a crowd, polite and desperate all at once, formed behind Aschermann's bakery and waited for the owner to slide a bag of the day's unsold bread out the back door.

By arithmetic alone, the Garretts faced a precarious future. The birth of a son, Richard, in January 1935, brought the family to seven, with three of the children in diapers. While raising this brood, Lizzie and Edward played benefactors to relatives in even more dire condition. They raised one cousin after his mother died, rescued another from an alcoholic father, and took in a third for months while his mother recovered from pneumonia.

Generosity was another name for doing more with less, redistributing literally pennies within the family budget. Instead of seeing a Saturday-night movie, the Garretts stayed home and read. Edward got hold of a secondhand rolling machine to save the cost of store-bought cigarettes. To keep enough food on the table, Lizzie made the hour-long trip by bus to the Italian section of Yonkers, which had the cheapest groceries around, and mastered the art of roasting the same chicken she had earlier boiled for soup.

Lizzie had already been turned down for relief. She sometimes helped a doctor deliver babies in Crotonville, and squeezed about two months' work from an old employer in Manhattan, preparing the man's brownstone for occupancy between his summer and winter vacations. Frugal as Lizzie was, the intermittent money never lasted long enough. She cashed in the insurance policies that she and Edward, who both had been forced to drop out of grade school to start working, had meant for sending their children to college.

Eventually, Lizzie found a wealthy family that needed a maid, falling back on the subservience that had sustained her as a seventeen-year-old orphan. Every Monday morning she lugged her suitcase two miles to the Croton-Harmon station and the train to New York. Every Friday night she came back, flourishing at least a few necessities—socks, underwear, rolls of toilet paper. Then she tied on her apron and set about baking bread and cooking stews to last the week while she was gone.

Edward got work only after snowfalls, when the railroad hired men to clean the tracks. Afraid each storm might be the last, he would keep shoveling and sweeping for days, finally staggering home chilled by his own sweat. On one occasion, unable to cobble together the bus fare of thirty-five cents, he walked fifteen miles to White Plains, the county seat, looking for a public works job. He located the appropriate office, filled out an application, and was told the only openings were for registered Republicans.

By default, then, he managed the household. Edward was not averse to such duties; once, he had taken great joy in teaching Edith how to cook a dinner of lamb chops. But years had passed since there was money for such a luxury, and the indignity of sitting home unemployed, being supported by his wife, compounded Edward's natural stoicism into a kind of silent rage. There were only so many repairs to be made around the house; there was only so much wood to be split for the stove. Many nights he buried his anger in cowboy magazines and Zane Grey novels, but it burst forth just often enough for his quiet never to be mistaken for contentment.

●　●　●

The fears and defeats the Garretts endured arose from more than the Great Depression itself. They were living in a place—Ossining, specifically, and Westchester County, more generally—whose political leaders answered economic collapse with Panglossian forecasts of private recovery and attacks on the very notion of activist government. In this thinking, the county's ruling Republicans mirrored their national party.

"An ailing body cannot be cured by quack remedies," the GOP's 1932 presidential platform maintained. "This is no time to experiment upon the body politic or financial." Not even the electoral disaster visited upon Herbert Hoover that November shook the party's certainty, for four years later Alf Landon's platform asserted the New Deal had "destroyed the morale of our people." To the contrary, these putatively demoralized people were spreading Democratic dominion from the White House and Congress into town halls across America, even in such Republican strongholds as Westchester County.

Its gilded image notwithstanding, Westchester suffered demonstrably during the Depression. It had grown to a population exceeding half a million in part by assuming a level of debt surpassed by only a handful of major cities, and the illusory boom invited a more precipitous plunge. Factory jobs fell by nearly half between 1928 and 1933, and even such professionals as architects and engineers wrote in distress to the president. Within a decade of the stock market crash, the number of families on home relief rose from 17 to 2,075. After the federal government erected a camp for the homeless, it reached capacity almost immediately and began turning people away.

One of the clearest measures of the Depression's impact on Westchester could be found in the annual reports prepared by its Department of Child Welfare, documents rich in both statistics and anecdotes. During 1930 and 1931 alone, the department's caseload leaped by a total of 581 percent. In one of the most prosperous counties in America, parents without work were surrendering their children to boarding homes by the hundreds. Many arrived carrying the diseases of destitution—impetigo, scabies, and ringworm. Meanwhile, in a strange symmetry, an unprecedented number of families were asking the department to approve their homes for foster placements. The motive was less to show mercy than to offset their own financial woes with the monthly stipend paid for each child.

Year after year child-welfare officials pleaded against the assumption that poverty derived from some failure of character, the same assumption that decades earlier had driven Lizzie's mother from Liverpool. "We have had to help families who previously have managed their own affairs," the 1930 report noted. From 1932: "Assets diminished or exhausted and patience worn. . . . Larger numbers of people who have never before asked for help." And 1937: "These families do not present themselves either as columns of numbers or settlement classification; they come as human beings in distress, with jobs gone, and in need of food or on the point of eviction from their homes."

For its part, however, the Republican majority on the county board complained that the child-welfare department was spending *too much* money, that the children being parceled out to boardinghouses were dressed *too well*. The board cut the caseworkers' pay, then laid off many of them. At the same time that a record number of families were applying for aid, the department was forced for the first time to shunt some onto a waiting list and to reduce the allotments of coal, groceries, and rent money to the rest.

A decided ambivalence showed both in Westchester's own work-relief program and in its relations with the early New Deal agencies. The Emergency Work Bureau, the county body from which Edward Garrett had fruitlessly sought a job, received only $500,000 in funding during the direst years of the Depression. The figure lagged fully $300,000 behind the amount that New Rochelle, a city with one-tenth the population, was devoting to work relief. As a result, the bureau could employ only half of those whose plight it considered "most urgent." And the jobs lasted only four or five months because the bureau itself regularly ran out of money and had to close temporarily. Until advised the practice was illegal, the county intended to pay its work-relief recipients in scrip, the financial instrument normally favored by company towns and tenant farms.

Westchester was not alone in finding its own resources inadequate to the sudden immense needs. For that very reason, other communities welcomed the New Deal's various work programs, pleading with the Roosevelt administration to send them jobs. The elected officials of Westchester, however, regarded the New Deal as thinly disguised socialism and, perhaps worse, a bonanza for their Democratic foes.

The Civil Works Administration provided a representative example. Launched in late 1933 to create more than four million short-term jobs, pumping close to $100 million into the economy, the CWA delivered thousands of positions to Westchester County, primarily in construction. One project alone, just across the Hudson River in Orange County but accessible by bridge, hired six thousand men to build roads. The private economy, too, benefited, with the CWA signing large contracts for bus and rail transportation of workers to the site.

Such an infusion of jobs and money might have appeared a boon for a county that could not find employment for half those seeking it, that was stanching aid to children, and that required a vast camp for the homeless. Yet the public statements and private correspondence of the period suggested otherwise. The county board passed a resolution in January 1934 favoring the continuation of CWA jobs only through the winter. Thereafter, the board agreed, the jobs should be "decreased gradually until the unemployed can be absorbed in other public works projects or by private employers." Interestingly, at the very same time the county felt so sanguine about economic recovery, officials from the blue-collar city of Yonkers wired Washington: "URGENTLY REQUEST THAT THERE BE NO REDUCTION IN CWA WORKERS HERE. CONDITIONS WARRANT AN INCREASE. UNEMPLOYMENT STILL AT PEAK. NO INDICATION OF IMPROVEMENT."

Similar appeals poured into Harry Hopkins, the CWA administrator in Washington, from throughout the state, from the Bronx to Buffalo, from the rural counties of the Southern Tier to factory towns like Elmira. Attica asked for sewers, Binghamton for a hospital, and Cobleskill for a library. At bottom, all were asking for jobs for the jobless. The correspondence from Westchester, however, took a rather different tone. A group of homeowners in Hartsdale petitioned President Roosevelt to withdraw the CWA's plan to build an emergency landing field, contending that the facility would lower their property values. Congressman Hamilton Fish, a Republican whose district covered much of the county, demanded that Hopkins investigate a CWA project pruning diseased trees in White Plains for taking away business from a private contractor. The only time New Rochelle's city manager wrote to Hopkins was to request a job for himself.

These disparate actions all indicated a larger, more formal animus toward the New Deal. The officials of New Deal programs in Westchester, who had been installed by the county's Republican regime, largely opposed them. A man from the Westchester village of Mount Kisco wrote to Hopkins that when he applied for a CWA job, he received a lecture that "the N.R.A., the C.W.A., and the President's monetary program was [sic] a complete failure." The letter continued: "It is unfortunate the personnel of the C.W.A. in Westchester County is composed of people selected from a political group who are directly opposed to the National Administration . . . [and] are making a concerted effort to defeat the President's policies." A few months earlier a member of the Democratic National Committee had approached Hopkins with virtually the identical complaint.

By design, the CWA disbanded in March 1934. But only fourteen months later, a larger and more permanent successor reached the county, hiring the unemployed to paint murals, build schools, and (Westchester being Westchester) catalogue chauffeur's licenses. Few programs would so personalize the New Deal or so lodge themselves in a generation's memory as the Works Progress Administration, the WPA. And none other, in the lives and politics of the Garrett family, would figure more decisively.

• • •

In late June 1934, on Edith Garrett's last day of eighth grade, the new girl she had been noticing for several weeks on the school bus finally walked over to introduce herself. The gesture relieved Edith, who was at once too shy and too streetwise to make friends easily in Ossining. Betty Cypher was the girl's name, though the other kids called her Wimpy or Wee for her pixieish frame. It turned out she was just three weeks younger than Edith.

That summer the pair roved as tomboys together. They swam in the Croton River and fished in Teatown Lake; they ran through Quinn's orchard, hiked along the Croton Aqueduct, and hunted deep in the woods for tiger lilies. These they presented to Lizzie Garrett, who arranged the flowers in a milk jug.

In the next few years, as they moved through their teens toward womanhood, Edith and Betty shared other diversions. They collected deposit bottles from the Crotonville dump to raise the money for movie tickets, and then, from their seats at the Victoria, swooned together over Dick Powell. They worked side by side at Newberry's. Betty even dated that handsome Charlie Carey before he became Edith's sweetheart and fiancé. At the time, he'd been put off by Edith's red wedgies.

The closer Edith drew to Betty, though, the more little details pricked her curiosity. Betty's family lived in a bungalow in Crotonville just down the hill from the Garretts, but they rented in a neighborhood where most people owned homes they themselves had built. And the Cyphers had come there not from New York but from a more central, more desirable part of town. Then, too, there was the matter of Betty's father. She spoke of him often enough, but Edith had never seen him. If she has one, Edith found herself thinking, where is he?

Lizzie's words only sharpened the sense that something was wrong. As often as the Garretts welcomed Betty to their table for stew or goulash or a Sunday roast, Lizzie insisted that Edith never, ever let the Cyphers reciprocate. "Don't you eat off those people," she said, her voice hushed with pity. "They have a hard time goin'."

Obedient as Edith was, she strained against the order. She adored Betty's mother, whose name was also Edith, for her gentle manner and her readiness to listen, calling her not "Mrs." but "Mama." Mama Cypher, for her part, often invited Edith for meals. Time after time Edith excused herself, saying, "My mom said I have to go home." And Lizzie Garrett, as the Cyphers knew, was not a mother to be defied. But finally, in the summer of 1935, Edith said yes.

It was still daylight when Edith reached the bungalow, but as night descended every lamp and fixture stayed dark. The Cyphers, once again, had lost their lights. Mama Cypher said nothing of it. Instead she opened a card table on the front porch, laid a linen cloth across it, and arranged settings with candles, fresh flowers, and matching dishes. And in that one evening, with its amalgam of elegance and want, Edith received her first hint of the Cypher family's almost epic fall.

At the beginning, Edith Cypher was not a Cypher at all, but a DeFontaine, descended from French nobility and fathered by a renowned Civil War correspondent turned drama critic for the *New York Herald*. The family entertained the likes of Sarah Bernhardt and Oliver Wendell Holmes, who both signed young Edith's autograph book. She made a correct marriage, to the organist from the Cathedral of St. John the Divine, but four years later her husband died. Not long afterward, while visiting the daughters of a prominent family in Ossining, Edith met Arthur Cypher.

He was a townie, the son of a sewing-machine salesman, earning his own living as a railroad detective. He presented himself, however, as quite the dandy, tall and nearly regal in cashmere coat, black homburg, and gray suede gloves. On the streets of Ossining, people saluted Arthur Cypher as "Senator." Years later Edith said she had fallen in love with his perfect teeth.

Little else about him, it soon became clear, qualified as flawless. By 1920, Arthur and Edith had produced five children, Betty being the youngest, and lived in a clapboard shack without electricity, running water, or even glass in the windows. It fell to Edith to support the family, raising chickens and tending a garden, because Arthur had begun to wander. He might vanish for two or three months without explanation, one day materializing with a cut of meat and a Caruso record under his arm.

Perhaps to better anchor Arthur, perhaps to erase their own shame, relatives from both sides of the family bought the Cyphers a four-bedroom home with shake shingles and a fieldstone hearth, and filled it with wicker furniture and brass beds. All Arthur had to do was pay the monthly mortgage. But most of the time he was either wandering again or drinking at home. Once Betty and her older sister Marie returned home from an errand to buy their father cigarettes to discover their mother sprawled before the fireplace, sobbing, mouth bloody from his blows. Sometimes, women appeared, from as close as Chilmark or as far as Florida, one asking Betty how she would like to attend school in Europe, another offering the child a quarter to brush her hair and tell where Daddy was. Edith tried threatening Finkelstein the shoe merchant, who sold Arthur bootleg liquor, with a rusty old pistol. But she never dared press for a divorce. "I had five kids," she later told Marie. "Where was I to go?"

With Arthur or without him, the Cyphers went in all respects downhill. Shortly after the stock market crashed, a banker from across the street repossessed their house. They rented among the prison guards and domestics on the flats beside Sing Sing, and from there slid even further, as far as most of Ossining was concerned, to the "Hell's Kitchen" of Crotonville. Arthur was by then living with a lover in Washington.

The family bounced through three different cottages in Crotonville, each barely equipped to withstand winter, suggesting either a search for lower rent or flight from an unpaid landlord. With every move, Mama Cypher hauled the horsehair trunk containing her autograph book and a satin wedding dress adorned with pearls, artifacts of a vanished opulence.

She found work only on commission, selling dresses door-to-door, but people without money for food were hardly about to indulge in frills. Her own children wore clothes others had discarded, which Mama Cypher cut and resewed to fit, and she patched their shoes with cardboard from boxes she begged downtown. Even glue-on soles, at ten cents apiece, were too expensive.

At the best, Mama Cypher served her children potatoes fried in lard or bread thinly topped with mustard. Once, in desperation, she slaughtered Betty's pet chicken for a meal. But most often, Betty and the rest went to school unfed. Then Mama Cypher would tramp all the way into town to plead with her sister-in-law for a few jelly sandwiches to deliver to her children at lunchtime. And Betty, her hunger barely abated, would think to herself, I hope Mrs. Garrett invites me for dinner tonight.

It was a prayer Lizzie answered scores of times. But such acts of kindness, no matter what Herbert Hoover and Alf Landon thought, could not rescue an entire family. One or two times, when things were bleakest, Mama Cypher had told her children that for their sake she might apply for relief. Beaten and betrayed by her husband, reduced from high society to the lowest rung of subsistence, she viewed welfare as the final indignity. But one morning in the summer of 1936, Mama Cypher pulled on her blue dress, the last decent one she owned, and trudged to Town Hall.

She did not get welfare that day. She came home instead with a job from the WPA.

Mama Cypher was hired as a seamstress in a small garment shop. The sewing room, as it was delicately called, occupied a storefront just across the street from Ossining High School, and now Betty and Edith, before riding the bus home, could admire her through the plate-glass window. It was as if Franklin Roosevelt himself wanted all of Ossining to see the women he had put back to work.

Clad in smocks and kerchiefs, several dozen stitched away. They sat at their machines in rows, four or five in a line, rarely breaking the rhythm of assembly. Each seamstress reached back for the pieces to be joined and forward to guide them beneath the needle. Then she dropped the finished garment, each tethered by thread to the next, into a basket of goods awaiting separation and pressing. After all the misery Mama Cypher had borne, the rumble of motors and hiss of irons and slapping of belts against pulleys must have sounded oddly soothing.

This one sewing room, of course, formed part of a much larger social and economic experiment. The shop produced clothes, towels, and bedding for institutions and individuals who could not afford them; it provided business for cutters, shippers, machine repairmen, and, ultimately, cotton farmers. And the sewing room in Ossining was but one of 10,259 opened by the WPA. What the place meant to the women it employed may have been best expressed in a letter that the welfare commissioner of one upstate New York county wrote to the district WPA supervisor:

Let us forget the monetary value. The social benefits resulting from this work cannot be reckoned in terms of silver or gold. No word picture can adequately portray the rehabilitation and transformation taking place in some of these women, after a few months association and contact with other people, coupled with the sense of achievement of being able to procure a few of the things in life so essential to their happiness. Not frivolities but necessities, which cannot be obtained without money. One woman bought a comb, a broom, scouring powder and disinfectant, when she received her *first* check. The food order she had been getting her groceries with, simply could not be stretched to include these items.

With Mama Cypher's pay, the lights burned again in the bungalow. Milk and eggs appeared on the breakfast table for the first time in years. The old staples of bread and potatoes now made side dishes to stew meat or hamburger. Instead of sewing Betty's clothes from shapeless hand-me-downs, Mama Cypher bought enough organdy to fashion her daughter a prom gown.

But what Edith Garrett would remember most were Friday afternoons, when Mama Cypher got paid. Edith and Betty met her after school outside the sewing room, and then they strolled along Highland Avenue, down the hill of Main Street, left on Spring, and into the Crystal Restaurant, the Greek's place. There Mama Cypher treated them all to clam chowder. Clam chowder could make you a Democrat for life.

• • •

As if the Garretts required any further demonstration of the New Deal, they got it in 1937 when the WPA hired Edward. After all the years of enforced idleness, he flung himself into the physical release of construction and road building. All around town, in fact, the family could see the WPA, in the artist painting a Hudson River scene on the post office's wall; the crew rebuilding an elementary school so dilapidated it had been dubbed the "chicken coop"; and the men inspecting gravestones in Sparta Cemetery, Ossining's oldest, as part of a project compiling a master list of all 8,800 Westchester County war veterans. Some of the older boys in Crotonville reported to the Civilian Conservation Corps, and Edith could not help noticing how much healthier they looked after a summer of outdoor work and steady meals.

Neither Edith nor her mother, Lizzie, harbored any illusions that the Depression was over. The newspaper published a list of homeowners behind in their taxes, and real-estate speculators seized on it as a guide to bottom-fishing. From her post in the toy department of Newberry's, Edith saw mothers agonize on Christmas Eve the way her own had just a few years earlier. They would hover over some modest gift, a checkers set or a Popeye ring-toss game, pick it up and handle it, then return it to the counter and depart with a longing, backward glance. Others paced on the sidewalk, beating mittened hands against worn coats, waiting for eight o'clock, when Mr. Luce the manager would cut the prices.

At home, however, the difference of five years and one president was profound. The Garrett family's radio ritual had shifted from Father Coughlin, by now a venomous critic of the New Deal, to President Roosevelt's fireside chats, all hope and reassurance. Lizzie took Edith into Manhattan to shop at S. Klein's, a discount department store she elevated with the nickname Madame K's. Nine years after building what was meant to be a rudimentary summer cottage, Edward could finally afford to shape it into a permanent home. He built a combined living and dining room, for which Lizzie purchased secondhand furniture, and replaced the locust tree stilts on which the home had been perched with a concrete foundation. The process took months of evenings and weekends, but at its end the Garretts boasted one of the few houses in Crotonville with a cellar.

It became the social hub, both for neighbors and for visitors from the city, and New Year's Eve seemed to fall every summer Saturday night. Lizzie brewed root beer for the children and the real stuff for grown-ups, and Edward turned his voice to Tin Pan Alley and Irish ballads. At two or three in the morning they cooked bacon and eggs for the stragglers. Then the adults flopped onto the couch and the kids filled the attic. Once, when Edith returned from a date with Charlie Carey, she found her cousin Nora asleep in the bed she shared with her sister, Helen. So Edith simply dozed off in a lawn chair.

Through Charlie's mother, who kept books in a butcher shop and knew the rich folks among its customers, Lizzie found a maid's job right in town. Now she had both the stable income and the spare time to take her first steps into politics. Her role was not partisan at the start, at least not overtly, but more an example of what would later be known as community organizing.

For years, Crotonville had been nursing its grievances. Without sewers, the hillside was studded with outhouses. The roads remained unpaved and gutted, some not even recognized by the town. A single two-inch pipe provided water for several hundred residents. The latest slight, the one that drove Crotonville into action, was the opening in 1937 of a sixty-eight-acre park near one of the choicest sections of town, Briarcliff. In truth, Ossining's officials had had no choice; a man named Ryder, who had grown wealthy selling blasting powder during construction of the aqueduct, donated his farm to the town. But to Crotonville, given a one-acre dump for recreation, Ryder Park resonated with all the issues of class, religion, ethnicity, and political persuasion. "They put everything," Edward Garrett said, "on the *other* side."

So he and Lizzie and several dozen of their neighbors formed the Crotonville Civic Association. It met, all too appropriately, in the neighborhood's wildly overcrowded one-room schoolhouse, and nearly all its members were Irish Catholic, Democratic, and working poor, people who almost proudly called themselves "the forgotten citizens of Ossining." Whatever their agenda formally included, the evening usually gravitated by its end to pinochle and euchre, coffee and cake. These displaced New Yorkers, steeped in the culture of Tammany Hall, naturally mingled social life and politics.

Years, even decades, would pass before the association won the full complement of modern public works for Crotonville. But in the very immediate future lay a local election of tremendous interest to Lizzie Garrett and Crotonville, one that served as a kind of municipal plebiscite on the New Deal.

• • •

By most measures, the off-year election of 1937 seemed insignificant. The White House and every seat in Congress had been filled the previous year, as had the governor's mansion in Albany and most of the state legislature. The biggest race in Ossining that fall was for supervisor. As the town's chief executive, the supervisor controlled local relief payments, no small power during the Depression, and served on the county board. But those factors alone could hardly explain the phenomenon building from Labor Day into early October.

Under the laws of the time, voters needed to register anew for every election, and the number was soaring toward a record for a municipal campaign. On the last two days of registration, October 15 and 16, each party sent extra workers into the streets to meet the demand, and by the end, some 7,788 citizens had signed up, representing two-thirds of the entire adult population of Ossining.

What drew them was a campaign that could fairly be called epochal. The candidates stood as almost direct opposites, and their antagonism reflected not simply personal character or philosophy but the way the Great Depression and the New Deal had polarized the political universe. What academicians would someday call "realignment" was rippling through the hills and gulleys of Ossining.

The incumbent supervisor, Republican William Jackson, operated a Ford dealership in town and was said by some to be a millionaire. He could afford horses, a summer home, and excursions to South Carolina to hunt quail. Jackson seemed a compassionate man, when compassion could be expressed by individual acts. The story was told that when he saw a waifish boy slump against his showroom's window during a blizzard, Jackson motioned the child inside, wrote a note, and instructed him to carry it to Markowitz's dry-goods store. It promised payment for new shoes, galoshes, and a winter coat.

But in his official capacity, Jackson revealed a less munificent side. Under his aegis, the town foreclosed on homes with overdue property taxes and then sold them off. He grew so incensed with the cost of relief—$85,000 in 1937, up from $7,300 in 1928—that he appointed a committee to ferret out what he called "chiselers." A subcommittee report made the following suggestions, among others, for the investigation:

> That the political affiliations of the recipients should be checked up on . . .

> The list [of all recipients] be used to consult the various banks in Ossining, and if possible in Yonkers, to see if relief recipients have accounts . . .

> That the Telephone book be searched to see if relief recipients have telephones . . .

> The list also be used in contacting the contractors in the vicinity, who are in a position to know about laborers . . .

> That co-operation be sought from the public, through the newspapers as to the names of supposed "chiselers" being handed in to any one on the main committee, the information to be confidential.

In the end, after several months and $1,000 in expenses, the committee identified five questionable cases from a total of three hundred. But that report arrived after the election. What was more relevant to the campaign was the suspicion that propelled the probe.

The distrust felt personal to Lizzie Garrett. She, after all, had once applied for relief. So had Mama Cypher. Were *they* chiselers? And the Cyphers were just one of several families Lizzie knew who had lost their home. Moving through Ossining, from home to work, on rounds of errands, she commonly saw furniture piled on the curb. The idea that the government itself was putting folks out seemed inconceivable.

A man named Hugh Lavery agreed. He was running against Jackson for supervisor, and in the course of the race he was to become Lizzie's political hero. Naturally, she also admired Franklin Roosevelt and Al Smith, but they were simultaneously too immense and too removed to seem approachable. Hugh Lavery was someone she could see strolling up Main Street at lunch, greeting so many people it took him a half hour to cover two blocks, someone she could hear at rallies at France's skating rink. Edith and Betty Cypher usually went, too, consuming the oratory along with the free doughnuts.

Lavery knew he functioned as a sort of proxy for the Democrats whom New York had placed on the national stage. On campaign rounds, he liked to introduce himself with the phrase, "Shake the hand that shook the hand of Al Smith." The syllogism made for expedient politics, but it also touched a truth. Like Smith, Lavery was a child of the Irish-Catholic working class who maintained a fidelity to his origins, whatever lofty circles he ultimately entered.

The son of a guard at Sing Sing, Lavery had gone to college and law school on borrowed money, and had postponed his marriage for four years until he could repay the debt. He entered politics in 1932, running for State Assembly with the goal of securing pensions and a forty-eight-hour workweek for prison keepers like his father. Defeated in his initial race, Lavery won the next four times, and in Albany absorbed the gospel of activist government and public works, especially as it had been refined by Robert Moses during Smith's years as governor. Lavery introduced the bill establishing the state authority that ultimately erected the Tappan Zee Bridge across the Hudson, a linchpin of Westchester's postwar development.

And, again like Smith, Lavery knew just how to balance reform philosophy with machine technique. It was a style that New York expatriates like Lizzie could easily appreciate. Lavery was especially renowned in Crotonville for having won leniency in municipal court for several neighborhood boys arrested for stealing and slaughtering a cow. Others remembered the rally Lavery held during one race for Assembly, when he was deadlocked with his opponent and down to his last hundred dollars. He converted ninety of it into singles and spent the other ten on a barrel of beer. Then he instructed an aide not to tap the keg until he had finished addressing the crowd and to make sure that every last listener, before he wobbled home tipsy, be awarded a fresh dollar bill.

Against Jackson, Lavery mounted a door-to-door campaign never before seen in a supervisor's race. He shook hands outside the prison gates when the guards changed shift each afternoon at three-thirty; he plied the sidewalk bordering the Hudson Wire Company, probably the largest private employer in town; he visited all ten volunteer firehouses, traditional seats of political influence, placing the president of one hook-and-ladder company on his ticket as a candidate for town council; he reminded a Columbus Day audience of several hundred Italians that in the state legislature he had helped pass a law permitting towns to raise money for celebrating the holiday; and he spoke at rallies and card parties in Crotonville, telling the citizens they would be forgotten no longer. About the only thing he didn't do was campaign in Briarcliff, saying, "There's no votes for me there."

With his endless activity, Lavery presented a vivid contrast to Jackson, who at fifty-three was twenty-two years his senior and bedridden for much of the campaign with asthma, a severe cold, and, perhaps, a case of overconfidence. After all, Jackson had held an increasingly powerful series of offices for fifteen years, and in Ossining registered Republicans outnumbered Democrats by a two-to-one margin. The town's daily newspaper, the *Citizen Register,* endorsed not only Jackson but also the Republican assault on the New Deal as the enemy of recovery. Ossining needed "a steady hand at the wheel," the paper editorialized, "at a time when returning prosperity might lead to unsound governmental spending and when ever-increasing State and Federal taxes make economy at home essential."

In Crotonville, as in the Hollow, the North Side, and the other blue-collar sections of Ossining, people knew firsthand that whatever semblance of prosperity they enjoyed had derived directly from the New Deal. The New Deal was Edward Garrett building roads and Edith Cypher sewing clothes; it was the money for stew, a cellar, a daughter's prom gown. As a Democrat, Hugh Lavery could only gain by the association. But he pressed further into the politics of class division, specifically denouncing Jackson's foreclosure program in one of his last campaign speeches. Culminating a crowded and exuberant three-hour rally, he declared that the incumbent Republican "proposes to freeze out the mortgagees, take property off the rolls, and place it under ownership of the township—property on which the town can't even sell tax liens—and pay considerable legal fees for just this sort of thing. I can promise you one thing. If I am elected, if the Democratic ticket is elected, we will do not any such thing as that."

By November 2, 1937—Election Day—Franklin Delano Roosevelt himself was apparently watching the Ossining vote. The president had returned to his family home in Hyde Park, about forty miles north along the Hudson, so he could monitor local races throughout New York State more closely. He viewed them, press reports said, as a barometer of the New Deal's popularity.

Ossining flocked to the polls. By noon, fully one-third of the registered voters had cast their ballots; the final turnout surpassed 85 percent. Having begun the campaign with a deficit of 2,500 votes, based on partisan registration, Lavery wound up winning by 685. Crotonville swung about eighty of them into the Democratic column from the previous supervisor's election, just two years earlier. If Jackson needed a reminder of why he had lost, it arrived the next morning, when the New York State Department of Labor announced it would soon open an unemployment office in downtown Ossining.

Election Night belonged to Hugh Lavery. Overcoat open and hat held aloft, he marched at the head of a victory parade. More important, he remained supervisor through eleven more races, twenty-two years, falling from office just as, beneath the political surface, the New Deal coalition was starting to crack.

There is no indication that Lizzie Garrett attended the victory parade in 1937. She may well have had Betty Cypher over for dinner, or any of several cousins. Yet her political life had been transformed. If Al Smith had made her a Democrat, and Franklin Roosevelt had guaranteed she would stay one, then Hugh Lavery convinced her to do more with her beliefs than just vote. In the mid-1940s, the local Democratic Party chose Lizzie as a committeewoman. Almost instantly, she found Edith an annual job as an election judge, which would last a half century. And when Lizzie scaled the hilly streets of Crotonville, preaching the New Deal gospel door-to-door, she brought along her son Richie. Just past ten, the youngest in the family, he was, in her mind, old enough to start learning.

Chapter Five

The Physics of Cynicism
(Joseph Obrycki)

Two FLIGHTS ABOVE THE CLATTERING TROLLEYS OF EASTERN Avenue in Fell's Point, the lights of a single room snapped on. It was nearly eight o'clock on the Sunday evening of January 15, 1933. The sky had darkened hours ago, and the breeze blew raw and clammy off the harbor. Blue laws had locked the doors all day on Budacz's radio shop and Dembowski's Lunch Room, the Sonia Beauty Salon and Adamski the florist. Anyone moving down the block now was surely headed for the last brick row house before the alley, Number 1818, headquarters of the Polish-American Democratic Club of the Second Ward. On poker nights, they would have climbed the side staircase, coins jangling, to the third floor, where the chairs had armrests and the Coca-Cola cooler brimmed with home brew. The attraction this time, the obligation, more like it, was the regular monthly meeting. So each man halted at the second landing, turned into a deep, narrow room set at the level of streetlamps, and unfolded a wooden seat.

With his spectacles and brilliantined hair, the shopkeeper Jan Pfajfer presided. Among the regulars were Frank Kocjan the electrician and Tom Siemek the butcher, stocky men stuffed into coat and tie for the occasion. Simon Jarosinski, an insurance agent, arrived in a double-breasted suit, wearing the diamond signet ring he had picked up from a friend's pawnshop for just $15.

Joe Obrycki appeared, too, moving lightly as the party dancer he once had been. With the racetracks idle, Sunday was his day of rest from the rigors of bookmaking. He usually slept off his Saturday-night card game while his daughters went to Mass at Sacred Heart of Mary, and in his single rite of domesticity joined them for a supper of meat loaf and mashed potatoes. Occasionally, he took the family driving, to Ocean City or Middle River on fair days, or, in later years, to visit the brother-in-law in prison for tax evasion. But by early evening, clad in a freshly starched shirt, hair gleaming black with dye, Joe would excuse himself from the family, drive to Fell's Point, and resume his second profession of politics.

The times clamored for the attention of these men, the leaders of an immigrant, working-class neighborhood. Only months earlier, five thousand of Baltimore's garment workers had struck, hundreds of them blockading the trucks of a company heading to a yellow-dog shop across the state line. Seamen littered the saloons and missions along the wharves, jobless after years, replaced by novices desperate enough to ship out for a dollar a month. Entire families from Fell's Point vanished for the winter, following the migrant trail to pack seafood along the Gulf of Mexico, not to resurface in Maryland until the tomatoes reddened toward harvest.

Those who stayed scratched out a living—cobbling shoes, mending clothes, sharpening scissors, baking cookies for a wedding reception. The women of Little Italy sold homemade macaroni for ten cents a pound, and even at that the hungry lined up at dusk, handing over a penny or two for a sack of broken noodles. Near the cotton mills of the Hampden-Woodberry district, most slowed and many stilled, factory hands stripped the hillsides for firewood.

But in Joe Obrycki's clubhouse on this particular night the members buzzed with their own urgent issue. The annual banquet, a final accounting revealed, had lost $1.30. It had been controversial enough to sell tickets for only $2.50, a concession to hard times, and now the consequences showed: one hundred tickets, no profit. The news must have rankled the members since they knew few other means of raising money, just the odd smoker or oyster roast and the practice of skimming a dime on the dollar from the poker pot. And it evidently awakened some dormant feud because halfway through the next matter, a recitation of the mail, order collapsed. The minutes, rendered as usual in fractured Polish, proved in this instance equal to the event:

The recording secretary had not finished reading the letters when citizen Miedzianoski took the floor [saying] that that is not in order, that citizen Pondo had been removed, and citizen Skalenski and citizen Slowik stood up for citizen Pondo and stated that President Pfajfer did not remove citizen Pondo from the Board of Governors, only he himself didn't want to, but citizen Skalenski also didn't want to, but the problem was that citizen Miedzianoski stood and spoke through the president's permission and wouldn't listen.

Next citizen Strzygoski took the floor and began to speak, but citizen Miedzianoski stood and began to interrupt citizen Strzygoski and began to call citizen Strzygoski obscene things and he did the same to citizen Miedzianoski. But citizen Miedzianoski began calling him indecent names and a lot of discussion ensued . . . So the president waited for order but could not do so, no one would listen.

So the president adjourned . . .

The next month's meeting, while less profane than its predecessor, remained every bit as self-absorbed. There was talk of sending a delegation to the inauguration of "Freklyn dylano Ruzwelt," but not about the Depression that had elected him. In the meetings to come, the club's members argued over endorsing a Polish candidate for city council against the wishes of William Curran, their boss. They dithered about paying a $60 league fee for their boys' basketball team. They mulled over whether a monument to Pulaski planned for a nearby park ought to be limestone or granite. In saluting one another as citizen, they may have harked back to the idealism of Polish nationalism, but theirs was the realm of minutia.

Within it, Joe was building a career, from Sunday-night meeting to Sunday-night meeting and on all the nights in between. He bankrolled favors on the street and built loyalty in the clubhouse. Such an imperious figure at home, in the ward he never spoke merely to be heard, never created needless enemies in a shouting match, instead earning a reputation for business sense and meticulous organization. Keep your word; deliver what you promise—that was the way to rise in Baltimore politics. Issues were only for radicals and reformers, in other words the powerless.

Over exactly a decade of the Great Depression, from the first entry of minutes in December 1931 until the Pearl Harbor attack, only once did the club's discussion touch upon the enveloping national catastrophe. The moment came in April 1932, as a ragtag assemblage of 11,000 war veterans was marching toward Washington to plead for early payment of a bonus due in 1945. At Joe Obrycki's urging, the club petitioned Maryland's delegation in Congress to reconcile with the "Bonus

Army." That advocacy protrudes as one of the few selfless acts of Joe's political career. "He was always for the underdog," one observer put it, "as long as it was for him, too."

So far as the minutes reveal, neither Joe nor anyone else in the club ever spoke of the CWA or CCC or WPA, the New Deal programs that might have given work to the jobless who abounded in Fell's Point. A strike by hundreds of seamen in 1936, so violent that a half dozen wound up floating dead in the harbor, passed without comment. The attempt one year later to organize steelworkers was noted, but only insofar as club members resolved not to become involved.

These men were not ignorant or uninformed. When the Nazis invaded Poland in 1939, Joe and his colleagues raised nearly $1,500 for war relief, and one club member wrote of being "affected by the call of blood and fired with the desire to aid." Yet they seemed unmoved by the disaster on their doorstep, insulated from its harshest effects. Amid an epidemic of eviction, dispossession, and bank failure, the Second Ward club owned a building worth $8,000, just fitted with new windows and wallpaper, and held another $5,000 in savings. As banker or editor, undertaker or attorney, most of its members belonged to the local elite. For the rest, "Uncle Willie" Curran could deliver a patronage job, at the very least watching the polls on Election Day.

Joe Obrycki knew more comfort than most. True, his family sat down some evenings to a dinner of milk and crackers. Two nurses boarded in the household for a time. And Corinne, the eldest child, started working summers at age eleven, boxing the pesticide called Harris's Roach Pills. But there was never the slightest concern she might need to drop out of school and help support the family, a common enough scenario in the Depression. Joe already had her trajectory charted: Patterson Park High, University of Maryland, law school, personal counsel to him. "You just come down to the courthouse," he would say, "and look at all the money that's there."

She need not have looked nearly that far. At home one warm evening, with the front door open to admit a breeze, Joe heard the family dog bark at a stranger outside. "Someone's tryin' to break in," he blurted, "and I've got a thousand dollars in the back bedroom." The Obryckis listened to the Roosevelt's fireside chats on their neighborhood's first crystal set, which would later be supplanted by its maiden TV. When Joe tired of his Studebaker, he replaced it with a Cadillac, sniffing whenever he spotted his former model, "They ought to get those wrecks off the road."

Joe just happened to be doubly blessed. Bookmaking so thrived during the Depression that the Maryland legislature at one point debated legalizing it to lift the state's economy. And public service, too, had its dividends. Or as Joe once instructed his younger daughter, Vilma, "There's no such thing as an honest politician." Then he laughed.

Joe Obrycki was a man of his milieu. In his arrogance, calculation, and almost willful detachment from the genuine issues of the era, issues that battered and wrenched an industrial district like Fell's Point, he embodied the political culture from which he had sprung. Never would the elected leadership live down to the city's degraded standards more starkly than during the New Deal, when so much should have been possible.

• • •

On March 27, 1931, marked on most calendars as Good Friday, Baltimore celebrated "Self-Denial Day." Summoned at noon by church bells and firehouse whistles, citizens by the thousands carried purses, wallets, and fists of loose change to drop boxes that had been set up in stores, movie houses, and libraries, and even on street corners. The money was meant for the city's poor and jobless. And when the counting was done, the total came to $69,000, a measure both of personal generosity and political bankruptcy.

Few other cities would dare raise Lenten sacrifice to the status of public policy, but it fairly typified official Baltimore's response to the Great Depression. The city fathers could hardly fail to notice the scale of suffering. By early 1931, unemployment in the city stood at nearly 20 percent and the caseload of private charities had doubled within a year. Nineteen different breadlines operated. Hunger marchers carried their campaign for relief to city hall and the State Capitol. There the Democratic governor, Albert Ritchie, responded with words that could have come from Herbert Hoover's mouth: "Sometime, somehow, the problem of unemployment will be answered. What is necessary now is for business to recognize the problem belongs to it and not the state."

The Democrat who was elected mayor in 1931, Howard Jackson, ran not as a champion of the masses but as "a businessman's businessman." True to his slogan, he chose a balanced budget over spending on relief or public works. When Ritchie declared a statewide bank holiday for nearly three weeks in early 1933, leaving many people without the money to buy food, Jackson refused to redeem municipal paychecks, saying, "City Hall is not in the check-cashing business." His version of a jobs program called for each city employee to donate a day's paid work each month to an unemployed understudy. The city council proposed running "charity sweepstakes" at local racetracks and giving relief recipients garden plots instead of food parcels. As the relief load soared in

1934 toward 260,000, nearly one-third of the city, Baltimore simply halted benefits to hundreds of blacks and homeless persons.

What was most striking of all in this Democratic city was Mayor Jackson's studied ambivalence, if not outright hostility, toward virtually every jobs program created under the New Deal. In a few other big cities, notably Boston as ruled by Mayor James Michael Curley, the machine resisted the Roosevelt administration as a rival to its control of public employment and thus Election Day fealty. But even there the New Deal eventually took hold. And far more often, as the political scientist Steven P. Erie writes, "relief programs such as the WPA . . . meant popular neighborhood projects and services as well as patronage jobs, enhancing the machine's vote totals."

Not even self-interest, apparently, altered Mayor Jackson's policies. With more than 800,000 residents, Baltimore requested only $1.7 million from the Public Works Administration, exactly the same amount as New Rochelle, population 54,000. As of January 1934, only sixty-eight men in the entire city were working on PWA projects, and municipal officials, threatened by Washington with a cutoff of funds, insisted they were having trouble finding enough jobless people. Barely half of the eligible men and women found duties with the Works Progress Administration, and both the Civilian Conservation Corps and the National Youth Administration had hundreds, if not thousands, of positions go wanting.

"The W.P.A. was a God send through our President," a Baltimorean named Lloyd Brooks wrote to Eleanor Roosevelt in 1936, but "from what I can see here, it does not seem to be carried out here locally as intended by our President."

There were ample reasons, if often objectionable ones, for Baltimore's performance. The most powerful politicians in Maryland included two vigorous intraparty foes of Roosevelt—Governor Ritchie, defeated by him for the 1932 nomination, and Senator Millard Tydings, who beat back the president's personal crusade to unseat him in 1938. By hiring blacks, New Deal programs eroded Baltimore's customary segregation, and so presented more of a risk to the local Democratic Party than did heightened unemployment. Labor unions, among the most loyal supporters of the New Deal, had long been an anathema.

Most of all, the political culture of Baltimore was predicated on one party and no issues, save for self-preservation. The Republican opposition was hardly going to champion the New Deal. As it was, Mayor Jackson governed under incessant pressure from a large conservative lobby called the Taxpayers' War Council, which stood ready to attack any increase in municipal spending. So during the Great Depression, as New York brought forth a Fiorello La Guardia and Chicago an enlightened boss like Jacob Arvey, Baltimore watched Howard Jackson and William Curran wage their version of the Hundred Years' War.

"Many civic-minded citizens," a writer from *Esquire* observed some-what later, "finding the choice of candidates offered at election time by the political overlords very distasteful, simply do not vote and thus abdicate to the rough-and-tumble boys." At a time when a local election in Ossining, fiercely pitched on issues of class, could draw three-quarters of all registered voters to the polls, the usual showdown be-tween Curran and Jackson attracted one-third. Between elections their rivalry moved into city council meetings, with the unelected Curran writing scripts for his proxy, Council President George Sellmayer. As a later mayor of Baltimore, Thomas D'Alesandro Jr., writes in his memoirs:

> On one occasion Sellmayer came to the bottom of the page of a Curran attack and innocently read out "turn the page"—the instruction Uncle Willie had written. Another time when Sellmayer was reading an espe-cially rough attack on Jackson, the city solicitor grabbed the paper out of his hands and defied Sellmayer to continue. Of course Sellmayer couldn't.

As the year 1939 opened, Jackson and Curran girded for battle once more in the real election, the April primary, in which the mayoralty and every seat on the city council would be contested. In the First District, which included Fell's Point, Uncle Willie chose someone new to recite his lines, a neighborhood politico by the name of Joe Obrycki.

• • •

In many ways, Joe appeared an ideal candidate for council. As both ward heeler and professional gambler, he enjoyed a certain visibility, and in both roles he had excelled at organization. All the admiration the community once held for Aleksander, five years dead and nearly sainted in memory, now devolved upon his firstborn. That Joe actually lived outside the district mattered little. Canny as always, he still used the candy store as his legal address and spent far more time there than at his home. Only one problem loomed. The campaign would carry Joe beyond the known world of Fell's Point into neighborhoods of Jews, Czechs, and Italians; the newspapers would be watching and asking questions. And what exactly would Joe present by way of résumé, back-ground, qualifications? At the age of thirty-six, he had never held a legal job.

So Joe took a step down to take a step up. Curran situated him in the vast brass and marble courthouse downtown, the very hive of patronage, with a clerking job in the marriage-license bureau. The position paid much less than numbers and bookmaking, of course, but it required Joe to show up for only a few hours, scribble out some forms, and then decamp for Fell's Point and the real work of getting elected. He had been, in Baltimore political jargon, "perfumed."

In the campaign's major race, Jackson was defending his mayoralty against Curran's latest surrogate, a Claude Rains look-alike named Charles Buck. Once in a rare while, something resembling an issue surfaced. Buck might complain about taxes getting too high, and Jackson, normally such a foe of government spending, would advocate a five-year, $5 million program of road paving. In advertisements, Jackson even claimed the bridges, roads, and schools built by the WPA as his own achievements. More characteristically, he forced each city fireman to contribute $2 to his campaign, while Curran wrung $5 apiece from the court clerks. The challenger accused the incumbent of threatening to halt relief to any clients who dared vote against him.

On the electoral undercard, 109 candidates scrambled for eighteen council seats, three from each of six districts. Predictably, chaos prevailed. Joe's own political club splintered over endorsing him, and a total of five Poles wound up running. The district, with its dissonant mixture of religions and nationalities, had long been called the "Fighting First." Rather than unite its tribes behind one slate under the flag of class, Curran routinely fielded six or seven contestants for three council openings, promoting a different "favorite son" in Little Italy, Jewtown, Fell's Point, and Bohemian Canton. The idea behind the so-called bobtail ticket was to draw the maximum votes to the mayoral aspirant at its top. Any candidate elected to the council, after all, would obey his boss as blindly as the next; the whole bunch of them were, in Baltimore parlance, "Muldoons."

Joe campaigned by doing what he had always done, except more of it—fixing parking tickets, giving away garbage cans, persuading landlords to forgive overdue rent. With the "walk-around money" from Curran, he hired runners by the score to course through the neighborhood, from row house to pushcart to saloon, passing out palm cards with a portrait of Joe, eyes alert and head slightly cocked, as if attending a petitioner that very moment. One day he sent his younger daughter, Vilma, to school with an armload of balsa-wood airplanes, the fuselage of each emblazoned, "Vote for Obrycki."

Yet Joe seemed visibly miserable with the personal side of campaigning. For so many years he had waited for people to approach him, weighing their troubles and needs like a sovereign, that now he could barely bring himself to play the suitor. He would stand alone and impassive in the midst of an oyster roast, all boozy bonhomie, until a handler forced him from table to table for halfhearted gab. It was simpler, and less strenuous, to run on Aleksander's coattails, as an article in the weekly newspaper *Jednosc Polonia* made explicit:

> It is expected that young Mr. Obrycki will gather to himself the votes of all those and their children who today are indebted to the late Mr. Obrycki. Paying the son for the father, you should do the decent thing.

Election Day dawned blustery and cold, the streets puddled from an overnight storm, but as always it proceeded in Fell's Point with an air of festivity. By five-thirty, Joe's runners crowded the Second Ward club, receiving their assignments and dollars for bribes. In waves through the day, they knocked on doors, dispensed sample ballots, and arranged for baby-sitters and rides. A single voter might be set upon by four or five runners at once. Palm cards and flyers swirled in the wind, drifting onto sidewalks and collecting in gutters. By law the bars remained closed, so the club tapped a keg, welcoming at dusk the same runners it had sent out at daybreak, all itching now for the tally.

Standing at the center of this political circuitry, Joe Obrycki must have been worried. For one thing, the ballot worked against him. Through minions on the Board of Elections, Mayor Jackson had ensured that the Democratic insignia—a hand with index finger extended—pointed to his name. The design made him and his slate of council candidates look like the only Democrats in the race. (Naturally, Jackson called it a "mere accident.") Then there was the glut of Polish opponents, Kosakowski and Gutkowski, Siemek and Krysiak, so reliant on the same finite constituency that the first chore when campaigning outside it was to teach non-Poles how to pronounce their names. In an editorial a few days before the primary, *Jednosc Polonia* predicted, "All will be lost because of a split vote." This, it despaired, was what caused Polish jokes.

As the night lengthened, the results revealed not merely loss but disaster. Jackson won reelection with nearly two-thirds of the vote, taking even Fell's Point. And Joe finished fourth, behind two Germans and a Jew. With 6,413 votes, he fell barely 600 shy of landing in one of the eighteen leather swivel chairs that were, literally, city council seats.

Late that night Lillian Obrycki returned home from the clubhouse to find her daughters awake, still in school dresses, and anxious for word. "Dad didn't win," she said. As for Joe, he groused to his favorite sister, Marie, "Dumb Polacks didn't vote for me."

Aleksander Obrycki, in death Joe's greatest asset, would never have so slurred his own people.

• • •

As Anne Schanze would later remember it, she met Joe Obrycki when she stopped for a drink at his bar. It was late 1944, and he had just opened a tavern on East Pratt Street near Fell's Point. Waiting tables at an Italian restaurant for $15 a week, raising two children and meanwhile divorcing their philandering father, Anne appreciated the refuge. She appreciated, too, the gentlemanly manners of the owner, and his taste for gold watches and French cuffs. On New Year's Eve, by her recollection, he asked her to work for him, and some months later he rented the second-floor apartment to her. They were friends.

Joe's daughters and political associates perceived a slightly different version of the situation. In theirs, Anne Schanze strutted into the picture, blonde and buxom, eleven years younger than Lillian Obrycki. These people believed Anne was Joe's mistress—something that she vehemently denies even in the 1990s.

In any event, it seems clear, Anne became the linchpin of the life Joe built after his single, futile sally at elective office; she was present as he made book, delivered favors, attended political functions, and, half-way by accident, founded one of Baltimore's renowned restaurants. The relationship between Joe and Anne served, in the eyes of many, as the emblem of his ethos. It took a particular sort of husband to escort a young, attractive, and available woman alongside his wife to the same receptions, the same weekends by the sea. At one particular tea dance, Lillian and Anne appeared wearing identical hats.

Joe's curious linkage to the women typified the duality of all his endeavors. The new bar, for instance, was not meant as a bar at all. Brass rail and mahogany counter aside, it served foremost as the new headquarters of Joe's gambling business, replacing the family candy store. The regulars went by nicknames like Nookie, Yorkie, and Buckles, arriving from their rounds pockets bulging with orders. Instead of a jukebox spinning Sinatra and the Dorseys, this bar tapped its feet to a radio reporting each win, place, and show. Such was the money sluicing through that periodically a gambler would pull Anne aside, say, "Two dollars on the winner," and then tip her whatever the victorious horse paid. In one night she could match a month's pay from the Italian joint.

Joe left it to his younger brothers, Mitchell and Eddie, to collect and record the bets, freeing him to play the *wielka szyszka,* the big cheese. With Curran appointed state attorney general in 1945, Joe possessed more clout than ever, and the vanity to match. Once American trade with Japan resumed, his cotton shirts gave way to silk, each mono-grammed across the breast pocket. He even shaved his armpits, ex-plaining to Anne, "So I don't offend nobody."

Thus refined, he met his public. One afternoon the supplicant could be a Greek fellow who bought a building in Fell's Point and installed a bar, refrigerator, and new bathrooms, only to be denied a liquor license. "Joe," he would complain, "I put in all this money." So Joe would reach for the wall phone and dial a number from memory and ask for "Mr. Curran." A few days later, after Uncle Willie had pulled the appropriate levers, Joe would motor off to Annapolis, the state capital, to conclude the transaction.

Or the visitor might be a contractor covetous of a paving deal with the city, now that Baltimore was growing again. Joe would pour them both a Canadian Club on the rocks, and they would disappear into the kitchen, drawn by the aroma wafting from a pot of oyster stew. The contractor, as he told his tale, would drag a finger across the creamy surface, taste it, smile, reach for a ladle, and slurp down several more samples. Through it all, Joe would nod, grin, and promise intercession. And when the contractor left, Joe would rinse the ladle and mutter, "You goddamn son of a bitch."

Patience had its recompense. Curran moved Joe from the marriage license bureau to a higher grade of sinecure, as a bailiff in Orphans Court. Even in a courthouse of marble pillars and stained-glass skylights, guarded by the goddesses of mercy, truth, courage, and other virtues only intermittently observed in the local version of justice, the Orphans Court set the criterion for elegance. It was a jewel box of a room, with an oak parquet floor, desks fashioned from rare St. Jago mahogany, and a mural of Cornwallis surrendering to Washington, commissioned from a Parisian master and unveiled by the French ambassador.

Through its splendor shuffled hacks and factotums and rewarded loyalists, probating a will or hearing a contest between heirs, attracting little more attention than police court in Fell's Point ever received. As a bailiff, Joe wrote out the daily schedule, arranged the judges' papers, swore in the witnesses, and declared, in his most public moment, "Court's in session." Of his work ethic, this insight persists: When Frank Miedusiewski replaced Joe after his death in 1970 and was found busy at eleven o'clock one morning, a colleague remonstrated, "What're you still doin' here? Joe Obrycki would be gone by nine-thirty."

If correct in spirit, the account may err slightly in timing, since by most recollections Joe was visiting Anne Schanze in the morning. He generally arrived at court about eleven and left by noon, often for lunch with more rarefied company than he had hitherto enjoyed. He was part of Curran's daily "Roundtable" at Miller Brothers Restaurant, the collection of judges, lawyers, and clerks who determined the award of every courthouse job from janitor upward. Then, with Jack Pollack enthroned as Baltimore's most powerful boss, Joe joined his entourage at the corner table of the Emerson Hotel. When Pollack threw his annual Christmas party, with its heaps of shrimp and crab, its swing band and top-shelf liquor, Joe brought Lillian and conscripted a bald, dumpy bookie to escort Anne on a "double date."

With all this stature of a sort, it was serendipity far more than plan or necessity that transformed Joe into a restaurateur. Early on, his bar had served Maryland blue crabs steamed in spices, but only as an aspect of its lawful veneer and a proven way to raise thirsts and beer sales. Still, he applied to this sidelight the same industry that characterized him in gambling and politics. Instead of buying crabs in the Baltimore markets, some of them days out of the water, he drove to the Eastern Shore for the most recent catch. Then he steamed them, only six at a time, in fresh spices rather than a tinned mix. His obituary in the *Sun* would include this malapropism of a boast: "He never served dead crabs."

Thanks to one early customer, a newspaper cartoonist, word spread in press and political circles. In time, mayors, entertainers, and professional ballplayers would frequent Obrycki's Olde Crab House, and Joe would tell any audience how he shipped dinner to Dorothy Lamour in Hollywood. He even engineered a simultaneous crab feast in Paris, San Francisco, and Fell's Point, airlifting the crustaceans like so many C rations. The restaurant's fiftieth anniversary would merit coverage in the *Sun,* although its true origins had by then been encrusted by lore, just like Joe's own.

In the middle 1940s, though, such revisionism lay ahead. Joe practiced the physics of cynicism. Infidelity, criminality, and corruption formed a unified field of misshapen values, each predictive of the others. The man who could greet clients with such unflagging sycophancy walked his youngest sister up the church aisle and, before the altar, told the navy petty officer about to marry her, "How can I do this to a man who's serving his country?"

Joe's reign depended on the complicity of his subjects, some bulldozed and some bought. It depended on Lillian enduring humiliation to the point of an ulcer. It depended on the beat cops, fully aware of the real business of his bar, averting their eyes in exchange for a dozen crabs. It depended on people never leaving neighborhoods where, like his daughter Vilma and her boyfriend, Jack Maeby, they did not personally know a single Republican, and so could not imagine voting any way but Democratic.

The rules were not Joe's alone. They governed politics well beyond Baltimore. To a greater or lesser degree, every big-city Democratic machine counted on stasis for survival—on quiescent blacks, on timid immigrants, on a feudal reliance on the boss for jobs and favors, on material needs so basic a few bucks or a chicken could buy a vote. From the 1840s to the 1940s only the faces in the tenements had changed, not the conditions of life or the price tag on loyalty.

But the world would not long remain so immutable. Jack Maeby, a star quarterback for Patterson High School, was leaving Baltimore, first for the Army and then Bucknell University in Pennsylvania on a football scholarship. He would return home barely long enough to marry Vilma, then whisk her away with him to the frontier of suburbia.

Chapter Six

Worth Two
(Silvio Burigo)

Oɴ ᴛʜᴇ ʙʟᴜsᴛᴇʀʏ ᴀꜰᴛᴇʀɴᴏᴏɴ ᴏꜰ Mᴀʀᴄʜ 23, 1935, ᴅᴜʀɪɴɢ
New Rochelle's most disastrous stretch yet of the Depression, the Chamber of Commerce held a parade. From the corner of North and Main,
the center of the city, promenaded drum corps and school bands, police
astride motorcycles, soldiers brandishing rifle and bayonet, a float that
featured a jungle scene. It was altogether the largest such celebration
since the doughboys had marched in 1918. The procession moved four
miles northward, from the shopping district past the high school and
into the exclusive neighborhood of Bonnie Crest before finally arriving
at its destination, a vacant lot with yellowed grass a foot tall. There, a
contingent of officials and businessmen lifted new spades to break
ground for a model home, the civic elite's answer to hard times.

"All of you are aware, the continuation of the present business
depression is in no way due to a lack of money," declared the Chamber
of Commerce's president, an automobile executive named Eastman,
dressed for the occasion in a derby and double-breasted topcoat. "If we
could eliminate this fear, this dread of spending, and if the public by
and large would start to improve their homes . . . we would have prosperity in a fortnight."

Over the next four months the model home rose, a New England colonial with three bedrooms, two baths, a fireplace, a sun porch, and even a finished basement divided into laundry, workshop, and wet bar. Merchants could not furnish it fast enough, donating chintz drapes, a china hutch, a console radio, and a concert piano. After the last bit of trim had been dabbed, the model home opened its doors eleven hours a day for eight weeks, attracting visitors by the thousands.

But the only boom it ever generated was for the fortunate handful of men on the construction crew. The model home drew crowds for the same reason movies like *Top Hat* or *The Gay Divorcee* packed the RKO Proctor: It offered people mired in poverty a diverting glimpse of abundance. The only problem, of course, was that the film always ended, and with it the fantasy.

Few knew the reality better than Silvio Burigo. It was fine for his wife, Delia, to visit the model home, and to peruse all the houses being sold for back taxes, fine for her to talk about how $5,000 could get the whole family out of the walk-up it now occupied for $35 a month. But on odd jobs as a janitor or night watchman, Silvio could afford nothing more.

Despite what the Chamber of Commerce fellow said, it surely looked to Silvio as if there was too little money. Who could afford a model house for $8,500 when work relief paid $55 a month? It hardly mattered that Local 86 had recently negotiated for a weekly minimum wage of $67 because virtually no construction jobs existed at any pay. Even on the model home, a rare lode, nonunion plumbers were hired, even invited to march in the parade. Little galled Silvio more.

When he read the *Standard-Star,* New Rochelle's daily newspaper, the headlines crowed, "BUYING DEMAND FIRM IN COUNTY," "FUTURE BRIGHT IN REAL ESTATE." Yet in one month of 1934 the city had recorded $6,000 being spent in the building trades; before the Depression the figure once soared as high as $1.5 million. A few contractors, baffled at how else to find customers, sold new homes by lottery, fifty cents a chance. There was probably more work to be found in *de*struction, as the city razed houses it had acquired through foreclosure and then been unable to unload.

In the West End, it sometimes seemed, the industrial world was reverting to a subsistence economy of barter and foraging. A family raised and slaughtered its own pig for a season's meat. A blacksmith sharpened tools in exchange for food. A young girl pulled on a muslin slip sewn by her great-aunt for a Christmas gift, only to discover the word "SWIFT" faintly printed across the front, residue from the fabric's original role as a meatpacking sack. The girl was Silvio Burigo's daughter Lorraine.

During the twenty-six-month span from August 1938 through September 1940, a period that was documented in a union ledger, Silvio worked as a plumber exactly once. Even the most successful of his brethren in Local 86 went jobless well over half that time. All the union could offer these men was the unpaid task of monitoring the few private construction sites to determine if they were complying with the contract.

Silvio rarely located more than one of these sites in a month, and the experience harrowed him. Contract or no contract, most sites functioned on the crudest application of supply and demand. With jobs scarce almost to the point of nonexistence, contractors routinely wrung kickbacks from employees, added hours to the workday, and salted crews with cheaper, nonunion labor. It was only logical, then, that they also barred Silvio or any other union inspector from the sites. He would wait for hours at the perimeter, often volleying insults or threats with the boss, until the men broke for lunch and he could approach them. But these plumbers were hardly inclined to inform, not even to that "dear sir and brother," Silvio Burigo.

So he went home as unemployed as before and chastened besides. He would not work, it seemed, until he chose to betray the union. That option was unthinkable. But so, too, was life in a household starving for income.

For years Delia and Silvio had fought over money. And at points, their conflict had seemed almost comical, like Maggie and Jiggs on the radio. More than once, Delia forged a bill from the milkman to try to weasel a few dollars out of Silvio. But the Depression, with its prospect of unending want, magnified even their mildest spats into blood feuds. Delia bought used magazines from the Salvation Army and filled a scrapbook with the glossiest advertisements—a gleaming kitchen meant to sell Armstrong tile, rose-cheeked brides for Camay soap. These fantasies of affluence inflamed Silvio. "What're you cuttin' out paper dolls for?" he shouted from his armchair. "You got things to do."

By 1933, Delia began disappearing. Once she asked a cousin to watch Lorraine for a few hours and did not return for several days. Other times her absences stretched for weeks, as she fetched up with relatives in Hoboken or an Italian radio-theater troupe in New York. The price of this chaos appeared most clearly one day in 1934, when six-year-old Lorraine stumbled down the street. A neighbor, hurrying to her aid, discovered she had put the wrong shoe on each foot. No one had ever taught her the difference. Nor, for that matter, did she know how to tell time.

Determined as Silvio was never to reveal weakness, in these moments of despair he often sought out his aunt Virginia, who lived just five houses farther up Sickles Avenue. It was she with whom he had found refuge as an orphan twenty-five years before, and who still invited him for Christmas dinner. As much as he joked about her domineering style, dubbing her "the sergeant," he felt secure unburdening himself in the comfort of her kitchen. Now, as she sat in a chair, he knelt and sobbed into her apron.

"Let her go, let her go," Aunt Virginia advised.

"I can't," replied Silvio. "I love her so much."

The birth of a daughter, Mary Jane, in 1935, reunited the family only briefly. The search for construction work carried Silvio from state to state, and during one of his treks Delia took the baby and fled, leaving behind ten-year-old Seely and Lorraine, only seven. Loath to quit a job in the midst of the Depression, Silvio sent $10 each week to Lorraine to manage the household. With the money came orders to account for every dime.

Recalling a dish she had seen her mother cook, Lorraine threw cubed meat and a cow's knuckle bone into a stockpot. After an hour she served it to Seely. "That's not soup," he informed her. "That's water." Seely did little better, stretching scrambled eggs with so much milk he produced a custard as bland as it was pale. The two of them had no choice except to grimace and swallow. The only thing worse than wasting edible food would be bearing Silvio's wrath if he ever found out.

Eventually both Silvio and Delia returned from their separate travels and negotiated a peace based less on affection than on a mutual stake in survival. Once, when Silvio needed money to reach a steam-fitting job several hundred miles away, Delia solicited it from her relatives. The first, an uncle who owned a butcher shop and had enjoyed free plumbing service from Silvio, refused; the second, a painter who was himself out of work, somehow scraped together a loan. Typically, Silvio resisted, but Delia pleaded, "They're helping you out. Take the help."

He did and he remembered. In the years to come, Silvio never so much as tightened a joint for the butcher. But he brought the painter's son into Local 86 and personally trained him. By then, after World War II, it actually seemed possible to make a living as a plumber again.

• • •

Through every vicissitude of the Depression years, one element of Silvio Burigo's life remained stable. Local 86, even when it could not find him work, provided fellowship, identity, and political direction. Silvio responded with an almost religious sense of obligation. Not once between 1933 and 1941 did he miss paying his dues, a precious $3 or $4 per month, and only a job out of state could keep him from attending the weekly membership meeting. In June 1939, Silvio won election to the local's executive board, and served in leadership positions until his death almost forty years later.

In all that time, Silvio's roles as union man and Democrat remained closely intertwined. However discontented he later grew with welfare-state liberalism, he would leave the blasphemy of voting Republican to his descendants. Silvio Burigo's politics, a longtime friend and coworker said, consisted of "labor, labor, and labor." Or as he himself often put it, "The Republicans are for the rich. They don't know what it is to be hard up."

While Franklin Roosevelt reigned as Silvio's hero, the Depression itself created the conditions for an alliance between blue-collar ethnics, the vast number of them Catholics or Jews, and a Protestant patrician. Silvio himself rarely spoke in such grand terms, being far more absorbed in daily struggles, but he gladly adopted the doctrines of his union, the United Association of Journeymen Plumbers and Steam Fitters. And through its monthly magazine, the *Journal,* the United Association espoused an agenda shared by virtually all its fellow unions within the American Federation of Labor.

For a union that occupied the conservative end of the labor movement, the United Association nonetheless saw in Herbert Hoover's America a nation starkly divided between "valuable and valiant" workers and "plutocrats," "bourbons," and "industrial despots." For several years before Roosevelt won the presidency, the union advocated many of the specific programs he would introduce as elements of the New Deal—massive public construction, slum-clearance projects, control of working hours, repeal of Prohibition, banking reform. Only months into Roosevelt's first term, the union reversed its previous positions and began to urge federal relief payments and unemployment insurance.

Behind the declaration of class warfare, the union was actually pleading for reform as a moderating force. Like Silvio himself, the plumbers' union and the AFL regarded the organizing efforts of the Communist Party and the Industrial Workers of the World with horror. As skilled craftsmen, the self-described "aristocrats of labor," members like Silvio held themselves apart, too, from the rank-and-file of the assembly-line, mass-production unions that in 1935 would form the Congress of Industrial Organizations. Before there was the New Deal, the United Association understood one of its central premises: Capitalism had to be saved from itself. As Thomas E. Burke, the union's general secretary, argued in the United Association *Journal* editorial in April 1930:

Hungry men can not reason.

Communists are aware of this fact—hence their ease in staging unemployment demonstrations, not for purpose of relief but for hate propaganda.

Trade unionists are not in sympathy with this program, but they disapprove [of] Cossack tactics of police who are ordered to ride down hungry men.

To say unemployed have sympathy with Communism is to ignore the law of cause and effect. These demonstrations will cease if these men are employed.

President Roosevelt struck his essential compact with organized labor on June 16, 1933, when he signed into law the National Industrial Recovery Act. It was a sweeping piece of legislation that appropriated $3.3 billion for projects of the Public Works Administration and set codes for wages, hours, and conditions in the private sector. The codes would be overseen by a new agency, the National Recovery Administration, soon to provide one of the icons of the New Deal, a blue eagle grasping bolts of lightning above the vow "We Do Our Part." But the most salient words for the union movement, the passage some would call "labor's Magna Carta," appeared at the outset of Section 7a: "[E]mployees shall have the right to organize and bargain collectively through representatives of their own choosing."

With that single decree, the president reversed a precipitous decline for organized labor, whose share of the American work force had fallen from 12 percent in 1920 to less than half that in 1933. The AFL doubled its membership, to about four million, in the first year of the NIRA. The number of strikes, many turning on the issue of union recognition, tripled. Writing in the September 1933 edition of the *Journal,* Burke reflected both the drama and the hyperbole of the moment:

Men who have never dared consider joining a union now come forward openly, eagerly and joyously, to join with their fellows in a great humanitarian movement of labor for the betterment of its conditions and for the enlargement of the whole scheme and sphere of human life.

This great influx of workers into the unions of America is one of the great inspirations of our time. It is a picture of the opening of the gates of freedom. It is emancipation before our eyes.

Strife and rhetoric in combination created a deceptive image of union radicalism on the ascent. "WILL THERE BE A LABOR REVOLUTION?" *Fortune* magazine asked in a 1933 headline. In reality, many employers utilized the new law to establish compliant company unions, and the short-lived National Labor Board lacked any direct power of enforcement. Far from exciting labor to militancy, the NIRA invited it to become government's partner in a temperate consensus.

"People talk about a Roosevelt revolution," Sidney Hillman, the president of the Amalgamated Clothing Workers, told his union's convention in 1934. "They make me laugh. A year ago revolution was a distinct possibility. Today we hear no more of that sort of thing. The New Deal has changed all that." Lloyd Garrison, the first chairman of the permanent National Labor Relations Board, called organized labor "our chief bulwark against communism and other revolutionary movements."

Even in the West End of New Rochelle, so distant in most ways from Washington, the coalition between the Democratic Party and big labor could be seen, felt, and measured. The Fourth Ward, normally considered a Republican stronghold despite its concentration of trade-union members, had rebelled to support Roosevelt in 1932; four years later it gave him a two-thirds majority and a 1,200-vote margin, enough for Roosevelt to become the first Democrat to win New Rochelle in a quarter century. The leadership of the local Democratic club, meanwhile, passed from Cosmo Tocci, a classic padrone who made loans from his pocket and played Christopher Columbus in the holiday parade, to his son, Salvatore, a prototype of the new boss. A construction laborer himself, Salvatore forged his network of voters and precinct workers among comrades like Silvio Burigo in the building-trades unions. As if to remind them of the ultimate source of their protection, Tocci adorned the clubhouse with the NRA eagle.

The image became obsolete on May 27, 1935, when the Supreme Court struck down the NRA as unconstitutional. But just six weeks later President Roosevelt signed an even stronger protection for the right to organize, the Wagner Act. It emboldened labor in such epic confrontations as the sit-down strike by autoworkers in Flint, Michigan, and underlay the first union contracts with industrial corporations on the scale of General Motors and United States Steel. The Wagner Act on the surface had radical implications, suggesting ways for labor to exert as formidable a force as capital on the American economy. But as it was practiced, the law tended to moderate confrontations between union and management by confining them to the areas of wages, hours, and benefits. And the goal of raising wages, labor itself took to arguing in the years to come, was to raise consumption, to help *spend* America's way to prosperity.

Roosevelt relied increasingly on unions for power and votes. Virtually alone, organized labor endorsed his misbegotten scheme to enlarge the Supreme Court. More important, it lobbied, pressured, and campaigned for the so-called Second New Deal, which produced the Works Progress Administration, the most famous of all public jobs programs, and the Social Security Act, the cornerstone of the modern welfare state. After nearly six years of mass unemployment among its members, the AFL no longer viewed a nationalized pension program as a threat to its own package of benefits. Nor did organized labor's concern that the WPA undercut private wages sway its larger enthusiasm for the program. If anything, the severe recession that began in mid-1937 left union members, especially in the building trades, more reliant than ever on public works.

Issue after issue, month after month, the United Association *Journal* published snapshots of union crews on federal construction projects. October 1937: Locals 16 and 464 in Omaha pose outside the brick garden apartments of the Fontenelle Homes, built by the WPA. April 1939: Local 760 of Sheffield, Alabama, assembles on the site of the Guntersville Dam, part of the Tennessee Valley Authority. August 1939: Local 369 of Oklahoma City stands atop a classroom building at Oklahoma A&M, which had its campus expanded by the Public Works Administration. In their mix of the formal and the jocular, these snapshots evoke the spirit of a wedding or a family reunion; the men look grateful to be back at work, getting their hands dirty again. For a United Association member like Silvio Burigo, nothing could have made a more persuasive advertisement for the New Deal, Franklin Roosevelt, and the Democratic Party.

In New Rochelle, too, Silvio saw Washington's hand. From an office on North Avenue, one of New Rochelle's busiest streets, the Civil Works Administration dispensed several hundred jobs in fields ranging from nursing to filing to sewing. Aunt Virginia's son, Martin, a surrogate brother to Silvio, fought fires in Idaho with the Civilian Conservation Corps. The Works Progress Administration, lacking any large construction projects in New Rochelle, hired the jobless to paint murals, maintain parks and roads, grade the grounds of public buildings, and teach night-school courses in subjects from drafting to psychology to English literacy, the last so vital to Italian immigrants seeking citizenship.

One of the modest construction jobs the WPA did assume, building a gymnasium for the Better Boys Club, affected Silvio personally. The club was the epicenter of youth in the West End, the place to learn how to box or repair a radio, maybe even to wear the purple and white uniform of the Eagles baseball team. For Silvio, the product and now the patriarch of a tumultuous home, the club offered a safe haven for his children. Seely spent almost every afternoon there, building himself into a semi-pro third baseman, and Lorraine joined him for the Halloween costume party and the Friday-night movies—a serial, a cartoon, and Tom Mix feature, all for three cents.

In the end, what mattered most to Silvio and his fellows was the peace of mind that went with having a job. By creating work where there had been none, the New Deal dashed the political wisdom of the West End. For years the neighborhood's tradesmen had dependably if begrudgingly "voted the chicken," casting Republican ballots as the prerequisite for employment on municipal projects and with politically connected private contractors. Now they understood a different equation: Democrats equal jobs. All that remained was to act on it.

• • •

On September 12, 1939, a brief item appeared in the *Standard-Star*. Tucked on an inside page, well behind the war dispatches from Poland and barely ahead of the "Club News," it reported that on the previous evening the Democratic candidate for mayor, city council member Stanley Church, had addressed a rally in the West End. There, he advocated the construction of large apartment houses. Neither the place nor the subject was as innocuous as it seemed. In New Rochelle, "apartment" served as one of the code words of class politics, dividing owner from renter, WASP from ethnic, Republican from Democrat. And in the West End, Church saw the fulcrum of electoral power.

This was a neighborhood of renters or owners barely dodging foreclosure, of construction workers still jobless or underemployed, of people like Silvio Burigo. In national elections, it was true, the Fourth Ward had already shifted parties, but in a local contest it had never been pried loose from the Republicans. For a Democrat to win a vote there, then, was to seize one from the other side; it was, as the phrase went, "worth two."

By this time, it is generally argued, Franklin Roosevelt's hold on America was slipping. Despite the billions of dollars poured into public works, the national unemployment rate stood above 17 percent. In the midterm elections of 1938, the Democrats had lost eighty-nine seats in Congress. An emboldened opposition of Republicans and southern Democrats defeated even comparatively mild measures on housing and spending, effectively leaving the New Deal to wither. Running in 1940 for his third term, Roosevelt would defeat Wendell Willkie by less than five million votes in the closest popular vote since 1916.

Seen from the West End instead of Washington, however, from the bottom instead of the top, Roosevelt and the New Deal were still seeping into the political soil, permeating it, and transforming both government and governance for decades to come. The realignment of American politics in the 1930s was nothing but the concept of "worth two" writ large.

In Stanley Church, the emergent Democratic majority presented a flawed if fervent apostle. Excluding two patronage positions with New Deal agencies, Church had never really worked, though he variously claimed careers in law and public relations. He had courted scandal by eloping, at age thirty-seven, with an eighteen-year-old who would be the first of three wives. The last thing he did before bed every night, she said, was comb his hair and check the mirror.

But in seven years on the city council, and two previous runs for mayor, Church had been cultivating a following in New Rochelle's working-class districts, fusing a coalition of blacks and ethnic whites. He was not, by most recollections, a brilliant man, but he was a shrewd and tenacious one. Blacks and building tradesmen accounted for two-thirds of the relief cases in New Rochelle. And Church found a single issue, discrete and knowable, that could excite their resentment.

It was water. The wealthiest family in New Rochelle, the Iselins, owned the water company serving the city. That company was, in the most classic sense, a monopoly, and a monopoly controlled by people who lived on an estate called Sans Souci, socialized with Belmonts and Astors, and elicited bows of serflike deference from locals as they toured in a horse-drawn carriage. In the early 1930s, Church discovered that these barons were gouging the city.

He did not attack them by name; that would have been foolish. As benefactors of churches, schools, and even the city government, the Iselins had accrued much good will and political influence. So Church simply delivered the numbers, and let them tell the story of power and privilege. The Iselins sold their water at a markup of as much as 366 percent. They charged customers more than twice what the municipally owned water utilities in nearby towns did. Even the fire department had to pay $150,000 per year.

At Church's behest, the city filed a formal protest in 1932 with the state Public Service Commission. Three years and sixty-six hearings later, the commission ordered the water company to cut its rates by one-quarter, saving New Rochelle's consumers $245,000 annually. Triumphant once, Church mounted similar crusades against the gas and electric company and several commuter railroads, revisiting the same villains like shrines over a forty-year career.

Silvio Burigo appreciated these attacks, especially at the outset. Having lost his electricity once, he knew the difference even pennies made in a utility bill. He had other reasons, too, to admire Church. Back in 1933 the city had tried to fire its garbage collectors, many of them Italians from the West End, in order to hire a less expensive private outfit. Allying himself for the moment with the Socialist Party, Church fought back the plan. Much of his 1939 platform aimed at creating jobs in construction, not by trying to kindle a private recovery like the Chamber of Commerce with its model home, but by turning government to the task—expanding use of the WPA, loosening the zoning restrictions on apartments, and creating a public authority to build subsidized housing. Public housing was one of the economic tonics the plumbers' union most strongly prescribed. Silvio read the editorials in the *Journal;* he saw the snapshots, like the one of the local from Omaha. Those guys were working as plumbers, not night watchmen, like him.

Church made certain not a soul missed his message. In the Tammany Hall tradition he led a "balanced ticket" including an Irishman, a Jew, several Italians, and two women, allied by issues of class. Every night and all weekend he rang doorbells, especially in the tenement districts, here telling a joke with a punch line in Yiddish, there trading God-talk with a black Baptist minister. With the West End so vital to Church's prospects, Salvatore Tocci led him from church carnival to Holy Name Society breakfast, from the Columbian Civic League to the North Italy Society, from a bridge party at the YMCA to a house meeting at Jennie DiBenedetto's.

Heads invariably turned. With his high forehead and strong jaw, Church exuded a Cary Grant sort of dash, and his blonde, blue-eyed wife had modeled. And like the actor he had intended to become, Church rehearsed for the role. He memorized the names of five thousand voters and scoured the letters-to-the-editor column of the *Standard-Star* in search of issues to appropriate and meetings where he could put in a surprise, star appearance.

But something more than crass ambition animated Stanley Church. When he stepped into a cold-water flat dressed in a suit and tie, his wife in gabardine at his elbow, when he praised a piece of furniture or an aroma from the kitchen, he was offering the simple respect that New Rochelle's lower classes rarely enjoyed. He may have grown up in relative comfort, the son of an export manager in the dry-goods trade, but his own parents had been threatened with losing their water and lights during the Depression. Eventually a bank foreclosed on their home. As Silvio might have put it, Stanley Church knew "what it is to be hard up."

His opponent, George Roberts, had barely a clue. The son and namesake of a longtime Republican leader, and the product of private schools, Roberts worked as a banker and served in desultory fashion on the city council. Profiling him during the campaign, the *Standard-Star* managed only the faint flattery that while Roberts "never has been one of the more loquacious members . . . his laconic remarks are readily understood." He fairly shrank from Church's sort of door-to-door campaigning, explaining to one audience, "I have a large family to support and it is imperative for me to be at my place of business during the day."

Not that the old order exactly abdicated. On October 23, fifteen days before the election, a Teletype clattered out a message at the New York City police headquarters. The Westchester County sheriff, who happened to be the Republican Party chairman in New Rochelle, was requesting the criminal record of Stanley Church. In all likelihood, the sheriff knew no such record existed. But simply by asking for it, he could resurrect a twenty-year-old rumor that Church had once been arrested as a Peeping Tom.

Instead, within hours of the Teletype, Church presented himself voluntarily at the county jail for fingerprinting, careful to have the press in tow. He called for Governor Herbert Lehman, an intimate of President Roosevelt, to investigate the county sheriff. And the *Standard-Star,* in a front-page editorial, urged Republicans to vote for Church as a protest against the dirty trick.

They voted, in droves. In the West End, the line wound down Fourth Street from the poll in Silvio's cousin's garage, past the tomato patches brown with autumn, past the backyard chicken coops, and past the Democratic clubhouse once decorated by the NRA eagle and now festooned with posters of Stanley Church. New Rochelle assigned fifty police officers, nearly one-third of the force, to manage the crowds throughout the city. Only the presidential elections of 1932 and 1936 had brought out more voters, for, as Church said, "They don't come out when they're satisfied."

All night the dissatisfied streamed into his storefront headquarters— carpenters and masons, small shopkeepers, a sprinkling of liberal doctors and lawyers, hundreds in a room built for dozens. District leaders rushed in with results from more than sixty polls, and those numbers filled a grid posted along one wall. The Third Ward, the wealthy "back country," went to Roberts—no surprise there. Nor was it news that the Second, heavily Irish, voted Democratic as usual. But in the Fourth something was happening. The ward's black districts, Republican since Lincoln, came in heavily for Church. Then the Italian districts reported, and everyone realized this was not just a victory but a rout.

In a city with 60 percent Republican registration, Church took nearly two-thirds of the vote. The Fourth Ward delivered close to half of his winning margin. Church's supporters seemed to understand that they had captured more than one office. For Tocci and Kenny and Moskowitz, for Tiernan and Gotti and Duberstein, and for Silvio Burigo, too, Church's victory represented their own ascension. It had taken seven years since Franklin Roosevelt was first elected, but now, in the most complete sense, the New Deal had finally reached New Rochelle. In the person of Stanley Church, it would not fully relinquish its hold until 1970.

"We have a new mayor," one district leader cried out. "We won this election. Let's sweep the Republicans out."

With flags, torches, and corn brooms, the crowd cakewalked through the streets, moving past the slumbering banks and department stores downtown and climbing the Union Avenue hill into the West End. Roused by the racket, people hung out the windows of their railroad flats, gathered on tenement stoops, and joined the procession in housecoats and bathrobes. It turned up Fourth Street and halted outside a raincoat factory that had served as the West End's Republican headquarters, where it jeered at the handful of laggards.

A few buildings away, clustered around the kitchen table of their third-floor apartment, the Burigos heard the din. "That's the victory celebration," said Silvio, as if he had always been sure. So they ran to the parlor windows, Lorraine and Seely and even Delia, who had voted for Stanley Church because he was so handsome. And they gazed down on the street in amazement, at the firebrands brighter than streetlamps. This was no Chamber of Commerce parade arranged by a hired planner; this was spontaneous, from the bottom up. "Look at that," Silvio said with approval. "Look at them brooms. They're sweeping the city clean."

• • •

On the morning of November 24, 1943, while a backdrop of bloody stalemate continued along the Gustav Line dividing Italy, the commander of the United States Navy submarine base in Groton, Connecticut, bestowed an award for meritorious civilian service on one Otto Epstein, a plumbing subcontractor. The honor, by extension, belonged to Silvio Burigo, too, for he had worked for Epstein in the vast wartime expansion of the base. Theirs was a mission that had proceeded virtually around the clock for weeks, months, and years, pausing only for air-raid blackouts and, on one occasion, a gunpoint intrusion by marine guards who mistook a crew of steam fitters for saboteurs.

The war years were itinerant ones for Silvio, years of following jobs from the New England coastline to the far side of the Mississippi, of sleeping in boardinghouses or Quonset huts, of reaching his family only by postcard or pay envelope or, once, a tiny souvenir bale of cotton. But these were years of work. With military construction abundant and the ranks of skilled plumbers and steam fitters thinned by the draft, contractors were constantly broadcasting jobs through United Association locals. After a dozen years of fitful and menial labor, Silvio grabbed every chance, even conquering his fear of heights to climb high-tension towers at one base. Exactly what a plumber was doing up there remains unclear; the incident endures as a testament to Silvio's hunger for a job.

The scale of these bases dwarfed anything Silvio could have conceived; for him a junior high school had seemed epic. Fort Chaffee rose from the ridges and valleys of Arkansas into a military metropolis of more than 35,000; the project required 3,000 yards of cloth ribbon, 15,000 gallons of paint, 1 million pounds of nails, and 40 million board feet of lumber just to prepare the site for construction. There, as in Groton, the construction workers earned decoration, sharing in the Army-Navy Production Award conferred upon their general contractor for having completed the 73,000-acre camp months ahead of schedule and millions of dollars below budget.

On the Groton submarine base, crews had filled in a lake, moved a state highway, and literally peeled the surface off hundreds of acres of hillside. Within four years nearly two hundred buildings had sprung up, forming a city complete down to its soda fountain and barbershop. The very air throbbed with endeavor. Generators heaved, jackhammers rattled, and hot rivets snapped like a machine gun's report as they were hammered into place. "It could make you go wacky," one plumber would later remember. Besides a head numbed by the racket, Silvio might well end the workday coated with tar from weatherproofing pipe or smeared hobolike with sweat and dust from the trenches. It took all the energy anybody could muster just to hoist a few beers at Pippy's or the Kozy Korner.

What the toil provided, beyond thirst, sore muscles, and an expression of patriotism, was a renewed sense of worth. A supervisor at the Groton submarine base recalled having this conversation with an electrician just retrieved from the legions of the unemployed:

I said, "I'm glad to see you pitch in and do this work so well, even though you're not gettin' paid much." He said, "Harold, that's the only way I know to work. I wouldn't be worth a darn doin' anything else if I let myself go. I work as hard here as anywhere."

The impression exists, partly through Roosevelt's own words, that wartime mobilization replaced Depression-era public works in one clean stroke. In December 1942 the president presented the WPA an "honorable discharge," saying it had fulfilled its purpose; a year later he said "Dr. New Deal" was retiring in favor of "Dr. Win-the-War." But actually the two practiced in concert. On the bases where Silvio worked, private crews hired under War Department contracts labored alongside contingents from the WPA and the CCC. Bricks and girders for construction teams traveled over roads hewn by men fresh from relief rolls.

Whatever else World War II was, it was, on the home front, an utterly Keynesian exercise in deficit spending and public works. Between 1939 and 1944 unemployment fell from 17.2 percent to 1.2 percent, the lowest in modern American history. The average weekly industrial wage nearly doubled to $45.70 during roughly the same period. Corporate after-tax profits climbed to $10.8 billion annually from $6.4 billion. The fuel for this engine was the $288 billion the United States poured into the war effort, which would more than quintuple the federal debt between the Pearl Harbor attack and V-J Day.

By itself, the Groton base absorbed more than $3 million, recycling thirty-four cents of each as wages. Silvio Burigo's share amounted to perhaps $50 per week, a modest sum for modest hopes. With the young men at war, construction workers tended to be like him—middle-aged, old enough to have accumulated debts and humility. What Silvio wanted most was to reassemble his family, grown to six with the birth of a daughter, Carole Ann, in 1944, and to restore a semblance of security.

Having dragged the family from walk-up to railroad flat to relative's spare room, and moved nearly a dozen times in as many years in the quest for cheaper rent, Silvio could now afford the previously unimaginable expanse of six rooms. The Burigos got their own telephone. Eating out with her mother and sisters at the Traffic Diner, Lorraine tasted navy bean soup for the first time in her life. Purchases that would seem trivial a decade later gave survivors of the Depression reason enough for gratitude, gratitude that ultimately obtained to the president.

The war conflated Roosevelt's roles as employment agent and commander in chief. At the same time Silvio was building military installations, his son, Seely, was serving in the 75th Infantry, having been thrown almost straight from officers' training at Brooklyn College into the Battle of the Bulge. A man who normally dismissed religion with the comment "You don't need to go to church to be a good person," Silvio now joined his older daughters for nine o'clock Mass at Blessed Sacrament, praying for Seely's return. A cousin, only a year older, had already perished, shot down on a bombing raid over Germany.

Then, one morning in early 1945, the doorbell rang. Silvio lumbered down the three flights of stairs, only to find himself facing the angel of death in the prosaic form of a Western Union deliveryman named Bam Cataldo. Accustomed, perhaps, to the terror his appearance inspired, Cataldo quickly reassured Silvio that, by the color of star on the envelope, he could tell Seely was alive. He had been wounded, it turned out, by a German sniper.

Once it became clear Seely would recover, and have a Purple Heart and Silver Star to show for his injuries, the family could even joke about how he had caught the bullet in his butt. Everyone, that is, except Delia, who blamed Roosevelt personally for the injury. She just wanted her boy home and married off. All that would happen soon enough. But before the Germans and Japanese surrendered, before Seely sailed home to marry his sweetheart, attend Fordham on the GI Bill, and show his kid sister Mary Jane the nighttime lights of Manhattan, the nation would shudder at a death occurring far from the field of battle.

• • •

Silvio Burigo read two newspapers every day, the *Daily News* with his morning coffee and the *Standard-Star* after work, while chewing an unlit Phillie cigar. In the late afternoon of April 12, 1945, as he flipped the pages, a radio prattled in the background. All the chatter distracted Silvio, but Lorraine rarely missed her favorite soap, *Stella Dallas,* or afterward, with a twist of the dial, *Jack Armstrong, the All-American Boy*. It was Lorraine, then, expecting amusement, who first heard the bulletin that Franklin Delano Roosevelt had died. Minutes later, amid a crowd of neighbors gathered on the sidewalk, she asked no one and everyone, "What do we do now?"

At nearly the same moment in Baltimore, Jack Maeby was hurrying from high school to the factory where he helped fabricate bomber wings. Nearing the newsstand the Nardone brothers ran, or had run until they both went to war, he noticed a truck dumping bundles of the *American,* much later than usual. First his eyes found the word "EXTRA" and then the headline beneath. After his shift he would talk about it with his girlfriend, Vilma Obrycki. For now he could only think, My God, what'll happen to the country? The father is dead.

And in Ossining, Edith Carey glanced out her window and noticed Pop Graber next door lowering the flag outside his grocery. Anyone's tragedy was everyone's in tiny Crotonville; Edith herself had a husband and brother in the service. She walked out onto the stoop and asked, "Pop, what're you doin' that for?" As he turned to speak, she spotted the tears draining down his cheeks. "The president died?" she blurted. His answer apparent, she wondered, What's gonna happen to us?

Two evenings later, on April 14, the funeral train pulled out of Union

Station in Washington, bound for Hyde Park and burial. It would pass through Baltimore, New Rochelle, and Ossining, literally through the lives of three families. Nearly thirty years would elapse before they discovered one another, through the children who, paradoxically, would set out to dismantle the Roosevelt legacy. But on its somber journey the train gathered and joined them, just as the New Deal politics of the fallen president had.

Ten minutes before midnight the train reached Baltimore. With the platform of Pennsylvania Station closed to all but chosen dignitaries, people massed along the tracks, one stretch running through Fell's Point. Many waited five hours in the rain. A few laid coins on the rails, to be smashed by the funeral train and kept as mementos. A man named Terrence Jensen, who worked in a defense plant, told the *Sun*, "President Roosevelt was a man for the common people. He is the best friend you and me—people who work with our hands—ever had."

At 7:14 the next morning, the train rolled through Ossining, tracing the same route along the Hudson that Abraham Lincoln's funeral train had taken some eighty years earlier. One hundred people stood on the platform, among them a war photographer and a railroad mechanic who had been waiting since five o'clock. After the last car vanished, all of them filed away, silence instead of words forming their tribute.

Between Baltimore and Ossining, between Fell's Point and Crotonville, the train had made a special, prolonged stop in New Rochelle. The twenty-minute pause allowed for a change of locomotives as the train shifted from a branch line to the main for the final leg northward. Because the same routine applied every time Roosevelt had traveled from the White House to Hyde Park, seventy-eight trips in all, New Rochelle had grown almost proprietary about the president. Admiring his train in the switching yard, squinting for a glimpse of the great man, had somehow rendered him familiar.

On this dank morning Stanley Church was already waiting on the station platform, clutching a waist-high wreath. With Secret Service agents and local police standing guard, three hundred people lined the tracks and more spread across the flanking bluffs. One of them, a black man, lifted his voice into a spiritual as heads all around him bowed.

From the front porch of the Burigo house, high atop the Birch Street hill, Lorraine peered over the shingled roofs of the Tuite and Columbo homes, across the vacant lot where her father grew lettuce, and down into the switching yard. At seventeen, a junior in high school, she could not even remember another president. It was all because of President Roosevelt, crippled in his wheelchair, that she brought three cents to school every week for the March of Dimes.

Dressed in pajamas but incapable of sleep, Lorraine had been anticipating the train the entire night, moving between the parlor with its radio and a wooden chair on the porch. Delia wanted no part of mourning; reader of tea leaves that she was, she took Roosevelt's death as revenge for Seely's wounds. But Silvio had stayed with Lorraine for hours, from his easy chair uttering the eulogy, "He was the best. He was for the poor people." Then, toward daybreak, even he dozed off.

Finally, the train crept into view, seventeen cars stretched behind a locomotive draped in black. Lorraine folded her arms onto the porch railing, pressed her chin against them, and widened her eyes. It was six o'clock, the sky edging from black to taupe, granting just a bit of vision. Every coach remained dark, impenetrable to her gaze, every coach except the first. She caught sight of two soldiers, maybe part of the honor guard, alighting from it to stretch their legs. Then, through a bright square of window, she could make out the tip of the casket, covered by a flag.

When the train pulled away, life barely resumed. Mayor Church had declared thirty days of mourning, thirty days of flags at half-staff. This being a Sunday, the stores that had closed in honor of Roosevelt's funeral the previous afternoon remained locked and shuttered. Yet in the midst of this trance of grief, one institution flourished. Late in the afternoon of April 15, the New Rochelle Democratic Committee held one of the largest meetings in its history. A rabbi, a Catholic priest, a liberal Episcopal vicar, and an African Methodist Episcopal minister all extolled the late president to the audience, and in their collectivity offered a symbol of the coalition he had forged. In death as in life, in heroic death perhaps more than in fallible life, Franklin Delano Roosevelt could turn out the vote. Or so the Democratic Party, presiding over a nation soon to be prosperous and at peace, believed.

Part Two

The Fault Line

Chapter Seven

Voices from Downstairs
(Richie Garrett)

In all ways save one, the attic of Lizzie Garrett's house seemed to her son Richie a sanctuary. Everywhere else in Crotonville he saw the evidence of war—stars affixed to windows, bedsprings piled for a scrap-metal drive, pins stuck in the wall map at Pop Graber's store, each indicating the last known station of a neighborhood soldier. Sometimes Richie gazed from his front yard, high up a hillside, to the rumpled green land across the Hudson, thinking that was where his older brother Jack was fighting with the armored outfit called "Hell on Wheels." It was the closest he could come, as a boy of eight or nine, to visualizing "overseas," the word he heard each evening when his parents switched on their Philco for the news.

In the attic, though, childhood persisted. It was a small and separate place, a triangle of floor and arching roof, decorated with snapshots of baseball sluggers. During the summers Lizzie covered the bare planks with mattresses and blankets for sleep-overs, and spread supine across them might be Richie and his brother Eddie, and their cousins Joey and Marian, Jean and Phil. The air ripened with the scents of pine resin and mothballs, and amid the clutter treasures abounded. Here lay a cherry wood Victrola, nearby it the steamer trunk Lizzie's mother had carried from Liverpool. There sat the cigarette machine Edward Garrett had bought during the Depression, in which Richie now tried to roll the remnants of butts he plucked around the house. With a hand-cranked projector, the children watched Mickey Mouse flicker spastically against a bedsheet. On nights when lightning cleaved the sky, Eddie spun ghost stories by flashlight.

A trapdoor connected the attic to the kitchen, serving as an orifice between the worlds of child and adult, play and war. Even with the door shut, light pushed through its seams and voices intruded. On the night of August 6, 1945, when Richie was ten years old, he heard in those voices a somber weight, a gravelly tension, some texture palpably different from that of all the conversations he had eavesdropped on about battles and casualties. Sixteen hours after a B-29 dropped an atomic bomb on Hiroshima, the first reports of its destruction had begun to appear. In the afternoon edition of the *Citizen Register,* Lizzie and Edward read the account of "horrific havoc," of a weapon with "2,000 times the blast of the largest bomb ever used before." Far more graphic descriptions would emerge in the coming days, but this one gripped them enough to make them ask, "What if the other side had it?"

Richie could not make out all their words, and some of them, like "atom," he did not even understand. But the timbre alone spoke. A panic seized him, a primal horror that a bomb could fall on him any night. Lying on the mattress, he drew himself into a ball, knees pressing into chest, arms locked over knees. Then he shook for a long, long time. This was worse than his recurrent nightmare, the one about the stranger with the coal black eyes, because he could not simply shriek himself into consciousness.

More than a singular fright, Richie had received a political awakening. His evolution over the next decades into the Garrett family's most ardent liberal could be traced to the terror of a boy hearing voices from downstairs. "We had so much war in our time," he would say decades later. "Our whole life was war or the talk of war."

The first soldier in Richie's life was his older brother Jack, who enlisted in January 1941, when Richie was a few weeks shy of six. It seemed, in a child's elastic sense of time, that one day Jack was repairing cars down at Susse's Garage, then he was home on leave from Fort Benning, and then there was a letter from someplace called Tunisia. The letters stuck in Richie's memory, less for their censored contents than for the ritual of agony and relief that surrounded the daily mail. He watched his mother and all the other mothers of sons at war—Mrs. Hoyt, Mrs. Tuttle, and Mrs. Breen—as they scudded downhill to the mailboxes planted along Old Albany Post Road, the closest thing Crotonville had to a main street. The ones who discovered V-Mail inside had a way of pinching it, lifting it to an ear, and twirling it just a bit, as if to coax out a voice. The rest trudged home with backs stooped and shoulders slack.

Lizzie harbored more worry than most, for she had already seen Jack nearly die. That was when he was three or four, stricken with pneumonia, and the Sisters of the Sick Poor would lay him on the living-room couch with the windows open to ease his breathing. With the scare over, it became almost a family joke how Lizzie favored the boy; every time Lizzie made a roast, Edith chided, "Jack gets the blood gravy, Edie gets the water." Lizzie rued the day Jack signed up for the army, wishing he had been rejected like his friend John Hoyt.

Not that it would have mattered in the end. The marines gladly sent Hoyt to the Pacific, while Jack fought from the Kasserine Pass in North Africa through Sicily, D day, and the Battle of the Bulge. Sometimes, in a manner that amazed Richie, a gift arrived—a string of rosary beads blessed by the pope, a card for his eighth birthday with a picture of a cowboy. But months passed, too, with no mail, gaps Jack partially explained later with the story of being separated from his unit and hiding in a swamp from German patrols. Once or twice during these droughts, creeping through the house with a child's stealth, Richie spotted his mother crying over a sink of soaking dishes. To see even the matriarch frightful was to see order made chaos.

Then his sister Edith's husband, too, went into the military. Charlie Carey had played the surrogate brother to Richie, teaching the boy his own hobby of photography, imparting the mysteries of enlarger and developing tank. But all along Charlie had been aching to serve. Turned down by the army for his poor vision, he did eye exercises every night, something involving a thimble that Richie never quite fathomed, until the navy accepted him. The evening of Charlie's farewell party, Richie sat on his bed and sobbed.

Some compensation came in the sense of common purpose. Richie's father galvanized metal in the "dip shop" of an aircraft factory. His oldest sister assembled instrument panels for planes. His mother shipped packages of food, clothes, and shoes to relatives in England and Ireland. Richie watched PT boats, manufactured in nearby Haverstraw, skimming across the Hudson on their test runs, and cannons moving by flatbed railcar to the ammunition depot near Bear Mountain. During one promotion the Victoria Theater offered free admission to anyone donating scrap metal, and Richie conscripted one of Lizzie's cooking pots for the cause. When he cheered John Wayne, triumphant and unmarked, he imagined Jack Garrett.

But the home front trembled with fears of its own. There were fears the Germans would bomb the Croton Reservoir, fears they would infiltrate the Hudson with U-boats. It took the best jokes Edward Garrett knew to calm Richie during the enforced blackness of air raids. Not even the movies offered total escape. When the newsreel turned to the war, people searched the screen for the face of a son or husband or brother, and once a mother demanded the projectionist stop the film for a closer inspection. Even a family that received precious V-Mail could only know for certain its soldier was alive three or four weeks earlier, when the letter had been sent. Reassurance, then, was fleeting, granted and withdrawn in a single gesture of caprice.

The first two servicemen from Ossining died even before Pearl Harbor, during the fury of mobilization. Four months after the attack, a machinist's mate, Donald Low, became the first claimed by the conflict itself, his ship sunk in the North Atlantic. Barely an issue of the *Citizen Register* appeared without a prominent article about the death, injury, capture, or disappearance of some local soldier, invariably accompanied by the military portrait of a very young face. On a single day, like August 8, 1944, a reader would find the front page crowded with such headlines as "SGT. WRIGHT IS KILLED IN BURMA," "HOYT INJURED IN BATTLE," "PFC. BITTNER IS WOUNDED."

As a matter of statistics, not simply local emotion, Ossining suffered beyond its portion. Washington determined the town's draft quota by tallying all its young men—including nearly two thousand in Sing Sing who were not eligible to serve—and the body count reflected the skewed arithmetic. Ossining lost seventy-five men and one woman from a 1940 population of 16,600, prisoners excluded, giving it a mortality rate nearly 50 percent greater than the nation's.

Crotonville claimed two of the dead among its own. More unnerving for Richie, both had been friends of Jack's, and so were reminders of his own brother's peril. Charlie Parker, an army lieutenant, died in the Philippines on March 14, 1945, four days after mailing his final letter home. The story around Crotonville was that he had thrown himself on a Japanese grenade to save his platoon. Charlie had a wife and a son twenty months old, and before the war he had worked as a bank teller. Richie remembered sitting in a tree watching Charlie and Jack play baseball on the field below; he remembered a teenager who loved to canoe, and who had taught him to swim by tossing him into the Croton River and shouting, "Paddle your arms."

Then there was Clifford Bale, whom everybody called Stinky. He was the practical joker, the guy who would slap Richie on the back of the head and be strolling blithely along by the time the boy whirled around to look for the culprit. Evacuated from Guadalcanal with tuberculosis, Stinky convalesced with an aunt in Crotonville between treatments in various military hospitals. One day Richie paid him a visit. Stretched on a couch, eyes sunken and skin pallid, Stinky wheezed to him in a husk of a voice, "How ya doin', kid?" It was the last time Richie saw him alive.

As an altar boy, too, Richie found himself proximate to the dead. His parish, St. Augustine, numbered eight of its parishioners among the war's victims, and for one of them he served the Requiem High Mass. Whatever heroism was supposed to mean, Junior Downey seemed to personify it. He had enlisted in the marines four months out of high school and joined the battle in the Pacific at the age of nineteen. For swimming with a vital message between two islands, all the while under Japanese fire, he was awarded the Bronze Star by Admiral Nimitz himself. Then, after American forces had captured Saipan, he drew the assignment of routing out the remaining Japanese snipers from caves. Ambushed and twice wounded, he died providing cover fire for his comrades.

On October 7, 1944, nearly three months later, Ossining gathered to mourn him. Richie arrived at St. Augustine early that morning and prepared for the Mass. He lit the candles; he set cruets of wine and water on a marble table; he placed the host on the golden plate called the paten, and balanced it in turn atop the chalice. Then, inside the sacristy, he arrayed the priest's vestments. For other masses, for saint's days or great feasts or changing seasons, the robes might show color—purple during Lent, gold at Christmas, white for Easter. For the Requiem, however, the priest would wear black. In theological terms, the garment served as an emblem of sorrow at the death of someone loved, and it reminded believers, too, that before heaven came purgatory, the time of purification from sin, even for a fallen soldier just twenty years old.

Clad in his cassock and surplice, Richie preceded the Reverend Edwin Duffy to the altar. His arms hung heavily, the way they did after pushing a wheelbarrow of rocks for his father. Even at the best, serving Mass riddled him with butterflies. He had labored to learn the altar boy's responses, finally inventing English sound-alikes to help him remember. *Dominus vobiscum* . . . Dominic got all the biscuits. On this day of all days he felt an added pressure, a duty to be perfect, as if his performance might somehow salve the Downeys' pain. A phrase he had heard from the grown-ups came to him now—"the weight of the world."

As Father Duffy led the Mass, Richie answered in hushed tones, and over his own voice swept those of Sister Consolata and the girls' choir. It was a relief, perhaps the sole relief, for Richie to regard the priest and the nun. The Reverend Duffy had taught him Latin in parochial school with a gentle and patient touch. Sister Consolata, so conciliatory when her young singers struggled, always reminded him of the Statue of Liberty.

The solemnity of the moment could not be avoided, only endured. Twenty feet from Richie, at the head of the center aisle, lay the casket, covered by a flag. In the pews flanking it grieved Downey's parents, his sisters, and a brother just one year older than Richie. The Gold Star Mothers of two wars, a Greek chorus, huddled together a few rows back. And around Richie echoed Father Duffy's voice, intoning the plaintive Gregorian chants. Some promised eternal rest, rebirth after death. The most famous, though, Dies Irae, the one that had so inspired Mozart and Verdi, seemed to speak of the war that had dominated a nine-year-old's life.

> Dies irae, dies illa
> Solvet saeclum in favilla
> Teste David cum Sibylla.
> Quantus tremor est futurus
> Quando judex est venturus
> Cunchta stricte discussurus.

> Day of wrath, that day
> The world dissolves into fire
> as both David and the Sibyl foretold.
> What a terrible future tremor
> When the judge comes
> Who will judge all things strictly.

With the liturgy completed, Richie and another altar boy stepped toward the coffin. One bore a censer, the other a vessel of holy water, and behind them strode Father Duffy, clasping to his chest the book of prayers, the *Rituale*. As incense wafted down the nave and drifted among the pews, they slowly walked around the casket. The priest sprinkled it with holy water, the drops briefly beading and then soaking into the flag. From the nuns in school Richie had learned to conceive of holy water as washing away sin, nourishing Christian life, dousing the fires of hell. Yet in this moment he could think only of tears.

As a pious boy, he believed in heaven, envisioning it as a sort of family reunion, a place where you could visit all your favorite aunts and uncles for as long as you wanted. He had heard Father Duffy preach, "The Christian attitude toward death is one of joy—joy at the thought of another person reaching his goal and spending eternity with God."

The choir's final passage sang of angels and paradise. But not image or word or music could lift his misery. Only one thought offered solace, and it was a thought Richie entertained with guilt, even sacrilege. Thank God, he told himself, contemplating the coffin of Junior Downey, it wasn't Jack.

Richie received his wish on June 29, 1945, when the army discharged Technical Sergeant John M. Garrett at Fort Dix, New Jersey. As quickly as Jack could reach New York City, he dialed Ossining 556J, the party line his family shared with the Gilligans. Richie answered, then fetched his father from across the street, where he was repairing Nanna Walsh's house. The family conspired to keep Jack's return a secret from Lizzie until he himself could surprise her. It happened early the next morning. She came home from an overnight job nursing at a mental institution to find the slender, ruddy figure of her eldest son, blue eyes glinting. She wept and howled and hugged, and her crying infected Eddie and then Richie, all of them expelling four years of anguish.

As word spread, the celebration began, attracting far more people than the Garretts had chairs. For seating, someone grabbed a few two-by-twelve planks from a house under construction and laid them across sawhorses in the cellar. Wooden kegs of beer arrived from Tom and Phil's tavern. One of the summer renters, an amateur comedian related by marriage to Stinky Bale, told his Jap jokes. One by one, the revelers rose in song, some sentimental, some lewd, all bursting with brio. Richie had a song of his own, not to share aloud but to shelter within. From the time he first heard it on the *Breakfast Club* radio show, he had clung to it as fiercely as his altar boy's Latin.

> There'll be blue birds over
> The white cliffs of Dover
> Tomorrow just you wait and see
> There'll be love and laughter
> And joy ever after
> Just you wait and see.

For a time, the promise seemed to be honored.

• • •

As much as it can be dated to any single event, the postwar era in Crotonville began on May 8, 1947, when the American Legion granted a charter to Post 1597, named in honor of Charlie Parker and Stinky Bale. No other institution, not even St. Augustine, would so shape life in the neighborhood. As cohesive as Crotonville was, it had always lacked a focal place; the closest thing was Pop Graber's store, with its back room, beer cooler, and three-seat outhouse. But once the legion post bought the one-room schoolhouse, closed for a decade by then, Crotonville found its social and political hub, its polling place and wedding-reception hall and much more. It was known simply and familiarly as Parker-Bale.

Within its first six months the post built a community skating rink, held a Christmas party for children, threw a costume dance in the downtown ballroom once used for Bund meetings, and sent cash and gift packages to patients being discharged from the nearest Veterans Administration hospital. Much else would follow—clambakes and blood drives, drums corps and softball teams, oratorical contests, corned beef and cabbage suppers, and, most memorably, the New Year's Day parade.

The procession started about seven in the morning, after a full night of drinking. The survivors set forth from the post, swinging a bell at the end of a two-by-four to announce their approach, and proceeded house by house, demanding at each to be served a drink and surrendered the man of the family. They pulled him, if necessary, from under the covers or out of the closet, and sometimes made off with a leg of lamb from the kitchen. By midafternoon, their sotted circuit complete, they met their wives at the Delmar Tavern for dinner and several more rounds.

In more sober moments Parker-Bale assumed the agitating role of the Crotonville Civic Association. The neighborhood still needed sewers, garbage pickup, and its own park. Now, in the automotive age, a new concern arose: Old Albany Post Road, a favorite spot for stickball as the only level street in the neighborhood, had a speed limit of fifty-five miles per hour. The post drew up a petition for a lower speed limit, which was signed by sixty-eight of the ninety families in Crotonville. Lizzie Garrett pleaded their case before the town supervisor, Hugh Lavery, by now her old friend.

For Lizzie, Parker-Bale provided a political base, and hardly the only one. Running bingo night at Roosevelt Hospital, selling poppies door-to-door on Veterans Day, and catering a dinner for the Dominican sisters at the Mariandale convent, she combined good works and smart politics. From the Legion of Mary to the Order of Eagles to the St. Augustine PTA, she volunteered almost to the point of omnipresence. While shopping with Lizzie, Edith often watched her mother greet seeming strangers, whispering in their wake, "You don't know her." To which Lizzie snapped, "Don't tell me who I know," and recited the passerby's biography.

All a Democrat needed to win Crotonville was Lizzie's endorsement;

Republicans rarely bothered canvassing in the district. In her wool suit, feathered hat, and high heels, which she wore into her seventies despite an arthritic knee, Lizzie led candidates house to house, nimble as a goat on the steep, rutted roads. "This is a good friend of mine," she would say to a prospective voter. "I mean a *good* friend. And he'll be good for us." Sometimes the pitch was even more brusque: Grab the candidate by the elbow, like an exhibit for show-and-tell, and order the listener, "Vote for him."

She proved what political scientists would later confirm, that political allegiance in the postwar years was less a function of issues than heritage. People in Crotonville were Democrats because their parents had been Democrats and their parents had been Democrats because of religion and class. Edith Carey received one of the shocks of her life when, as an election judge in 1947, she encountered a registered Republican wearing a nun's habit.

Not only did Crotonville help return Hugh Lavery to office as supervisor for what would eventually reach eleven terms and twenty-two years, it also held fast for Democrats at the presidential level. It is impossible to determine the exact votes, since the election district containing Crotonville expanded and contracted with periodic redistricting and residential development nearby. But in the best years—for example, Lyndon Johnson's race against Barry Goldwater in 1964—the neighborhood by some estimates went 90 percent Democratic. Even in Dwight Eisenhower's 1952 and 1956 landslides, including ballots from outside Crotonville itself, the election district voted Democratic by 15 percent more than the surrounding town or county. What made this party loyalty most striking was that Westchester was becoming one of the most important and populous Republican strongholds in the nation.

The very isolation of Crotonville buffered it from the vast changes of the period—suburbanization, increased affluence, massive college education, white flight, the movement into northern cities of rural southern blacks. Crotonville still held June Walks, like the ones in San Juan Hill a quarter century before. Houses rose as they had before the Depression, with money loaned by relatives and the donated muscles of neighborhood men, thanked for their labor with sandwiches and beer. What amounted to an economic boom was the opening of a General Electric management-training center that hired the blue-collar people of Crotonville as housekeepers, waitresses, and cooks.

Even the issue that defined postwar politics, the crusade against suspected Communist subversion, failed to inflame Crotonville. There were opportunities enough for it to do so. The riots surrounding two concerts in 1949 by the radical black singer Paul Robeson occurred in

Peekskill, just ten miles away. Julius and Ethel Rosenberg, convicted of passing atomic secrets to the Soviet Union, were executed in Sing Sing. Centered as it was on its American Legion post, Crotonville received plentiful warnings about the enemy within.

The legion's eponymous magazine, in fact, provided a barometer of the transformation from World War II's common front to the Cold War. In April 1946, *American Legion* wrote of the "big reserve of good will toward us" in Russia and ran a wartime photograph of American GIs shaking hands with their Red Army cohorts. Nine months later, as Stalin was consolidating the Eastern Bloc empire, an article typical of many to follow offered advice on "how to spot a Communist." Gossipy features on life in Hollywood gave way to an analysis headlined "HOW COMMU-NISTS MAKE STOOGES OUT OF MOVIE STARS." For its members, the American Legion depicted a nation whose colleges, labor unions, and mass media were being undermined, whose crusading anti-Communists were themselves the subject of a left-wing witch-hunt. One article in particular, entitled "Our New Privileged Class," anticipated the very way Barry Goldwater, George Wallace, and Ronald Reagan would ultimately wield class as a cudgel against liberalism:

> In the whole tongue-tied crew brought before the House [Un-American Activities] Committee in 1947 in connection with Soviet espionage and infiltration, there was no farmer or workman or so called "common man." Without exception they were college graduates, Ph.D.'s, *summa cum laudes* and Phi Beta Kappas from Harvard, Yale, Princeton and other great colleges.

Crotonville was not immune to these emotions. When a bartender outside the enclave refused to serve those he called hillbillies and when a baseball league charged $500 for the neighborhood team to enter, it felt the lash of class discrimination. But Crotonville still experienced class as an economic division—haves versus have-nots—rather than the ideological split between "elitists" and "populists" that the conservative theoretician Jeffrey Bell would frame in the 1980s. Communism never drove Crotonville to as much activity, or even verbiage, as more local indignities. During the Cold War, Parker-Bale settled for sending a few members to show its colors at the anti-Communism rallies sponsored by the Ossining Women's Club. People supported Senator Joseph McCarthy and the House Un-American Activities Committee in a passive manner, and felt nothing in that stance contradicted their Democratic loyalty or New Deal beliefs.

To a great degree, they were correct. Many liberals concurred with the right wing that Communists were trying to undermine American institutions, and differed only on the extent of infiltration and the means to be employed against it. The most influential liberal organization of the postwar years, the Americans for Democratic Action, led the effort to discredit Henry Wallace's 1948 presidential candidacy as a tool of international Communism. ADA hailed the Marshall Plan for rebuilding Europe as "the last chance for world peace" and endorsed the Truman Doctrine of "support[ing] free peoples who are resisting attempted subjugation by armed minorities or by outside pressures." Among those who carried the ADA message throughout the nation in 1947 was a charter member named Ronald Reagan.

The essential dispassion Crotonville held for the subversion issue became most apparent in the late summer of 1949. It was then, on August 27, that Robeson was to give his concert at the Lakeland Acres Picnic Ground outside Peekskill. Although he had sung there three times before without incident, he had created a furor in the months leading up to this engagement with a speech to a Paris conference on world peace. The Associated Press reported that Robeson had compared the American government to Nazi Germany's and said it was "unthinkable" that American blacks would fight a war against the Soviet Union—a misrepresentation of what Robeson said in the speech, but an accurate rendering of his private beliefs. Against the backdrop of Mao Zedong's victory in China, the Soviet explosion of an atomic bomb, and the trial in New York of eleven alleged members of the Communist Party for conspiracy to overthrow the government, the Robeson concert escalated into a bit of Armageddon.

By all logic, the struggle *should* have swept up Crotonville and Parker-Bale, for the opposition to Robeson centered on veterans' groups and Roman Catholics. An assemblage of five hundred, from members of American Legion and Veterans of Foreign Wars units to students from St. Joseph's High bearing the school banner, halted the concert by blocking roads to the site and attacking audience members, many of them black and Jewish. For some participants at least, the violence gave cause for pride. "Our objective was to prevent the Paul Robeson concert," a spokesman for a legion post in Peekskill said, "and I think our objective was reached." Bumper stickers soon appeared, declaring, "WAKE UP, AMERICA! PEEKSKILL DID."

For Robeson's second concert, on September 4, the opposition among veterans was even more organized: Fourteen separate posts united as the Associated Veterans Group. Robeson himself enlisted security from leftist unions, and 750 police officers were assigned to the site. Robeson succeeded in performing, but once the show ended, a riot erupted that left 146 people injured. While the concert would later become an almost mythological tale of persecution for the American left —retold by E. L. Doctorow in *The Book of Daniel* and T. Coraghessan Boyle in *World's End*—the mainstream opinion of the time blamed Robeson and his followers. A grand jury impaneled to investigate the riot declared that Communists had intended to stir "racial and religious hatred" for propaganda purposes. Even such liberals as Eleanor Roosevelt denounced Robeson and the counterdemonstrators in equal measure.

Why, then, would the members of Parker-Bale not have enlisted in the battle? As a small and relatively new post, it may have been overlooked in the planning. But the members, as individuals, knew the protest that was building, especially after the first concert. In part, they were preoccupied with their own insular projects, decorating graves in local cemeteries and helping World War I veterans collect their pensions. But they decided at least partly on principle. The radicals in their midst seemed more worthy of ridicule than violence; nobody in Parker-Bale could imagine the Jews of "Communist Hill," as they called one left-wing enclave nearby, forming the revolutionary vanguard. And the race hate that permeated the opposition to Robeson offended some gut-level tolerance in Crotonville, perhaps born of its own role as Ossining's doormat, perhaps from many residents' origins in the polyglot neighborhoods of New York. "It was not our business to get involved," Parker-Bale's commander said years later. "We weren't the Ku Klux Klan." Recalled another member: "Parker-Bale was a calm outfit. We saw enough in World War II. Throwing rocks, wrecking people's cars was not gonna help."

Inaction, in this case, amounted to action. The Peekskill riots contributed to a national climate in which even anti-Communist liberals could be painted as pink. Absenting itself from the turmoil hardly made Parker-Bale a radical redoubt, but the decision probably stopped the post, and the community it typified, from being driven rightward. That shift would come a generation later, and for reasons to which international Communism was only incidental. For now, in the 1950s, a certain stasis prevailed in Crotonville. If the neighborhood did not nurture or celebrate dissidence, it at least accepted idiosyncrasy from within, and so allowed Richie Garrett to gravitate toward liberalism.

• • •

From the very birth of the Parker-Bale post, Richie spent nearly as much time there as did its members. He watched the Friday-night movies the veterans showed for kids and sold soda when his mother ran the auxiliary's bingo game. As the members overhauled the century-old school-house for the modern age, installing stairs and banisters, and replacing a dirt floor with poured concrete, Richie fetched tools, lugged trash, and did any errand to allow him nearness to these men, his idols.

He worshiped Jack most of all. Fishing, chopping firewood, lying in hammocks and talking, he relished their togetherness. Yet even at twelve or thirteen he could see in his brother something ineffably awry. It was less the physical damage—the shrapnel that formed abscesses on one armpit—than the edgy, jittery way Jack had about him. He hated wearing khakis or going camping, saying he'd had enough of both in the army. And that was just about all he would say about the army, to Richie or anyone else, even his wife. Jack stuck his Bronze Star medal in a drawer and never explained what he had done to deserve it. Only when he had drunk himself past inhibition might a story slip out; once he told his wife about reaching to pull a soldier from a tank that had been hit by German fire and having the man's flesh crumble in his hand.

John Hoyt was even more extreme. Everybody had called him Nutsy as a joke before the war, but now, home from Iwo Jima with a plate in his head, he seemed genuinely disturbed. His benders ended not in confession but violence, most often against his wife. One day Richie's best friend, Al Riel, found Hoyt pummeling her in an open lot along the Old Albany Post Road, shameless in the public spectacle. Al wrenched Hoyt off her, but then the wife started yelling at him for interfering. So he withdrew, saying, "That's the way you want it? Go ahead. Hit her again, John."

Little in the world around Richie prepared him for the wounds of these returned soldiers. Two more wars would pass before doctors diagnosed and named post-traumatic stress disorder. For now, the Memorial Day parade was glorious, formal, and bloodless; the movies at the Victoria presented a war that was both righteous and uncomplicated, producing only martyrs and heroes, not broken survivors. In their separate ways—Jack with his silence, Hoyt with his rage—both men held Richie at a distance. Moving through his teens toward adulthood, Richie wondered how these guys he remembered playing football and going fishing before the war could have come home so inexplicably haunted.

Then he got to know George Tice. George was not a Crotonville native, but after the war he took a job managing the gas station next to Hudak's custard stand and rented a house in the neighborhood. As an army veteran, he made his way naturally enough to Parker-Bale, and he coached its youth softball team. Richie Garrett played center field and he also loved singing, which happened to matter, because one day George heard him practicing harmonies and offered some advice. At that point the relationship between the teenager and the grown-up, twenty-five years apart, subtly shifted from that of coach and player to one of friendship.

Each was, to a degree, an outsider. Richie had a pensive, artistic temperament inconsonant with the brash, raucous style of manhood in Crotonville; he was the sort of teenager who read the newspaper's editorial page and knew a special spot in the woods just for thinking. George wrote poetry, painted landscapes, and had a way of looking scrubbed and pressed even while digging in his garden. There were vague stories of a sweetheart back in England or a fiancée killed in an auto accident and a few mutterings that this blond-haired blue-eyed ladies' man might actually be queer.

Most important to Richie, George wrote songs. He and his brother-in-law Manny wrote them together, and a famous rhythm-and-blues group, the Orioles, even recorded one called "Is My Heart Wasting Time?" Nothing could have impressed Richie more, for he dreamed of life as a singer. Self-taught in bel canto, George served in an informal way as Richie's first private tutor. Sometimes he let him record on the crude record-making machine he and Manny used for their demos. "You got a hell of a voice," he would say. "Use it."

One evening in 1952, when Richie was seventeen, he and George were drinking in Tice's house. It was little more than a converted chicken coop, but George had adorned the walls with his oils and charcoals, and transformed planks and cinder blocks into shelves for his personal library. The two had been downing wine for several hours, and as Richie knew from nights at Parker-Bale's bar there came a threshold in drunkenness when the war stories flowed out as steadily as the liquor flowed in. Now, for the first time since he had known George, the subject of World War II arose. George told a story of flying a glider carrying supplies and reinforcements to paratroopers in Normandy during the D-day invasion. Descending into what he thought would be meadow, he found himself hurtling instead toward rows of tree trunks several feet tall. Gliders smashed against them, their plywood skin shattering, and the men who survived the crashes staggered upright into a field of German fire. Of the 250 troops on his mission, he said, fifty or sixty survived.

What George was describing and Richie hearing, each in a fragmentary way, was one of the grisly subplots of D day. The tree trunks were called *Rommelspargel,* Rommel's asparagus, and they formed an integral element in the general's defense against the Allied assault. French civilians at German gunpoint had felled the trees and stripped them of their limbs about fifteen miles inland, then planted them in prospective landing zones along the Norman coast. From trunk to trunk ran cables, set to trigger mines and bombs. And from aerial reconnaissance photos, taken directly overhead, the trap could not be discerned. It is difficult to identify the exact operation George Tice recounted, and it is possible he exaggerated the number of deaths. But in the Normandy invasion, nearly one in five glider pilots was killed, injured, lost, or captured, and for the entire war the pilots registered a casualty rate of roughly 25 percent, far higher than any branch of the service. With little hyperbole, they called their gliders "flying coffins."

In any event, George was not giving Richie a lecture in military history. He was talking about heroism. Heroes were what his commanding officer had called the survivors. What George thought then, what he told Richie now, what he had been carrying with him for nearly a decade, were two questions: "My God, what is he talking about? Why is he praising me?"

The words turned Richie's thoughts instantly to Jack. In all the tales Jack had spun about his army buddies or his friendships with the locals in Sicily or Belgium, he had carefully avoided mentioning combat itself. Now Richie recalled one of the few stories Jack had let escape, about the disaster in the Kasserine Pass, when Americans with equipment from World War I lumbered into battle against the Afrika Korps.

"Why don't you put this down on paper?" Richie said spontaneously to George. "Let's work this out."

So they did, mulling each phrase and line, gradually filling a sheet on one of the notepads George had scattered throughout the house, wherever the muse might alight. Forty years later Richie could still recite the poem verbatim, for it had answered not only George's needs but his own, what he called "the hunger that boils inside, the hunger for life and peace, the hunger for 'Why?'"

> Don't call me hero.
> Don't raise your voice in praise
> Of deeds I have done,
> Or cover me with glory
> For a battle won.
>
> I'm here and breathing
> Which is proof enough I didn't fight
> Quite hard enough to die.
>
> If you must praise a hero,
> If you must fill your ears with empty words
> To satisfy your hunger to be heard,
> Then travel over there today.

Who fought the battle
Hard enough to stay—
They are your heroes.
They who traded blood and sweat and toil
For a muddy, cross-marked mound of foreign soil—
Make your speech to them.

And, what is more,
Convince them
There's glory in a war.

Deeply as that night affected Richie, it did not on the surface alter his life. He played tackle for the Ossining High Indians and stocked shelves after school at the A&P. He and Al Riel went on double dates with the Margada sisters. During his senior year of high school he enlisted in the Marine Corps Reserve. It was either that, Richie knew, or wait around to be drafted.

The Korean War struck him as one worth fighting, a moral calling as clear as World War II. Here was an undeniable instance of Communist aggression and an armed rescue sanctioned by the United Nations. Thirteen young men from Ossining died in the cause, and several of Richie's older friends saw combat. In the end, he never got closer to Inchon or Pork Chop Hill than war games in North Carolina. The one time his unit was placed on red alert, the prelude to departure, a stalled round of peace negotiations abruptly resumed. One week later, on July 27, 1953, both sides signed an armistice.

With his remaining duty largely confined to weekends, Richie enjoyed the fruits of a booming nation. He rose from polisher to salesman for a Buick dealership in Ossining, and followed Jack into reinforced-steel construction. Such a labor shortage plagued major projects that Richie was able to work "on permit," as the phrase went, paying the union a dollar an hour in lieu of dues and earning the wages and benefits of a full member. On the longest and largest jobs, like the Tappan Zee and Throgs Neck Bridges, he brought home upwards of $600 per month, more than twice the Crotonville norm.

Some of the money went into his bachelor life, with its convertible, custom suits, and nightclub excursions; he once chatted with Teresa Brewer at a Westchester cabaret called the Log Cabin and inadvertently tripped Tony Bennett coming down the aisle at the Copa. It was to their world that Richie aspired. "Being in the spotlight," as he put it, "and making people like each other better."

Richie studied both piano and voice, at one point with a coach who had students at the Metropolitan Opera, and bought arrangements from Mitch Miller himself. In time, his venues graduated from the Parker-Bale bar and Crotonville weddings to local clubs with a band called the Flying Five. But Richie discovered that applause left him more embarrassed than encouraged. Perhaps he feared surrendering to the sin of pride; he had grown up, after all, eating oatmeal and beets and sifting the wood-stove ashes for unburnt "clinkers" to be fired the next day. Then, in 1960, Richie married. Five children would follow in eleven years, and singing could no longer compete with reliable money, with "the idea of a refrigerator and paying your bills."

Life might have accommodated itself to exactly such a routine had not Richie hit a patch of unemployment just after finishing work on a high-rise in the fall of 1962. During the lull he got a call from his father, who was by then the superintendent of St. Augustine Cemetery. At seventy, Edward was trying to avoid the most physical work, but the cousin who helped him had just dropped dead digging a grave. "Give me a couple of weeks till I get someone," Edward offered, and Richie, both dutiful and short of cash, consented.

By the time the two-week spell ended, winter was arriving, and with it the usual slowdown in construction. "Why don't you stay till things pick up?" Edward asked, and again Richie accepted. It was a miserable winter—"cold as the hinges of hell," Richie would later recall—and one day he found Edward in his Ford, trying to warm his hands on the heater.

"Are you all right?" he asked.

"I can't handle it anymore," Edward said. "It's getting too much."

A few months later, on a Tuesday early in spring, Edward failed to appear for work.

"Where is he?" Richie asked his brother Eddie, who had also been drafted by the old man.

"He retired."

"When?"

"Yesterday."

Later that day the monsignor drove up from St. Augustine to offer Richie the job. "I'm not gonna work like my father," he protested, "like a slave." But before the monsignor headed back, Richie had agreed. A former car salesman himself, he had to admire the priest's gifts of persuasion. So Richie inherited his father's job and also the graveyard nickname of Digger. And through circumstance and filial loyalty he found himself, unknowingly, about to bear witness to war's damage once more.

• • •

At the beginning, in the years before Vietnam, St. Augustine Cemetery seemed to Richie Garrett not a morbid place but a lush and comforting one. Tucked off a county two-lane about three miles from Crotonville, its fifteen acres rambled down a hillside and along a freshwater brook. At the fringes tulip trees soared a hundred feet skyward, and thick stands of honey locusts, red maples, and chestnuts formed the lower canopy. The woods teemed with game—pheasant, partridge, deer, cottontail, and wild turkey. Trout, perch, and turtles abounded in the stream. It was no wonder the Boy Scouts visited the graveyard to study wildlife.

From his office in a brick hut or at a pause in his labors, Richie appreciated the pageant of seasons. In early autumn, hawks beyond count circled high above the hilltop before taking aim south in single file. Spring announced itself with the return of red-winged blackbirds to the marsh, the damp air vibrating with their song. In summer and winter, the headstones magnified temperature, radiating heat or cold.

Most of the time death, too, abided by the natural order. Father passed before son, mother before daughter; family plots filled slowly, generation by generation. Richie learned how to share sympathy while still conducting business. He offered wide berth to the peculiarities of mourning. One day a woman approached him with a box containing a brand-new Stetson and explained that in a dream her late husband complained of being cold. Richie looked to his father, there for company and advice, and Edward said softly, "Bury it." So Richie pierced the sod at the gravesite, dug down three feet to the top of the vault, and there laid the boxed hat. The next day the woman returned and told Richie, "He's satisfied. Nice and warm."

The work itself moved by organic rhythms. Only when facing the rare day with more than two burials would Richie hire a contractor with a backhoe. Otherwise he dug graves by pick and shovel, the "Irish anchor" and "guinea banjo," spreading his energy evenly across the hours. Edward loved telling the story of winning a bet worth his weekly pay against a man who swore he could dig a grave in ninety minutes. Well before time expired, the challenger spent himself faint. "Ease up, lad," a helper, Pat Conway, always advised Richie. "Make haste slowly."

The only untimely death in those early years was of the occasional child who had been struck by a car. And it was exactly such a death, in a strange way, that commenced the chain of events that would bring Vietnam into Richie's consciousness and revive all those decades-old terrors. The victim was Richie Carey, the youngest child of Richie Garrett's sister Edith. One day in March 1961, when Richie Carey was four, the boy crawled under a parked car to retrieve a balsa-wood airplane. While he was beneath it, the driver returned and started forward.

Richie Carey's death especially anguished his oldest brother, Michael. He was the one who always came home from school with a candy in his pocket for Richie, the one who bought him a kitten from the pet store where he worked. That day, he found Richie on the street, not yet dead. In the aftermath, Michael started fighting, cutting school, and hanging out with the wild children of a couple of local drunks. Then he fired a .22 at an empty boat cruising the Croton River, and someone called the police. The case went to municipal court and the judge, an old friend of Charlie Carey's family, agreed to drop the charges if Michael would join the army and leave town.

At five o'clock one morning in October 1962, Edith and Charlie drove him to the Ossining train station, the same platform from which Jack Garrett had departed for Fort Benning twenty-one years before. After a two-year stint divided between bases in Alaska and Germany, Michael re-upped and received his orders for Vietnam. Home on leave just before shipping out, he was sitting one day on the green bench outside Jack's house, usually the place for reliving a morning's fishing, with Jack and Richie. Now the subject turned to Vietnam. "This is going to be a dirty, dirty war," Jack told his nephew. "We have no business in it."

The words did not register with Richie as deeply then as they would later, for his own political beliefs were still coalescing. Beyond a firm sense of himself as a Democrat, he felt pulled between poles—of patriotic duty and pacifistic revulsion in wartime, of belief in the "domino theory" and puzzlement at why one corner of Indochina should matter so greatly. Even as a teenager he had tried to separate support for Joseph McCarthy's aims from disgust at his means; it had shattered him to decide finally that an Irish Catholic could be evil. Richie responded strongly to John F. Kennedy not only for his youth, religion, and ethnicity, but also for his ability to embody both Cold Warrior and compassionate liberal. In the early 1960s, such congruence was still both possible and popular.

Then, in the last week of December 1966, Richie received a call from the Waterbury and Kelly Funeral Home. The body of First Lieutenant Timothy J. McCarthy, the first child of Ossining to be killed in Vietnam, had come home. On New Year's Eve, after a Requiem High Mass, he was to be buried in St. Augustine Cemetery.

The name conjured a face, and a vague memory of a quiet, bright boy hanging around Pop Graber's store. The McCarthy family did not live in Crotonville, but its children had attended St. Augustine School and so knew plenty of classmates and friends from the neighborhood. The son of a Sing Sing guard who had emigrated from Ireland, Timmy had been a pudgy and bookish boy who once devoted an entire summer to reading *The World Book* encyclopedia from "A" to "Zworykin." But he grew sturdy, handsome, and popular—cocaptain of the football team, student council member, and steady beau of a Jewish girl in a faintly scandalous pairing. He won admission to Villanova, as fine a college as a working-class kid from Ossining could ever dream of attending, and graduated in June 1964, less than two months before Congress passed the Tonkin Gulf Resolution, in effect the declaration of an undeclared war.

Suddenly vulnerable to the draft, Timmy could have sought the partial refuge of the reserves, as did several of his friends. Instead, he leaned toward applying to Officers Candidate School. One night before he made the final decision, some of his drinking buddies, veterans of the Korean War, lured him to a favorite bar. There they tied him to a chair and barraged him with reasons not to go to war. He could teach; he could keep his deferment. Unconvinced, Timmy earned his commission and went off to Vietnam to command a platoon.

He wrote to his family and friends nearly once a week. Most of the letters diminished the danger, describing instead Thanksgiving dinner in the field or asking about retirements, new jobs, or vacation plans on the home front. But gradually he started signing as "Tim" instead of "Timmy." And in his last letter to his best friend, Wayne McCormack, he told of running "into the meat grinder." It was a letter at odds with itself, partly a work of a professional soldier's detachment and partly a confession of a greenhorn's fright. What it described, in essence, was the tragic farce of two platoons of virtual teenagers trying to surprise a veteran army long skilled in jungle warfare:

> The 2d and 3rd [platoons] were working together and set up an ambush on a well-traveled trail. The first night they saw five and killed one of them. . . .
>
> About 9:30 after the 2nd gave up or lost sight of NVA and returned to a location 300 meters from the 2nd they saw some new NVA and started SW again. They moved on the NVA but were hit with automatic weapons from a hill and called on the 3rd to move down to help.
>
> The 3rd moved down but were hit by a large force and were overrun in a matter of minutes. The 2nd was still unable to free itself.
>
> All this time my platoon was moving to come to the aid of the rest. We had a long way to go and did not know exactly where everyone was.
>
> We arrived just in time to save what was left of the 2nd platoon. As we got there the NVA left the field.
>
> The count is still going, so far it is well over 100 NVA. But we payed [*sic*] a big price for it.

The 3rd was wiped out. Only two men are still alive. The 2nd had 14 men walk off the field. We suffered 33 KIA and about 12 WIA for the company. . . .

It's comforting to know that everyone back home is working on little ones. You, Johnny D and Tommy K are expectant fathers. The reason I say that it's comforting is that [I'm] out in the woods 80 days now, so long I get to feel that I'm getting it put to me. But I guess I'm not the only one.

Several weeks later, on December 20, 1966, Timmy McCarthy's own platoon fell into an ambush. Just when the troops seemed to have secured a landing zone near An Khe, hidden North Vietnamese forces rained fire on them. Calling on a field radio for reinforcements—his antenna serving as a bull's-eye for snipers—Timmy took bullets in the back and the side. He was twenty-five years old, and in the military portrait that appeared in the *Citizen Register* his cheeks still betrayed a hint of childhood chubbiness.

On the day mourners filed through the funeral home, lingering over the open casket that had called upon all the undertaker's talent, Richie Garrett set about digging Timmy McCarthy's grave. He would be buried in the section of the cemetery reserved for war veterans, a slope near the main gate that faced the setting sun. Over it loomed the granite figure of a doughboy, left knee slightly bent, hands clasping a rifle. The statue memorialized George De Barbiery, an infantry sergeant in World War I, killed in France at the age of twenty-eight. Nearby, in a family plot, lay the mother who outlived him by fourteen years.

Richie shoveled the snow off a rectangle of sod, and using metal pins and mason's line marked a site eight feet long by three wide. With a spade, he cut the turf into one-foot squares, and lifting them exposed the bare earth. Then he shouldered pick and shovel and leaned into the task. Even working with a helper, his old friend Al Riel's father, Charlie, Richie toiled the entire day. By sundown, with his head barely breaking the surface of the ground, only the frosted breath rising from the pit proved its current occupant was alive.

Early the next morning, during the Mass at St. Augustine, a truck arrived with the concrete vault, which two workmen slowly dropped into the grave. Richie assembled the planking and the lowering device for the casket, and covered the lumber and dirt mounds with rugs of artificial grass. Then there remained nothing but the wait.

The funeral cortege, a hundred cars long, crept from St. Augustine past the bakeries and pizzerias of the Hollow, beyond town hall and the public library as it scaled Croton Avenue, and finally into the open land outside the village border. All along the route, spectators lined the curbside in silence, both attracted and humbled by the novelty of local death in this newest war.

Finally, the hearse turned through the graveyard gate and into Richie's gaze. Car after car followed, parking along every foot of curving roadway, the backlog idling onto Hawkes Avenue even as the service commenced. In his khakis and work boots, Richie retreated from the gravesite as clusters of mourners claimed the space between every monument and headstone. There was a girlfriend from Ossining and a girlfriend from California; there were Irish immigrants, hair graying and clothes black, who had journeyed to America with the elder McCarthys; there were the pallbearers, most close since grade school, who had spent so many other New Year's Eves with Timmy drinking Bud and feeding the jukebox for "Shout."

From his remove, Richie could not see much of the service, but he knew well the rituals of a soldier's burial—the military escort, the honor guard, the flag-draped coffin. He added his voice as the assemblage recited the Our Father and the Hail Mary, and he stood at attention as the guardsmen fired their three volleys and a lone bugler blew taps. Then, after the last mourners had departed, when only the military escort remained, he drew toward the grave. With one touch of a lever on the lowering device, the coffin descended into place.

All Richie had done before the service he did again now in the opposite order, the symmetry of labor like his own private rite. He peeled the green rug off the planking and dirt, let two men from the vault company fasten its lid, shoveled earth back into the pit, and restored the squares of sod. Atop them he laid the floral arrangements in futile defiance of winter. Nothing would grow for three months, and it would take just as long for the army to supply the headstone. By that time, Timmy McCarthy's grave would no longer be the only one in the first row, the row for those killed in Vietnam.

In the chill dusk of the last day of the year, Richie thought about the morning after. It wasn't the happy-ending kind he had in mind, sunshine after the rain and whatnot. Funny, George Tice had once written a song like that about World War II called "Storms Blow Over." But that was before he glided into Normandy and Rommel's asparagus. No, this morning after was of the hangover variety, miserable and unrelenting. You wake up the morning after World War II and it's Korea, Richie told himself. You wake up the morning after Korea and it's Vietnam. Richie wanted to believe in the war and in the government that had marshaled its young men to fight it. At thirty-one, he still remembered the lessons of civics class "the way you remember a song or the smell of your mother's cooking." But burying Timmy McCarthy meant contemplating the man Timmy McCarthy might have become, and peering into that chasm filled Richie with dread and despair.

He was not nearly so alone as he might have believed. During 1966, the year just ending, American forces in Vietnam had doubled in number to 398,000. In concert with the escalation, antiwar sentiment had burgeoned from campus avocation toward mass movement. It was the year of Operation Rolling Thunder, a billion-dollar bombing campaign that failed to subdue North Vietnam; it was the year of the Fulbright committee hearings, three weeks of nationally televised clashes between openly skeptical senators and some of the architects of the containment doctrine. By the time of Timmy McCarthy's interment 6,643 other American soldiers had died in combat.

Each death sent its own tremors through the survivors. Pride or rage, sacrifice or waste, the responses veered to irreconcilable extremes, capable of dividing a nation or torturing a soul. Timmy McCarthy's father, for instance, erected a pole to fly the flag that had covered his son's coffin, yet burned every letter from Vietnam he could find. As for Richie Garrett, he remained utterly loyal to Crotonville and Parker-Bale, both of them growing conservative. But when the occasion soon arose for him to choose a side—and sides were rarely clearer than in the late 1960s—he would line up with the doves.

Chapter Eight

Recessive Genes
(Silvio Burigo/Lorraine and Frank Trotta)

I N THE YEARS AFTER WORLD WAR II, FRIDAY WAS A NIGHT OF two rituals for Silvio Burigo. First he sat down with his family to a dinner of buttered macaroni or *pasta e fagioli,* meatless in obedience to the Holy Roman Church, and then he did something truly religious. He went bowling.

From his bedroom closet he withdrew the team shirt of McGovern Plumbing & Heating, its back adorned with the felt portrait of a toilet. Although the shirt was cut to be worn open-necked and over the belt, Silvio insisted on tucking in the tail, buttoning the collar, and even wearing a tie, as if the game deserved a degree of formality. Then he drove downtown, skirting Arnold Constable and Benjamin's For Men and the other pricey stores, and entering a stretch of Main Street that catered to workingmen. There squatted Sears with its khakis, tools, and steel-toed boots and then Strauss Auto Parts, stocked with everything from spark plugs to hood ornaments. Farther along beckoned Rudy's Diner and the Sawdust Trail tavern and finally Silvio's destination, Roger's Bowl-o-Bar.

It was an elemental place, an oblong expanse the size of a supermarket, with sixteen varnished tongues of maple stretching in place of scuffed linoleum aisles. Teenagers still set the pins by hand and the score was tallied with paper and pencil, not projected overhead. As a matter of choice, the bar kept neither television nor jukebox and served beers brewed in Brooklyn and Newark. Beneath the low ceiling, the air grew furry with the smoke from a hundred cigars.

Past the counter where Silvio rented his shoes and the rack where he hefted his ball, he would find Davey Heinz, Charlie Brown, and Freddie Nero, all plumbers and his partners in the obsession entitled the New Rochelle Industrial League. The Bowl-o-Bar hosted other leagues, recreational and co-ed by design, boisterous with gutter balls and giggles and flirtation, but this one belonged to men grave about their sport. When the cops bowled against the firemen, or Griffin Ford faced Soundview Chevrolet, rivalry bristled. Conversation halted with each shot, as any distraction was assumed to be sabotage, and the foul line came under incessant surveillance.

At season's end, a bar in the West End threw the blowout that passed for a banquet, and the champions carried off trophies and cash prizes. Middling in all but his passion for the game, Silvio returned home every year empty-handed. But he was not unrewarded. For him, his teammates, and so many others in the industrial league, bowling meant more than a night out with the fellas. It was recreation, and recreation was a function of disposable income, and disposable income was a luxury Silvio had never before known.

Friday nights offered other clues, too, to this unprecedented comfort. Silvio bowled not for Local 86 but for a plumbing contractor—the boss, his putative enemy. How many contractors, after all, had demanded kickbacks for work during the Depression? Or hired nonunion crews? And kicked Silvio off the site when he tried to inspect? Now prosperity was lubricating the grating gears of class struggle, and in its microcosmic way McGovern's sponsorship attested to the new comity between labor and management. Even the cigars, so ubiquitous in the Bowl-o-Bar, were more than cigars. For Silvio and his union brethren, a cigar symbolized a measure of status and leisure; it was rolled by someone else and smoked in repose. The first chore for many an apprentice plumber was to buy his journeyman a White Owl.

Silvio rarely lit his cigars, and friends joked he was too cheap to spend a match. In many ways, it was true, he never stopped looking over his shoulder, as if the Depression might sneak up and suckerpunch him. The tumult of both his childhood and his marriage only magnified his caution. Even physically he seemed divided between the potbelly and double chin of a burgher and the piercing, hungry eyes of a waif. If Silvio Burigo was turning conservative, it did not mean he was turning Republican. It meant that, for the first time in his life, he had something to conserve.

The years immediately after V-J Day had jarred Silvio along with millions of union members. He lost his steady job building military bases as the armed forces contracted for peacetime. With defense contracts being canceled at a pace of $15 billion per month, Ford laid off 50,000 workers and Boeing 21,000. Organized labor, restive after its wartime truce with management, struck such basic industries as steel, coal, and railroads. While prices rose abruptly for basic goods, shortages still denied consumers meat, coffee, refrigerators, and especially housing.

But the economy did more than rebound as the market gorged on savings accounts and shopping lists that had grown vast during years of rationing. The gross national product rose 150 percent between 1945 and 1960. Even when adjusted for inflation, wages climbed more during the 1950s than in the previous five decades combined. Seventy-five percent of American households owned a car by 1960, and 90 percent had a television. Most important for those like Silvio in the building trades, six in ten families now owned a home.

Even in the booming 1920s, construction virtually ceased in the winter, with contractors loath to pay for heating unfinished buildings. Plumbers like Silvio, hostage to the fitful pattern, never dared spend the money they had saved in the warm months. Instead, like the coal pile in the tenement of his childhood, the reserve had to be hoarded and budgeted until spring arrived. Now the contractors had so many projects backed up they could not afford to hibernate. So they hung canvas sheets as exterior walls, lit portable propane heaters, and ordered the work to proceed, weather be damned. Not only could Silvio earn money the year round, the heaters were also handy for warming his lunch.

Westchester County and with it New Rochelle was enjoying a period of unparalleled development, as the middle class and corporate capital began their flight by freeway from New York. Union Carbide, American Telephone and Telegraph, General Foods, and New York Telephone all built headquarters in Westchester by the mid-1950s. The total value of business construction in the county for the year 1952 alone approached $90 million. The people who filled those new offices needed places to live, and so home building surged, too. Between 1950 and 1960 the population of New Rochelle leaped by nearly one-third, the largest increase of any community in a county dizzy with growth. Public monies further fed the bonanza. Drawing variously from local, state, and federal coffers, New Rochelle spent $14 million expanding schools, $3.6 million installing storm drains, and $2.7 million creating a combined city hall and school administration center, replete with Greek columns and bronze doors.

From the Standard Products ribbon factory to the Holy Name of

Jesus Church, from the Ursuline School to the 7-Up bottling plant, Silvio rarely laid down his tools. With a seller's market in labor, both his income and his influence climbed dramatically. Between 1930 and 1945 the hourly wage for a journeyman plumber in Local 86 had risen only fifteen cents, to $1.80. By 1950, it stood at $2.70 and by 1958, $4—a difference in thirteen postwar years of 122 percent. Along with higher pay, the local won a shorter workday, cracking the eight-hour barrier that had withstood bargaining for decades. Atop all these gains the national union introduced pension, health, and welfare benefits.

Such was the power of Local 86 that when its plumbers discovered New Rochelle High School purchasing shower panels manufactured in a nonunion factory, school officials returned them to avoid a strike. Like his comrades, Silvio would not even enter a home under construction on the day a lineman was installing the telephone; he deemed any worker without technical expertise, even one carrying a union card, to be a lower form of labor, if not of life itself.

Clout transferred readily into politics. From union halls in New Rochelle to hotel suites in Albany, candidates for offices as lofty as governor aggressively sought union endorsements. Even one local could deliver ten or fifteen men, who could in turn reach a hundred times as many—hanging posters, ringing doorbells, sending pamphlets to everyone on the family Christmas-card list. Silvio played a one-man phone bank, dialing his way through the union roster, repeating endlessly, "He's for labor. Give him a break."

At a national level the plumbers' union exerted force disproportionate to its rank and file of roughly 300,000. A former plumber, George Meany, led the American Federation of Labor and later the merged AFL-CIO. Dwight Eisenhower selected the United Association's president, Martin Durkin, as his first secretary of labor. Even after Durkin had left the administration with no small acrimony, Eisenhower found it expedient to help lay the cornerstone of the new AFL-CIO headquarters. Only the Roman Catholic Church and several Baptist denominations claimed the loyalty of more potential voters than did the mega-union.

In these halcyon years, Silvio finally loosened a lifetime's reins on his wallet. He bought Birch Street's first television set in 1949, and three years later indulged in a maroon Chevy, the first new car in his life. On many Sundays he drove around Westchester with Carole Ann, his youngest child, pointing out Peach Lake, where he and Delia had honeymooned, and then the high schools he had helped build in Armonk and Lewisboro. It was hard to tell which landmark made Silvio more sentimental. Passing the schools, he would slow the car, indicate the cornerstone, and ask Carole Ann, "How'd you like to go there?"

It was, of course, little more than a fantasy that Silvio Burigo could situate his family in John Cheever country, and yet in the flush 1950s a union plumber could believe certain fantasies came true. Silvio's friends treated themselves to hi-fis, tape recorders, and the ten-horsepower motors that transformed a rented rowboat into a pleasure craft. So many plumbers hunted that a chronic shortage struck the construction industry the first week of deer season. In the outdoors column of the United Association *Journal,* Silvio saw not only the usual snapshots of weekend fishermen brandishing ten-pound bass but of plumbers skiing and scuba-diving, hobbies once unimaginably rich for blue-collar blood. Simply a look at the *Journal*'s covers over the postwar generation gave proof a golden age was dawning. They metamorphosed from grainy, almost grim portraits of oil refineries and auto plants to illustrations of household cheer in a Norman Rockwell mode to full-color photographs of vacation spots. "Our Nation's Capital—City of Trees, Monuments and Tourists," went one typical paean, followed in the next issue by "San Francisco—Crossroads of the World."

The taste of ease brought about a salient change in what might be called union culture. The goal of organized labor shifted from struggling for a foothold to guarding the niche that had been captured. In the affluent society, plumbers were not quite affluent themselves, and that created an important distinction between their acquisitive surface and a deeper, abiding insecurity. Long before the term "trickle-down economics" had been coined, they depended on a version of it, waiting anxiously for drops of private capital or public investment to drip to their station. And that station felt too new, too tenuous, too hard-won to be shared readily. Silvio Burigo was a craftsman, after all, not a philanthropist.

His livelihood depended on excellence at his craft. On a construction site, a plumber always strung twine to mark the outer limits of a wall within which his pipes would run. Most would glance once at the plans and then place the string; Silvio checked and rechecked and checked yet again, pacing through the trenches with a sheath of blueprints and a hundred-foot tape measure. "You're in the wrong place," he once curtly informed a sheet-metal worker clamping together a duct. "My cast iron goes there." Indignant at first, the man discovered he had misread the plans by six inches.

Silvio might spend one hour stringing a single wall, just *preparing* to lay the pipe, and to some builders, undoubtedly, his painstaking approach looked like a boondoggle, a scheme to prolong the job and inflate everyone's paycheck. But Silvio knew that with even a slight error in aligning the pipes a wall or floor might need to be torn out, and the plumbing reinstalled, Sheetrock rehung, and concrete repoured. That hardly made for a bargain. Besides, he treated a construction site no differently than his own kitchen floor, which he would order his children to mop a second time if their first effort left behind streaks.

In other ways, too, Silvio set an example. Already accomplished as a plumber, he studied drafting and design in middle age. Loath to lose time from a job sitting in the john, he would drop his pants over a five-gallon bucket and send his apprentice for toilet paper. When a coworker on a large site suggested Silvio walk off with a few pipes and fittings for a bathroom at home, Silvio all but burst a vessel with rage. "That's one thing I don't believe in," he shouted. "You got a salary. You give a day's work. That's *all*. Buy the goddamn stuff."

Along with industry and honesty, Silvio considered fidelity to the union a cardinal virtue. As treasurer of Local 86, he personally visited any member behind in his dues, sometimes to intimidate him into paying but more often to arrange a compromise so the plumber would not lose his union card, the passport to employment. If necessary, Silvio himself fronted the money. Social life revolved around union affairs, from clambakes in City Park and dances at Glen Island Casino to national gatherings. Rather than miss the United Association convention one year, Silvio skipped a granddaughter's wedding; his daughter Carole Ann rescheduled her own nuptials to avoid a conflict with Local 86's weekly membership meeting, knowing which aisle her father, forced to choose, would walk down. At those family occasions Silvio did attend, he argued so relentlessly with his brother Jimmy the electrician about who belonged to the better union that their sister Vincenza usually fled the room, muttering, "Them guys, them guys."

In the union even more than at home, Silvio enjoyed the status of patriarch. He as treasurer, Wesley Brown as president, and George Grimm as business agent formed a dynasty that governed Local 86 uninterrupted for more than thirty years, from the Great Depression to the space age. And it was generally accepted that Silvio could have assumed the other positions, nominally more powerful than his own, had he merely declared the desire. When Grimm retired as business agent in the early 1970s, Silvio chose his favorite among three candidates vying for the job and escorted him to the home of virtually every member of the local. They received Silvio almost reverently, husband and wife practically colliding in the scramble to see who could take his coat and hat first, who could serve up the cake and coffee. In the election, Silvio's man carried 90 percent of the vote.

Most important, Silvio affected the local's future. As director of apprenticeship, he oversaw the education and training of prospective members. Nothing made him prouder—and nothing would ultimately make civil rights groups more outraged. For apprenticeship as practiced by Local 86, among countless others in the building trades, raised the bitterly divisive question of whether it perpetuated a high standard of workmanship or just an all-white preserve of lucrative jobs.

The United Association established the Joint Apprenticeship Program in 1948, and its collective operation by union locals and plumbing contractors demonstrated on a grand scale the same spirit of partnership as did Silvio's bowling team. Within six years of its founding, the apprenticeship program included a summer school held at Purdue University, with courses ranging from craft skills to liberal arts, and a technical competition among apprentices, the pipe trade's version of the Olympics. The AFL considered the United Association approach a model and touted it in a nationally broadcast documentary.

Silvio operated on a more narcissistic premise: Every apprentice in Local 86 reflected on him. So he worked on his students as carefully as he worked on his pipes, albeit with far less patience. Once he asked an apprentice if he was comfortable in high places. "I don't know about bein' on a skyscraper," the young man replied timidly. To which Silvio roared, "Can you climb a fuckin' ladder? That's all I wanna know." Another time an apprentice interrupted Silvio in mid-lesson with a question. Silvio lowered his head, peered over his glasses, and scowled. "Learn the method," he snarled. "Then ask."

Beyond the temper lay both talent and commitment. Silvio not only administered the program but taught many of its classes as well, spending innumerable nights in a workshop so drafty the windows were covered with cardboard. Fedora atop his head, cigar jammed into his cheek, he moved from table to table, showing how to read plans and rough out designs, how to compute angles and solder joints and comply with the building code. From other instructors, personally recruited by Silvio, the apprentices learned labor history and the gospel of solidarity. Ten thousand hours of paid fieldwork still lay ahead before anyone reached the level of journeyman, but a critical process was already under way. In the world of a union plumber, circa 1955, the dingy classroom on Horton Avenue served a purpose not unlike the Indian sweat lodge or bar mitzvah bimah: There the tribal elders initiated the next generation into manhood.

Seely, the only son in the Burigo household, did not follow Silvio into the trade, instead pursuing the glamour of professional baseball and, when that eluded him, the stability of civil service. Silvio's eldest daughter, Lorraine, tried, practicing on the elbow joint beneath the kitchen sink every time table scraps clogged the drain, but he told her,

"There aren't any woman plumbers." So the apprentices Silvio trained, the people he would be accused of favoring at the expense of qualified blacks, were his surrogate children. And like all children they represented a parent's only hope of immortality.

• • •

In October 1945 a naval aviator named Frank Praete returned to New Rochelle with the wife he had married and the son she had delivered during wartime. His brother, also a flier, came home with his new wife. Two sisters had wed servicemen as well, and all of the couples settled with the Praete parents. With the birth of more children, the household swelled to thirteen, packed from cellar to attic. Yet none of these veterans could afford a home or a decent rental in New Rochelle, still suffering from the demolition of vast swaths of housing that had slipped into tax delinquency during the Great Depression. Even two rooms in a boardinghouse commanded $80 a month.

All through the city the soldiers who had defeated Hitler and Hirohito were reduced to sleeping on couches. For New Rochelle, their plight amounted to a civic embarrassment; for Mayor Stanley Church, it opened a political opportunity. He had won election in 1939 partly on the promise of building public housing. Two years later he had managed to create a municipal housing authority, the legal entity necessary for borrowing money and undertaking construction. There the initiative stalled. Private homeowners complained that the subsidized apartments would drive down the value of their property. The very notion that New Rochelle needed public housing offended the city's self-image. "It seems strange to use the word 'slums' in connection with a residential community," one of Church's allies wrote, "least of all with 'The Queen City of the Sound.' "

Several hundred men like Frank Praete swayed the argument. Not even the most conservative homeowner wanted to look ungrateful by forcing war heroes to languish in dependency or borderline poverty. Shrewdly, Church appointed a Veterans' Emergency Housing Committee, which secured both federal and state funds for two projects totaling about 150 units. Frank Praete and his wife and son moved into one, paying $35 a month for four rooms in a prefabricated barracks. The project blossomed into a genuine neighborhood, peacefully integrated by race, ethnicity, and religion, jovial with bridge games and progressive dinners. Even a brief rent strike in 1949 was almost humorous: The veterans were incensed by a plan to paint their buildings gray, complaining, "We had enough of that shit in the service."

The success of the veterans' housing led directly to the construction of New Rochelle's low-income projects. More important, it inaugurated the era of modern liberalism in New Rochelle, an era in which public spending on public works no longer required a catastrophe like the Great Depression for justification. An activist government with brick and mortar in hand seemed a self-evident good—good for the poor, who would be uplifted; good for the affluent, who would no longer be endangered from below by crime and disease; and good for the trades-men in the West End, who would earn union wages erecting the monu-ments to forward thinking. Indeed, plumbers from Local 86, if not Silvio Burigo himself, installed the pipes in New Rochelle's housing projects.

Yet just when liberalism appeared most consensual in New Rochelle, it was sowing the seeds of its own fragmentation. Programs of public housing and slum clearance inevitably raised the subject of race, for it was blacks who disproportionately populated the poorest urban dis-tricts. Far from seeming a problem to liberals of the era, the plight of blacks presented them with an opportunity to further expand the New Deal coalition.

In the late 1940s, as New Rochelle was building its first housing projects, the issue of civil rights divided America by region rather than party. Millions of blacks had streamed from the rural South to the urban North during and after the war years. Liberated from Jim Crow and newly enfranchised, they held the swing votes in Ohio, Illinois, and New York, among other states crucial to any presidential candidate. Both parties vied for their loyalty.

The Republicans had more than the legacy of Lincoln to recommend them. Under Governor Thomas E. Dewey, New York became the first state to create a Fair Employment Practices Commission. Senator Robert A. Taft, Dewey's chief rival within the GOP and the nation's most promi-nent conservative, sponsored legislation to fund public housing. North-ern Democrats thus feared that the segregationism of their southern colleagues might cost the party power far outside Dixie. It took a coali-tion of young liberals such as Mayor Hubert Humphrey of Minneapolis and Joseph L. Rauh Jr. of Americans for Democratic Action and big-city bosses including Jacob Arvey of Chicago and Ed Flynn of the Bronx to wedge a forceful plank on civil rights into the Democratic Party's 1948 platform. When southern delegates walked out of the convention in protest, Rauh, for one, considered their desertion a boon to the party.

For New Rochelle in particular, civil rights presented the safest of battles. The city rested hundreds of miles from the South's bastions of legal segregation and from the risks, both physical and psychic, of taking a stand. Its own black community formed barely one-eighth of the population, and included a substantial and conspicuous middle class. Even the poorer blacks seemed familiar and unthreatening, because so many worked in white homes as domestics. If anything, the proprietary tone of the early civil rights struggle, the presumption that enlightened whites were doing something *for* incapable blacks, held a particular appeal. New Rochelle was as prosperous as postwar suburbs got—it had the greatest buying power of any community its size in the nation, according to a 1951 survey—and liberals chronically worried about affluence creating moral complacency. Thus they found it useful to have a social problem or two around, provided it was finite, uncomplicated, and easily solvable.

Partly for idealistic reasons and partly to hold the black votes in his coalition, Stanley Church turned race relations into a personal cause second only to utility rates. Whatever the motive, he acted precociously. As early as 1943, when the nation's armed forces were still segregated, he formed the Mayor's Interracial Committee, later renamed the Council for Unity; on May 6, 1948, only months before the issue of racial equality ruptured the Democratic convention, he declared Civil Rights Day. New Rochelle established a Human Rights Commission not simply to wax idealistic but to investigate complaints of discrimination aggressively.

What most distinguished New Rochelle's racial liberalism was that it far exceeded the official acts of government. The spiritual authority behind Mayor Church issued from what were arguably the most important pulpits in the city—the First Presbyterian and North Avenue Presbyterian Churches and Temple Israel, a Reform Jewish congregation. Together, they approximated the national coalition that civil rights was assembling. It stretched from socially liberal Republicans of the Nelson Rockefeller stripe to former radicals settled on the Democratic left wing, from Christians imbued with the concept of good works to Jews sensing both kinship and shared self-interest with oppressed blacks. Put another way, the Jews had the numbers, comprising nearly one-third of New Rochelle's population, and the Presbyterians had the influence of an established elite.

Under their aegis, the ethos of racial enlightenment informed almost every aspect of daily life. Each new homeowner received a brochure from the Council for Unity entitled "Teamwork for Our Town." The *Standard-Star* published photos every time a black student in New Rochelle High was elected to school office; even an impromptu shot of a white child hugging two black playmates functioned as a visual homily, appearing beneath the headline "BROTHERHOOD KNOWS NO BOUNDS." Forty years before multiculturalism achieved vogue, the high school was offering both a course and a club devoted to race relations and the Council for Unity was paying for teachers to attend workshops in "intercultural sensitivity."

Not a city to deflect attention from its achievements, New Rochelle celebrated racial harmony in numerous public displays. There was "I Am an American Day," with speakers ranging from the liberal Senator Wayne Morse to the black boxing champion Sugar Ray Robinson; there was the Community Song Festival, featuring an ecumenical and interracial array of choirs, choruses, and glee clubs. The opera singer Marian Anderson, a civil rights heroine since being barred from Washington's all-white Constitution Hall in 1939, performed in New Rochelle two years before the Metropolitan Opera permitted her on its stage. After the Ku Klux Klan bombed Sixteenth Street Baptist Church in Birmingham in 1963, killing four children, a little-theater troupe raised money for rebuilding with a benefit staging of *John Brown's Body.*

Never would New Rochelle's vision of itself as a light unto the nation become more apparent than on October 18, 1954. The previous spring, the Supreme Court had struck down the doctrine of separate-but-equal education in *Brown* v. *Board of Education,* and in the new academic year boycotts against integration and attacks on black pupils had erupted in numerous schools. On that fall day New Rochelle hosted students from four of the most troubled schools, Southern in Baltimore and Anacostia, Eastern, and McKinley in Washington, so they could observe its high school as an object lesson in successful integration. Sixty-five different families clamored for the chance to house the ten visitors. Newsreel and camera crews recorded their every step, from homeroom to cafeteria to human-relations class. The *Standard-Star* spread the story across its front page for two days, approvingly quoting a Washington student who said, "Being at New Rochelle High School is like seeing a goal."

Little did that visitor realize New Rochelle would soon be branded the "Little Rock of the North." For decades, the city had contained a black slum of "squalid dwellings without sanitary facilities, often without electricity and hot water, infested with vermin and inhabited by families of eight or more," as one state report described it. The board of education in 1930 drew attendance boundaries for its twelve elementary schools that restricted virtually all the black students to one of them, not coincidentally named Lincoln. As the black community expanded, the board revised Lincoln's district to conform to the new border. It covertly permitted any white child at Lincoln to transfer to another school. By 1949, Lincoln was nearly 100 percent black, while all but one of the other elementary schools were at least 80 percent white.

The local branch of the National Association for the Advancement of Colored People, mincing no words, called the disparity "Jim Crowism." After years of pressure and protest the board proffered its solution: Knock down the current Lincoln School, a relic from 1898, and build a new one. Voters approved the necessary bond issue in 1957, but the black community refused to accept the same segregation in a fancier package. When seven black parents tried to register their children in mostly white schools in the fall of 1960, the police arrested them for loitering, and the Lincoln School case was bound for court. In January 1961, Judge Irving R. Kaufman of United States District Court, specifically citing *Brown* v. *Board of Education,* ruled that New Rochelle had "deliberately created and maintained" segregation. And while an earlier, more conservative city had first gerrymandered the elementary school districts, it was liberal, postwar New Rochelle, so self-satisfied, that, in Kaufman's words, "did nothing to alter the status quo or lessen the serious racial imbalance."

In striking ways, the case anticipated the vicious battles to come in Boston and other northern cities over school integration. New Rochelle never burst into violent opposition, but even its progressives advanced the same argument as the working-class Irish of Boston later would: The issue isn't segregation; it's neighborhood schools. The school board pursued vindication all the way to the Supreme Court, facing opponents en route as renowned as Attorney General Robert F. Kennedy and Thurgood Marshall of the NAACP Legal Defense Fund. Defeated at the lower levels and refused a hearing by the High Court, New Rochelle ultimately assigned Lincoln's students to other schools and razed the building, as if in destroying the evidence one expunged the crime.

"It is important," one school board member insisted, "not to fall into the intellectual boobytrap of equating the New Rochelle situation with that of the South." The *Standard-Star,* on its editorial page, despaired that "the impression follows to outsiders that we are a city of segregationists." Seeming to comprehend the city's shame, Judge Kaufman hailed the compliant New Rochelle as "a trailblazer." He may have been right in a less salutary way than he had intended. As the first northern city forced by a federal court to integrate its schools, New Rochelle supplied one of the legal precedents judges employed to order mandatory busing in Boston. In a more general way, the city had discovered liberalism's limits, if not outright hypocrisy.

Yet even the Lincoln School case did not fully explain why liberalism was hurtling toward a collision with people like Silvio Burigo. The litigation, in fact, contributed to the belief that New Rochelle consisted of two and only two communities, wealthy whites and needy blacks, pity and its object. Barely noticed in the center sprawled a blue-collar Italian community, constituting well over one-third of the city's population and experiencing race relations in a deeply complicated way. Even as many Italian parents sent their children to overwhelmingly white parochial schools, and as an Italian member of the school board spoke most vociferously against black "agitation," the three elementary schools serving the Italian West End were by 1960 the most integrated in the city. Social class put the Italians in proximity with blacks—and in competition against them—with an intensity the affluent liberals of the North End never knew.

The ground on which the New Deal coalition stood was cracking open, but for the moment nobody seemed to notice the chasm. Blacks, blue-collar whites, and upscale liberals were all continuing to vote Democratic, with their might never greater than in Lyndon Johnson's 1964 landslide. In popular culture, too, competing interests and contradictory agendas vanished amid the celebration of a "classless" society.

Every week for five years beginning in October 1961, as many as 35 million Americans saw precisely the portrait of New Rochelle that the city might have commissioned, in the form of *The Dick Van Dyke Show*. Indeed, the show's creator, Carl Reiner, lived in New Rochelle and shaped the leading man in his image. Rob Petrie was not a suburbanite of the gray-flannel, middle-manager variety but a witty, urbane television writer. With its sectional sofa, Princess phone, and pass-through kitchen, his home at 448 Bonnie Meadow Road advertised the bounty of postwar America. Most of all, Rob and his wife, Laura, behaved like liberals, so obviously so that critics often compared them to John and Jacqueline Kennedy. She wore Capri pants, he read Dr. Spock, and they played bridge weekly with a couple who were among television's earliest identifiable Jews. In one particular episode Rob became convinced the hospital had switched his newborn son with the child of a couple named Peters. His fears subsided only when he met the other father—a visibly middle-class black. "Why didn't you tell me on the phone?" Rob asked. The man answered, "And miss the expression on your face?" Broadcast in September 1963, less than a month after Martin Luther King's "I Have a Dream" speech and over the objections of network and sponsor alike, the episode amounted to New Rochelle's ultimate sermon to the country on humanity.

If much of the city genuinely resembled *The Dick Van Dyke Show*, then Silvio Burigo lived metaphorically in *The Honeymooners*. The comedy cast Jackie Gleason as a bus driver named Ralph Kramden, who lived in a walk-up, bowled in a league, belonged to a lodge, and threatened, however jokingly, to knock his wife "to the moon" with a punch. Tellingly, *The Honeymooners* had gone off the air in 1956. So far as the television industry was concerned, not merely the show but the way of life it depicted had ceased to exist, having been replaced by countless variations on the middle-class suburban theme. Reality, however, could not be quite so neatly manipulated. And the day was fast approaching, in places like the West End of New Rochelle, when Ralph Kramden would decide Rob Petrie was his class enemy, a goddamn bleeding-heart limousine liberal.

• • •

To most outward appearances, Mary Jane Burigo was a tomboy, the sort of girl who played stickball, lettered in three sports, and loved nothing better than sitting with her big brother, Seely, in the Polo Grounds bleachers. Inside, though, by high school she had begun to consider herself a socialist. Socialism, as she conceived of it, meant making everybody equal, wiping out distinctions between rich and poor, distinctions starkly apparent to Mary Jane every time she visited a classmate in the North End. An adoring daughter, Mary Jane acquired much of her class consciousness from her father, less by way of instruction than osmosis. Whatever gripe about the rich Silvio vented during dinner, whatever curse upon the Republicans he pronounced while reading the paper, Mary Jane silently absorbed. And the sum of Silvio's unintentional lessons led her, ironically, far to his left.

As a teenager in the early 1950s, the most frigid years of the Cold War, she admired Norman Thomas, the Socialist Party's candidate for president in every election from 1928 through 1948, and read the political philosophy of Eugene Debs, the Socialist standard-bearer earlier in the century. Even Mary Jane's pleasure reading tended toward the novels of Howard Fast. One in particular, *The American,* stirred her profoundly, for it connected labor to radicalism and transmuted history into a page-turner. The title character is John Peter Altgeld, elected governor of Illinois in the wake of the 1886 Haymarket riot. During a rally of workers striking the McCormick reaper works, one hurled a bomb into a wedge of advancing police, who then turned their guns on the crowd. Eight officers died in the violence and an equal number of anarchists were arrested, tried, and convicted of their murders. By the time Altgeld took office, four had died on the gallows, one had committed suicide in his cell, and the case had escalated into a radical cause célèbre on the level of Sacco and Vanzetti or the Rosenbergs. In an act of both principle and political suicide, Altgeld studied the trial and, declaring it tainted by false evidence and judicial bias, pardoned the three remaining anarchists. Mary Jane wrote a report for English class about *The American,* especially decrying how Altgeld had been "crucified." The teacher reprimanded her for reading "this type of book."

Undeterred in her idealism, Mary Jane joined the high school's Interracial Club. Since its founding six years earlier, in 1945, the club had played a central role in New Rochelle's campaign for racial harmony, providing the intimate, casual contact that was often overlooked amid ceremonies and speechmaking. "Shared experiences," the club's literature put it, "are the way to friendship." Those experiences ranged from weekend worship services to school assemblies to afternoon snacks at each member's home. For Mary Jane, the club also offered the chance to spend time around her best friend, a black girl named Jean Allen. They played field hockey together, and often walked home from school, and shared a class affinity stronger than racial difference. For most of Jean's life, her family had rented, just like the Burigos, and even when they bought a home it was in the working-class West End.

The Interracial Club held one of its dinners in the Allen house, and Mary Jane, assigned to provide the snack, searched the city for soul food. Then, a few months later, her time to play hostess arrived. Mary Jane asked her parents for permission, not even sure she needed it. Silvio would still be working in the late afternoon, and Delia was usually out, too, although Mary Jane rarely knew where. Besides, she was her father's favorite, the one he called Cookie, the one for whom he had endowed a bank account toward her wedding day. But when she mentioned the club's meeting, Silvio said, "Absolutely not. No way are we going to have anybody like that in our house."

In Jean Allen he was barring the all-American girl. She bounded through school as cheerleader and choir singer, softball player and band conductor, student council delegate and Junior Prom chairman. With her wool blazer, turtleneck sweater, and straightened hair, she looked positively preppie. Beneath her photograph in the school yearbook, a caption extolled "the sunshine of her smile." But "like that" meant only one thing, and Silvio never brooked dissent.

"I don't have anything against the colored," he told Mary Jane by way of conclusion. "I just don't want any in my house."

More ashamed than outraged, Mary Jane concocted an excuse for canceling the meeting and withdrew from the Interracial Club. A few more times the issue of race flared between her and Silvio, mostly on the infrequent occasions a word harsher than "colored" passed his lips. "How can you talk like that?" Mary Jane cried. Silvio looked at her, almost smirking, and muttered, "Oh yeah, sure. Who you kidding?" The unspoken assumption, a seminal one in the years to come, was that beneath their masks even liberals like Mary Jane held the same hate.

Mary Jane never asked her father exactly where, why, and how he had generated this malice. That he had it, however, many of Silvio's relatives and coworkers agree, even if they prefer the euphemisms "outspoken" or "opinionated" to blunter words. In their memories, rarely did Silvio actively disparage blacks, but even more rarely did he ever engage them. Over the years two black families, the Browns and the Abrams, lived down the block from the Burigos. The largest black neighborhood in New Rochelle abutted the West End, and Silvio had cousins who were among the handful of whites in Lincoln School. Yet none of the physical nearness ever evolved for Silvio into even a nodding acquaintance. Within a polyglot city, he moved almost entirely among reflections of himself, the blue-collar Italian Catholics of the West End, Local 86, and the North Italy Society. Understandably, what was most familiar felt most comfortable. Common heritage put iron in the backbone of the union, the neighborhood, and the mutual-aid society. This clannishness accepted, if not encouraged, Silvio's intolerance.

And blacks were not its only object. In one incident during the postwar years, Silvio believed a Jewish shopkeeper had cheated him. Many of the details are impossible now to determine: He may have been buying work clothes or he may have been buying boots; it may have been a military-surplus store or it may have been a dry-goods store. What Silvio's daughter Lorraine did remember decades later was that her father experienced the encounter not as an isolated dispute but as part of a pattern of Jewish deceit. Whatever the original sources of Silvio's antipathy, it grew pronounced enough that when Carole Ann prepared to marry a Jewish man in 1972, even converting from Catholicism, Lorraine worried aloud, "I hope Daddy doesn't say anything about the Jews."

One can only speculate about the extent to which Silvio's attitudes toward minorities mirrored those of his trade-union peers. The question also remains of how much those emotions governed his behavior. "If it was prejudice," Carole Ann said in retrospect, "it wasn't hate. It was stereotyping." This very distinction, between belief and conduct, private thought and public action, underscored many discrimination suits against organized labor. What is indisputable, however, is that in Silvio's burgeoning conservatism on other issues he accurately represented much of the rank and file. And, as with his feelings about blacks, a question from Mary Jane conjured his deepest convictions.

One night in the early 1950s they were watching televised hearings into Communist subversion. Mary Jane swelled with sympathy for the witnesses. Forty years later she could not explain the precise reason, but it may well have stemmed from her love for *The American*. By this time, Howard Fast had been imprisoned for refusing to name names before the House Un-American Activities Committee. Librarians across the country, under pressure from the American Legion among other groups, had purged his books from their shelves. He played the martyr with such certitude that even a fellow author and radical, Dashiell Hammett, chided Fast about his "crown of thorns." Only later would Fast himself admit he had "sold his soul" as a member of the Communist Party from 1943 to 1956.

"How can you believe all those people wanted to betray their country," Mary Jane asked her father, "even if they did belong?"

"Birds of a feather flock together," Silvio replied.

To him, Communist allegiance was not an intellectual exercise or an act of misguided idealism but an active and immediate threat. As much of a union diehard as Silvio was, the flurry of strikes in basic industries after World War II had alarmed him. It seemed possible that infiltrated unions could shut down the country and open the way for a Communist takeover. Like many skilled craftsmen in the American Federation of Labor, Silvio had long imputed radicalism to the mass-production unions of the Congress of Industrial Organizations. Even the CIO's expulsion by 1950 of twelve unions as Communist fronts served less to quell Silvio's fears than to redouble them. Here was proof of how far Moscow's tendrils reached. Why, then, should he doubt Joe McCarthy was right about traitors lurking in the State Department and the U.S. Army? Why would he not believe Whittaker Chambers over Alger Hiss?

Silvio's greatest hero in the labor movement, after all, aspired to be "the most rabid anti-Communist in America." George Meany had begun his working life as a plumber, a member of United Association Local 463 in the Bronx. As Meany quickly climbed through the echelons of trade-union officialdom, plumbers like Silvio proudly considered him one of their own, a brother in high places. The leaders of Local 86 met with Meany during his tenure as president of the New York State Federation of Labor. In later years, as leader of the AFL and the merged AFL-CIO, Meany made a point of regularly addressing the United Association convention, although it was only one union among the 142 under his jurisdiction.

From the waning days of World War II, a time when America and the Soviet Union were officially allies, Meany propounded an uncompromising anti-Communism. On April 5, 1945, he addressed the New York Central Trades and Labor Council, including representatives of the plumbers' union, about the AFL's decision to boycott an international conference of trade unions sponsored jointly by the Soviet Union and Great Britain. In answering the immediate question, Meany defined his abiding principles, delivering organized labor's equivalent of the "Iron Curtain" speech Winston Churchill would give eleven months later:

> We see no virtue in groveling in the dust of a false unity which would simply replace one form of totalitarianism with another. We do not

propose to be a party to the rigging of international labor machinery to be used as a medium of infiltration or the chocolate coating of any ideology among people who would choke if they knew the consequences of what they were swallowing.

In Meany's worldview, one that Silvio reiterated to his own family, trade unions were the tool Communism conspired to turn against democracy. The 1948 coup in Czechoslovakia provided Meany's parable of choice: "They controlled the trade union movement," he told the United Association *Journal,* "and within seven days they controlled the country." The message resonated with Silvio Burigo, and not simply because it transformed him from a tubby, balding, middle-aged plumber into a sentinel of freedom. It explained the chaotic world around him by arranging disparate events into a logical pattern. At the same time Eastern Europe was falling under Soviet hegemony, the CIO was ousting member unions as Communist-dominated and Walter Reuther was just winning a decade-long battle against Communists for control of the United Auto Workers. In a very real way, America must have seemed to Silvio the western front of the Cold War.

There was nothing new in Meany's vision of labor as the bulwark against Communism. Sidney Hillman and Lloyd Garrison, among many others in Franklin Roosevelt's circle, had espoused the same idea fifteen years earlier. For that matter, when Samuel Gompers founded the AFL in 1886, he had disowned his former Marxism to pursue a more pragmatic, respectable unionism. Far more than any precursor, however, Meany buttressed rhetoric with action. He barnstormed the United States in support of the Marshall Plan, arguing that rebuilding Western Europe and so girding it against Communism was worth "postponing the day when there will be sufficient goods to satisfy all the demands of our own people." Meany threw the AFL's estimable resources and energies into a worldwide labor alliance with a pro-Western ideology, the International Confederation of Free Trade Unions. When diplomacy failed, the option of destabilization loomed. In 1954, Meany implored Latin American nations to overthrow Guatemala's democratic government and assigned an AFL representative with ties to the Central Intelligence Agency to the country—ostensibly because Guatemala had permitted Communist control of trade unions. The CIA indeed engineered a coup later that year, which benefited not labor but the United Fruit Company, from which the ousted regime had expropriated 400,000 acres of land.

Economics as much as politics sealed the AFL's partnership with Washington in the Cold War. Just as it had during World War II, defense spending during this uneasy peacetime translated into union jobs. More than almost any other trade unionists, plumbers possessed skills required in the atomic energy and aerospace industries. The United Association *Journal* devoted lavishly illustrated articles to both the Honeywell and Titan missile systems during a three-month period in early 1960. Where the magazine once had published snapshots of plumbers on New Deal projects, it now listed recent government contracts, the vast majority of them from the military—$827,290 from the Army Corps of Engineers for barracks; $574,180 for additions to a Veterans Administration hospital; $351,700 for a storage building at the Naval Gun Factory.

As Meany saw it, military expenditures drove the economy; the money earned making guns would buy ever more butter. Speaking at a 1953 testimonial in his honor, he linked organized labor's social agenda of improved housing, education, and medical care to purchasing power, a power "largely based upon defense spending." To unintentionally macabre effect, a short story in the January 1953 edition of the *Journal* entitled "Family Bomb Shelter" similarly conflated brinksmanship and prosperity:

> Each afternoon thereafter was declared family time and the Shelly [family] basement became a beehive of activity, with even Frieda and Gwen learning to "sling mortar" for the cement forms and bricks that rapidly went into place. Al and the boys did the heavy work.
>
> Even Bert came over from next door to help supervise the job and sprinkle terse bits of wisdom among the workers.
>
> "Got t' hand it to ya', Al," he commented when the project was nearing completion, "most folks just talk about war preparedness, but what they need is more horsepower and not so much exhaust!"
>
> Al grinned.
>
> "You know, Bert," he chuckled, "I've sort of forgotten about this being a bomb shelter. Of course, it can serve for that, too, if it's ever needed—pray to God it's not—but since our family has found out how much fun it is to work together like this I've decided to turn the basement into a rumpus room. There's plenty of space for a game of shuffleboard, a pingpong table, and maybe even room for volley ball if the boys want to play it. War or no war, we can have the time of our lives down here—can't we kids?"

In a decade of bipartisan consensus on foreign policy, neither George Meany nor Silvio Burigo needed to switch parties to remain fervently anti-Communist. Right in New Rochelle, Stanley Church understood the political algebra. While his left hand pressed for rent control and lower utility rates and appointed the first black to a municipal school board in New York State, his right seized the subversion issue.

At his behest, New Rochelle passed a law ordering the arrest of any known Communist passing through the city by train. The board of education, deeply influenced by Church, closed its buildings to an array of radical groups. Once the political ally of local Socialists, Church now weighed an offer to chair the federal Subversive Activities Control Board.

At the national level, Silvio felt an even greater communion with Harry Truman than he had with Franklin Roosevelt. Truman's mixture of class politics at home and containment abroad, of Fair Deal and Cold War, paralleled Silvio's own duality. Temperamentally, too, Truman as the scrappy son of a big-city machine seemed familiar to Silvio in a way that the aristocratic Roosevelt, however admirable, never was. "He's a regular, common fella," Silvio said of Truman. "He's down-to-earth. One of us. Not a *pol*-itician." The United Association *Journal* hailed Truman as the emblem of "the millions of little men and women, the unsung, unheralded, average people"

The reason for the praise could be distilled to two words: Taft-Hartley. Two Republicans bore the credit—or the blame, to union members—for introducing the bill in 1947. The Republican majority in Congress, swept into power in the 1946 midterm elections, passed it. The New Deal was over, the victors announced. Indeed, Taft-Hartley reversed many of organized labor's greatest gains from the Roosevelt era, and the single most important of its provisions banned the closed shop, one in which only union members are hired. Other elements required union officials to certify they were not Communist; weakened the National Labor Relations Board; designated categories of unfair union practices; and allowed both the president and the federal courts in certain instances to curtail or outlaw strikes. Cried the unions in response: "slave labor."

When Harry Truman vetoed the Taft-Hartley bill he did more than earn labor's gratitude. The stand helped transform him from a beleaguered caretaker president to FDR's legitimate heir, from "go-along, get-along Harry" to "give-'em-hell Harry." Truman summoned Congress into session shortly after the 1948 Democratic convention, submitting legislation in the New Deal tradition on public housing, education aid, and rent control; he signed executive orders ending racial discrimination in the military and the civil service. During the whistle-stop tours of Truman's 1948 presidential campaign he missed no opportunity to wage class warfare with a ferocity that harked back as much to Andrew Jackson as to Franklin Roosevelt. "The Democratic Party puts human rights and human welfare first," he declared in one typical speech. "These Republican gluttons of privilege are cold men. They are cunning men. . . . They want a return of the Wall Street economic dictatorship."

Deemed a sure loser in opinion polls, Truman scored one of the most famous upsets in American presidential history. In the process, he led the Democratic Party back into control of both houses of Congress for the next four years. Labor, Jews, and Catholics all remained solidly Democratic, and blacks voted for Truman in greater numbers than they ever had for Roosevelt. The Republican candidate, Thomas Dewey, actually polled a smaller percentage of the popular vote against Truman than he had against Roosevelt in 1944. The two fringe candidates, Strom Thurmond on the right and Henry Wallace on the left, split less than 5 percent of the vote between them. After inciting fears of a Southern bolt from the Democratic Party, Thurmond's Dixiecrats took just thirty-nine of 127 electoral votes in the region. The coalition had held.

In the next presidential election the AFL broke its nonpartisan tradition to endorse a candidate. And the union chose not Dwight Eisenhower, a certifiable war hero almost incidentally running as a Republican, but the Democrat routinely derided as an "egghead," Adlai Stevenson. The combined AFL-CIO repeated the endorsement four years later. Silvio, too, voted futilely for Stevenson both times.

Even with Eisenhower in office, however, the Democratic Party could plausibly claim victory. A Republican may have won the White House by a landslide, but he was willing to accept much of the New Deal's legacy. Eisenhower increased Social Security benefits in 1954 and 1956, raised the minimum wage by one-third in 1955, and spent $1.3 billion on slum clearance during his two terms. "Social Security, housing, workman's compensation, unemployment insurance, and the preservation of the value of savings," the president said, "are the things that must be kept above and beyond politics and campaigns."

Yet at the very moment of comity, of stasis, Silvio Burigo had within himself the ingredients of political realignment. He was a man opposed to any compromise with Communism, a man worried about losing his precarious bit of prosperity, a man indifferent at best to black claims on the national conscience. Only the enduring memory of the Great Depression and the New Deal and the overarching moderation of the Democratic Party kept the forces of change within Silvio latent. But in the next generations, as embodied by his daughter Lorraine and her husband and their firstborn child, those recessive genes would spring into dominance.

• • •

In late September 1953, about two weeks after Lorraine Burigo had married Frank Trotta, a letter arrived at the frame house in which they rented the attic. The communication appeared official, coming on thick bond paper imprinted "County of Westchester," but the content could hardly have been more personal.

> Heartiest congratulations on [your] recent marriage.
> We are happy to note the union of two of our fine local families.
> May health and happiness attend you thru a marital lifetime of constant romance.
> My warmest personal wishes and—
>> Keep courting!
>> Salvatore Tocci

Seventeen months later a similar piece of mail reached the Trottas, now the parents of Frank Jr.

> Heartiest congratulations on [the] recent birth of your son. We are happy to note the continuance of our fine local families.
> May health and happiness attend your son through a long lifetime of success. May he bring honor to your house.
> My warmest personal wishes.
>> Salvatore Tocci

Salvatore Tocci had played baseball with Silvio Burigo back in the 1920s and led Stanley Church through the West End as ward leader during the Depression. Now he was writing in his roles as a city supervisor and concomitantly a member of the county board. Each evening, in fact, he spent two hours cranking out just such letters, to newlyweds and mourners and recent parents, to the all-county shortstop and the *Standard-Star* paperboy-of-the-month and the scholarship winner at Blessed Sacrament High. Not all of them could yet vote, but someday all of them would, and Salvatore Tocci intended for their every ballot to be cast for the Democrats.

In Mr. and Mrs. Francesco Trotta, as he inscribed the envelope, Tocci must have assumed he was reinforcing rather than convincing. Bloodline, social class, and past practice all identified them as loyal Democrats. Lorraine was her father's daughter not only as a matter of genealogy but also as a form of imitation. She rooted for the Giants because he rooted for the Giants. She added food coloring to her tomato sauce so it would redden to the shade he preferred. She hovered beside the sink as he shaved and washed after work each afternoon. Naturally enough, she mimicked his example in politics, too, casting the first presidential vote of her life for Adlai Stevenson in 1952. "I'm a Democrat," Silvio had often put it. "They're the workingman's party. I'm a party man. I vote the party line."

Silvio's intransigence as a parent ensured that Lorraine would never see a world beyond the West End, one that might challenge assumptions and overturn habits. On the day in 1946 when she graduated from high school, he had informed her, "Legally, I don't have to support you anymore. You're on your own." She wept and asked, "Where'm I gonna go?" and, by way of compromise, he agreed to let her rent her own bedroom at $10 a month. "Thank you, Daddy," she gushed.

Drawn to military nursing during wartime, Lorraine now studied for the entrance examination to the Waves. She passed and brought the enlistment papers to Silvio. "Whaddaya gonna do with all those men around?" he huffed. "You'll be a bum."

Without his signature to sanction her escape, Lorraine could think of only one alternative. In the last weeks of high school a recruiter from the New York Telephone Company had visited and shown a film. Two scenes stayed in Lorraine's mind. One had a woman relaxing on a footbridge over a stream in what was evidently midafternoon. "What are you doing here?" a friend inquired. "I have split hours," the woman replied. "I don't have to go back till later." The other scene showed the same woman at a dance. "This is great," Lorraine had whispered at the time to her friend Jean. "We'll meet guys."

Within two weeks of leaving high school, then, Lorraine abandoned her dreams of travel and profession. She started work as a switchboard operator for $26 a week, and she would remain with the phone company for thirty-eight years, miserable every single day. With perhaps forty operators in a room cooled by only floor fans, the place stank of sweat. The earpieces pinched. One part of the headset, dangling onto her blouse, always left stains. Supervisors stalked the aisles, snapping, "Shut up," if they heard any social conversation, and timing operators' visits to the bathroom, needling those deemed too slow, "You got a kidney problem?"

At the end of the first week Lorraine asked a longtime operator, "When do you have the parties and the dances with the men?" Mystified, the woman answered, "What parties? What dances?"

All Lorraine or anyone else there had was the job itself. The company refused to hire women except as operators or clerks, and the operators' union itself was a management creation, hardly inclined to press that issue or any other. Still, the women took home a paycheck every Thursday night, and the money formed a vital second income in their blue-collar households. The most educated operators in the room, ironically, were the only two blacks, who both had college degrees and presumably had traded down to find employment at all. By their presence alone, they represented a threat to the ethnic working-class franchise. Occasionally, when a position opened, a supervisor would slip beside Lorraine and whisper, "You know anybody?" The implication, she understood, was anybody white. Another time a white operator groused loudly to her supervisor, "You gotta change my seat. It smells here." The black coworker beside her, instantly aware of the implication, shot back, "You white people smell, too. Only you don't know it."

All the tension repelled Lorraine. With students seated in her high school classes by alphabetical order, she had often studied without incident next to a black girl, Hyacinth Brown. Early in Lorraine's working life, before the Lincoln School case and the Local 86 suit, civil rights struck her as a purely southern issue and a simplistic one at that. Why have two sets of water fountains or bathrooms? Why not let everyone vote? Segregation made no sense to her. Even in the late 1950s, when Frank Jr. as a precocious three-year-old asked her what the word "integration" meant, Lorraine demonstrated by mixing salt and pepper. For a northern urbanite, almost irrespective of political party, the solution could seem just that innocuous.

So nothing yet disturbed Lorraine's sense of herself as a Democrat, least of all her choice in a husband. Frank Trotta lived next door to the Burigos on Birch Street, and one of the consequences of his being sixteen years older than Lorraine was that he had been able to vote three times for Franklin Roosevelt. Frank's father, a blacksmith, had been a Republican until the Great Depression turned the entire family into Democrats. The elder Trotta lost his shop on mortgage payments and found work only through the WPA. The seventh of ten children, Frank discarded his dream of becoming an illustrator to change tires and paint cars for a series of gas stations. As three brothers went to war, he toiled in the tool crib of a factory converted to defense contracting, and grew so involved with the union he was elected shop steward. Whatever his doubts about organized labor, and he harbored a few, they vanished when the pay clock clicked into overtime.

The next decade saw only minor change. Frank left the defense contractor to assemble pocketbooks in a factory and then to clean telephone company offices in southern Connecticut. Along the way he voted twice for Adlai Stevenson, less as an act of intellect than of reflex. But Frank's custodial job created problems at home since he and Lorraine, working different shifts, owned only one car. So Frank listened carefully on the day in 1959 when his brother-in-law, the maintenance manager for New Rochelle's public housing projects, told him the civil service exam was about to be given. Frank assumed "lower-type people" lived in the subsidized buildings, but, from the Depression, he knew the poor needed somewhere to sleep. Besides, he could easily walk or catch a ride to the projects. First he took the test for a machinist's position, failing because he read poorly, and then passed one to become a laborer.

Soon after, Frank reported for his first day of work at the Robert R. Hartley Houses. There he would see Democratic liberalism and its best intentions literally from the inside out.

Chapter Nine

Address as Destiny
(Vilma and Jack Maeby)

ONE MORNING IN THE LATE SPRING OF 1951, VILMA OBRYCKI heard a knock at the door of her family's home in Baltimore. She groaned and wondered, Who'm I gonna have to get rid of now? With warm weather, the salesmen had descended like cicadas, chirping the virtues of vacuum cleaner and aluminum siding and encyclopedia set, and always it fell to Vilma to sweep them back into the street. Her mother was already at the restaurant, peeling shrimp and patting crab cakes, and her father was sleepwalking through his rounds in Orphans Court. So Vilma, twenty-two years old and counting the days until her wedding, put down her book and left her sunlit spot in the kitchen to trudge to the front door to say no. This visitor, however, bore neither a sample case nor a smile.

"Does Joseph Obrycki live here?" he asked.

"Yes."

"Well, here," he said, passing Vilma a sheet of paper folded into thirds. "Would you give him this?"

Only after closing the door did she glance down at the page and see the word "Subpoena." Not quite sure what it meant, and thus un-alarmed, she laid the subpoena atop the dining-room table with the rest of the day's mail.

There it sat, undisturbed, until Joe returned home in the early afternoon. He did not intend to stay, just to change from his business suit into a sport coat and tie for greeting guests at the crab house. Vilma halted him by the mail pile and said, "There's a subpoena for you." He picked up the sheet, unfolded it to read the contents, and snorted out a laugh. Then he said, "Don't worry, Vilma. I'm gonna take the Fifth." For the next two days he paced through the house, repeating the mantra, "I refuse to answer on the grounds it may incriminate me."

Joe had good reason to rehearse. He wasn't in trouble with the beat police, so easily bribed, or even a state court, ultimately controlled by the Democratic boss, William Curran. He had been summoned by the United States Senate's Special Committee to Investigate Organized Crime in Interstate Commerce—the famous Kefauver committee. For much of the previous year the committee had traversed the country exposing both rackets and political corruption, and beaming its hearings on the new mass medium of television to tens of millions of Americans. At its most entertaining the Kefauver investigation unveiled a demimonde of mobsters named Greasy Thumb and Trigger Mike speaking a patois of "bagmen" and "ice" and "the fix." More important, in probing numbers and bookmaking in thirteen major cities, the committee revealed just how extensively criminals had infiltrated the Democratic Party's urban machines. In July the committee planned to turn its scrutiny to Baltimore, a city rich with all the requisite vices.

Yet as the hearings drew closer, Joe betrayed barely a ruffle. With his courthouse position and the crab house's success, he was earning more of his living legitimately than ever before. Since seeing a brother-in-law jailed for evading income tax, he had habitually overpaid his own, the better to deflect attention from the money he still made gambling. More to the point, Joe had a connection. One of the senators on the Kefauver committee, Herbert O'Conor of Maryland, like him owed obedience to Curran, for three decades the boss of state politics. Not only had Joe delivered money and votes to O'Conor's campaigns, for senator and earlier for governor, he had regularly dealt with him on patronage as well. The clubhouse hack and the congressional statesman, seemingly so distant, socialized at the same political dinners and greeted each other by first name.

So Joe went about life as usual. He danced at Vilma's wedding to Jack Maeby on June 23, and presented them with a honeymoon in the Poconos, paid for by the city's preeminent boss, Jack Pollack, and his entourage. In the afterglow, Joe bragged about how much food he had bought for the reception. Not even Pollack himself had laid out such a spread for *his* daughter's wedding. And Joe made sure everyone knew that he, generous guy that he was, had shipped the leftovers to an orphanage. The subpoena, as a topic, had disappeared.

Sure enough, when the Baltimore hearings opened on July 2, the name of Joseph Obrycki did not appear on the witness list. It is impossible to determine whether O'Conor interceded on his behalf, but to this day politicians who were close to both men consider it plausible. In any event, the Baltimore sessions proved to be anticlimactic, focusing mainly on "news services" that supplied racing results to bookmakers. Television skipped the proceedings and the newspapers outside Baltimore reported mere paragraphs. But Jack and Vilma Maeby, back from the mountains, noticed one very familiar figure in the press coverage, Willis H. King, whom they knew as Buzz. Two years earlier, as a favor to Joe, King had found Jack a summer job.

Home from college, Jack was spending the season with the Obryckis at the shore resort of Ocean City and needed to make money for his next year of school. Sympathetic, Joe led him to a nightclub named Rick's Raft and explained the young man's dilemma to the burly, graying man in charge. "Don't worry, kid," Buzz King said in his gruff version of the paterfamilias. "We'll find you a job if we have to put a flashlight on your head and make you a lighthouse."

A few hours later an underling of King's walked Jack down the boardwalk to a cigarette store with no cigarettes. The job, he explained, was to stand at the counter and look busy, so that meanwhile, behind a false wall, the slot machines could whirl away undetected. Much to the shock of his boss, Jack actually stocked and sold a great many cigarettes that summer, and his presence, as expected, staved off the police. For doing so little he made the staggering sum of $40 a week and, Damon Runyon reader that he was, thrilled to the raffish allure of it all.

Now, with King on the witness stand, the charm vanished. Here was a man who refused to state his business for fear of self-incrimination and claimed ignorance of his own tax returns; here was a man who just happened to have loaned $5,000 without collateral to an officer on the vice squad and kept 2,475 pairs of dice "as a hobby." The gallery laughed then, but no one laughed as the committee counsel led King through an inventory of the arsenal police had discovered in his home —a twelve-gauge shotgun and a sawed-off twenty, a .38-caliber pistol and three Colt automatics. Just for target practice, King explained, and shooting rabbits.

As much as Joe's subpoena, Buzz King's testimony forced a clarity on Jack and Vilma Maeby that was both painful and liberating. Running numbers, making book, and buying votes no longer seemed occupations only incidentally illegal, not so different from sewing clothes or packing vegetables like the rest of Fell's Point. They were genuine crimes, backed by weaponry and filled with contempt for civilized law. As they began their adult lives, contemplating where they might raise their own children, Jack and Vilma surveyed their surroundings in moral as well as geographical terms. A person could take the Fifth but a city could not, and Baltimore incriminated the Democratic Party.

• • •

The dirt gridiron of White Swan Park lay four blocks from the row house where Jack Maeby was raised. Just to ensure that none of the football players or fans overlooked the benefactor of their recreation, a seven-foot-tall painting of a white swan hung beside the entrance gate. It was the symbol of the neighborhood's Democratic club. Someday football would carry Jack away from the one-party politics of Baltimore and introduce him to the startling concept of free choice, but during his childhood in the 1930s it served as one more reminder of how the machine insinuated itself into every fiber of society, always demanding a mindless vote in return.

Jack had an uncle, Emil Sandru, who starred as a single-wing tailback for the local semi-pro team, the Millburn Blackjacks. Like the rest of the roughnecks wearing the striped black and red jerseys, Emil got his pay indirectly from Jack Pollack, the rising boss. In return, Emil stood every Election Day outside the polls at Public School 228 handing out what appeared from a distance to be flyers. The one time Jack Maeby actually entered the White Swan Club, following the uncle he so admired, he saw otherwise: The sheets were ballots with the appropriate boxes already marked.

On the football field, a tailback like Emil weighed myriad options every time he took a snap. He could run, he could pass, he could hand off; with its array of fakes and reverses, the single-wing offense demanded both a hunter's reflexes and a magician's sleight of hand. The Emil Sandru of Election Day, as Jack came to realize, surrendered all the autonomy and high style of his sporting life for the programmed responses of a robot. Yes, that was the word Jack could not shake: "robot."

Jack did not arrive at this insight until he left Baltimore for the military and then college. The discoveries he made in the larger world, about both himself and his city, anticipated what he later learned from the Kefauver committee. For Vilma, the hearings offered the first glimpse of a rot that threatened to engulf her. Jack experienced them more as confirmation of the disgust already building in his soul.

Enlightenment came in the perverse form of the draft. Graduating from high school in February 1946, Jack was immediately grabbed by the army and assigned to the Signal Corps base in Fort Monmouth, New Jersey. His comrades in the training unit hailed from the distant precincts of Atlanta and Philadelphia, and most had entered the military after college, only adding to their worldliness. Politics made a natural subject, especially around election time, and as Jack sat on his footlocker during bull sessions and poker games he shrank with inadequacy. Nothing had ever caused him to ask why he was a Democrat; coming from Baltimore, where the Republicans existed solely as a civics class abstraction, he might as well have asked why he breathed. Now he began wondering who these Republicans were and what exactly they stood for.

Jack could hardly bring himself to utter such ignorant questions, and he ducked any chances to talk about Baltimore, a city he increasingly viewed through skeptical eyes. Somehow the war, fought continents away, had inflicted damage at home. Not far from the Maeby house, the Glen L. Martin aircraft factory had burgeoned from 3,600 employees in early 1939 to 32,000 less than two years later. Appalachians thronged to the unskilled jobs, pitching up in barns and cars, trailers and tents, and the "hot-sheet" boardinghouses that rented the same bed to workers on different shifts. Eventually, the government and the company threw together a district of frame houses as flimsy as they were small, meant only as temporary quarters. But after the war, even with the factory cutting jobs, the Appalachians stayed. While their neighborhood was officially christened Aero Acres, as a postwar eyesore Jack knew it as Hillbilly Heights.

His girlfriend, Vilma, no longer dared walk alone in Fell's Point, the sentimental home to her family. The Broadway market, once butcher and greengrocer to the neighborhood, teemed with prostitutes and rats. Farther down the street, the surge in wartime shipping supported a miscellany of missions, flophouses, and dives, dubbed Nickel Town for the deep schooner of beer five cents could buy. A reporter for the *Sun* counted forty-seven bars in just two blocks, places with names like Jew Fanny's, Mary Widow, and the Barbary Coast. Among the multitude of drunks, there even existed a separate caste of untouchables called smokehounds for their drink of choice, a cloudy mixture of water and denatured alcohol.

In less obvious ways, which Jack could not have been expected to recognize, Fell's Point teetered between decency and decline. It boasted a high percentage of home ownership, strikingly so for a working-class area, and an abundance of sturdy brick row houses that would lure gentrifiers two generations later. But nearly all its housing stock dated from the nineteenth century and was worth barely half the citywide average per building. Two of every three residents lacked a private flush toilet, and three of four had no central heating—rates as low as those in the West Baltimore black slums. When a city commission in 1943 studied what it termed "the menace of blight," analyzing some one hundred residential tracts, Fell's Point wallowed among the most endangered dozen.

The only solution around was cosmetic. It went by the name Formstone and consisted of dyed concrete that was slathered across the face of a row house and then rolled with a mold to resemble separate blocks of limestone and sandstone. Convinced by salesmen that such was the stuff of modernity, homeowners buried marble portals and stained-glass transoms beneath the facade. What Formstone could not disguise was an overarching entropy, a corrosion spreading from Fell's Point outward through working-class East Baltimore. No single calamity befell the surrounding area, but an assortment of lesser blows slowly tallied—a playground vandalized twice during Holy Week, cars stolen by a gang called the Hot Wirers, a seventeen-year-old boy stabbed to death in a park by his kid brother.

So Jack Maeby was not long for Baltimore. On leave from Fort Monmouth near the end of his service, he had gone drinking with his childhood friend Flavio Nardone, who was on strike at a shipyard. In one saloon, a man recognized them from the football team at Patterson Park High. "What're you doin' tomorrow?" he asked.

"Nothing," they replied.

"The junior college is startin' football practice. Why don't you come out there?"

Jack and Flavio did, and by day's end the coach had arranged for them to take the entrance exam. Baltimore, as it turned out, was a recruiting haven for Bucknell University in Lewisburg, Pennsylvania, and after one season Flavio transferred. The next year, on Flavio's recommendation, the Bucknell coach offered Jack a full scholarship.

Traveling north along the Susquehanna that fall of 1949, Jack formed part of the rising postwar meritocracy. He may have earned his place among the elite as a quarterback instead of a scholar, but he shared more than a little with the Jewish kid from the Bronx riding the subway to City College. The whole Baltimore contingent at Bucknell, in fact, moved with a certain unmistakable sense of purpose. As children of the working class, they had no family money to cushion mistakes or indecision; as veterans of Bastogne and Kwajalein, they knew something of leadership and loss. One evening a group of them burst into a student court that was trying a freshman who had been discovered without his required beanie. Turning the interrogation lamp onto the upperclassman judges, the veterans announced, "That's over. We're here to get an education."

Even in a historical moment of such flux, however, Bucknell spoke of money, tradition, and privilege. Compared to a Princeton or Williams, of course, it seemed strictly middlebrow, but the only other campus Jack had ever seen was the converted high school of Baltimore Junior College. Nestled in a valley among the Alleghenies, Bucknell unfolded with quadrangles, towering oaks, and geometric paths. Century-old Taylor Hall had been designed by the same architect who planned the United States Capitol's dome, and the more recent buildings emulated its Greek Revival style. Outside the president's residence grew kwanzan and princess and golden rain trees, exotic species whose very presence was considered part of a Bucknell education.

The university entitled its yearbook *L'Agenda* and sponsored an ornithology club and a daily conversation hour in German. Mandatory chapel attendance, like freshman beanies, was headed for history. While a preponderance of students came from small-town Pennsylvania, they were frequently the children of bankers or merchants. Enough others represented the right kind of suburb, Cynwyd and Short Hills and Mamaroneck. Jack's class counted among its men a Bramley and a Boyd and an Ellsworth, a Harvey Hamilton Bush and a C. Graydon Rogers— names that suggested if not entitlement then at least the pretense of it.

Many a newcomer like Jack Maeby might well have withered in insecurity or bridled with resentment. What was he but the son of a wire maker who never finished high school? What was he but a jock recruited to supply bread and circuses? But Jack's father had preached to him class escape instead of class consciousness, brandishing as evidence the hands he could never scour clean of factory grime. "Use this," he had always said, indicating his head, "instead of these." The very future so many of Jack's peers back in Baltimore craved—a stable union job at Bethlehem Steel in Sparrows Point—loomed for him as a hell of drudgery and routine.

When Jack's new friends at Bucknell asked about his background, he offered only fuzzy answers. On the occasions they visited him in Baltimore, he met them in the Obryckis' neighborhood, more presentable than his own. Classmates assumed he wore sweatshirts and sneakers because he was an athlete, not a scholarship kid too strapped to afford cashmere sweaters and saddle shoes. Popular as Jack was, he avoided the favored hangouts, the Bison and Pardoe's, rather than reveal he did not have cash enough for a hamburger.

On several memorable occasions, however, the portals swung open to admit him to a finer world. After a football game against Franklin and

Marshall in Lancaster, a fraternity brother's family hosted Jack for dinner. He coveted their servants, their cars, and, perhaps most of all, their ineffable assurance. And much less than that could impress him. Invited home by a classmate from Reading, Pennsylvania, the son of a knitting-mill foreman, Jack found his eyes returning again and again not to furniture or an appliance but the lawn. Never had he seen so much grass in Baltimore, except on the field of Memorial Stadium.

These moments delivered the same epiphany. Being upwardly mo-bile, Jack began to believe, meant being Republican and conservative. As for what else being Republican and conservative meant, Jack learned from Professor Russell Headley.

Of all the professors at Bucknell, Russell Headley seemed almost predestined to become the mentor to a working-class athlete with mid-dle-class dreams. A small-town grocer's son, Headley had gone to the Ivy League only thanks to a scholarship. In college, he had wrestled, and after graduation he had taught, mostly in public high schools. When in middle age he undertook doctoral studies, he paid the tuition with a second job in a steel mill.

So he made quite the outsider on the Bucknell faculty. He preferred tutoring a pupil over pie and a Coke to sipping sherry with the depart-ment, and treated ballplayers from unlettered homes as potential schol-ars. Jack took nearly every course Headley taught, most important "The History of Economic Thought." There Headley introduced him to Adam Smith and the *Wall Street Journal* and a withering critique of activist government. Little in sixteen years of education astounded Jack more than learning that Washington actually paid farmers *not* to grow crops. The unimpeded marketplace, Russell Headley maintained, would best solve its own problems. When a student as obedient as most of the nation to John Maynard Keynes said, "That can't be right," Headley simply turned Socratic and asked, "Why not?"

The concept of a free market resounded for Jack with more than financial connotations. Everything in Baltimore, he believed, was utterly *un*free. For all the choice offered between two factions of the Demo-cratic machine, the elections were travesties worthy of a Soviet satellite. Labor unions, supposedly the voice of the workers, just ordered them around like a second boss. You had to join up, you had to pay dues, you had to strike when the union said strike. He remembered how his friend Flavio had survived on handouts from relatives during the ship-yard walkout, only to have the union settle after months of picketing for essentially the same offer it had initially scorned.

Having transferred to Bucknell as a junior, Jack had only two years to leap into the middle class. With the inspired impatience that animated so many fellow veterans, he attacked a major in commerce and finance along with varsity sports, college government, fraternity membership, and a job as dormitory proctor. Never in four semesters did his first class start later than eight in the morning. During football season he went directly from his last class to the practice field to the training table to his desk, studying until his head drooped in exhaustion. By the time he graduated, he had earned selection to *Who's Who in American Colleges and Universities,* won the presidency of the Student Faculty Congress, and filled eight lines of type in *L'Agenda* with various other accomplishments.

None of these achievements dictated a precise direction, however, and in Jack's final months at Bucknell a time of reckoning arrived. Professor Headley had been using Jack as one of several assistants in research on Descartes, and he had extolled him to colleagues at the Massachusetts Institute of Technology. They, in turn, offered Jack a partial scholarship to study for a master's degree. Jack was to marry Vilma only weeks after graduation, and had intended to enter a management-training program with Montgomery Ward. Now, suddenly, a prestigious alternative dangled before him, waiting only to be plucked.

Jack faced a choice not simply between a job and education, or between business and academe as a career, but between two entirely different types of status. As an economist he would belong to an elite based on intellectual accomplishment, one that the conservative commentator Michael Novak in 1972 would critically brand the New Class. As a manager for Ward's he would secure an immediate place in the fiscal middle class, the very population Novak and others would someday enlist against the intelligentsia. Naturally, Jack Maeby at twenty-three did not conceive of himself as part of the currents of history. Everything necessarily felt personal. And since graduate school seemed to him just a way of "postponing reality," he drove one morning in July 1951 to the Montgomery Ward warehouse and distribution center in central Baltimore. In so doing, he was metaphorically registering as a Republican.

• • •

As Jack Maeby decamped rightward, Vilma began migrating in the opposite direction. As he abandoned the Democratic Party, she believed in its redemption through the ever greater exercise of liberalism. Someday they would contend for the political soul of their daughter, Leslie, but for the moment what mattered most was that both were vacating the electoral center, however imperfectly embodied by Joe Obrycki and the Baltimore machine. The issue that stirred Vilma's compassion, that pulled her to the left, was one that would ultimately fracture the Democratic coalition: race.

For a city with 200,000 blacks in 1945, Baltimore managed to effectively obscure them from white eyes. Restricted almost entirely to the single ghetto of Upton, barred from shopping in the downtown department stores, and denied virtually any job except domestic service, blacks existed as a sort of fleeting vapor. Through her childhood Vilma glimpsed them only as maids changing streetcars downtown, "Arabbers" peddling vegetables from horse-drawn carts, and church ladies wandering down the alleys, beating tambourines and singing "That Old Rugged Cross," hoping for grace in the form of loose change.

The virtual eradication of a black presence from white Baltimore attested to a rare, if informal, instance of bipartisan cooperation. The Democratic Party actively legislated against blacks, three times passing laws to enforce segregation in housing, and even though none of the measures survived court challenges they hardened the private pattern of restrictive covenants. Both the city and state divided public sector jobs by race, leaving few above the level of janitor for blacks. For more than eighty years after the Civil War, the Republicans, the party of Lincoln, refused to mobilize blacks, permitting them at political gatherings only if they sat at their own tables. A doctrine of separation every bit as ironclad as apartheid governed pools, amusement parks, skating rinks, movie houses, public schools, the state university, the municipal bar association, and more, in some cases well into the 1960s.

But in 1943 something had happened to Vilma. She entered Patterson Park High School, and she rode there every morning on the Number 26 trolley. She picked it up along Eastern Avenue, a block from her house, but the route originated several miles to the southeast, in a neighborhood of steelworkers and servicemen called Turners Station, one of the few pinpricks of black settlement outside West Baltimore. A handful of black students were always sitting on the trolley when Vilma boarded; they seemed quiet and clean and they kept to themselves. How long they had already been traveling toward school Vilma could only guess. A half hour? An hour? More? All she knew was that after forty minutes, when she alighted near Patterson Park, they stayed in their seats, continuing forty-one more blocks to Dunbar, one of the black high schools. When Vilma rode home at day's end, she spotted the same kids. They had begun their journey while she was still hanging out at the Arundel ice-cream parlor.

Hindered by shyness and social custom, Vilma never spoke to any of the black students. But in simply riding a trolley with them, noticing they carried lunch bags and homework much like her own, she was engaging in the kind of mundane, incidental association against which segregation conspired. Tacitly accepting her black peers' humanity, Vilma could hardly countenance their longer trip to school. And the commute barely hinted at deeper inequalities. Fifty years after the Emancipation Proclamation, the Baltimore school commissioner warned against providing blacks with "the so-called higher education that unfits [them] for the lives that they are to lead." Maryland spent nearly three times the money educating white pupils as blacks, a 1920 survey found. Into the early 1950s, black public schools routinely operated at twice their capacity, shuffling students through on split shifts, while the most elite white schools refused to let blacks even attempt the entrance exam.

After Vilma graduated, and stopped riding the Number 26 trolley, she continued to encounter blacks personally. None became a friend; years later she could not recall many of their names. But for the child of a Polish family in a blue-collar neighborhood, any such dealings were exceedingly rare. Blacks were seen, if at all, as competitors for jobs. The earliest immigrants in Fell's Point, primarily Irish, had used fists and fire to drive out blacks who caulked ships. Nearly a century later, when Bethlehem Steel tried to train fifteen black riveters, seven thousand white workers struck.

If anything, Vilma's experience more closely paralleled those of the Jews on Baltimore's northwest side, who would become the city's most outspoken white advocates for civil rights. Like them, Vilma came from a family whose small business and relative affluence afforded contact with blacks. These blacks, it was true, occupied subservient positions, but they moved through the most intimate quarters of the family's life. For all the inequity built into such relationships, they engendered a certain kind of trust.

Within eleven months spanning the summers of 1952 and 1953, Vilma gave birth to Jack Jr. and Leslie. Although the new family was living with the Obryckis, so Jack could save for a down payment on a home, Vilma could barely manage an infant, a toddler, and chores with her chronic asthma. She hired a black woman to clean the house and do the wash once a week, and in the process acquired an emissary from the unknown world across town.

The women met against a backdrop of bold civil rights activity. Nine black students in 1952 endured beatings and abuse to break the color barrier at Polytechnic High School, the city's best. Meanwhile the local NAACP was demanding that the federal government halt millions of dollars of redevelopment aid to Baltimore until public housing was integrated. Even in its skewed form, urban renewal forced a reckoning with the appalling conditions in black slums. One could hardly pick up the

Sun without finding the latest exposé about battered row houses lacking plumbing or heat, beset by vermin and tuberculosis, spilling their garbage and excrement into narrow "squeeze-gut" alleys. *The Saturday Evening Post* likened the poorest neighborhoods to a leper colony.

Adrift in diapers and bottles, Vilma barely noticed, and the cleaning lady was hardly inclined to raise such volatile topics. Instead, she enlightened Vilma by example. By working briskly and wordlessly, she was a living refutation of Joe's standard rants about shiftless blacks, and even when Vilma's mother, Lillian, offered her lunch she brought her own. Sometimes she brought her three children as well, and they clustered at her feet, obedient and abashed, only daring to smile when they played with Jack Jr.

Occasionally, as Vilma fed Leslie and the cleaning lady ironed, they talked about being mothers. Something in the way the black woman spoke about wanting her kids to excel in school caught Vilma. It was not simply the sentiment or the underlying values, but the actual elocution the cleaning lady employed. She sounded too educated to be pressing shirts and scrubbing toilets. Regarding this woman, not much older than herself, Vilma beheld a life stunted by forces she was only beginning to comprehend.

Then, one week, Vilma gave the cleaning lady a few bags of used clothing, and suddenly the membrane between missus and maid, white and black melted. "You have no idea what this means to me," the woman blurted. "The clothes you give me are things I don't have to buy." Bits of her life spewed forth—how the money from cleaning just covered the rent, how her husband worked nights and she hardly saw him, how she had to bring the kids with her if he got overtime.

The cleaning lady returned the next week, her mask of propriety firmly restored. A few months later Jack and Vilma moved away. But in the years to come, years that saw the family living hundreds of miles from Baltimore, the racial education of Vilma Maeby proceeded, this time in the kitchen of Obrycki's Olde Crab House.

With the restaurant's success, it moved in 1961 from Pratt Street to a larger setting on Lombard. No longer could Lillian Obrycki and Anne Schanze, Joe's wife and his "Friend," between them handle all the food preparation. So the Obryckis hired three black women from the Winchester-Sandtown neighborhood a half mile north, which was shifting from Jewish to black at the time and was always being mentioned as a candidate for urban renewal. Their names were Laura, Dora, and Susie, and few in the family bothered to learn any more than that. They were just three middle-aged ladies in housedresses and aprons, reaching for hairnets when the health inspector arrived. All Joe cared about was their willingness to take minimum wage.

Officially, the women's duties went no further than peeling shrimp and shelling crabs, tasks considered sufficiently unskilled for a black. In fact, they concocted the crab soup and clam chowder, spicy dishes that helped establish the restaurant's reputation. Lillian, herself the veteran of decades of unappreciated labor, repaid their talent with friendship. "Miss Lil," the women called her in return. When Vilma stopped in the kitchen during her visits to Baltimore, they would hug her just because she was Miss Lil's little girl.

One afternoon Vilma asked Laura how to make clam chowder, her personal specialty. As Laura started reciting the recipe, Vilma lost track and asked her to write it down. A few moments later she received a page of misspellings and indecipherable scribbles. Ever her mother's daughter, Vilma said thanks graciously.

The image, though, remained. For Vilma Maeby, the Number 26 trolley and the garbled recipe for chowder and the glimpse of a stoic maid's desperation made the evil of race hate immediate and concrete. They also made the need for liberalism manifest. To Vilma's mind, the Democratic Party could hardly embrace civil rights quickly or aggressively enough.

• • •

As Jack Maeby, management trainee, soon discovered, all human endeavor fell into two realms. There was the Montgomery Ward way and there was the wrong way. And the Montgomery Ward way was Sewell Avery's way. Nearing eighty when Jack became his employee, Avery had assumed the chairmanship of Ward's as J. P. Morgan's candidate, and he had turned efficiency and caution into record sales during the Great Depression. Nicknamed Gloomy, he never stopped anticipating another Black Friday, hoarding corporate assets toward half a billion dollars. Those who disagreed disappeared. Over the years Avery purged four presidents and forty vice presidents and shrank his board from a contentious fifteen to a cowed nine. Now Jack was learning what the sovereign desired.

It started with clothes. A Ward's manager wore a two-piece suit in navy or charcoal, a blue oxford shirt, and a rep tie. Those who deviated received a reprimand from the personnel director, with the unspoken sense that in the Chicago headquarters Avery himself was grinding his teeth in displeasure. And a Ward's manager, at least as Jack understood it, owned a home in the suburbs. So after his first year of training Jack paid a thousand dollars down on a brick house in a place called Irvington.

Irvington was the brainchild of a developer, Irving Ditty, who mercifully chose not to immortalize his surname. Tethered by streetcar to central Baltimore by the turn of the century, Irvington grew in blocks of brick. For the elite, Ditty erected Victorian homes with generous yards, and for those whose ambition exceeded their means, he installed the narrow row houses dubbed "blind" for their dearth of windows. To move into Irvington was not simply to change address but to arrive, as Russell Baker recalls in his memoir *Growing Up:*

> I'd never dreamed of living in such splendor. Besides its four bed-rooms, it had a living room twenty feet long, a dining room more than ten feet in both dimensions, and a "sun parlor" that overlooked an expanse of green, tree-shaded parkland through which flowed a small stream. There was a front porch big enough to accommodate a glider. In the kitchen sat a gleaming white refrigerator that made its own ice cubes. I would never again have to worry about the icebox pan overflowing. The cellar floor was covered with blocks of inlaid lino-leum tile. The house's most magnificent feature, however, was the bathroom, with lavender fixtures, green wall tiles, and—wonder of wonders—a shower over the bathtub. For the first time in my life I could take a shower right in the house.

On a January morning in 1954, Jack Maeby and family unlocked the front door of their own home. By this time, Irvington exemplified not rarefied luxury but comfort accessible to the masses. It attracted workers from the high end of blue collar and the low end of white collar, the steel mill foreman and department store saleslady and telephone com-pany clerk. Jack filled the profile. He bought the corner house at 728 Bethnal Road with a GI Bill mortgage for $9,000, and he shaved $700 off the purchase price by painting the walls and varnishing the floors himself. Even at that, Irvington was a stretch; the monthly mortgage payment of a hundred dollars consumed nearly half of his salary.

What sacrifice won him was a niche in the middle of the middle. His new house, built after the war, fell between the Irvington extremes of Victorian and "blind" row. It contained three bedrooms, a tiled base-ment, and both refrigerator and range; the living room gaped so wide Jack worried only how to furnish it. From the picture window, from the back porch, from the sloping lawn he planted with azaleas, Jack contemplated a world that was prosperous and fair. Just a few blocks away the campus of Mount St. Joseph High School stretched verdant as a park. The Frederick Road trolley ran directly downtown, but who needed downtown anymore? One of the premier stores, Hochschild's, had opened a branch nearby, anchoring the first shopping center in greater Baltimore. Now, at last, Jack owned a home to which he could invite his Bucknell buddies, unashamed.

So great was his sense of achievement that he overlooked the fact he was still living in Baltimore. Irvington was not a separate town, although it had been one until being annexed piecemeal in 1888 and 1918. Jack's misapprehension was revealing. Hillbilly Heights, the Appalachian slum that to him embodied urban blight, actually lay in the suburbs. Irvington, the suburban idyll, sat within the city. "City" and "suburb" had ceased to designate geography; each word now connoted values, prospects, a particular future.

Montgomery Ward fit into the brighter of those futures. The warehouses and distribution centers that formed the core of the company might squat on city concrete, right beside the transit barns in Baltimore's case, but the products they shipped were meant to sate the suburban appetite. Formally, Jack was learning how to manage inventory, oversee employees, and budget a department; but all those discrete skills aimed, finally, at supplying the American Dream—in the form of an Airline Portable radio or a Pert Bolero dress or a Rocketrike tricycle. Back in 1946, a diplomat had joked that America could win the Cold War by bombing Russia with Sears catalogues. Less than a decade later the United States Information Service indeed began sending both Sears and Ward catalogues to embassies overseas with orders that they be prominently displayed.

An ambassador could just as well have exhibited Jack Maeby himself as an advertisement for corporate capitalism. It was not that he had consciously decided to submit his life to Ward's direction, but he possessed all the traits of a manager—intelligence, discipline, leadership, and the physical presence necessary for respect on the loading docks. Ward's kept promoting him and raising his salary. Jack advanced from first-line supervisor to floor manager to head of an ever larger series of departments. By the end, he had spent his entire career with one company, and had seen his paycheck rise over those thirty-five years from $57 a week to $1,500. He had become, too, the sort of political thinker Sewell Avery would have appreciated, a foe of big labor and big government, a reliable Republican. Hadn't "Gloomy," after all, once defied Franklin Roosevelt's War Production Board so adamantly that the police had to oust him from his office, still clutching the arms of his executive chair?

As a mere management trainee, Jack had no way yet of foreseeing his longevity with Ward's. But when the company transferred him in the summer of 1955 to its Chicago distribution center, he readily complied. It was a rite of upward mobility for a promising young manager to be posted in Ward's capital city. Besides, with two toddlers in the family and Vilma pregnant again, Jack was not about to quit a job just to stick around Baltimore. Psychologically, if not physically, he had already left on the day he moved into Irvington.

• • •

Within the Chicago distribution center, Jack Maeby could easily forget any other place on earth existed. Rising eight stories and sprawling across 2 million square feet from a railhead to a dining salon set with china, it regarded the outer world only through its loading docks— suspicious, heavy-lidded eyes. One aisle ran spinelike the length of the building, and at Sewell Avery's dictate it was to be kept clear of impediments. Even now, unseated as chairman during a hostile takeover struggle, he often inspected unannounced. Starting at the front of the building on Chicago Avenue, he would march to the rear at the banks of the Chicago River. Then he would urinate into the water, return to his office, and call down wrath on anyone who had left a forklift parked in "Avery's Aisle."

In his own position, Jack traversed the entire edifice, both in terms of geography and class. Climbing stairs for the exercise, he bounced every day from his office beside the docks to the ordering department to shipping and receiving to the top management suites, from first floor to third, back to first, up to eighth. How many orders were going out? How much tonnage was coming in? Were any boxcars or trucks left from yesterday to be unloaded? Was any given department exceeding its budget for payroll? He needed to answer those questions on a daily basis, first for himself and then for his superiors. It was symptomatic of his straddling act that beneath the suit and tie required for audiences with executives, he wore, at least in winter, thermal underwear for the arctic winds strafing the freight bays.

No matter how separate and self-contained the vast building seemed, however, the city still encroached. The ghetto poverty so hidden from Jack in Baltimore confronted him every working day in Chicago, literally from across the street. Without realizing it, he had placed himself in the midst of an experiment in "slum clearance" and "urban renewal," an experiment that would fail in grand, notorious fashion. What Jack witnessed of the debacle would inform his attitudes toward both the black underclass and the Democratic liberalism meant to rescue it.

That Jack arrived in Chicago halfway through the sequence of events made a difference. For there had been a time when the neighborhood around the distribution center was a Sicilian slum called Little Hell and when poverty and crime were not so neatly conflated with blackness. The district had risen from the scorched earth of the 1871 Chicago fire into a jigsaw of plank tenements crammed two or three to a lot. Their first occupants, Swedes, gave way to Sicilians as the century turned, and the conditions only worsened. As a writer for the *Chicago Tribune* later described it:

> Little Hell was a rabbit warren of vermin-infested, garbage-strewn alleys, gangways and dangerous streets in which residents endured a rate of violent crime 12 times that of non-slum neighborhoods. There were no parks or playgrounds and few yards for children to play in. Half the rotting tenements that housed the residents had no bath or shower facilities. Whole families were living in makeshift, dirt-floor basement apartments partitioned off with cardboard.

The Chicago Housing Authority began razing Little Hell in the late 1930s to allow construction of low-income housing. Far from being the high-rise, all-minority projects of later infamy, the Francis Cabrini Homes would consist of 568 garden apartments, integrated on the formula of one-quarter for blacks and three-quarters for the Italians who had been displaced by demolition. Under federal pressure after Pearl Harbor, however, the authority turned the entire development into housing for migrant defense workers. And virtually all of them were black. For a time the Italians succeeded through protest and intimidation in restricting blacks to their original portion of the apartments. But they could hardly prevail indefinitely, not with a war to be won and southern blacks flooding into Chicago and its factories at a rate of 15,000 per year. By 1949, blacks constituted 40 percent of the population in the Cabrini Homes, and twice that proportion in the adjoining neighborhood.

Six years later, when Jack arrived, he found no Italians except a handful of grandfathers sipping grappa in the last white bar. The familiar demons of Little Hell—tuberculosis, infant mortality, and juvenile delinquency—now wore black faces. The houses, all soot stains and weathered wood, tilted into one another, chimneys listing and eaves bowing, broken windows patched with rags. In a neighborhood with 1,200 more families than units of housing, life necessarily played out its tragedies on the public stage of the street corner.

The ghetto intruded most directly into Jack's existence through theft, of a curious sort. At least once a week the receiving supervisor appeared in Jack's office to file a nearly identical report: One of the locals had hopped onto the loading dock in full daylight and snatched the nearest box. A hi-fi, a pair of loafers, a three-pack of T-shirts—it didn't matter. Jack would have expected a certain amount of cunning, of stealth. This was brazen, as if the point was not only to take but to mock. One other thing struck Jack: Every single thief was black.

Wanting to spare Vilma worry, he never told her about the incidents. She heard of race only elliptically. It was the implicit element when Jack shambled through the door at eight or nine and groaned, "It was a lousy day" or "Jake was acting up again" or "We had to let two of 'em go." Nearly all the "time-card people" Jack managed were black, and he considered most to be decent and reliable. But a layer of front-line supervisors below Jack dealt directly with those men, every Wednesday passing out pay envelopes with wisecracks and backslaps. Thus buffered, he never came to know any of them in the personal way Vilma had come to know the cleaning lady and the crab house cooks.

Instead, Jack encountered the black failures, observing them in almost clinical detail. To fire any employee, he had to construct a case of absenteeism, alcoholism, or insubordination airtight enough to withstand the inevitable union grievance. The scenario rarely varied: Some guy from the neighborhood would fill out an application and get hired for handling freight or stock. It was unskilled labor, but it brought a weekly check, paid vacation, and profit sharing—incentives aplenty in Jack's mind. After a week or two, though, the man would start showing up a half hour or an hour late or not at all. Then Jack would have to shift a merchandise examiner to the loading dock, the outgoing orders would back up awaiting inspection, and some superior would give *him* hell for falling behind schedule.

So Jack never wasted any time getting sociological about the ghetto. None of his superiors pitied him for being stuck with these losers. Why should he weep for them? He got paid for performance, calibrated in timetables and budgets, and evaluated by a corps of efficiency experts. When he fell short, there was no raise, no promotion, no 10 percent bonus at Christmas. "Those people," Jack would say later, "were getting into my pockets."

Coming and going from the job, passing blocks of battered tenements and scores of idle men, Jack felt at his most charitable a profound incomprehension. How could people tolerate such misery? Why didn't they do something about it? He thought of his own childhood household, not poor but hardly rich, always abuzz with scrubbing and painting. Jack himself had started working at thirteen, laying concrete blocks for foundations, then unloading trains at a can factory, and after that bucking rivets at an aircraft plant. What was his title and salary at Ward's but a reward for years of dutiful labor? What was his home in the suburb of Park Ridge, with peonies in the garden and hamburgers on the grill and kids swinging in the yard, but a testament to gumption and grit?

When bulldozers and wrecking balls leveled the tenements just north of Ward's distribution center in the late 1950s, Jack dared to hope.

Thirty-six acres of the neighborhood was being cleared for the Cabrini Extension, and the finest architects in the city had been retained to create it. They designed fifteen high-rises, the state of the art in public construction, all cushioned by parkland with five hundred trees and ten thousand shrubs. With 1,925 units, the extension would form the largest public housing development in Chicago, a fact that was still deemed a superlative. Even Jack, conservative as he was turning, thought perhaps the tenants would treat a brand-new apartment better than a decades-old tenement. Maybe they would show some pride in the property; maybe that pride would carry over to a work ethic. If nothing else, the construction had improved his own life. With the adjacent blocks pummeled and the residents scattered, theft from the loading docks halted.

By the time the Cabrini Extension opened in 1958, Jack had left Chicago, having been promoted and transferred to a warehouse just outside Albany, New York. But he learned quickly enough what became of the new projects. Returning to Chicago twice yearly for performance reviews, he heard how gang members covered the buildings with graffiti, and vandals tore off doors and shattered windows. When Ward's disgorged its workers on Wednesday afternoons, each carrying a pay envelope full of cash, thugs jumped them in the company parking lot. Soon it had to be fenced and patrolled. A few years later a former colleague phoned Jack to say a sniper had just fired from one of the Cabrini buildings into Ward's home office, across the street from the distribution center. After a while nobody bothered calling Jack with the latest incident: Felony had lost its novelty.

When the adjacent William Green Homes were completed in 1962, the combined project contained 3,500 units and 15,000 tenants in an archtype of what some blacks came to call the "vertical reservation." Indeed, Cabrini-Green solved a political problem—the violent opposition to public housing in white neighborhoods—even as it incubated social ones. Tenants joined "self-protection" bands to use the laundry rooms. Rooftop gunmen slew two police officers on patrol in the summer of 1970. A survey two years later discovered that murders, rapes, robberies, and assaults occurred in Cabrini-Green at three to six times the citywide rates. By 1985, the percentages of unemployed workers, families on welfare, and single-parent households dwarfed those of Little Hell at its most pathological.

All that Jack had seen, heard, and felt during his three years in Chicago led inescapably to a political conclusion. He had arrived there only months after Richard J. Daley assumed office for the first of six terms as mayor. In Daley's early years especially, before Martin Luther

King's 1965 fair-housing protests and the police riot during the 1968 Democratic convention, pundits and citizens alike routinely proclaimed Chicago "the city that works." Whenever Jack heard the term, he rolled his eyes and waited for the subject to change. The Montgomery Ward job had immersed him in a Chicago that Daley, much like Baltimore's mayors, shielded from white eyes, a metropolis of crime, violence, and despair. Paradoxically, Jack shared his outrage at the Daley machine with the blacks and liberals who most ardently opposed it. Vilma had even voted for Dwight Eisenhower in 1956 largely as a protest against Adlai Stevenson's ties to the Chicago Democrats. But she, like most liberals, believed in reforming the party from within by pushing it to the left. Jack preferred to vote Republican and throw the bastards out. Before long, in the shadow of yet another Democratic machine, he would have his chance.

• • •

The first time the west wind blew across the pigpens of Constantine's farm and down Timberland Drive, Vilma and Jack Maeby recoiled with what could delicately be called culture shock. In the fall of 1958, they had just moved into a brick split-level home in Colonie, New York. The map and the relocation experts at Montgomery Ward told the Maebys that Colonie was a suburb of Albany, but it looked to them more like a misplaced chunk of Iowa. Tractors rumbled down roads that wound along the routes of Indian paths. Cattle grazed on the pasture that doubled as a baseball field. The shopping district called Four Corners amounted to three gas stations and a grocery.

Timberland Drive jabbed into the landscape as a block-long spike of suburbia. The mothers, none of them working, met on play dates with their toddlers or outings to Saratoga Lake. Each morning they paraded to the corner, kids in tow, to await the school bus. Passing them, waving good-bye, drove fathers like Jack on their incremental way up in the world—a contractor and an engineer, a music professor and a power plant supervisor. At day's end, the men returned, to chat driveway to driveway about lawn mowers and Little League.

Many of the neighbors, the Maebys soon discovered, had recently arrived from Albany, following Central Avenue out from the city of their upbringing. There was nothing unique in such migration. As the manifestation of status and upward mobility, the suburbs exerted a nearly gravitational pull on the postwar generation. Jack and Vilma had lived in Irvington and Park Ridge for precisely such reasons. But a deeper affinity bound them to their new friends, one that revealed itself quite by accident.

Five-year-old Cathy Nicolla across the street was Leslie Maeby's best friend, so, naturally enough, both sets of parents socialized often over the barbecue grill. One night Cathy's mother, Mary Ann, started telling a story about her college days. As a senior majoring in education at St. Rose in Albany, she was assigned to student-teach a history class at Vincentian Institute, a nearby Catholic high school. The curriculum included the subject of political machines, and Mary Ann told the pupils what she herself had learned in a political science course, that Albany had one. She explained how the machine doled out cash and favors for votes; she even told how the ward heeler in her own neighborhood, knowing she and her fiancé were short of money with both in college, had offered her a bribe.

The next day the education department chairman at St. Rose summoned Mary Ann and ordered her to recant the lesson and apologize to the class. She refused. The chairman proceeded to draft a retraction for her. By then, Mary Ann realized she had somehow provoked the machine's wrath; the price of integrity, she worried, could be her diploma. She slunk to the classroom and, with the chairman standing outside the door to ensure her compliance, recited the statement. Later she learned exactly what had happened. Her pupils had repeated the lesson about Albany's machine to their parents, many of whom sold their votes to it for food, coal, or jobs; the parents, in turn, had deluged both St. Rose and Vincentian with protests against one neophyte's embarrassing candor.

Hearing the story, Jack and Vilma felt not the abrupt sting of shock but the dull throb of a chronic ache. Another city, another machine, and of course it was Democratic. They had barely heard the name of Albany's boss, Dan O'Connell, yet they knew him already. He was Howard Jackson and William Curran and Richard Daley, all the tyrants of their past. One element, however, had changed. The people on Timberland Drive did not vote Democratic. Maybe their parents had; maybe, before they left Albany, they themselves had. But now they were, in Jack's phrase, "nouveau Republicans."

Very quickly in Colonie, Jack and Vilma acquired the local attitude toward Albany, a mixture of ignorance and disdain. They drove the five miles downtown perhaps twice yearly, just to treat the kids to the Shrine Circus or the Indian exhibit at the museum. One of the rare neighbors who still shopped in Albany had her purse snatched in a department store. Only when the store shut down five years later did the bag turn up, hidden behind a display case with the driver's license left undisturbed. Every trip to downtown Albany from Colonie required rolling up the windows and locking the doors for the passage through Arbor

Hill, a black ghetto just within the city border. Jack and Vilma never feared Arbor Hill as much as they grimly recognized it with the same sense-memory that had found Dan O'Connell so instantly familiar. A slum, like a boss, meant the Democrats were in charge.

With its shopping malls, industrial parks, and exemplary schools, Colonie was in most ways growing to be independent of Albany. Politically, though, it clutched the city next door in a strange embrace. Colonie needed Albany to supply embittered expatriates like Mary Ann Nicolla and to destroy neighborhoods like Arbor Hill; it needed Albany, the dominion of Democrats, to furnish the most compelling reasons for becoming a Republican.

Over the fifty-five years O'Connell ruled Albany, ending only with his death in 1977, his machine infested every facet of life, legal and otherwise. If you wanted to gamble, you played the machine's baseball lottery. If you wanted to keep your liquor license, you bought Hedrick's beer, from O'Connell's own brewery. If you wanted a low tax bill on your house, you bribed the assessor. More than anything, if you wanted a job you mortgaged your vote. The O'Connell version of patronage was like public works without the work. One reporter calculated that the Albany courthouse required seventy-two janitors for six floors while the Empire State Building somehow managed with sixty for its 102. If all other inducements failed, O'Connell's minions delivered ballots from legions of what one scholar called "the dead, the departed, even the unborn."

So pervasive was Albany's corruption, it spawned a species of jokes. One concerned the judge who summoned a defense lawyer to the bench. "The plaintiff slipped me five thou to decide the case his way," he explains. "Here's my idea: How about you giving me five thou, too, and I'll decide the case on its merits." While serving as governor of New York, Mario Cuomo offered this story: Dan O'Connell washes ashore on a desert island to find one other man and a single coconut. They decide to vote on who will eat it, and O'Connell wins by 110 to one.

The bard of Albany, William Kennedy, could hardly have invented better material for his cycle of novels. He had begun his writing career as a reporter for the Albany *Times-Union*, one of the few institutions willing to defy O'Connell, and he understood exactly what was being sacrificed to the picaresque pageant of machine rule. "Dan's Democracy was always like that: more dictatorial than democratic," Kennedy put it in a retrospective essay. "For anyone dealing with Albany this created, at worst, a feeling of fear, at best a respect for unleashable power."

Mary Ann Nicolla knew the sensation all too well. For Albany refugees like her, the children of dutiful Democrats, both idealism and dignity rested in reaction against the machine. Education and affluence had lifted these people above dependence on a municipal job; their own homes sat beyond the reach of ward heelers and capricious bureaucrats. Like Jack Maeby, they vowed never to perform as robots.

The change in attitude would not have mattered so greatly, in Colonie and in America, had it not been accompanied by an epic shift in population. As far back as the 1920s, when O'Connell took power, Colonie was voting Republican as predictably as Albany was voting Democratic. But in 1930, Albany held seven times the population of Colonie, a margin of 110,000; fifty years later the gap had nearly vanished. From the lonely cul-de-sac of Timberland Drive, set amid farms, fields, and twisting two lanes, Jack and Vilma Maeby in the late 1950s were seeing the last vestiges of a small-town, almost midwestern style of Republicanism. In its stead would rise the prototype of a modern Republican suburb, the core of a reborn party.

• • •

The story of the emerging Republican majority, to appropriate a phrase from the political analyst Kevin Phillips, starts with good soil. And no soil is better than farm soil, the sort Colonie occupies for most of its fifty-seven square miles. It is flat on the surface and sandy below, and it drains without man-made assistance. A developer inclined to build houses could ask for little more. Faced with rocks or clay, with water that has nowhere to go, he would have to wait for the town to spend millions on sewers. In sandy farm soil he could get away with a septic tank and start selling right away to the burgeoning middle class.

In precisely that way in the late 1940s Colonie's postwar housing boom began with the development called Latham Heights Park, rising beside a nineteenth-century hamlet named for an innkeeper. A few years later a tract of so-called slab houses appeared beneath the unduly effete rubric of Burns-Whitney Estates. Each home squeezed onto a one-fifth-acre lot, lying without basement atop a concrete foundation. The price was $5,990, with a stove and refrigerator included, and a membership store offering special prices for union members waited just down the road. In the decade of the 1950s, the population of Colonie nearly doubled to 52,760, and, more important, the residential density in certain areas reached the critical mass that attracts commerce.

Sure enough, the Latham Corners shopping center opened in 1956, making it the inaugural mall in metropolitan Albany. Where the silos and barns of a dairy farm had recently stood there now spread 300,000 square feet of stores, led by J. C. Penney and Grand Union. People drove from as far as Saratoga and Schenectady to shop and to gawk. On a nearby stretch of Route 9, long empty except for the Crossroads Diner, sprouted a hardware store, carpet dealership, and supermarket. Not long after, branch banks and hamburger franchises seized the remaining frontage. Between 1950 and 1960 the value of taxable property in Colonie climbed by three-quarters to $75 million.

Thanks to such development, the residential tax rate stayed low while the amenities mounted. Colonie erected a second high school by 1958, and in the years to come built a new library, a golf course, an Olympic-size pool, and even a municipal jogging trail. Compared to tired old Albany, Colonie portrayed itself as the bustling upstart, brimming with pluck and elbow grease. In political terms, it presented the image of private enterprise acting wisely when least fettered. And since a Republican town supervisor and an all-Republican town board had overseen all this enhancement, they reaped the votes of approval.

But what might be called the hidden history of suburban America, and certainly of Colonie, was one of immense intervention by activist government. Federal policy helped create the suburban culture of home ownership and automobile travel. Moreover, many of the key programs originated not with the Republicans who would ultimately harvest suburbia's ballots but with Democrats.

Woodrow Wilson signed into law the first federal income tax, establishing exemptions for "interest on indebtedness" and "other taxes." Thus a homeowner could write off both mortgage interest and property tax while a renter received no such advantages. By 1984, the total of those deductions swelled to $53 billion per year, at least fourfold more than Congress spent on public housing. "Put simply," the historian Kenneth T. Jackson writes, "the Internal Revenue Code finances the continued growth of suburbia."

The New Deal, too, lent powerful incentives to suburban growth. Founded after the harshest months of the Great Depression, the Federal Housing Administration aimed to stimulate employment in the building trades by insuring long-term mortgages written by private lenders. In so doing, the FHA also made home ownership more attractive than ever before. A mortgage backed by the FHA tended to have a longer duration, lower interest rate, and smaller down payment than a purely private instrument.

The FHA plainly favored neighborhoods segregated by race and class, instructing its underwriters to weigh such factors as "stability," "adverse influences," and "inharmonious racial or nationality groups." The agency went so far as to specifically recommend areas with "subdivision regulations and suitable restrictive covenants," the provisions commonly used to bar blacks. After the Supreme Court outlawed such covenants in 1949, the FHA with some reluctance stopped insuring mortgages augmented by them. Still, a disproportionate share of the $119 billion in mortgage insurance it issued through the mid-1960s went to suburbs that were overwhelmingly white.

Through the Veterans Administration, too, Washington fueled suburban growth. The VA did not evaluate neighborhoods in writing mortgages, but in practice the money followed the returning soldiers into suburbia, where billboards cried, "GI? $1 DOWN!" Taken together, loans from the FHA and the VA figured in half the home purchases in suburbia during the 1950s. Through the GI Bill, the VA also allowed millions of veterans to attend college, further securing their place in the middle class. An act of government transformed higher education from being the bastion of an elite to an agency for the multitudes.

Washington engaged in social engineering on a similarly grand scale in the interstate highway program. A 1956 law committed the federal government to paying 90 percent of the cost for a 41,000-mile system. The resulting roads gave city dwellers both the means and the motives for leaving, as they shook, darkened, and severed urban neighborhoods. The direction of public policy itself turned dramatically away from mass transportation and the cities. Between 1946 and 1980 federal aid to highways totaled $103 billion compared to $6 billion for rail service. Those staples of suburban life—Dad driving to his office in the city, Mom filling the station wagon with groceries—owed their ease less to Henry Ford than to Uncle Sam.

All this mobility, both upward and outward, presented a threat to the Democratic Party. The machinery of activist government, so vital in surmounting the Great Depression and defeating the Axis powers, had created the most unexpected of enemies: mass affluence and the complacency that came with it. Deprived of the issues of poverty and class, still a decade shy of fully seizing the banner of civil rights, the liberals of the 1950s groped in search of a compelling domestic cause. Writing in 1953, the historian Arthur M. Schlesinger Jr. saw the dilemma clearly:

> For the new voting generation, "Don't Let Them Take It Away" was an irrelevance. To say "You never had it so good" to young men and women who never had it any other way seemed, in a sense, a betrayal of the American promise; they wanted to have it better. . . . The classical maxim is that a revolution devours its children. But in this case, as Murray Kempton brilliantly observed, the children devoured the revolution.

Colonie demonstrated that irony in action. It was a Republican stronghold that had grown prosperous on the tax-and-spend policies of the welfare state. Seen as at least partially the product of big government, the town might trace its modern history to the day in December 1959 when the first leg of the Adirondack Northway interstate highway opened. The segment ran five and a half miles from Albany into northern Colonie, cost $9 million, and set off a bonanza of both speculation and construction. Not only did the Northway reduce the commute into Albany from thirty or forty minutes to less than ten, it placed Colonie along what would become the primary route from New York City to Montreal. Land that was selling for $1,000 per acre before the Northway's construction fetched ten times the price once the interstate was completed. With such a return possible, few farmers could resist the offers of developers, and a commercial corridor grew along the interstate.

Activist government, in the form of highway construction and improvement, did not end with the Northway. State and federal agencies spent about $150 million during the 1960s and early 1970s on routes linking Colonie to Albany and Troy. The taxable value of property in Colonie soared by 72 percent during the period. Even what seemed a modest project bore stunning results. One of the streets that parallels the Northway in Colonie is Wolf Road, a two-lane skirting a country club. Ostensibly to create a service road for the interstate, the federal and state governments paid $3.5 million to reinvent Wolf Road as a four-lane divided highway. With the expansion under way in 1966, an 869,000-square-foot mall, anchored by Macy's and Sears, burst from the fairways and greens. Meanwhile, two department stores in downtown Albany folded, unable to compete.

Colonie's role during the swirl of development consisted largely of standing aside, of deliberately declining to regulate the massive wave of construction. From 1932 until 1966 only an extremely general zoning ordinance governed land use. A comprehensive land-use plan, devised in 1972, was never made legally binding. During the years of Colonie's most vigorous growth, then, its elected officials weighed a trade-off: development and property taxes or aesthetics and order. The cluttered, jumbled commercial strips along Central Avenue and Route 9 attested to the choice.

Residential neighborhoods blossomed from the same combination of Washington's money and Colonie's indulgence. In the recollection of realtors who sold homes in Colonie during the 1950s and 1960s, about three-quarters of the buyers utilized either VA or FHA mortgages, a proportion significantly higher than the national average. Colonie never knew a Levitt and Sons, a developer capable of throwing down houses by the thousands; instead, small builders without tremendous cash resources produced Capes, ranches, and split-levels in clusters of ten or twenty. The town made a major concession in not requiring home builders to install sidewalks or to pay the full cost of water (and later sewer) connections.

When another government was paying the bill, though, Colonie eagerly added improvements. The town contributed only one-eighth of the $80 million cost of expanding its sewer system in 1969 under a federal environmental program. In later years, Colonie aggressively sought community development block grants from the Department of Housing and Urban Development, receiving an average of better than $500,000 per year from 1978 through 1993.

While Colonie's citizens rightly reviled Dan O'Connell's bloated payroll, they depended almost as greatly as his minions on government jobs. The 1980 census found that 17.3 percent of Colonie's labor force worked in public administration—not much less than Albany's 21.6 percent and nearly quadruple the statewide rate. Besides a college degree, all that separated a state bureaucrat from one of those ubiquitous janitors in the Albany courthouse was that he owed his position to a Republican, Nelson Rockefeller. As governor from 1959 through 1973, Rockefeller characterized himself as being a social liberal and a fiscal conservative. In fact, he operated a public works and public employment apparatus that any Democratic boss would have envied. State spending in the Rockefeller years ballooned 434 percent, or nearly ten times the cost of living. New York's per capita debt jumped fivefold from $128 to $646.

As relentlessly as Colonie's Republicans cast O'Connell as Beelzebub, demonization alone could not explain their party's hegemony. Nor is it sufficient to contend, as William Whyte did in *The Organization Man,* "Something does seem to happen to Democrats when they get to suburbia." Behind the appearance of such individual conversions, Colonie's Republicans consciously assembled a machine of their own. It was not, of course, called a machine; it was an "organization," a term altogether more sanitary. And while the party appealed to voters' disgust with O'Connell and their financial caution as first-time homeowners, neither factor truly drove the engine. The gasoline of the machine was the gasoline of the town itself: development.

What happened in Colonie, particularly in the years after the Maebys arrived, the years when Leslie came of age politically, replicated itself from Atlantic to Pacific. Nassau County outside New York City, Orange County outside Los Angeles, and Du Page County outside Chicago all flourished in large measure thanks to federal investment, and all converted the wealth from growth into Republican power. From suburban Republican strongholds would emerge national politicians as prominent as Congressman Henry Hyde of Illinois, Senator Alfonse D'Amato of New York, and even, in a less direct way, Ronald Reagan, with his base in Southern California. At the very time the urban Democratic machines were creaking, tottering, and toppling, the Republican Party was taking hold of the suburbanites who would constitute, with the 1992 election, the majority of presidential voters.

These "organizations" avoided, in most cases, the grotesqueries of buying votes and stuffing ballot boxes. They did practice patronage, but generally on a smaller scale than in cities. Instead, the suburban Republican machines wrung political advantage from real-estate development. Speculators, contractors, and construction tradesmen, among others, depended on site-plan approvals, zoning variances, and the myriad other minute actions of local government in order to break ground and thus make money. By dint of the Republican advantage in the suburbs, the party often held the majority of seats on the zoning boards, planning commissions, town councils, and other bodies charged with passing judgment on proposed projects. The result was that developers cultivated Republican politicians with donations and assistance. Nothing broke the law, but everything conspired toward one-party rule.

Colonie presented the most extreme example possible. No Democrat had ever won a council seat, and the last Democratic town supervisor left office in 1931. Thus the pattern of unchallenged Republican power was already established by the time after World War II when the town exploded with private development. One could measure the resulting alliance in, among other places, the program for the town GOP's annual dinner. The advertisers in the 1973 edition, for instance, included engineers and surveyors, developers and contractors, paving companies and real-estate lawyers. The livelihood of every single one in some way hinged on the actions of Colonie's elected officials.

By the standards of a state or national party, the money raised with a local souvenir program seems minimal. At this level, however, it covered a large share of the year's campaign costs. It reelected Republicans and perpetuated the closed circle of development and politics. The Democrats, in turn, represented the worst conceivable investment. They claimed, as of 1968, 14 percent of Colonie's registered voters. Their candidates had to pay for handbills, palm cards, lawn signs, and bumper stickers from their own pockets. Party headquarters was the chairman's basement, decorated in a rathskeller motif. Public records of campaign expenditures in local elections go back only to 1980, but there is no reason to doubt they accurately reflect the relative strength of the parties in earlier years, too. In a 1980 race for a State Assembly seat, the Democrat raised $2,667 and the Republican $12,750. During 1983, a year with elections for supervisor, town council, and the county board, the Colonie Republican Party spent $32,363. The incoming leader of the Democrats inherited a war chest of $67.

For the Maeby family, the result was an amazing case of historical symmetry. Jack and Vilma had become Democrats because they grew up in Baltimore surrounded by nothing but Democrats. Now their children would mature in a suburb every bit as monochromatically Republican. In either generation, individual choice played a strikingly small role in political identity. The process was more one of address as destiny.

• • •

During their first seven years in Colonie, the Maebys lived a suburban life that made sitcoms seem like cinéma vérité. Leslie and her sister, Colleen, brought a friend's boa constrictor to school one morning for show-and-tell, and after hearing about it at lunch all the mothers locked their children home in terror. Vilma ran a school fair with rides on a fire truck, and wore her cashmere coat and leather gloves for shopping trips to Colonie Center. Jack planted maples, oaks, and evergreens, and when his son and namesake started playing Pop Warner football he helped coach.

For all those signs of permanence, Jack was still renting on Timberland Drive. Tenancy had started as a hedge against disliking the house, and then it became a way of staying flexible in case Montgomery Ward issued marching orders. By 1965, though, all the children were well into school, and Jack was turning down any promotions that meant moving. The time had come to buy.

No longer did Timberland Drive seem equal to the Maebys' aspirations. The south side of Colonie, the less expensive section adjoining Albany, was filling with the white flight from Arbor Hill. Vilma especially feared that the district's high school was becoming "a greaser school." So she and Jack looked on the north side, where the high school was only seven years old and decidedly upscale. They found a new split-level on a looping lane flanked by willows and spruces. True to the era, Jack used a VA mortgage to buy a home that might otherwise have hovered beyond his reach, paying down $600, or barely 3 percent, of the $19,900 price. On the front lawn he planted a pine Vilma had uprooted during a family vacation to Schroon Lake.

Quickly they befriended the neighbors. Vilma bowled in a league. Jack earned unending gratitude for cleaning up after the family setter. The kids skied down the hill of an adjoining estate, now maintained by the state for its education commissioner. It was a life that did not raise disquieting questions or encourage iconoclasm, not even as the counterculture arose.

Yes, the newscasts featured the usual gloom and doom, and all Jack had to hear were the words "Northern Boulevard" to know that whatever had happened had happened in Arbor Hill. One of his superiors' sons, a theology student, went south as part of the civil rights movement and wound up being arrested for playing baseball with blacks. Nor had the political differences between Jack and Vilma vanished. If anything, now that he was a registered Republican and she was free of infants and toddlers, the debating season ran from January to December. They split in both the 1960 and 1964 presidential elections—she for Kennedy and Johnson, he for Nixon and Goldwater—and argued ideology every time Jack grumbled about the latest tax bill.

"I could live with socialism," Vilma said during one scrap. "I wouldn't mind paying taxes to help people live better."

Socialism, Jack countered, robbed workers of incentive.

"You know who the first socialist was?" she shot back. "Jesus Christ."

Their rhetoric accurately reflected the tone of the 1964 presidential campaign. Goldwater opposed the Civil Rights Act of 1964, suggested that Social Security be made voluntary, and proclaimed in a nationally televised speech, "Extremism in the defense of liberty is no vice." Johnson's campaign exploited the trigger-happy image of Goldwater in a commercial showing a nuclear bomb exploding as a little girl picks flowers.

On its surface, the election appeared a rejoinder to Jack. Whatever Cabrini-Green and Dan O'Connell had done to turn him conservative, the rest of the nation seemed not to have shared. Lyndon Johnson won forty-four of fifty states and 486 of 538 electoral votes. His landslide swept away thirty-eight Republican seats in the House of Representatives and 530 in state legislatures.

But in truth, Barry Goldwater lost the same way Al Smith had, by creating the conditions for another to win. Just as Smith in defeat had remade the Democratic Party from agrarian to urban, with all that implied in ethnicity and religion, so Goldwater shattered the Grand Old Party's Yankee mold. The changes only started with his victory in the South, "solid" for the Democrats never again. Goldwater actually raised the Republican vote in the blue-collar Catholic sections of Detroit and Gary. He essentially matched Richard Nixon's 1960 performance in neighborhoods of working-class Italians, Irish, and Jews in New York and Boston.

Among the voters who fled from Goldwater were the old, affluent linchpins of the Republican aristocracy. In their absence, a modern and more conservative party could lay claim to populism. Kevin Phillips, for one, soon predicted the appeal of such ideology in a "new suburbia" of "subdivisions populated by salesmen, electricians, and supermarket managers," many of them Catholics and Jews. His description sounded a lot like Colonie.

For the moment, however, the rumblings and gratings of political realignment sounded distant from 29 Eberle Road, the Maeby sanctuary. When things went well, when the immediate world felt orderly and right, those at the helm got the credit on Election Day. That meant, even more than any president, Nelson Rockefeller, the one figure in whom Vilma and Jack found political congruence. Two of their neighbors, a printer and an engineer, worked for the state. Many others in Colonie held some job in the governor's two giant building projects, a modernistic office complex to house his bureaucracy and an Albany campus for the state university. Soon enough, the Maeby children would be old enough to attend it.

Beyond voting, neither Jack nor Vilma practiced politics. Leslie might never have either, except for Pop Warner football. A man named Fred Field had two sons on the team, and among their coaches was Jack. Perhaps the two men met after practice, when the station wagons pulled up in the autumn dusk. Perhaps it was during the potluck lunch always held for the visiting team at the American Legion hall. Whatever the exact moment, only afterward did Jack connect Fred Field the parent with Fred Field the politician, the one always in the local papers.

A member of the town council, Field was running in the fall of 1968 for a State Assembly seat. His goal seemed quixotic, to put it kindly. The district had been drawn by the Assembly's Democratic majority to lump Colonie with their own strongholds; the incumbent assemblyman was one of O'Connell's confederates. Field intended to at least put a scare into the machine. He had plans for rallies and functions and door-to-door blitzes, and he needed some pretty young female volunteers. "Field Girls"—that's what he would call them. How convenient that his wife directed the Pop Warner cheerleaders. One of them was Leslie Maeby. In her pleated skirt and pom-poms, she had unknowingly launched her political career.

Chapter Ten

Fence and Basement
(Silvio Burigo/Lorraine and Frank Trotta)

JUST BEFORE FRANK TROTTA SR. TURNED FIFTY, IN THE FALL OF
1962, he bought a house. It stood two stories on a street one block long
in a section of New Rochelle bounded by an interstate highway and
railroad main line. Chunks of plaster had fallen from the walls in several
rooms. So inconsistent were the front steps—some of them four inches
high, others nine—that Frank Sr. cracked that the mason must have
been a drunk.

Still, 33 Birch Street was the home that the Trottas had been saving
for during nine years of marriage, not a way station of a "starter house"
but a place to stay and raise their boys. It bore testimony to all the nights
Lorraine had handled a switchboard at the telephone company, and all
the days Frank Sr. had hauled trash and swabbed floors in the Hartley
Houses project. Certainly, it surpassed their first house, which had not
even had a heating system. So the Trottas threw a party on Frank Sr.'s
birthday, Halloween, covering the wall holes with cardboard cutouts of
pumpkins.

There was plenty of company right on Birch Street. Seven different
houses held members of the Trotta or Burigo families, twenty-eight
relatives in all. In a duplex next door to Frank Sr. lived his father-in-law,
Silvio Burigo. Cautious as ever about money, Silvio was still renting the

apartment he had first taken during World War II. Even with his three oldest children adults and two of them married, he had college costs to pay for his youngest, Carole Ann.

Shortly after five each morning, a windup alarm clock rattled Frank Sr. awake. He showered, brewed coffee, and tugged on the navy blue uniform he kept on a bedroom chair. Always he slipped a few pencils and a small screwdriver into the breast pocket. Then he walked the dog to Cheech's store and bought the *Daily News,* which he deposited on the kitchen table for the family. From the refrigerator he grabbed the olive loaf sandwich that Lorraine had fixed for his lunch after coming home from her shift past midnight.

By the time Frank Sr. was climbing into his car at 6:15, Silvio Burigo was sitting down to eggs sunny-side-up in his kitchen. He and his wife, Delia, had come to an accommodation after decades of friction, and part of their truce involved her making his breakfast. Now in his sixties, Silvio wore dentures and bifocals. He had quit cigars in favor of butterscotch candies after his son, Seely, suffered a heart attack. But whenever there was work, Silvio reached into the bedroom closet for his Dickie's work clothes, woven tough as a canvas sail, and packed last night's leftovers into a black metal lunch pail. By seven-thirty, his Chevy was rolling away.

The morning rituals of two workingmen went nearly unnoticed on a block that expected all its fathers to labor. Their routines receded into the backdrop of daily life on Birch Street, along with the rumble of traffic and the clatter of trains, noises so steady they became a kind of silence. A job was a job, regular and predictable, nothing worth putting down the evening paper to discuss.

For Frank Trotta Sr. and Silvio Burigo, at least for the first few years they were neighbors, work seemed almost that uncomplicated, the sum of its wages and hours, its paychecks and vacation days. Then time passed, not a lot but enough, and the janitor and the plumber, in their parallel lives, found themselves careering into confrontation with liberalism.

• • •

A plywood fence girded the rectangle of land from which a Macy's store and shopping mall would rise in downtown New Rochelle. The fence stood eight feet tall and was locked across its single gate, sealing Silvio Burigo into the domain of his choosing. From eight in the morning until three-thirty in the afternoon the place quaked with labor. Hammers rang and saws whined. Generators roared as bulldozers huffed diesel breath. Shanties and trailers, each the encampment of a separate trade, perched along yawning excavations. Kerosene stoves burned against the winter chill as if this setting of cinder block and steel beam were a citrus grove besieged by frost. Only when a journeyman sent his apprentice for coffee or a truck lumbered in with tubing or pipe did the outer world briefly penetrate the peculiar sanctity.

In these final weeks of January 1967, Silvio moved around the grounds with particular dispatch. He was the plumbing foreman for the mall, and the day to pour foundations was fast approaching. A single error, once trapped in concrete, could never be corrected; an entire floor or wall would have to be battered to rubble to permit an expensive, embarrassing second chance. With a ruler as his scepter, he strode from trench to trench, knowing which would lie beneath the movie theater, which the bookstore, and which the public toilet. He measured the placement of stakes and twine, ripping loose those that violated the blueprints. Once satisfied, he oversaw the installation of cast-iron pipes for sewage and water, and tin sleeves for gas heat.

At least once each day Silvio needed to report to the contractor, to assure him the work was proceeding faultlessly and on schedule. So thirty minutes after inspecting a spot, he circled back for more scrutiny. With a favorite plumber, perhaps a former student in the apprenticeship school, he might share a trick, such as how to squeeze oil into a joint before soldering so the hot lead would not touch a hidden water drop and explode. The rest he drove like recruits at Parris Island. "We don't do this kinda work," he would rail at the plumber who sloppily fastened a joint. To the plodder, he would shout, "Get a little more move on." And for anyone who objected to his standards, Silvio offered a stock response: "You don't like it, get a job somewhere else."

Few threats better muzzled an ingrate. The "mall job," as everyone in the building trades called it, was the windfall they had been anticipating for more than a decade. Between Macy's, fifty-eight smaller stores, and a municipal garage for nearly two thousand cars, it would cost upwards of $25 million, with the bulk of the money going into the pockets of construction workers and the cash registers of suppliers. Better still, this job wore the perfume of virtue. Macy's and the mall, city leaders predicted, would save downtown New Rochelle from ruin at the hands of a competing shopping center in White Plains. The new businesses would create three hundred permanent jobs, putting $5 million yearly into the local economy, and pay another $1 million directly to the city in annual property tax. Why else had Washington agreed to underwrite most of the expense as urban renewal?

For Silvio, the job represented the capstone to a career. He was sixty-four now, with nearly a half century of toil behind him, and feeling his own mortality. Old age in Local 86 was a comfortable enough proposition. He could work three months of the year, enough to keep adding to his pension, and still teach the apprentices. The mall project, as large as any Silvio had undertaken outside wartime, would grant him one last, vast legacy to show off to the grandchildren.

Then the strange, defining day of January 25 dawned. It was warm that morning, warm as May for the fifth morning in a row. Jasmine was blooming and women were sunbathing, and twenty demonstrators were gathering outside the construction site's gate as Silvio arrived. For the moment, their presence seemed no odder than any other aspect of false spring. They had appeared a few other times lately, carrying signs and chanting slogans about how the unions discriminated against blacks. The same bunch had similarly protested during the construction of a subsidized housing project three years earlier, failing utterly in their attempt to shut down the work.

Inside the fence, gladly unable to see or hear their antagonists, Silvio and his crew waited for the concrete trucks. Today the foundations were going to be laid. The pipes fit in flawless patterns. Around them reared plywood forms demarking the walls. The fluky weather was a boon, even if it had brought out the marchers. Concrete poured in frigid air tends to crack later because its water freezes before evaporating. But concrete poured on a sixty-five-degree day will dry slowly, smoothly, with strength.

As the first truck approached, mixer churning, the demonstrators drew together in a tight circle, blocking the opened gate. The driver halted. Two or three more trucks, also bound for the mall project, soon clogged the street behind him. Cars braked, horns bleating. Police cruisers sped toward the scene. A leader of the Teamsters Union local dashed from the construction site onto the street and right up to the fender of the first truck.

"Drive right through them," he ordered the union man at the wheel. "Or get off the job."

Having heard the command, the protesters swarmed closer to the truck's front fender. Workers squeezed out at the edges of the gate and hoisted themselves atop the fence. Amid the din of sirens, shouts, and idling engines, the first driver put his truck into gear and started to move —backward. "I don't get paid for this shit," he hollered to his union boss. "I'm going home."

Far from defusing the confrontation, his decision escalated it. The protesters refused to clear a path for his exit, bellowing in jubilation, "Hell no, we won't go. We will not be moved." Several white men, presumably from the job, jumped a black demonstrator and dragged him into the street. "Let go of me," he shrieked. Some police officers rescued him, and others shoved into the crowd, wrenching bodies loose before a mass brawl could erupt.

In the aftermath, six protesters, three of them clergymen, faced charges of disorderly conduct. The president of the Westchester County Building and Construction Trades Council said, "They just want a lot of publicity." With his city's commercial future suddenly in jeopardy, the mayor of New Rochelle begged George Meany to mediate. Silvio Burigo found himself less enraged than bewildered, less contemptuous than confounded. As he had told his daughter Mary Jane some years earlier, "I don't know what they're complaining about. We got treated the same as them."

His observation raised profound historical questions. Was there a difference between being a black trying to crack an overwhelmingly white union in 1967 and an Italian like Silvio trying to crack an overwhelmingly Irish one forty years earlier? Was there a difference between being the orphaned child of immigrants and the descendant of slaves? And what was government to do about any of it?

Instantly, Silvio stood at the very fulcrum of the national debate on civil rights. The battleground was shifting from South to North, from direct action to litigation, from segregation by law to segregation by habit, from voting rights to economic equity, from equality of opportunity to equality of outcome. Put another way, the Democratic coalition was cleaving, perhaps irreparably, along the fault line between its constituencies in organized labor and in the civil rights movement. The same party that had once legitimized the union cause with activist liberalism, in the form of the National Industrial Recovery Act and the Wagner Act, was now alienating it with a newer brand that framed issues by race instead of class.

The mall controversy did not look so complex and divisive at the time. It looked, in fact, deceptively simple. The unions were wrong; the unions were racist; the unions would have to change or be changed. What most demanded reform, in the eyes of labor's critics, was exactly the sort of apprenticeship training Silvio directed. Such programs, the argument went, protected neither merit nor quality but a white monopoly on gainful jobs. Nearly a decade would pass before affirmative action, with its doctrine of present redress for past injustice, reached from blue-collar redoubts like the building trades into colleges, graduate schools, and the professions. Until then, northern liberals would find it as painless to condemn a Silvio Burigo as a Bull Connor.

Indeed, as the winter of 1967 wore on, the fence around the mall site assumed a new meaning for the construction workers within. No longer did it contain and thus celebrate their talents; now it barricaded them from a hostile populace. By February 1, the number of demonstrators had grown from twenty to 150, and four days later some three hundred assembled for a prayer service on the steps of city hall. More trucks were turned away and more people were arrested. The police department's lone paddy wagon practically served as a commuter bus, as the more enterprising protesters, released before lunch on their own recognizance, often raced back to the picket line in time to be booked again by supper.

The mall protest became a mass movement with touches of the *Social Register*. From across barriers of race and denomination marched preacher and salesman, probation officer and bookkeeper, engineer and English teacher. The *Standard-Star* compiled a daily list of the "prominent citizens" observed picketing and devoted an entire article to the appearance of a former mayor's wife. "We just are not going to let the truck in," she told a reporter, "if we have to throw ourselves against the wheels." Much of the rhetoric sounded shriller still. "Bigotry," a speaker at one rally declared, "seems to be winning a fight here in New Rochelle." A vice president of the National Council of Christians and Jews compared the construction site to Dachau. For people so concerned that the Lincoln School desegregation case had unfairly blemished their reputation, New Rochelle's elite spared no hyperbole in castigating those, like Silvio Burigo, who had literally built their city.

In the end, all the marching and singing, all the prayers and calumnies, amounted to a sideshow. The demonstrators intended to press their cause not on the street but in the courts. Within weeks of the protests, the New Rochelle Human Rights Commission submitted a formal complaint to the corresponding state body, which possessed the power to hold hearings and render judgments on its own and to solicit remedies and penalties from the courts. On March 24 the state commission officially adopted the complaint as its own. In the infelicitous locutions of law, the state charged Local 501 of the International Brotherhood of Electrical Workers, Local 38 of the Sheet Metal Workers' International Association, and Local 86 of the United Association with "unlawful discriminatory practices relating to the acceptance of Negroes as journeymen, relating to admission of Negroes to their apprenticeship training programs, and relating to the failure to establish on-the-job training programs."

The moral core of the complaint could be found on the penultimate of its five pages. The words there derived not from a statute book but a speech delivered by President Lyndon B. Johnson at predominantly black Howard University nearly two years earlier:

Freedom is the right to share, share fully and equally in American society, to vote, to hold a job, to enter a public place, to go to school. It is the right to be treated in every part of our national life as a person equal in dignity and promise to all others.

But freedom is not enough. You do not wipe away the scars of centuries by saying now you are free to go where you want, work where you desire and choose the leaders you please. You do not take a person who for years has been hobbled by chains and liberate him and bring him up to the starting line of a race and then say, you are free to compete with all the others, and still justly believe you have been completely fair.

Thus it is not enough just to open the gates of opportunity. All our citizens must have the ability to walk through those gates.

Three human rights commissioners assigned to the New Rochelle case would ultimately decide whether a president's oratory applied to the issue at hand. Yet simply by citing the speech, with its eloquent allusions to a tragic past, the plaintiffs had proven one point. Their suit against Silvio Burigo and his peers, however spontaneously it seemed to have arisen, was anything but a historical accident.

• • •

There existed a place and time in America when the preponderance of black tradesmen provoked not a whisper of protest. The place was the South, the time was before 1865, and the blacks who constituted fully 85 percent of the artisans were slaves. With emancipation and the right to be paid for their labor, blacks would never again hold more than a fraction of the skilled jobs they had once dominated. They would pay in violence and controversy even for that share. In the former Confederacy, Jim Crow's reign restricted blacks to sharecropping and domestic service; above the Mason-Dixon line, a black with acumen or ambition collided with the latest immigrant off the boat.

As one of the progressive forces in America, the union movement from its outset espoused racial justice. The Knights of Labor favored integration, partly out of idealism and partly out of pragmatism. It was a standard trick of bosses to drive down wages and shatter strikes by hiring black workers barred from unions. Similarly, the AFL denounced discrimination from its founding in 1886, and four years later passed a resolution declaring that it "looks with disfavor upon trade unions having provisions which exclude from membership persons on account of race and color."

Yet a contradictory impulse equally animated labor from the start. The AFL admitted segregated unions and defended them against pressure from government or the federation's own racial liberals. The early apprenticeship programs, including the United Association's own, sought to raise wages by limiting the supply of skilled workers. In effect, if not by intent, these programs barred blacks from the ranks. The years immediately before the New Deal found labor with so few allies and so many fears that it struck a Faustian bargain with the conservative southern Democrats in Congress to pass the Davis-Bacon bill in 1931. Understood narrowly, the law safeguarded wages during the Depression's massive unemployment by requiring that all public works projects pay the prevailing scale—more often than not union scale. In practice, however, Davis-Bacon guarded against integration by outlawing the substandard wages that gave a contractor his sole incentive for hiring blacks.

The AFL's ideals aside, then, its craft unions evolved into almost wholly white bastions. One of the United Association's most powerful outposts, Local 2 in Brooklyn, counted three black journeymen among several thousand members in the early 1960s. Around the same time, the carpenters' union in New York maintained a separate Harlem local for blacks and the electricians refused to admit them altogether. The 1950 census found only 2,190 black apprentices in the entire nation, and a decade later the number had risen by a grand total of one. Only in the unskilled roles of laborer or hod carrier did blacks hold a substantial share of construction union jobs. The building trades, the labor and civil rights activist Herbert Hill insisted, were "feudal enclaves in a postindustrial society."

As early as the 1930s, the federal government was being drawn into the incipient conflict. The Public Works Administration required contractors who were building subsidized housing for blacks to maintain a certain percentage of blacks on the construction crews. But, importantly, the agency did not differentiate between unskilled labor and skilled crafts or between union and nonunion workers. The pressure for presidential intervention grew as World War II neared and blacks streamed off farms into defense plants. A delegation of civil rights leaders, foremost among them A. Philip Randolph of the Brotherhood of Sleeping Car Porters, threatened a mass march on Washington to protest discrimination in the newly revived private industries. At least partly in response, Franklin Roosevelt, on June 19, 1941, signed Executive Order 8802, creating a wartime Fair Employment Practices Committee to investigate job discrimination.

Roosevelt's action presaged a series of more expansive measures, and one Democratic president after another contorted himself trying to please two increasingly irreconcilable sets of supporters. Harry Truman failed in his effort to establish a permanent Fair Employment Practices

Committee, in large measure because the AFL aligned with conservatives of both parties in opposition. Signing an executive order in March 1961, John F. Kennedy introduced the term "affirmative action" into the federal vocabulary, but only as a synonym for nondiscrimination. Title VII of the Civil Rights Act of 1964, the first of Lyndon Johnson's great domestic achievements, forbade bias in unions and apprenticeship programs as well as workplaces. But the agency formed to oversee the provision, the Equal Employment Opportunity Commission, lacked the direct power to litigate, punish, or enforce.

So much political compromise inevitably produced a muddle—legally, ethically, and even semantically. The giants of organized labor routinely signed this or that pledge against discrimination, trooping to the White House for one such ritual in 1962. Virtually in the instant the ink dried, they were assured that, naturally, nobody expected them to give minorities preferential treatment. But what exactly was "discrimination"? Was it deliberate segregation or the absence of integration? And what was "preferential treatment"? Soliciting minorities to join unions? Letting them learn a trade on the job rather than in an apprenticeship program? Promising to hire them in certain numbers?

One of the seminal events of the civil rights era revealed how wide the chasm was growing. The March on Washington in August 1963, ultimately remembered for Martin Luther King's "I Have a Dream" speech, actually claimed as its two goals "freedom and jobs." The primary organizer, Bayard Rustin, was A. Philip Randolph's protégé, and shared his commitment to integrating union labor. Addressing the crowd of 200,000, Randolph largely articulated a common agenda for civil rights and organized labor, from Medicare to a higher minimum wage to guaranteed full employment. But as he was defending "our struggle in the streets," even likening it to the union movement's own, he leaped from the Birmingham bus boycott, the lunch counter sit-ins, and the Freedom Riders to the building trades. "It was not until construction sites were picketed in the North," he declared, "that Negro workers were hired." He went on, "Those who deplore our militance, who exhort patience in the name of a false peace, are in fact supporting segregation and exploitation."

The liberal end of the union movement, personified by Walter Reuther of the United Auto Workers, marched at the head of the procession and followed Randolph at the microphone. But craft unions saw nothing to celebrate, not in being compared to the bigots who turned fire hoses, billy clubs, and attack dogs against nonviolent protesters. Exactly one week before the march, the United Association had issued this preemptive defense of its apprenticeship system:

There is only one standard for entrance into the United Association and that is the man's qualifications. We do not believe in rejecting an applicant because of his race, color or creed and we likewise cannot be expected to admit an applicant *because* of his race, color or creed. . . .

We have a voluntary program. We intend to keep it so. That means we will accept no dictation from any government agency. . . . We reject any imposition of quotas based on racial or population percentages by any government agency or private pressure group. We consider quotas undemocratic, unreasonable, unwarranted, and unworkable.

Randolph had been indisputably correct on one point. Debate was giving way to confrontation. In 1963 alone, protests against building-trades unions flared in Cleveland, Philadelphia, and Elizabeth, New Jersey. New York shook with demonstrations at the construction sites for two housing developments, a university medical center, and a hospital in the center of Harlem, the capital of black America. Six hundred fifty picketers were arrested at the site while others held a six-week sit-in at city hall. When contractors hired even a token number of black trades-men—at the Bronx Terminal Market in 1964 and the Gateway Arch in St. Louis in 1966—white union members struck. "This proves there's no difference between New York and Alabama," one black minister said, "between New York and South Africa."

The acrimony of the era was embodied in the relationship between George Meany and A. Philip Randolph. Back in the 1940s, when discrimination seemed only a southern affliction, Meany had threatened to move an entire AFL convention from a Houston hotel that refused a room to his black union brother. In later years Meany ordered every member union of the merged AFL-CIO to negotiate for a nondiscrimination clause in its contract. He threw all his lobbying muscle behind the 1964 civil rights bill, even as its southern foes plied labor with the siren song of "quotas." Yet when Randolph attacked the AFL-CIO's internal record—the segregated locals in the South, the scarcity of blacks in the building trades—he was considered family no more. In a showdown at the AFL-CIO convention in 1959, Meany shouted from the podium, "Who the hell appointed you the guardian of all the Negroes in America?"

These allies turned adversaries were the direct progenitors of the mall controversy. Meany had begun his career as a plumber and always regarded the union's apprenticeship program with particular pride. Randolph, too, was familiar with the United Association and its ways. Having decided the construction unions would never reform themselves, and that Meany would not force enlightenment upon them, Randolph had formed an organization called the Workers Defense League. It aimed to prepare black applicants for apprenticeship tests, to beat the building-trades unions by their own rules. In 1966, with ground soon to be broken for Macy's, the league assigned a man to New Rochelle.

• • •

When members like Silvio Burigo described Local 86, they called it a "father-and-son local." They uttered the phrase with the same warmth they might use to recall the "mom-and-pop grocery" where they had bought gum balls and red hots in childhood. If anything, the web of kinship extended well beyond fathers and sons to brothers, nephews, cousins, and grandchildren. In the West End of New Rochelle, few values surpassed "taking care of your own," and no better way existed than finding a relative a decent job.

The results filled the union roster. In March 1951, for instance, Local 86 tallied 362 members. Fifty surnames accounted for nearly one-third of them, from six Mullinses to four Larussos to three Fogartys. And that only told the patrilineal story. The new apprentices included a Lifrieri who was family to the Donderos on his mother's side and a Girone who was Silvio's wife's relation.

As Silvio saw it, a trade union could perpetuate itself in no other way. "If there's a father who's a plumber," he explained once, "what else should a son do? What else will he know? His father comes home and talks about the jobs he does. He drives around town and says, 'I worked on that building.' " The father in the parable, of course, was Silvio himself.

So when the economy boomed and room opened at the bottom of the union ladder, the leaders of Local 86 never dreamed of advertising for apprentices. They spread the word over cards at the North Italy Society or after Mass at Blessed Sacrament; they knew who among one another's children would be graduating soon from high school or getting discharged from the army. For years, the local did not bother with an application form; a sheet of paper, scribbled with name, address, and telephone number, simply went into a file drawer. Until 1965, when the state objected, any blood relative of a union member or plumbing contractor received ten extra points on the entrance exam.

In Silvio's mind, none of this compromised quality in the least. To the contrary, he brought his daughter Carole Ann to watch him teach, and after she went off to college in 1961 he conscripted Seely's kids. George Meany, his hero, had once expressed Silvio's fierce pride best: "I'd like to put some of those college professors through the plumbers' apprentice school. They talk about a plumber as if he was some kind of meat head. Well, it might not have been Shakespeare, but it wasn't any cup of tea, either."

Besides, Local 86 had sound reasons for guarding its franchise. The collective memory of plumbers like Silvio traced back to the first Croton Dam, when Italian immigrants toiled for even poorer pay than blacks received. The men of Local 86 knew of the Italians who had built the railroad through New Rochelle, squatting in hovels beside track traveled by the wealthy, They remembered being forced to "vote the chicken" and put a matchstick in a hatband as the promise of a kickback. Yes, the Great Depression had taught caustic lessons about what a labor surplus did to wages and solidarity.

Even in the robust economy of the postwar years, Silvio endured periods of joblessness. He held thirty or forty years of seniority, and a leadership position in the local, and surely he could have pulled rank. But his sense of integrity forbade it, so he waited to rotate back into employment. Every morning he donned his work clothes and heavy boots, just in case, and went to the union hall in hopes a contractor might appear, the same way he had in the 1930s.

These idle times exacted a toll beyond the financial; they summoned all the old ghosts of helplessness and insecurity. Unemployment was a misfortune to be whispered about, to be hidden from the children. But even Silvio's youngest daughter sometimes overheard. When Carole Ann was in the fourth or fifth grade of parochial school, her teacher invited every pupil in class to write a prayer request on a strip of paper. Since it was May, the month of the Blessed Mother, the class marched to a grotto outside the parish church and gathered before a statue of Mary. There the teacher burned the papers, sending their wishes heavenward. Carole Ann had asked for a job for Daddy. Attending a state college years later, she felt his sporadic unemployment so keenly that she skipped meals rather than ask for money from home. On the one occasion she requested what for many New Rochelle offspring would have been spare change—$50 dollars for a trip to Florida over spring break —he turned her down with no small loss of face. "I am still out of work," wrote the man who wanted few things more in life than the reputation of being a good provider. "And things do not look too good for the immediate future."

Blacks rarely entered into Silvio's thinking, much less consumed it. Nobody in Local 86 was stopping a black from becoming a plumber; nobody was burning crosses or wearing white sheets. It was just a matter of the blacks waiting their turn the same way the Italians had waited for theirs from the Irish. Weren't there Italians in Local 86 who had had to Anglicize their names or spend ten years instead of five playing gofer as an apprentice? The notion that blacks had suffered, and were still suffering, from a uniquely virulent and persistent sort of hate baffled Silvio. Once, years earlier, Mary Jane had suggested to him that blacks unlike Italians "can't change the color of their skin." Silvio muttered, "Where do you get these ideas?" ending the discussion.

As a matter of public policy, however, the topic could not be dropped so easily. So Local 86 conformed to the increasing number of state and federal regulations. It operated its apprenticeship program with Albany's approval. It certified to contractors on federally funded projects such as the mall that it did not discriminate. It even took the unprecedented step in the summer of 1966 of announcing before the Human Rights Commission that it was accepting applications for apprentices, although not a single black submitted one. At every turn, the United Association's attorneys assured Silvio and his colleagues that, in the words of one legal opinion, "there is no statute or executive order which requires that unions must go out and recruit apprentices from the members of such [minority] groups."

Local 86 observed the requisite social obligations of racial tolerance and Democratic unity. It had even turned out, under the umbrella of the Westchester County Building and Construction Trades Council, for a testimonial dinner to the craft unions' nemesis, A. Philip Randolph. On that evening in April 1964 at New Rochelle's Glen Island Casino, every actor performed to perfection. President Johnson sent a telegram and Josephine Baker a photograph. Randolph assailed "extremists," while the politicians sharing his dais predicted rapid passage of the civil rights bill. And before the crowd of 825 dispersed, its more luminous members posed for the *Standard-Star*'s camera. In one of the published pictures, Randolph stood beside Fred Wright, the business agent for Local 501 of the electricians' union. Less than three years later, that same Fred Wright would sit before a state tribunal to answer charges of job discrimination on the New Rochelle mall.

• • •

During the 1950s and early 1960s, a black child named Earl Forte was growing up not so many blocks from the Burigo apartment and learning a drastically different version of labor history. His father, having been rejected for membership by the sheet-metal union, was able to practice his trade only with a civil service position in the Brooklyn Navy Yard. An older cousin won entry to the operating engineers' union by passing for white. The surrounding households abounded in trained welders, bricklayers, and concrete finishers who could work union jobs only "on permit" as nonmembers. If they wanted to join a union, with its benefits and protections, they had to step down in skill and pay to the so-called mud job of laborer.

A football scholarship carried Forte to the University of Wisconsin, where he immersed himself in civil rights activity, and a subsequent stint in the Marine Corps taught him courage and discipline. Returning to New Rochelle after his discharge, he earned an appointment to the state police. So when the New Rochelle Human Rights Commission was looking for someone to monitor labor unions for discrimination, someone with knowledge of the field and an incontestable reputation, it stopped the search with Forte.

One of his neighbors, Napoleon Holmes, led the labor and industry committee of the New Rochelle NAACP. The son of a steelworker, he, too, was a former marine. He had first raised the job discrimination issue against New Rochelle's banks and police force, but he was turning his attention to the construction industry. Even entry-level labor in a building-trades union paid better than many factory or office jobs. The greenest apprentice in Local 86 earned $2.60 an hour, some 10 percent more than the average for all black workers in Westchester County.

When New Rochelle sold downtown land to Macy's in 1964, Holmes recognized that after years of delays and false starts the mall project was finally proceeding. Because it enjoyed Washington's dollars, it had to meet federal laws and executive orders on discrimination, however vaguely they were drawn. "The mall was our big opportunity," Holmes would say later. "Get black people in the unions then or never. And if we didn't get some of those jobs, nobody would work."

The prospect at first terrified the city's Human Rights Commission. Oh, shit, one member later recalled having thought at the time. We can't shut down the mall. We need this like a hole in the head. But the commission's chairman, Alex Miller, had withstood far graver danger as a field representative for the Anti-Defamation League of B'nai B'rith. In Atlanta, his last posting before New York, white supremacists had bombed a temple whose rabbi campaigned for civil rights. Miller realized the construction unions actually presented a convenient target. In the Lincoln School case, the whitest schools had served the most affluent and liberal families, dividing New Rochelle's usual civil rights alliance by race. The job discrimination issue, by contrast, would let white liberals reunite with their black allies against a common enemy. They had nothing to lose but their guilt.

Forte and Holmes undertook the research necessary to bringing the suit. From the onset of construction in October 1966 through January 1967, they waited by the gate counting heads. The unions representing carpenters, operating engineers, and laborers produced integrated contingents. But in an average week, not one black appeared among the plumbers, electricians, and sheet-metal workers. The Human Rights Commission, acting on the information, declared Locals 38, 86, and 501 "guilty of discrimination."

The finding, while devoid of legal impact, set into motion the increasing isolation of the unions. Macy's vice president for engineering and construction pressed the construction company and general contractor for the New Rochelle store to "fulfill the spirit as well as the letter of the law in providing equal opportunity." The general contractor in turn pressed the electrical subcontractor, who in turn pressed the electricians' union, which resisted any concessions. Between them, the Workers Defense League and the federal Department of Housing and Urban Development delivered thirty-two nonwhite applicants for membership to the unions. The league hired a curriculum specialist from Harvard to tutor these applicants for the apprenticeship entry exams. Meanwhile New Rochelle officials required bidders on the remaining portions of the project to guarantee they would hire at least two minority apprentices or trainees.

It mattered immensely that a plurality of New Rochelle, including the mayor, was Jewish. In these years before the Allan Bakke and Mario DeFunis cases raised the issue of reverse discrimination in white-collar environs, many Jews equated their historic battle against discrimination with that of blacks. Herman Schmier, for instance, as the city's assistant corporation counsel represented the Human Rights Commission in the mall case. A friend of Silvio Burigo's son, he considered Napoleon Holmes a "culprit." Yet in the blacks being repulsed by building-trades unions he saw a younger version of himself—a lawyer refused positions, a reliable tenant denied apartments, all because of anti-Semitism. The rabbi at Temple Israel could hardly have preached a more persuasive sermon on choosing sides.

Surrounded in both literal and metaphorical ways, the three union locals hardened their opposition. They stood alone, as they saw it, against black militants and white do-gooders, federal bureaucrats and cowardly contractors, the department store America loved for its Thanksgiving Day parade, and even the Ford Foundation as a prime benefactor of the Workers Defense League. As for the Democratic Party, its former loyalists spoke of it in terms of betrayal.

In so superheated a climate, the last chance at compromise vanished. Hostile as it appeared to the three locals, the Workers Defense League represented the moderate, accommodationist wing of the civil rights movement. Randolph and Rustin sought inclusion in American institutions, not their overthrow, and for precisely that reason were vilified by younger firebrands as Uncle Toms. The Human Rights Commission even abandoned its insistence that the unions accept blacks as apprentices, proposing instead a system of on-the-job training. Earl Forte, for one, was terrified the locals might accept. As firmly as he believed the apprenticeship programs discriminated, he admired their modern equipment and rigorous instruction. Without access to both, blacks would never excel at the building trades even if they did penetrate the unions. To Forte's relief, the three locals spurned the offer.

Along the fence, both sides raised the stakes. The unions transferred their few black members from other construction sites to the mall. Meanwhile Forte and Holmes obtained inside information from a black mechanic on the job. From his espionage they knew the day the foundations were to be poured, the ideal day for blocking the gate. As the initial standoff repeated itself several times during the succeeding weeks, the controversy pushed closer to violence. Relentlessly taunted as a "nigger" by the construction workers, Forte stopped picketing for fear he would throw a punch. Holmes received hate mail and parking tickets beyond count. And one day a young protester ventured away from the rest to confront an approaching bulldozer. Both a union official and a local NAACP leader dashed to the scene.

"Run him over," the union man ordered the driver.

"*You* get on the bulldozer and run him over," the NAACP member dared the official.

As the union man edged toward the bulldozer, the NAACP member unbuttoned his own coat to reveal a gun.

"Get in that bulldozer," he said, "and I'll shoot you."

• • •

On April 19, 1967, Silvio Burigo walked through the gate and spent his usual seven and a half hours measuring and eyeballing and hectoring. He must have felt preoccupied, though, for mere blocks away at city hall the state Human Rights Commission was launching its formal hearings on the job discrimination case. Only by the technicality of serving Local 86 as secretary-treasurer rather than president or business agent had Silvio escaped being personally named as a defendant. But those two men, Wesley Brown and George Grimm, respectively, were among his oldest friends in the union, and his partners in its leadership since 1939. And the ultimate object of the state's scrutiny, the apprenticeship program, belonged to Silvio more than to anyone else. That attention was what infuriated him most. To say the program discriminated was to call him a racist. To say a newcomer could learn plumbing on the job was to say he had wasted all those hours teaching. Nothing less than his reputation—for decency, rectitude, and talent—stood accused.

The task of defending it fell to two attorneys, Ernest Fleischmann and Ralph Katz, who represented all three unions. At bottom they intended to argue one point: How could the locals be breaking the law if they were obeying it? All the apprenticeship programs complied with state regulations; no less an authority than U.S. Secretary of Labor Willard Wirtz had told the mayor of New Rochelle so. Moreover, the federal law underscoring the case, the Civil Rights Act of 1964, said in Title VII, Section 703(j):

> . . . nothing contained in this title shall be interpreted to require . . . grant[ing] preferential treatment to any individual or to any group . . . on account of an imbalance which may exist with respect to the total number of percentage of persons [in any job, union, or apprenticeship program].

A statute is a block of words in a book, mutable only by the action of government. But a trial, as Katz well knew, occurs within a matrix of larger events. Had the state hearing commenced just a few months later, those events would have favored him. By then, the "long, hot summer" of urban riots and the near war between Jewish teachers and black parents in Brooklyn over community control of schools began robbing the civil rights cause of white sympathy. For now, however, the growing opposition to the Vietnam War was pushing the nation leftward on many issues. Legally, it should not have mattered that Katz's clients as "hard hats" fit the stereotype of Vietnam hawks. Still, he could not help worrying that before a panel of liberals—and who but liberals would be human rights commissioners?—conservatism would appear tantamount to bigotry.

Then there was the problem of language. Katz had defended enough construction unionists already to know how commonly many spoke of "coons" or "pickaninnies" or "niggers." He liked to think the epithets proved only that these men were products of their times, when they considered such slurs innocent slang. Practically, though, he dreaded the moment a client let one slip from the witness stand.

It happened on June 29, the last day of testimony, from the mouth of Fred Wright, the business agent for the electricians' local. By that time, though, Katz could hardly complain about a lack of context. The three commissioners had held thirteen hearings and accumulated two thousand pages of transcripts and evidence. They had heard from New Rochelle activists and Macy's executives, from subcontractors and state employment officers, from blacks who applied for union membership and union leaders who denied it to them. They had waded through wrangles over what constituted preferential treatment, whether state and federal laws permitted on-the-job training, and why the unions required that applicants obtain a "certificate of clearance" proving they had no criminal record when no local police department said it issued any such document.

The pivotal moment for Local 86 had arrived before then, on the raw, windswept morning of May 25, when George Grimm strode to the stand. Silvio could hardly have asked for a better surrogate. The men had been born two years apart, entered the union within four years of each other, and led it together for twenty-eight. How many times over the decades had Silvio eaten roast chicken at Grimm's house? How often had they mulled union business over beers at the dining-room table? Katz deemed Grimm the best witness possible for Local 86, the one most capable of destroying the troglodyte image of tradesmen. Grimm had studied architecture and labor relations at the college level and helped coach wrestling at Columbia University. Even in his mid-sixties, he wrestled and lifted weights to remain fit. He squeezed his own vegetable juices, cultured his own yogurt, and, most remarkable of all in the cigar society of union plumbers, did not smoke.

Fleischmann began the direct examination by leading Grimm through basic employment statistics. Local 86 had 335 members, of whom forty-five were currently jobless. The entire membership had not been working simultaneously since 1959. The last time the local had admitted apprentices, during the summer of 1966, it had pared the openings from twenty to ten because rising mortgage rates were slowing home building. Seven persons applied, Grimm testified, six joined the ranks, and not one had worked a day yet.

"Did any Negroes make application?" Fleischmann asked.

"No, they did not," Grimm replied.

To underline the point, Fleischmann had Grimm recall that Local 86 had sent notices of the openings to the New Rochelle Human Rights Commission, as well as to the boards of education and state employment offices in six communities. Then, abruptly, a commissioner, Ruperto Ruiz, interrupted with a question that pierced to the very heart of the case.

"He did not post any notice in a civil rights organization headquarters?" Ruiz asked Fleischmann.

"He did not post it either in churches or synagogues," the lawyer answered, bristling. "He didn't take television time. They didn't take radio time and make announcements to the United Nations."

"His efforts to notify people of minority groups," Ruiz said with an air of conclusion, "is limited to certain institutions."

"Limited to the minority groups that were interested," Fleischmann shot back.

When the state's attorney rose for cross-examination, she, like Fleischmann, moved quickly into statistics.

"Over the last twenty-eight years," Ann Thacher Anderson asked, "during the period you have been business agent, has there, to your knowledge, ever been a Negro journeyman member?"

"Not to my knowledge."

"Over the same period . . . has there even been . . . a Negro apprentice member of the local?"

"Not to my knowledge."

The next day numbers gave way to nuances. Anderson needed to demonstrate that design, not circumstance, had made Local 86 wholly white. She elicited from Grimm the basic requirements for incoming apprentices, and sought with mixed success to show whites had been admitted without fulfilling them. Grimm granted that the local had never tried to organize a particular plumbing shop that employed many blacks.

Anderson's attack finally distilled to the experience of Harold Morse, a black plumber whom a federal official had recommended to Local 86. Morse served, in civil rights parlance, as a tester, someone sent to apply for a job, loan, or apartment in the full belief that he will be rejected. That rejection, in turn, can be introduced before a court as proof of discrimination. Already the three commissioners had heard the testimony of several testers turned away from the electricians' local for not supplying the apocryphal "certificate of clearance" or failing to submit a birth certificate that the union had in fact already received. Rather than call Morse as a witness, Anderson extracted this account from Grimm.

Q: Did you contact Mr. Morse?
A: Yes. I wrote him a letter to come in.
Q: Did he come in?
A: Yes, he did.
Q: What happened?
A: He was asked if he had worked at the plumbing industry. He said, "Yes." I asked him, "How long?" He said, "Twenty years." I said, "Where?" He said, "Around." I said, "Who did you work for?" He said, "Well, me and another fellow did some jobs." I said, "Did you ever work for a licensed master plumber?" He said, "Yes." I said, "What was his name?" He said, "I can't tell you." I said, "Where did you work for this master plumber?" He said, "Around." I said, "Well, we have to have this information. We have to know that you have had a proper background in this business. We meet here every Tuesday night. When you get ready to give us the information, come in and we will proceed on your application."

Q: Did he fill out a formal application?
A: He never came back.

As evidence, the story of Harold Morse sounded ambiguous, if palpably painful. Was the union being fair or resistant? Was the applicant lying about his background or protecting a former boss from reprisal? Why exactly didn't he ever return and file the application? Neither Anderson nor Grimm ever answered, and the three commissioners never asked.

The pursuit of justice is not necessarily congruent with the discovery of truth, and Grimm's testimony suggested just how much of it eluded the state commission. The panel never learned, for instance, that many of the forty-five jobless plumbers in Local 86 were living seasonally in Florida while paying dues or were working only enough to enlarge their pensions or were turning down strenuous or cold-weather jobs because of their age or past injuries. On the other hand, the panel never learned that Earl Forte was exasperated by the failure of many young black applicants to present themselves on schedule at union offices or construction sites; he had resorted to playing both their alarm clock and chauffeur.

In the end, six months after the hearings closed, the state commission found Local 501 of the International Brotherhood of Electrical Workers and Local 38 of the Sheet Metal Workers' International Association guilty of discrimination, A judge in New York State Supreme Court in turn ordered both to commence programs of on-the-job training for minorities and to send regular compliance reports to the state Human Rights Commission. Four months later Local 501 was sued again.

Local 86 was found innocent. If the local could not find work for its most recent crop of apprentices, the commissioners wrote, it had just cause not to admit any more. But the acquittal made surprisingly little difference. Being charged with discrimination in the 1960s disfigured a reputation as completely as would being charged with child abuse in the 1990s; the public remembered only the allegation, not the outcome. Besides, federal and state laws were increasingly requiring construction unions and contractors on public projects, even those never accused of racial bias, to hire specific percentages of minorities.

So Silvio Burigo began soliciting applications from minorities, accepting six as apprentices by March 1968. He maintained their names on a separate list, which he sent as required to the state labor department. When the town supervisor of Rye asked if the local could belatedly admit a friend who had missed the deadline for applying, Grimm wrote back almost wistfully: "As you know, the selection of applicants for the apprentice program is under State law and supervision; we do not have a free hand in this as we did previously."

They still had a free hand, however, in the voting booth. An interesting thing had happened in New Rochelle in the fall of 1967. A Democratic candidate for city council, whose father had run for mayor ten times on the Socialist Party ticket, pursued and captured the Conservative Party line. Not surprisingly, his name was Doyle, for the Democratic-Conservative hybrid would prove a staple of New Rochelle's blue-collar ethnics in the years to come.

Silvio Burigo was a perfect example. He had stayed a Democrat for too long to defect; he voted in 1968 for Hubert Humphrey and in 1972 for George McGovern. Yet this product of the New Deal was bequeathing to his descendants a disgust with what Democratic liberalism had become—the force that treated him as a virtual criminal. And the turbulent 1960s were not done with his family yet. All through the mall controversy, Frank Trotta Sr. was working about a mile away in a housing project. Few places in New Rochelle had been conceived amid loftier ideals; put another way, few had further to fall.

• • •

Swaddled in mittens, mufflers, and overcoats, shuffling in place and beating arms against chest, some five hundred people shivered in line on the glacial morning of January 15, 1949. At its very front, the column disappeared down several stairs and into a cellar, the makeshift quarters of the New Rochelle Housing Authority. These suitors were doing something that would seem unimaginable several decades later: They were clamoring for the chance to live in a low-income housing project.

Inside the office, a woman named Issaght clasped her hands reverentially and beseeched the authority's chairman for an apartment. Her baby, she told him, had contracted bronchitis in the unheated attic the family now occupied. They shared a kitchen and bathroom with several fellow unfortunates. The day abounded in such tales, for the authority was selecting tenants not on the basis of first-come, first-served but on an evaluation of both need and character. Mothers presented their wedding license to prove they were married. Veterans submitted papers showing an honorable discharge. Those deemed provisionally eligible would still have to permit an examination of police records and an inspection of the hygiene and housekeeping in their current abode.

Yet they flocked by the hundreds, not just that Saturday the authority began accepting applications, but well into the next week. Even after turning away those who earned too much money or had not lived in New Rochelle long enough, the authority approved 493 families, or more than twice the new project's capacity. The Robert R. Hartley Houses consisted of five tidy brick buildings of forty-eight apartments each, fireproofed and centrally heated, scattered across a 6.5-acre campus. For a two- or three-bedroom apartment, a tenant would pay between $32 and $42 per month. That amounted to less than half the rate on the private market, a market so tight the *Standard-Star* carried fewer than a half-dozen advertisements for such rentals each day.

Public housing in New Rochelle was answering to a genuine groundswell. When the city council had defied Mayor Church in 1947 and refused to rezone land for the Hartley Houses, the public outcry forced it to relent. A rent hike in several tenements near the site brought protests from groups as diverse as the NAACP, the League of Women Voters, the Veterans of Foreign Wars, and the Third Ward Wallace for President Club. The first tenants in the Hartley Houses represented a wide sweep of race, religion, and ethnicity; they ranged from chauffeurs to cops, mechanics to firemen, garbage collectors to telephone operators. They comprised not an underclass to be quarantined but a working class to be embraced. As the state housing authority argued in its 1952 annual report:

> Building an environment of good living requires consideration of the goal that is sought. Are we seeking to perpetuate division in America by economic classes? Or do we seek to have families of various incomes living in proximity to each other . . . so that they may come to understand and appreciate the problems of each other? Which is democracy; which type of living did the founding fathers intend, which is better for the future of America in its fight against the "isms"?

America, in return, expected the tenants to comport themselves as model citizens. To live in public housing was to enjoy a privilege. It entailed responsibility and sacrifice, specifically the sacrifice of certain rights of privacy. The residents' manual of the Hartley Houses, for instance, required tenants to "report to the Management office at once all births, deaths, accidents, or the presence of contagious disease." Every six months each household had to surrender its income records. Hosting overnight guests required advance permission. The occupants of each floor risked a fine if they failed to sweep their common hallway, as did any parent whose child walked on the grass. Pictures were to be hung only with a particular kind of pushpin approved by the management. "Don't shake your mops out of the window," another rule read. "You don't want anybody else's dirt and nobody wants yours."

And those were just a handful of the written regulations. The management style, in flesh and blood, mingled elements of drill sergeant, dormitory proctor, and mother superior. The building managers conducted unannounced checks of each household every four or five months. Had the refrigerator been defrosted? Was the toilet scrubbed? The stove clean? The beds made? One manager knocked on doors at eleven o'clock at night to send home any boyfriend trying to spend the night with his steady.

Such intrusions could—and ultimately did—enrage civil libertarians and public interest lawyers. Plenty of the residents of the Hartley Houses, too, griped about them. Yet the many forms of meddling added up to a social contract between landlord and tenant, and in a larger way between those who paid taxes to the welfare state and those who received its benefits. The result was community. Mothers grew collard greens and cabbages in gardens beside the parking lot. Children earned Friday-night helpings of soda and cake for cleaning the hallways. Fathers stayed married and held jobs, and nobody considered either state anything but unremarkable. It was to this version of the Hartley Houses, one that seemed to fulfill liberalism's promise and validate its compassion, that Frank Trotta Sr. reported to work as a janitor in 1959.

• • •

Most mornings at six-thirty, ninety minutes before his shift officially started, Frank Trotta Sr. waddled in his stumpy-legged way down a ramp and into the basement of 81 Winthrop Avenue. This underbelly of dirt and concrete, itself unheated, harbored both the furnace for the Hartley complex and the janitors who tended it. The first obligation Frank fulfilled, even before turning on the space heaters in his own quarters, was to light the flames of three boilers. He liked to think of the steam coursing through the pipes and warming the bathroom tile by the time the first tenant to awaken staggered into the shower. Then Frank walked back outside, across a small plaza, and into 70 Winthrop to unlock the door and switch on the lights for the project's sole laundry room. It was not supposed to open until seven, but he knew working mothers counted on being able to wash a few loads before rousing the kids for school.

During the day ahead Frank might shine the brass mailboxes, hose down the sidewalks, sweep the stairs, mop the elevator, empty ashes from the incinerator, vacuum out the furnace pipes, and rake leaves, shovel snow, or cut the lawn as the season demanded. Then there were the duties he performed beyond the janitorial. His reading ability may have ruined his score on the civil service test for mechanic, and with it his chance for better pay, but few among the maintenance crew could equal him at repairing the riding mower or changing the elbow joint under a sink. And if one of his favorite tenants like Hazel Alexander seized upon him halfway hysterical, sputtering out a story about how she threw her husband's W-2 form down the trash chute by mistake, well then Frank would pick through three feet of corncobs, fish scales, and coffee grounds to unearth it.

With a demeanor pitched between stoic and curmudgeonly, Frank dismissed his own efforts. He was an early riser; he was handy; it was a job. His family, accustomed mostly to his grit and temper, would have been flabbergasted to know that his buddies at work nicknamed him Porky, as in pig, and a tenant described him as "a jolly little man." More than he admitted, Frank brought to the Hartley Houses a quality beyond a work ethic; he held an affinity for the tenants, and his commitment demonstrated it far more vividly than words ever could have. Economically, the residents were his peers. As of 1964 he was earning $3,900 annually, and had Lorraine not been making money, too, the family would have qualified for low-income housing. The maintenance crew, like the population it served, was racially mixed. One of Frank's comrades, in fact, lived with his family just one floor above the janitors' domain.

These men shared in the joys of the project, even created several themselves. Late every autumn the janitors raffled off a "basket of cheer," and throughout the year they collected rags from tenants to be sold to dealers for five cents a pound. The take from both paid for the annual Christmas party at 81 Winthrop, with soda and beer and sandwiches and ziti, and Frank's pal Mickey Circelli as Santa Claus bestowing dolls and toy trucks. For satisfaction, though, no ritual surpassed the subtle one of being assigned to repaint an apartment that had suddenly become vacant. That meant another family had bought a house. Frank admired the manner of such people, earnest and industrious as the old-country *contadino*. They never bragged about their grand plans; they just quietly cobbled together a down payment. Even if they had broken the rules—working a second job for cash and hiding it from the project management—they had honored the ideal behind subsidized housing. It wasn't a place to spend your whole life; it was where decent folks, strivers, could stay till they got a leg up.

Nobody, not a police officer or a social worker, not even the tenants themselves, understood the Hartley Houses as thoroughly as did the janitors. They saw the project in its totality and in its minutiae; they supplied its vital fluids and carried away its waste; they groomed it and bandaged it. If the housing project was a living thing, a sort of body, then the janitors labored from its innermost organ, its heart, the basement of 81 Winthrop.

A visitor would see only the front room, the office, with its gunmetal gray desk and cleaning-supplies company calendar. Off the dusky hall-ways past it lay the rooms for changing, washing, and relaxing at day's end beneath *Playboy* centerfolds and pipes wound with yuletide tinsel. Still other rooms held stoves and refrigerators, mowers and tractors, drums of disinfectant and heavy bags of rock salt. In corners, drawers, and boxes beyond number collected johnny bolts and bonnet assem-blies, motor oil and mopheads, and lug wrenches, rakes, and gas flex connectors.

Behind a door marked "Pipe Access Space" was the most revealing chamber, one the janitors called the "dirt room" for its earthen floor. At any given time the room might contain stuffed animals, a percolator, a snow shovel, an ironing board, stereo speakers, an extension cord, a basketball, roasting pans, and a hot-pink toilet-seat cover. These objects shared only two common traits: They had been thrown away by the tenants, and they had been rescued by the janitors, who thought them, with a modicum of repair, well worth preserving.

From the garbage Frank Trotta had scavenged a red leather recliner that became his virtual throne. All it took were new springs in the cushion and duct tape over the cracks. While the chair stayed in the basement at 81 Winthrop, most of Frank's other finds went home and, after a bit of tinkering, back into use. Various relatives inherited the typewriter, window fan, transistor radios, and vacuum cleaners. The Trottas themselves kept a bike that Frank retooled into a stationary exercise cycle.

Every one of these objects served a purpose beyond the obvious. They showed, as Frank put it, that when you get something for free it doesn't mean as much. They showed how easily you throw away things you didn't pay for. Literally speaking, the tenants had bought most of the objects; what Frank meant was that the money they had available for these items was the money they had saved thanks to subsidized rent or had been awarded by welfare. So the real villain in the parable of the "dirt room" was less the prodigal tenant than the government whose handouts invited the sins of waste and sloth.

Frank's cynicism built gradually and never so fully as to compromise his devotion to the job. But from the mid-1960s onward he increasingly measured the conditions and values of families supported by the welfare state against those of his own. Just before a new subsidized housing project opened on Main Street in 1964, Frank drove his family over for a look. Lorraine fell into awed silence at the apartments with two bath-rooms and tiled halls, and a stove and refrigerator fresh from the factory, glinting back light. Neither she nor Frank needed to utter aloud what both knew: This apartment for the poor shamed their first house, which they had struggled to buy with two incomes. That house had had a chicken coop in the yard and a coal stove for heat, which the family could only afford to replace with a furnace because Silvio installed it for free. Yet within weeks after visiting the new project, Frank was bringing home stories of shattered windows, graffiti, and excrement in the elevators, all as further evidence that government was helping the wrong people.

Later a series of explosions in the Hartley Houses incinerators occasioned similarly withering comparisons. Some government program was doling out free food, or so Frank assumed, because suddenly the tenants had so much of it they were throwing out the excess. And bags of flour, dropped down the rubbish chute, ignited like gunpowder. Flames blew out the incinerator doors and roared back up the channel, scorching the children usually delegated to take out the trash. What most outraged Frank, though, was not the fires or injuries as much as the cavalier attitude about perfectly good flour. In the Trotta household, food was counted like pennies. Frank and Lorraine ate potatoes and eggs for dinner, saving meat for their two sons. Visits to the butcher occurred only on sale days. A family splurge consisted of a bucket-to-go from Chicken Delight.

The same frugality applied to gas, lights, and water. Frank set rules: Put on a sweater instead of raising the heat; shut off the tap while brushing your teeth; don't run the faucet for a cold drink. It was a family mission never to exceed the monthly minimum on any utility bill. So naturally Frank seethed when he entered an apartment to make repairs and found the lights blazing, radio blaring, and television blinking, all because the housing authority paid the tab. Those who most needed lessons in thrift got only incentives to squander.

When had the Hartley Houses so degenerated? When had the working poor been outnumbered by the welfare poor? Frank could hardly designate a single pivotal moment. Was it the day he chanced upon a kid urinating in the elevator he had just mopped? Or the time Mickey Circelli found a fifteen-year-old girl waving a knife at her grandmother? Maybe it was when Franklin Jones, for ten years the executive director of the housing authority, dropped dead of a heart attack at forty-six. The job, quite literally, had killed him.

Frank could easily understand why. Just as the buildings and appliances were aging, turning twenty years old in 1969, the money for upkeep began draining away. Mopheads arrived now in lots of three instead of six. Rather than replacing broken stoves, the authority depended on Frank to rebuild them with secondhand parts. Graffiti spattered so many walls the janitors went through solvent by the fifty-five-gallon drum, and twenty minutes after scouring a patch it was often tattooed anew.

The project was a paradox, a dump with immaculate garbage cans. Only the thieves seemed to use them, for secreting their stashes; Frank fished out a set of stemware from one and brought it home to Lorraine. A complex that once fretted about zealous matrons shaking their mops out the windows now had teenaged mothers heaving their trash to the ground. The parking lot once bounded by garden plots bore a bumper crop of cigarette butts, blackened spark plugs, and pint bottles. The rooftops that janitors used to comb for baseballs clouted from the nearby diamond yielded junkies' needles. At one point a new custodian nettled Frank by never eating lunch with the rest. It turned out he was an undercover narcotics officer who ultimately found a large cache of heroin in a first-floor apartment.

The entire temperament of the Hartley Houses had grown hostile, and it was never more apparent than when Frank and his mates cleaned the parking lot. Invariably, a few dozen young men were idling there, smoking and drinking, maybe stripping a stolen car. Among them moved the janitors, hunched and grumbling, picking the litter, stuffing the cans, and toppling them into the garbage truck's maw. And in the banter that crackled occasionally between camps lay a profound and mutual sense of contempt.

"Why they need five of you on that truck?" one of the parking-lot crowd taunted the janitors one morning.

"At least we're doin' work. When're you gonna get a job?"

"If it wasn't for us makin' a mess, you wouldn't have no job."

Frank worried less about having the job than surviving it. The janitors stopped sponsoring the Christmas party at 81 Winthrop after two drunken, brawling tenants ruined it one year. A sniper with a pellet gun wounded a maintenance man cleaning the grounds. Another time the same fellow discovered a revolver in the grass. The very ritual that defined Frank, firing up the boilers before dawn, rendered him most vulnerable. One day, sure enough, three teenagers he presumed to be thieves in flight encountered him in a lonely basement tunnel. He retreated from them at knifepoint.

Then, one August day in 1976, the building manager summoned the janitors to clean an apartment that had abruptly become vacant. The tenant, however, had departed not as a home buyer but a murder victim. Frank and the others refused to enter the unit. The manager told them health regulations required that it be cleaned. So they donned rain boots, rubber gloves, and surgical masks and cracked open the door. Even for men accustomed to snaking clogged sewer pipes, the stench buckled the knees. They picked a path through mounds of soiled clothes three or four feet high to the spot where the body had lain. Blood, urine, and feces puddled on the floor, making a feast for maggots. Rats and cockroaches barely bothered to scatter. Oddly, when the janitors carried their sponges and buckets into the bathroom, they noticed a certain order. The room seemed not so much sanitary as undisturbed, like a place that had rarely been visited.

• • •

As intimately as Frank Trotta observed the demise of the Hartley Houses from the basement of 81 Winthrop, he saw the symptoms rather than the disease. When he and the other janitors and their friends among the longtime tenants bemoaned the maladies of the project—more crime, more vandalism, more unwed mothers on welfare—they knew at best only a fraction of the causes. The ultimate answers lay far from their view, inscribed in financial ledgers, court dockets, and volumes of federal regulations. Taken together, these forces transformed the Hartley Houses from a symbol of activist government assisting the worthy to an emblem of incompetent government indulging the worthless. In New Rochelle, as in the nation, no extension of the welfare state except Aid to Families with Dependent Children surpassed public housing as an indictment of liberalism.

Yet the deterioration of public housing began with a classically American debate between collective security and individual rights. Whether managed by a federal, state, or municipal authority, subsidized housing initially operated from the assumption that a public landlord, like a private one, could frame and enforce rules. It could decide who qualified for an apartment and who got evicted from one; it need not provide a spurned applicant or ousted tenant with stated reasons, advance notice, or an avenue of appeal.

Harsh as the system sounded, it represented a kind of statist liberalism, one that placed the development of a cohesive community above any single citizen's right to due process. Of course, the notion of what constituted cohesion or community varied wildly from place to place. Was it barring single parents or was it enforcing racial segregation? Was it limiting the percentage of welfare recipients or dictating residents' political opinions? Thus liberals devoted to individual rights went to war against a system of public housing that was, ironically, one of liberalism's proudest creations.

The grandfather of all the litigation to come arose from a project in Washington, D.C. Amid the anti-Communist fervor of 1954, Congress attached to a standard appropriations bill a rider requiring all tenants in federal housing to sign a loyalty oath. One tenant named Rudder refused, and when he was evicted he brought suit against the government. Ruling on Rudder's behalf in 1955, a federal district court declared that a public landlord cannot function in the same manner as a private one, that it must subscribe to the due process clause of the Fourteenth Amendment.

For more than a decade, the Rudder case remained what it superficially seemed, one turning on the issue of political freedom. But in a series of later suits, stretching from the late 1960s into the mid-1970s, courts cited its precedent in forbidding housing authorities to evict tenants without having "good cause" and offering a forum for appeal. The specific issue of an unwed mother's right to public housing reached a federal court in Little Rock in 1967, and the judge ruled that tenants must be admitted or evicted based on individual conduct alone, not membership in any larger category of humanity.

The effects of these rulings rippled through the country in two ways. First, the Department of Housing and Urban Development, the landlord for federal projects, incorporated the judgments on due process and tenants' rights into its own regulations. Second, state and local housing authorities tended to follow HUD's lead. Many communities, like New Rochelle, which had built certain projects with federal funds and others with state funds, dreaded the headache of jumping between two sets of rules. The Hartley Houses, erected with Albany's dollars and governed by Albany's laws, in actuality operated by 1973 under Washington's far looser reins.

The so-called rights revolution of litigation had begun directly eroding the powers of the New Rochelle Housing Authority in 1964. That year the authority evicted a single mother with three children younger than six for allegedly engaging in adultery. She sued in state supreme court to regain the apartment. While the judge upheld the housing authority's general right to oust an adulterer, he overturned the eviction, ruling that the woman's misbehavior remained unproven. Between the expense of arguing a case and the slackening of sexual mores, New Rochelle discovered, enforcing morality looked to be a losing proposition.

In 1970 the housing authority marched into court again, this time to defend one of the last pillars of selectivity still standing. The provision did not consider marital status, sexual activity, or anything remotely so controversial; it simply mandated that any prospective tenant have resided in New Rochelle for five consecutive years. Two women had recently been refused applications in separate instances. Had they been accepted, they still would have stood at the end of a three-year waiting list. Nonetheless, with a legal-aid attorney they sued in federal district court, charging the residency requirement violated the Constitution.

First that court and then the federal court of appeals ruled in their favor. Given the waiting list, the judgments hardly affected the projects themselves. But they contributed to a public relations disaster for those who supported subsidized housing in New Rochelle. Its early popularity had rested on a belief that local help would go to local people. Now the federal courts had saddled New Rochelle with one of the most corrosive images in the entire debate about poverty, public aid, and, inevitably, race. The two women who were now entitled to subsidized apartments were both recent migrants from the South receiving welfare. They embodied, and thus seemed to confirm, the racist stereotype of black parasites flocking to New York for the generous benefits made possible by white workers' taxes.

Already wearied by the two lawsuits, the housing authority essentially abandoned its standards of screening and discipline by accepting federal regulations in 1973. No longer did the agency determine if an applicant had a police record or knew how to keep house; no longer did a building manager surprise tenants with a white-glove inspection or midnight knock on the door. The percentage of single-parent households in the project rose steadily until hitting a plateau of 85 percent in the mid-1980s.

Meanwhile the Hartley Houses' financial woes had been swelling for years, and for reasons that might well have been foreseen. To pay for constructing the project, the state housing authority had loaned New Rochelle $2.8 million, which was to be repaid on a forty-year schedule. Since low-income developments were not intended to show a profit, the state each year forwarded aid to New Rochelle in almost exactly the amount of annual debt service. In essence, Albany was moving money from one pocket to another, through the medium of New Rochelle. The rent each local authority collected was expected, in turn, to cover its operating expenses.

What the state failed to anticipate back in the 1930s and 1940s was the future. As the buildings grew older and the costs of labor and material rose, the price of maintaining a project like the Hartley Houses outdistanced the revenue from rents. And only an act of the legislature could increase the state subsidy. The oil embargoes of 1973 and 1979 further magnified the problem by driving up heating costs. So did a piece of seemingly reasonable federal law. Under an amendment introduced by Senator Edward Brooke, a black Republican from Massachusetts, HUD was restricted from charging tenants more than 25 percent of their income in rent. As usual, most states adopted the federal standard as their own. The cap took effect, disastrously, at a time when subsidized projects were increasingly housing public-aid recipients. A quarter on every dollar of a welfare check could not possibly sustain the Hartley Houses.

As early as 1971 the New Rochelle Housing Authority was sagging under a $167,000 deficit and trying to balance its books with a monthly surcharge of $10 on each household. A four-month rent strike ensued, scuttling the plan, causing $24,000 in losses, and undermining the very culture of meeting the rent. By the mid-1970s, 45 percent of the authority's tenants were in arrears. In the fiscal year ending March 1, 1979, the authority showed a $403,000 deficit on a total budget of $1.2 million. The next year the shortfall came to $657,000. Fuel bills alone nearly equaled the annual state subsidy of $291,000.

That was why the janitors were receiving half the usual supply of mopheads and why Frank Trotta was conducting transplant surgery on stoves. That was why stairwells and lobbies were swabbed less often. Apartments that had been painted every few years waited until a tenant moved out. If a leaky roof got patched, then a balky elevator went unrepaired. And it may well have broken because the authority had tried to save money by reducing preventative maintenance such as lubricating the motor.

Such economies were utterly insufficient to the crisis. So the housing authority began diverting state aid from debt service to operating expenses, futilely begging Albany to release the next year's grant early. On November 1, 1980, the housing authority missed a debt-service payment of $51,545.66. One month later it skipped an installment of $68,947.50. On February 15, 1981, it fell behind by another $32,741.25. In all New York State, with forty-three different housing authorities, only one had preceded New Rochelle's into default and ignominy.

State law required that when a local housing authority failed in its obligations to Albany the municipality itself settle the debt. New Rochelle refused. The state threatened to recoup the $153,234.41 by removing that amount from a $1 million urban-renewal grant due to the city. New Rochelle refused again. This was no longer the city, awash in postwar liberalism, in which Stanley Church had called public housing "the first duty of government." It was no longer the city where, as recently as 1963, all eight mayoral candidates had favored the construction of more subsidized housing.

Church had retired to Florida in 1971 and been supplanted by Leonard Paduano, a Republican reared in the West End and supported by blue-collar ethnics like the Trottas and Burigos. Soon after taking office, Paduano led the city in a lawsuit to halt the state Urban Development

Corporation from erecting a high-rise across Main Street from the Bracey Apartments, the project the Trottas had visited in 1964. In letters to the *Standard-Star*, ordinary citizens reviled the plan, one calling the development agency a " 'Hitler Type' organization." Even liberals averred that New Rochelle already had enough tax-exempt property.

Lost in the rhetoric—in the formulation of race as a "wedge issue" —were people like Martha Davis. Her husband worked with Frank Trotta as a janitor and the Davises lived in the project themselves. Amid all the violence and rot, they kept a spotless apartment, its walls covered with photographs of children and grandchildren in graduation gowns. They remembered a time of open windows on balmy nights and azaleas blooming on sills. "Put all the ones that don't do right in one building," Martha once pleaded to the housing authority, "and leave the rest of us alone." But only a rare white person, conservative or liberal, knew the Martha Davises personally. And Frank Trotta, one who did, would soon be gone.

• • •

On Halloween 1982, Frank Trotta's seventieth birthday and his final day as a janitor at the Hartley Houses, he presented a fountain pen and a split of champagne to all forty-eight families in 81 Winthrop. Several tenants baked him a cake, and many more attended his retirement party at the senior citizens' center. Despite the physical danger, insufficient supplies, and ungrateful tenants, Frank had actually fought for and won five one-year extensions of the mandatory retirement age. He felt not simply affection, particularly for the older residents, but a sort of bunker camaraderie.

By then, his son and namesake was already grown. But the lessons of the Hartley Houses had subtly shaped his youth. Frank Jr. could recall that trip to the Bracey Apartments and the exercise cycle fashioned from a discard. He remembered the summer the government gave free lunches to kids in the projects and his father would bring home brown bags that had never been opened. He and his brother Joseph ate the sandwiches for snacks.

During that same period of the late 1960s, Frank Jr.'s grandfather, Silvio Burigo, was enduring the allegation he was a bigot. It was hardly the sort of thing he would mention to a child. The winter of the mall protests, Silvio and Frank Jr. shoveled snow together; the summer the state hearings concluded, they watched Seely's kids play Little League baseball. Silvio treated Frank Jr. to ice cream at Carvel and Blackjack gum from the supply in the glove compartment of his Chevy.

Silvio must have appreciated the diversions. Too much was changing too fast. Back in 1960, not so very many years earlier, the United Association's president had lauded exactly such developments as the Hartley Houses and the New Rochelle mall as godsends for blue-collar workers.

A clean, well-planned, orderly city is usually a prosperous city. New housing—urban renewal—both mean many jobs—not alone for the building tradesman but for the supplier as well. More wages in the community mean more buying power. Every retail store—every business—is bound to profit from a well-planned redevelopment program. Backing these programs is good citizenship and good business, too.

Frank Trotta Jr., an uncommonly observant teenager, already had his doubts.

Chapter Eleven

Senator Clearwater
(Richie Garrett)

IN FEBRUARY 1966, AS IN ALL THE FEBRUARYS BEFORE IT, Richie Garrett was waiting for the ice to melt. Silver sheets covered the Croton River and spread across the Hudson except for a channel the Coast Guard chopped clear. Somewhere underneath lolled striped bass and yellow perch and tommycod, teasingly unattainable, locked away until spring. In this impatient interval Richie might oil a reel, pour lead for jigs, scrape and patch the boat—worthy endeavors all, but no replacement for the contentment of being on the water. So when he received a vague, secondhand invitation to some sort of sportsmen's group, he hopped into the car with his angling partner, Augie Berg. Talking about fishing wasn't as good as fishing, but it beat talking about almost anything else.

The directions led them quickly from Crotonville into Croton-on-Hudson. Adjacent and yet alien, the town was known less for outdoorsmen than bohemians and radicals who once included Max Eastman, Isadora Duncan, and John Reed. Soon Richie and Augie found themselves in the living room of a journalist, Bob Boyle, staring at a bust of Ralph Waldo Emerson wreathed with a fleece strip of hand-tied flies. Where a coffee table might otherwise have rested there sat a 120-gallon aquarium stocked with bass, sunfish, and perch. On closer inspection, it also contained bricks, in a mordant comment on the Hudson's condition. Richie was a gravedigger and Augie a prison guard, and around them gathered degrees and credentials in the form of oceanographer, entomologist, orthodontist, law professor, and airline pilot. Months later Richie would be amazed to learn Boyle was Catholic, since, in his view, anyone who wore Brooks Brothers suits had to be Episcopalian. Clearly, this was not going to be just another rod and gun club yammering about scores at the target range and whether the hatchery truck had visited the local stream yet.

Boyle qualified as a veteran in the nascent environmental movement. Straddling the roles of reporter and partisan, he had been agitating most recently against the Consolidated Edison utility company's plan to construct a reservoir and hydroelectric plant atop Storm King Mountain along the Hudson. But that battle was being fought the old, mannerly way, by gentlemen conservationists and women in sensible hiking boots who aspired only to preserve a beautiful place. Tellingly, they called their organization Scenic Hudson. The product of military school and the Marine Corps, Boyle envisioned a more combative activism, and one that operated on the principle of ecology. The word was just beginning to penetrate conversational English and political discourse from the laboratories and lecture halls of the academy. It conceived of the natural world not as so many picture postcards but as an intricate web of interdependent life.

Boyle damned the Storm King plan for its threat to mutilate the landscape that had inspired the Hudson River School of American painters. More than that, though, he feared it would shatter the fragile balance of the river. Con Edison intended to continuously replenish the reservoir by vacuuming billions of gallons of water from the Hudson. With that water would inevitably come plankton, larvae, and small fry, the bottom rungs of a food chain that supported commercial and recreational fisheries generating tens of millions of dollars annually. Stopping Con Edison, Boyle believed, was only one environmental struggle among dozens crying for soldiers.

Launching the crusade simply, Boyle asked every man in the living room what he had seen on the river. Some talked about the vast fish kill in the spring of 1963 outside the Indian Point nuclear plant, a Con Edison installation several miles north of Ossining. Others mentioned the massive kills just downriver from Albany every summer, where the water was a broth of sewage, chemicals, and paper-mill pulp fit only for maggots and leeches. As if the Hudson were not beleaguered enough, now Governor Nelson Rockefeller planned to fill the shoreline for an expressway running ten miles from Tarrytown to Crotonville. The National Geographic Society had just published a map with the river marked black, consigned to being industry's chamber pot.

When Richie's turn came, he spoke with calm authority. His schooling had stopped at twelfth grade, he earned his living with pick and shovel, and he wore denim instead of Brooks Brothers, but he had spent his life on the water. Long ago the men of Crotonville had hacked a stairway of railroad ties into the hill descending to the Croton River, and every summer morning the women lugged children and picnic baskets to the beach at the bottom. As a boy Richie had ridden a fifty-pound snapping turtle, its mouth held by a wire bridle, and seined bait for commercial fishermen. As a teenager he had fished for stripers by daybreak bonfires and ogled girls all afternoon as they sunned on the boulders. Sometime late in high school he met Augie Berg, probably as a baseball foe, and they became fishing companions, ultimately sharing six rowboats and two outboards. Augie liked to sneak rods into Sing Sing, which hunched along the Hudson, so the inmates unloading coal barges could pause to drop a line.

Then, in the last few years, Richie had seen some disturbing changes. When he was working construction on the Chevrolet plant in Tarrytown, he noticed the paint shop flushing its excess down a stream and into the Hudson. He could tell by the river what color that day's Impalas were. Since Ossining had yet to equip Crotonville with sewers, rinse water from the neighborhood's washing machines tumbled through drain and culvert into the Croton River, foaming along the banks. Then there was the Penn Central's maintenance shop in nearby Harmon, dumping oil and solvents into the shallows of Croton Bay, one of Richie's favorite spots for bass. No matter how expertly he cleaned them, the fish tasted of diesel.

"And the thing is," Richie told the others, "when the sun hits the oil, it's all hues. Yellows and blues, like a rainbow. Beautiful. Except it's oil."

A grim laugh rumbled through the room, the same kind of laugh that had greeted the aquarium bricks. Such levity aside, the talk grew only more heated as the hours passed. Some wanted to stuff mattresses up the railroad's pipe, others to set fire to the oil it gushed. Richie could appreciate their impotent fury. As he saw it, God had created the waters and mountains and sky, but "that man-made product, the dollar bill, is the Almighty in this country." So what power could some local-yokel fisherman with St. Francis in his soul muster against a General Motors, a Penn Central, a Rockefeller? He felt as helpless to revive the Hudson as any of the bodies he interred.

Boyle, though, had an idea for fighting pollution within the system.

While writing about the environment for *Sports Illustrated* magazine he had stumbled upon a forty-year-old federal law, the Oil Pollution Act, and traced its origins to the even more obscure New York Harbor Act of 1888 and Federal Refuse Act of 1899. As Boyle read them, these statutes forbade dumping or discharging any foreign matter whatsoever into the Hudson or its tributaries. And whoever turned in a violator was entitled to collect half of any fine a court levied. Just to make certain he had understood correctly, Boyle submitted the laws to the Wall Street attorneys representing Time, Incorporated, and they concurred.

"They've never been enforced," Boyle told his audience of the laws, "but they've never been repealed." In other words, Washington blessed the environmental version of bounty hunting. This would be even more fun than sabotage.

Boyle also knew of at least one powerful ally, a freshman Congressman named Dick Ottinger. A liberal Democrat in the Republican heartland of Westchester, Ottinger had captured his seat partially by seizing the emerging issue of ecology. He proceeded to hire one of Storm King's most effective foes as a chief aide and to introduce several pieces of legislation aimed at protecting the river. The same Boyle who had registered Republican while living in Chicago as a personal protest against the Daley machine now led a group of GOP turncoats for Ottinger. The Congressman's cooperation, he told the fishermen around him, "is a given."

Thus the Hudson River Fishermen's Association was born. In the weeks to come, incorporation papers were filed with the state and an initial public meeting was planned, with Ottinger as the featured speaker. Flyers announcing the meeting appeared on telephone polls, supermarket bulletin boards, and commuter train platforms from Yonkers to Peekskill. Driving home with Augie from Boyle's house, Richie no longer felt isolated in his outrage. His public life had begun.

For years the rivers had granted Richie pleasure and serenity, antidotes to the sorrow that often gripped him during a succession of wars. Fishing was not a political act; it was an escape from anything so worldly. Now, with the Croton and Hudson befouled, ecology was pointing Richie toward liberalism just as surely as knowing George Tice or burying Timmy McCarthy had. Taking sides against a major railroad or utility company, against an immensely popular and profoundly wealthy governor were not isolated acts. They encouraged Richie in a broader way to dispute the wisdom of big government and big industry, to "question authority" in the parlance of the times, to identify his civic duty as dissidence.

As the Vietnam War ground on in carnage and stalemate, Richie believed more intensely than ever that it was a "money war," sending defense contractors home with fat paychecks while four of his working-class nephews served. Yet precisely because Richie had family in the armed forces, he kept his dissent to himself, wishing publicly for quick victory and safe returns. Stoic patriotism suited his temperament better than an antiwar march possibly could.

So in the battle over two rivers he loved, and in the larger environmental movement behind it, Richie Garrett's liberalism would find expression, fulfillment, and, finally, crushing failure. That night in February 1966 he could not possibly realize just how far these first stirrings of activism would carry him. But he did get one clue that he would be more than a mere bystander in history when the phone rang a few weeks later.

"Congratulations," Bob Boyle said.

"What are you congratulating me for?"

"You've been elected the first president."

"I can't handle that," Richie told him. "I'm just a gravedigger. I don't know if I'm capable."

"We're under the impression you're very capable," Boyle replied. "You know the river. Experience on the river is the greatest attribute to our cause." Then he paused, writer's brain searching for a phrase. "And we're going into conservation and recycling. That's what you do in the cemetery. Conserve and recycle."

• • •

Whatever St. Patrick's Day signified to the rest of Crotonville, green beer or the Manhattan parade or corned beef and cabbage at the American Legion post, it meant only one thing to Richie Garrett: Fishing season was under way, not as a matter of formal declaration but of hallowed tradition. The way most winters went, the last ice had gone out of the Hudson and Croton Rivers during the first days of March, and fish began biting perhaps two weeks later. St. Patrick's Day neatly conferred ceremony on nature.

Some fishermen would be calling the bait shops for bloodworms from Maine or prowling by flashlight for night crawlers. They might ply Croton Bay, where the water warmed soonest and the striped bass thronged. If the smelt were running, others would wade into the Croton River with their hip boots and dip nets. As for Richie and Augie, they knew a special spot a mile and a half upriver, way at the bottom of a gorge lined with oaks, locusts, and beeches. Years ago the wealthy had summered at an inn atop the northern palisade, and silent movies had passed off the granite cliffs and hardwood stands for Tarzan's Africa. Now it all belonged to Richie and Augie and the yellow perch, which were at their firmest and tastiest in the bracing waters of March.

Richie fished as usual on March 17, 1966. But on the night afterward, an uncommonly balmy night of southern breezes, excellent for catching smelt, he stood with scrubbed hands, groomed hair, and a church suit with pocket square at the podium of Parker-Bale Post 1597 to preside over the first public meeting of the Hudson River Fishermen's Association. On folding chairs before him sat sixty or seventy people, and between the rifle cabinets along the back wall leaned a dozen more.

From his singing career Richie knew how to hold a crowd, and he also knew the difference between being the headliner and the opening act. His brief words of introduction mattered less than his presence alone. It was no coincidence that Richie's more distinguished colleagues had selected him as their leader. Boyle was keenly aware that ridicule was one of the most effective weapons the environmental movement faced. He had heard Storm King's opponents disparaged as dilettantes more interested in trees and fish than in America's progress. Richie Garrett, incontestably earthy, vitiated that argument against the association. In time he would recruit members by the dozen from Crotonville, lathers and mill workers, roofers and housepainters, and the commercial fishermen he had known since childhood. Already he had opened Parker-Bale's doors to the association. Any foe would find it difficult to impugn the patriotism of a bunch of fishermen who met in an American Legion hall.

Richie surrendered the podium to Boyle, who in turn introduced the various founders of the association, each with his own specialty. The law professor talked about the harbor and refuse acts. The oceanographer spoke of the need for basic research into the Hudson's aquatic life. Then Dom Pirone, an entomologist by training, presented his slides. For half an hour snapshots flickered across the screen, showing sundry Pirone cousins landing stripers in the Hudson, chests puffed and backs arched as they brandished their catch. Frivolous as the slides seemed after the weighty matters of science and law, they documented an essential truth: The Hudson, black ink on the map notwithstanding, was still alive. And if it was alive, it was worth protecting.

That was where Dick Ottinger came in, literally and otherwise. In his off-the-rack suit, rumpled from trekking through five or six community meetings since lunch, he moved to the microphone. Although he was liberal, certainly more liberal than Crotonville as a whole, he faced an amenable crowd. John F. Kennedy was virtually worshiped in the neighborhood—his portrait hung downstairs in the Parker-Bale bar—

and Ottinger had served as one of his bright young men in the Peace Corps. With his lanky frame, high temples, and a stray strand of hair always drifting across his forehead, he resembled the slain president's brother Robert, now a senator from New York. Most of all, Ottinger had already proven himself an advocate for the Hudson. He had failed nobly at having a section of the river declared a national preserve, and still had a bill before Congress to put the entire waterway under the joint control of two states and the federal government, effectively diluting the power of both Nelson Rockefeller and Con Edison.

Rather than advancing his own agenda, though, Ottinger solicited his audience's. From the floor poured forth the tales of Indian Point, Storm King, Penn Central, fish kills, diesel oil, the expressway. "I'm working on an apartment house going up in Riverdale," said Jack Garrett, Richie's older brother, "and every day when I sit down for lunch on the sixteenth floor, I look down and what do I see but a lot of crap coming out of a pipe on the Harlem River. I want to throw up. Now who's putting this crud through that pipe and what can we do to stop it?"

Testy and raucous, these voices amounted to more than a gripe session. The men who fished for their livelihoods feared wholesalers would soon stop buying their shad, eels, and turtles, taken from such suspect waters. And recreation was too pallid a word for what the Hudson and Croton offered someone like Richie Garrett. Crotonville had no park, no playground, no Little League, and no money for resort vacations. It had two rivers. "Our Monte Carlo," Richie often put it. "Our Riviera."

Ottinger had budgeted ninety minutes for the meeting. He wound up staying past one in the morning, still fielding questions as he backed out the door. Tie loosened and collar unbuttoned, he steered his station wagon into the fog and toward Pleasantville, twenty minutes from Crotonville on the upscale side of the class divide. He drove, though, knowing he had bridged the difference. Richie agreed. He had found not only the central issue of his liberalism but a champion capable of articulating it on a national stage. He would never forget how Ottinger answered every last question from the fishermen, how he returned soon after to climb the steep streets of Crotonville, something no politician since Hugh Lavery had bothered doing, listening to beefs and shaking hands. The memory of those handshakes remained with Richie. Because Dick Ottinger, he knew, didn't have to shake anybody's hand, not with the family he'd come from.

• • •

By either nature or nurture, Richard L. Ottinger presented unlikely origins for a liberal Democrat. He was the son and nephew of Republicans, a rich boy reared with boarding school, riding lessons, and polo matches. His father made his fortune as the founder and president of a plywood company, touring his forests in vested suit and homburg. One uncle served New York State as a supreme court justice, another as attorney general before running for governor in 1928. And after Uncle Albert lost to Franklin Delano Roosevelt by 25,000 votes, a margin he attributed to Tammany Hall skulduggery, the very mention of the victor's name was banned from the Scarsdale mansion of Dick's childhood. The presidency did nothing to rehabilitate Roosevelt's image. In the Ottinger mind, the New Deal fairly reeked of socialism.

Through college at Cornell and law school at Harvard, through duty in the air force and seasoning in corporate law, Dick Ottinger continued to define himself as a Republican. Only when he moved to Pleasantville in 1957, at the age of twenty-eight, did he bridle at heritage. It happened after the town's Republican supervisor and chairman, in the course of a welcoming visit, reminded him that the tax assessor looked most unfavorably on homes owned by registered Democrats. So Ottinger became one, and shortly thereafter defeated the incumbent supervisor, launching his political career.

More than pique alone had stirred him to change parties. During his childhood he had heard even his father concede that government sometimes needed to intervene in private commerce on behalf of a societal good. The elder Ottinger, for instance, believed timber companies like his own should replace every tree they harvested, but he would only bear the cost if Washington required his competitors to behave similarly. From that example, Dick grew to see a role for an activist government in solving the social problems America was just rediscovering in the late 1950s, from rural poverty to urban blight. Seeking his own niche, Ottinger abandoned a lucrative legal partnership for the inglorious rank of contract officer in a foreign aid agency during the Eisenhower administration.

The position placed Ottinger in Washington with desirable expertise just as John F. Kennedy assumed office and was creating the Peace Corps. Ottinger helped shape the program and then directed several thousand of its volunteers in South America. So galvanized was he by the young president that for decades to come he hung beside his desk a copy of Kennedy's inaugural address with its famous admonition to "ask not what your country can do for you but what you can do for your country."

What Ottinger did was run for Congress in 1964. Seen logically, the candidacy appeared suicidal. The Twenty-fifth District, drawn from Westchester and Putnam Counties north of New York City, had never sent a Democrat to Congress. A three-term incumbent, Robert R. Barry, part of the Rockefeller family, was seeking reelection. Ottinger understood that he could not hope to unseat him by running as the social liberal he truly was. In a district where Democrats formed less than one-third the electorate, it behooved him to offer Republicans some reason to cross party lines.

He discovered it while poring over a map. From the industrial city of Yonkers to the commuter suburb of Tarrytown to the charming village of Cold Spring, the Twenty-fifth District shared only one element: the Hudson River. Ottinger had cherished its beauty since earning a Boy Scout merit badge for hiking the Croton Aqueduct, high on a ridge above the eastern shoreline. What stunned him as a candidate was learning how deeply working-class voters, people he associated with factories, taverns, and wakes, cared for the outdoors. That hike along the aqueduct, Ottinger would later realize, had taken him past Crotonville, a hundred feet from Richie Garrett's house.

Through luck and money, the river issue became his own. Luck arrived in the form of Mike Kitzmiller, a public relations man active in the Storm King dispute. Kitzmiller had shown a genius for attracting national media to the controversy with stunts like assembling an armada of fishing boats and pleasure craft to picket by water. In Ottinger, young, handsome, and energetic, he saw the person who could heighten the pressure on Con Edison by turning Storm King into a political issue. So completely did Ottinger grasp the cause that few voters ever realized Congressman Barry himself had taken part in the waterborne protest.

As for the money, Ottinger had plenty of that on his own. His family's foundation gave $20,000 to a professor of architecture at Columbia University who happened to be a friend of Ottinger's campaign manager. Under the pretext of objective scholarship, the professor and his students produced an elegant, full-color report on land use along the Hudson shoreline, showing how the present jumble of factories, tenements, and railroad rights-of-way could be transformed into public parkland. *The New York Times* trumpeted the report on its front page, inspiring editorials and essays that outdid themselves in lyrical tribute to the river. Charity thus benefited both public interest and self-interest. Ottinger had bought himself a platform.

He bought much more, spending the staggering amount of $193,000 on the campaign. In volley after volley of radio commercials, he returned to the plight of the river. One spot featured a fisherman reeling in his catch only to discover its tail had dissolved. "Why would our own incumbent Congressman vote over and over against pollution control?" asked the voice-over. Another advertisement, depicting Barry as the pawn of a reactionary fringe group called the Minutemen, provided an answer: Ruining the Hudson was a right-wing plot.

Only the presence of Barry Goldwater atop the Republican ticket let Ottinger dare such hyperbole. He tarred Barry with Goldwater's fervent conservatism, an ideology that distressed suburban New York's species of moderate, cosmopolitan Republicans. Dressed as nurses, Ottinger volunteers presented shoppers and commuters with bottles of candy pills to "cure the Barry-Barry disease." Raising another issue, Ottinger commercials lampooned Barry for maintaining only a motel room in the district while living in the California resort town of Rancho Mirage. "Richard L. Ottinger, the man from Pleasantville," one spot concluded. "He's proud to live among us."

On Election Day, Ottinger carried more than 55 percent of the vote, outpolling even Robert Kennedy. Goldwater or no Goldwater, residency issue or no residency issue, the new congressman would later say, "I swam into office on the waters of the Hudson River."

Once in Washington, Ottinger kept paddling. Mike Kitzmiller joined his staff with the charge of shaping legislation. At a time most freshmen were kowtowing to party elders, Ottinger introduced a bill placing any projects proposed for the Hudson in the next three years under the joint review of officials from New York, New Jersey, and the Interior Department. With the measure awaiting action in July 1966, he led a delegation of lawmakers on a six-hour cruise of the river, passing oil slicks, beer cans, frothing detergent, and dead fish. At one point the boat drew beside a huge drain pipe in Newburgh, and Kitzmiller announced, "That's pure sewage." To which an aide serving hors d'oeuvres replied, "Please, not while I'm passing meatballs."

Once again, The New York Times displayed an Ottinger gambit across its front page. With Robert Kennedy sponsoring the bill in the Senate, Congress enacted Public Law 89-605, better known as the Hudson River Compact, on September 26, 1966. The action came just in time for Ottinger's first reelection race.

Campaign literature listed the compact foremost among his accomplishments. Radio spots hailed him as "the man who's making the Hudson come clean." The congressman's wife, Betty Ann, wrote a book entitled, What Every Woman Should Know—and Do—About Pollution: A Guide to Good Global Housekeeping. The campaign even commissioned a theme song, set in a perfect bit of Zeitgeist to a Tom Lehrer tune.

If you sail from New York to Yonkers
You'll discover the industrial waste that conquers
Hold your nose, don't try to swim
'Cause you'll find that the Hudson
Is filled to the brim
With pollution, pollution
What're we gonna do?
Vote for Dick Ottinger
He'll clean it up for you.

In a midterm election dominated by a backlash against liberalism, with the Democratic Party losing forty-seven seats in the House while Ronald Reagan and Lester Maddox took governorships, Ottinger triumphed easily. Two years later, as Richard Nixon captured the White House, he won by his widest margin yet.

The essence of Ottinger's appeal, and its historical importance, lay in environmental issues. Like a handful of other national politicians, most notably Senators Gaylord Nelson of Wisconsin, Clinton Anderson of New Mexico, and Frank Church of Idaho, he recognized that concerns about pollution, conservation, and recreation transcended the traditional barriers of party and ideology. Which was hardly to say that environmentalism was an apolitical force. To the contrary, Ottinger and the others employed it to attract moderate and even conservative voters to a wider liberal agenda spanning civil rights, social programs, and opposition to the Vietnam War.

That effort marked a significant shift. It was a Republican president, Theodore Roosevelt, who had first elevated environmental issues to national prominence. Under the tutelage of Gifford Pinchot, a private forester turned activist bureaucrat, Roosevelt founded the U.S. Forest Service, expanded the national forest system to some 148 million acres, and began developing a system of wildlife refuges. A generation later the self-described "tree grower" Franklin Roosevelt incorporated environmental concerns into the New Deal. Working closely with Interior Secretary Harold Ickes and other New Dealers committed to conservation, Roosevelt formed the Civilian Conservation Corps, the Tennessee Valley Authority, and the Soil Conservation Service, and engineered the designation of millions of acres of federal land as national parks and monuments.

Still, environmentalism amounted to little more than a trace element in Democratic politics. The leading advocacy groups, from the Sierra Club to the Wilderness Society to the National Audubon Society, concentrated on preserving land and wildlife. Liberals of the postwar era, far from challenging the emerging consumer culture, prescribed economic growth as the cure to all social problems. Science and technology reigned as secular gods.

The concept of ecology began creeping into discussion with the posthumous publication of *A Sand County Almanac* by Aldo Leopold in 1949. "All ethics rest on a single premise," the professional forester and Wisconsin naturalist writes, "that the individual is a member of a community of interdependent parts." Then, in the summer of 1962, *The New Yorker* published excerpts from Rachel Carson's forthcoming book *Silent Spring*. A polemic underscored by fifty-five pages of references, *Silent Spring* painted a terrifying portrait of DDT and other toxic pesticides and insecticides infiltrating the food chain, poisoning even the milk of nursing mothers. Two senators and three representatives read portions into *The Congressional Record*, and the book soared onto best-seller lists. Inspired by Carson, millions of Americans began to question the consequences of progress.

These stirrings hardly occurred in isolation. The environmental movement, as it burgeoned, learned from the civil rights and antiwar campaigns. Gaylord Nelson, the architect of Earth Day, modeled it on antiwar "teach-ins." The Environmental Defense Fund and the Natural Resources Defense Council adopted the litigious tactics of the NAACP Legal Defense Fund. In its preference for direct action, Greenpeace borrowed Martin Luther King's methods of civil disobedience and nonviolent resistance. But more than specific techniques, the environmental movement shared with its companions an unsparing critique of America. As the journalist Philip Shabecoff writes:

> The links between the Earth Day activists and other causes of the 1960s, including the antiwar, civil rights, Native American rights, and feminist movements, were direct. Pollution and the exploitation of public resources to create private wealth were regarded as expressions of social inequity.

The environmental movement, however, held the political advantage of appearing more benign than the rest. It never rioted and looted, never occupied a college president's suite, and never declared one gender the oppressor. It wrapped itself in the virtues of clear water, clean air, and unspoiled land. Even its attacks on monopolies like Con Edison and the Penn Central touched the populist strains on both the left and the right.

Put another way, only by standing on a platform of environmentalism could Dick Ottinger have enjoyed the welcome he did on that

March night at Parker-Bale. The last time he had addressed an American Legion crowd, daring to denounce the House Un-American Activities Committee, he found himself instantly disinvited to a "Loyalty Day" parade. When he later debated a conservative congressman on the subversion issue, his staff feared enough for his safety to arrange police protection.

Yet Ottinger kept winning elections even as his own polling showed that 80 percent of his constituents opposed his dovish stance on the Vietnam War. In Crotonville, as accurate a barometer of blue-collar opinion as existed, he outdrew Hubert Humphrey in 1968 by a factor of 40 percent. And in no small measure his success both at the ballot box and on environmental issues depended on the Hudson River Fishermen's Association and Richie Garrett.

"He was a diamond in the rough," Ottinger later recalled of Richie. "The roughness was the blue-collar part. And the diamond was his dedication to the river." And each part enhanced the other. As Kitzmiller put it: "When we got a gravedigger on our side, the Hudson became a regular-people issue."

• • •

As his plane descended through the late morning haze of June 25, 1969, Richie Garrett pressed his face to the window and marveled at the ivory spear of the Washington Monument. Never before had he flown. Never before had he set foot in the capital. He was thirty-four years old, and until this moment Washington had existed for him only in memories of civics class, in the gray tones of newspaper photographs, and in the snapshot some couple from Crotonville took while motoring back from a honeymoon in Florida. Now he, "Harry Nobody," was coming to testify before Congress.

It was the latest proof of how drastically Richie's life had changed, of how much more deeply he was being drawn into activism. In just three years since that first night in Bob Boyle's house, the Hudson River Fishermen's Association had "mushroomed into an octopus," as Richie put it. The group claimed three hundred members, reached several times that many by newsletter, and espoused with equal vigor the joys of hooking stripers and polluters alike. Just recently, the group had distributed ten thousand copies of the harbor and refuse acts, inviting the general public to join in the bounty hunt.

When Richie picked up his phone, he often heard the whisperings of an informant. A voice at two in the morning from the Penn Central's maintenance shop reported, "We're gonna be dumpin' oil in half an hour." A trucker, hired to haul away a fish kill, tipped him off to its location. The mail spoke similarly. "Went fishing in the Croton River yesterday," one typical postcard said. "It was beautiful—*except* for pollution coming in hard below No. 66 Nordica Drive. Perhaps there is something that can be done to remedy this situation."

As president of the association, Richie provided its public face as well as its private ear. Armed with slides of oil slicks and endangered sturgeon, he carried the gospel of environmentalism from high school classes to yacht club luncheons to a German Catholic charity called the Kolping Society. He sat for interviews with the *Daily News, Reader's Digest,* and *Field and Stream,* and led journalists to the sites of illegal dumping and dredging. Johnny Carson invited him to describe the battle over the Hudson from the best-known couch in television. Concerned as only an Irishman could be with the sin of pride, Richie declined in favor of his new ally, the folksinger and radical Pete Seeger.

Washington, though, appealed to duty rather than ego. In an indulgence nearly as rare as flying, Richie hailed a cab for the ride from National Airport across the Potomac. On his lap lay the typewritten sheets of his statement, drafted over five or six nights with Bob Boyle. Outside the windshield, Washington was going to lunch, spilling from marble and granite quarters onto the sun-soaked green of the Mall. Richie could not help gaping like a tourist at the purposeful bustle of bureaucrats in poplin and seersucker, at the comely swish of career women in miniskirts.

For them this was a day without distinction. Thirty-one different committees and subcommittees were convening, taking up matters from Vietnamese refugees to coal mine safety to student extremism at an obscure Ohio university named Kent State. Warren Burger was presiding over the Supreme Court in his third day as chief justice, Earl Warren and his controversial liberalism having retired to California, and the Senate was debating how much money to allocate for food stamps.

The taxi left Richie outside the Longworth Office Building atop Capitol Hill. Ionic columns and neoclassical details aside, it was a punch line of a building, known among insiders for fitful elevators and stifling heat. Congressional freshmen who drew poor numbers in the lottery for office space resigned themselves to its upper floors, and panels without prestige conducted their business in its unadorned hearing rooms. In one of them, the House Subcommittee on Fisheries and Wildlife Conservation was preparing for its afternoon session.

Curiously, the place was packed, with perhaps seventy spectators and a contingent of press. Nothing in the official agenda seemed to merit such interest: The subcommittee was holding hearings into the effect of the proposed Hudson River Expressway on aquatic life. More important, what the nominal topic indicated was that Dick Ottinger was leading an insurrection of environmentalists against Nelson Rockefeller, billionaire governor and master builder.

Although Ottinger did not sit on the subcommittee, one of his closest friends in Congress chaired it. To much of the environmental movement, Congressman John Dingell of Michigan played the role of a predictable villain, defending the automobile industry against emission standards. Yet he himself hunted and fished, and he knew that many of the auto-workers in his district loved nothing more than pasting a trout decal on the pickup and fleeing the assembly line for a lake. And Dingell had the leverage to make his opinions matter: His subcommittee had drafted the Endangered Species Act and it controlled a share of the Interior Department's annual budget. Although Stewart Udall, the interior secretary, had already endorsed the Hudson River Expressway, he ignored the Dingell panel at his peril.

To defeat Rockefeller, Ottinger believed, it was essential to cast his highway not as a public improvement, not as a mother lode of jobs, but as the onerous imposition of an oligarch. The project, after all, had been approved first by New York State transportation officials who owed their appointments to Rockefeller and then by a regional planning commission chaired by his cousin. Ottinger had private correspondence, un-earthed in a related lawsuit, that revealed the degree of political incest. He had biologists and oceanographers prepared to testify that filling the shoreline would destroy spawning grounds and existing fisheries. He even had the president of the Ossining NAACP ready to testify that where the expressway was designed to return to dry land it would gouge a six-lane hole through the town's black neighborhood.

But it was Richie more than anyone else who had to fuse the issue of ecology with the issue of class, who had to play David to Rockefeller's Goliath. Heredity as well as history had prepared him for the role. The road Richie's father had driven decades earlier from San Juan Hill to Crotonville skirted the Rockefeller estate of Pocantico Hills, where family dictate kept it dark and thus treacherous. "Old John D," Edward would mutter. "He didn't want lights, so there aren't lights." Few campaign rituals maddened Richie more than the sight of Nelson Rockefeller slumming at a construction site. With delicious sarcasm, he mimicked the potentate pumping hands and rasping, "Hey, pal, how ya doin'?"

Now Richie settled into the witness chair, blinking back the flash-bulbs and then lifting his eyes to the lawmakers arrayed before him on a two-tier dais. He remembered all the hearings he had seen on television—the Kefauver committee, Army-McCarthy, and Bobby Kennedy sparring with Jimmy Hoffa—and realized they had looked exactly like this. The realization, far from intimidating him, brought a sense of honor. He still believed what he had learned about American democracy years ago in high school: An individual could make a difference; those men on the platform were public servants obligated to listen to him.

"I am simply just a citizen who grew up along the Hudson," Richie said at the outset. "I am glad to have the chance to speak before you, and to answer any questions you may wish to ask, because I care very much, as do many people, about what Governor Rockefeller and his highwaymen are planning to do to this wonderful river."

Richie talked about riding the turtle and seining bait as a boy. He talked about finding species from grass shrimp to sea sturgeon, fifty in all. He talked about the commercial fisherman who hauled in 8,000 pounds of bass in a single day. And he talked about the landfill and concrete Rockefeller intended to pour as far as a quarter mile into the fertile river.

"Are we, the people of the United States, to lose our fish because of a New York State highway?" he asked. "I guess so, if all goes to Governor Rockefeller's plans.

"This expressway, from what I can find out, was put over in a quickie bill passed by the state legislature. Nobody knew what was up, or what was to be filled in. As word leaked out, people raised hell, and then the state said it would make a landfill park next to the road.

"Park, shmark. Who wants a park with fishing piers when there won't be any fish?"

"Park, shmark." That grace note of slang and dismissal loosed Richie's temper. He bristled now with the scorn of underdog for top dog, an animosity bred over generations, vented most often in the Parker-Bale bar. The expressway had been "jobbed from start to finish." The state conservation department was "gutless" and "phony baloney." The commission led by Rockefeller's cousin, "a sad joke on the public if ever there was one," had perpetrated a "double shuffle." Richie stopped just short of emulating Bob Boyle, who had once slapped a dead striper across a congressman's desk.

Then, abruptly, he modulated his rage with sentimentality.

"People who love the Hudson," Richie told the subcommittee, "were supposed to take the count. I say no. Anything that Congress can do to stop New York from killing resources of the Hudson estuary will be like the Seventh Cavalry riding to the rescue on Saturday afternoon in the Victoria Theater in Ossining. You can do this, and I say that sincerely. . . . I am not a radical in asking for this. I am simply an American."

A few moments later Richie finished his prepared comments. Dingell did not excuse him, instead soliciting questions for him from the sub-committee. The chairman's intercession may not have appeared important, but in the subtext of a congressional hearing it sent a message. Even without a lobby behind him and a campaign contribution in his checkbook, Richie Garrett was to be taken seriously, not humored with the pretense of attention. In the end, it was he, not any of the congressmen, who had to leave in haste for a plane.

Richie could hardly take credit for killing the expressway project— a lawsuit involving an abstruse matter of dikes would ultimately do that —but he left a decided impression in Washington. The eighteen members of the panel, hailing from such distant states as Alaska, Minnesota, and Louisiana, may not have cared a whit about the Hudson. But they all cared about winning elections, and in Richie they had seen all the blue-collar voters who might be wooed with support for ecology. As John Dingell later exulted to Mike Kitzmiller, Ottinger's aide, "Where'd you get that guy? He's the salt of the earth."

The adventure in Washington, though, did cost Richie a fine afternoon of fishing. Late June was the time to cast for stripers off Croton Point or tramp through the marshes for soft-shell crabs or row into the reservoir for freshwater bass. Sure enough, as Richie's plane swept over the dammed lake on its approach to Westchester County Airport, he spotted a rowboat painted a familiar shade of lime green, with a lone angler aboard. That tiny figure was Augie Berg, as much of a landmark as the Washington Monument to Richie Garrett.

• • •

From the wheel of his Chevy Biscayne, a dinged and dented hand-me-down, Jack Garrett Jr. glanced at the jittery figure in the passenger seat, his uncle Richie. Out on the water, rod in hand, the man personified patience. Giving talks to outdoors clubs, he had always looked composed. Normally Richie would have savored a drive like this one, with the New York Thruway clear in the wake of rush hour and the trees just budding on the hills off either shoulder. So many times in childhood he had made a similar southbound trip to cheer his beloved Giants at the Polo Grounds.

Such pleasant memories receded at the moment. Never had Jack seen Richie so preoccupied, balling and spreading his hands, worrying the air like rosary beads. Once, twice, three times Richie read aloud the same lines from his speech, testing different cadences, asking Jack which sounded best. Should he keep the part about everybody getting in touch with nature? Boyle had cut it; maybe it should stay. What did Jack think?

What Jack thought was that it was lucky he had Wednesdays off from the post office because Richie was in no shape to drive. This particular Wednesday, April 22, 1970, was the first Earth Day, and Richie Garrett was to address the major rally in the largest city in the nation. In Union Square, where his mother had searched S. Klein's during the Great Depression for the bottommost prices of a bargain store, he would be sharing a podium with the prominent, the powerful, the entitled.

Exactly how this honor had befallen him remained something of a mystery. One day a few weeks earlier he had opened the mail to find a letter from Mayor John Lindsay of New York City, inviting him as president of the Hudson River Fishermen's Association to speak. The city and the group, it was true, had recently joined forces in the latest lawsuit against the Storm King plant. Like several other members of the association, Richie had become a regular visitor to the federal prosecutors based in Manhattan, whose territory included the Hudson Valley. The fishermen, in fact, had been bounty hunting with a vengeance.

Just six months earlier the association had collected half of the $4,000 fine that the Penn Central paid in pleading guilty to four counts of polluting the Hudson. Within a year the association would earn another $25,000 in a similar case brought against Anaconda Wire and Cable. Richie, Bob Boyle, and their network of environmental moles reported violators ranging from a battery manufacturer to a condominium complex to a Day Line tour boat. When the Penn Central persisted in dumping oil and faced renewed charges, Richie and Augie Berg walked a half mile along a trestle to the offending pipe, filled a jar with the discharge, and delivered it that same morning to a federal judge. The railroad ultimately signed a consent decree to avoid $75,000 in fines.

Almost as significant as the legal activity itself was the United States attorney who undertook it—Whitney North Seymour, a Republican who had been appointed by Richard Nixon. Seymour watched birds for a hobby and politics for a living, and he surely recognized the groundswell building for ecology. Nixon himself went on to create the Environmental Protection Agency and sign into law a half-dozen landmark pieces of legislation, foremost among them the Clean Air Act of 1970 and the Water Pollution Control Act of 1972. That a president without any prior zeal for environmental issues could cooperate with a hostile Congress on measures fettering private enterprise with government regulations showed that, at the very least, environmentalism had grown into a cause worth appropriating. Many conservatives and Republicans would later denounce the movement as excessive and absolutist, assailing exactly the type of aggressive litigation practiced by the fishermen's association, but for the historical moment they feared abdicating environmentalism to liberal Democrats. They had made that mistake twice already, with Social Security and civil rights.

Earth Day, beyond its educational mission, intended to be a show of political force. Richie Garrett hardly needed Seymour or Nixon as examples of the people ecology had won over. Right next to him in the Chevy sat an even more familiar one. Outraged by race riots and indignant at pressure on trade unions to integrate, especially on the lathers' local he had expected to enter, Jack Garrett had cast the first presidential vote of his life in 1968 for George Wallace. Then, in the very next moment, he had pulled the congressional lever for Dick Ottinger.

But if Richie wanted to tell any story in his brief time at the national pulpit, to invoke anyone's experience as a parable, it was his own. The environmental movement had converted him, if not from conservatism, then from isolation and pessimism. "I feel like *Mr. Smith Goes to Washington.*" He had written that sentence in an early draft of the speech, then surrendered it to Boyle's red pencil. Redundant, the journalist had insisted; the point was already clear. Richie hoped Boyle had been right. He would find out soon enough.

Jack pulled off the East River Drive and picked his way to a coffee shop on the perimeter of Union Square. There Richie met one of Mayor Lindsay's aides for coffee and final preparations. He wanted to know where exactly he would be speaking. What theater or auditorium was being used? None, the aide told him, the rally would be held outdoors, in Union Square Park. There was talk the crowd might hit 100,000. Richie's brain went blank with terror and awe.

For now, Fourteenth Street resembled its usual mercantile self, with buses and delivery trucks honking away, subways rattling into the cavernous station, and customers pursuing candy or loans or used books. Once Richie entered the park, though, he could tell an extraordinary event was unfolding. Schoolgirls had filled one entire corner with trays of geraniums and African violets. Tie-dyed banners, each a sunburst of color, fluttered from flagpoles. Atop a flatbed truck sprawled a "junk sculpture" of hubcaps, ice-cube trays, and traffic signs, all overseen by a mannequin wearing a gas mask.

As Jack broke away to find a vantage point for watching the speeches, the Lindsay aide led Richie into a holding area behind the stage. Suddenly he stood among the famous. Several cast members from *Hair,* the hippie musical basking in vogue on Broadway, escorted Richie onto the platform. He dropped into his chair, flanked by two unrelated Moores, the singer Melba and the game-show host Garry. Farther along sat others who would orate or entertain, from Leonard Bernstein to Pete Seeger, Margaret Mead to Arthur Godfrey. From his perch twenty feet above the park, Richie peered into the crowd. At first he could spot gaps, pieces of grass or sidewalk; then, as the noon start drew nearer, humanity pressed into every cavity. People balanced on fire hydrants, shimmied up lampposts, hoisted themselves into trees.

Edgily, Richie awaited his turn, third in a lengthy program. Then Garry Moore motioned and guided him to the wooden podium, its several microphones wound with daisies. And from that promontory, Crotonville regarded Woodstock. Keep your cool, Richie told himself, keep your cool. Through the mantra he heard a voice bellowing, "Richie! Hey, Richie!" Squinting into the noontime sun, and training his eyes left and right, he found a pair of waving arms. Attached to them was a fisherman from New Jersey, name of DiBlasio, who had just joined the association. Buttressed by the sight, Richie straightened the pages before him and began.

"God bless you all for being here today," he said. "My name is Richie Garrett, and I am president of the Hudson River Fishermen's Association. The association includes all sorts of members—writers, marine scientists, housewives, interested kids, commercial fishermen, and people who give a damn." He gave his best toastmaster's pause. "I happen to be a cemetery superintendent in Ossining, and I'm told I was elected because I'm the last guy to let anyone down."

A Borscht Belt dish served to Firesign Theater palates, the joke stirred only scattered laughs. Richie turned serious.

"I've missed a few opportunities in my life," admitted the man who had aspired to a life of nightclubs and ballads. "But I can't say that I regret it, because about a half-dozen years ago I got seriously involved in conservation, the environment. Since then, fighting for the Hudson River, I have felt completely fulfilled. The Hudson is my life. I'm not involved in fighting the dope problem or the crime problem. There's only so much of me to go around. But the way I figure it, clean water and clear air—a clean earth—is the most important issue of all. If you don't have a clean earth, there's no point in doing anything else. You might as well open up all the prisons and let everybody out so we can all choke to death together."

Richie's eyes rested on a passage he had been agonizing over all morning. Somehow he had wanted to raise the issues polarizing America, to offer environmentalism as a unifying cause. Boyle thought it unwise to remind an audience of all that divided it. Why jostle a bandwagon everybody was clamoring to board? Long slashes of red pencil, Boyle's handiwork, pierced the next several lines. Along the left margin, Richie had answered back in block letters, "TO STAY." So it did.

"Our country has its problems," Richie said. "Black versus white, hawk versus dove—you name it, we got it. But unless we can get in tune with the world again, put ourselves in touch with nature, nothing will ever be solved. Black or white, hawk or dove, we'll all drown in garbage up to our eyeballs.

"You can do the job. In fact, I know damn well you can. The fact that I'm up here speaking to all of you shows that a persistent voice can be heard. If anyone had told me five years ago, or even last year, that I'd be speaking here like this in Manhattan, I'd tell them they were out of their mind.

"Now that I'm here, let me tell you how to go about it to be effective. To start, do what you think you can do, and be honest. Sure, I want to save the world, but I've picked out a small marvelous piece of it to save, the Hudson River Valley, from the Adirondacks to New York Harbor. That's no small job—because every rotten thing that is being done to this country today is being done to the Hudson, times ten."

Richie recounted the battles against Con Edison, the Penn Central, and Nelson Rockefeller. He saluted Dick Ottinger and thanked God for the federal courts and declared, "You can whip Albany and shove the decisions right down their bumbling bureaucratic throats." Not even when a banner tore loose from the stage and blew onto him did Richie falter. He just shed the sign and ad-libbed, "That's how air pollution gets started."

From the crowd, Jack Garrett gazed up at his uncle in admiration. Not a shred of anxiety showed—no flapping hands, no awkward silences. These hippies with their peace signs and clenched-fist salutes loved having big business get smacked around, it seemed to Jack, and not even the suit-and-tie types amid them could work up much compassion for a commuter railroad that ran notoriously late and a utility company responsible for New York's infamous 1965 blackout. But Richie was doing more than preaching to the choir. What he exuded, and Jack could tell from the applause around him, was authenticity, something genuine on a day with its share of radical chic. Bob Boyle had been right to excise the line about Mr. Smith. Jimmy Stewart could only play at being the person Richie Garrett truly was.

"You have to get involved," Richie said, his seven-minute speech drawing to an end. "It's necessary that *you* get involved. One organization can't do it alone. Call your Congressman. Call your Senator. You can't wait until tomorrow. Today is the day we start. You're not just saving the river. You're saving your own lives."

Richie stood at the microphone, feeling a thunder of applause. Then he backed into his seat and heard Melba Moore blurt, "Jesus, that's powerful stuff you have there."

"It's the truth," Richie said. "It's all documented."

After several more speeches an intermission arrived, and Richie used it to politely escape. He said no thanks to a reception at Gracie Mansion, the mayor's residence, and to a night's free lodging in a Manhattan hotel. Instead, he and Jack found a saloon and drank a few beers as much in relief as celebration. Driving back to Crotonville, they switched the radio to the New York Mets, heirs to the old Giants. Tom Seaver was striking out nineteen that afternoon. Only the next morning did Richie begin to comprehend that he, in some way, had made even bigger news.

Fully 100,000 people, it turned out, had passed through Union Square Park during the course of Earth Day. Mayor Lindsay and some 200,000 more had strolled a section of Fifth Avenue that was converted for several hours into a pedestrian mall. A crowd of 25,000 gathered outside Independence Hall in Philadelphia, where a billboard carried the text of an ecological "Declaration of Interdependence," and 10,000 attending an outdoor rock concert in Washington received commemorative litter bags. Ten million students, *The New York Times* estimated, attended ecology teach-ins around the country. By *Newsweek*'s reckoning, more Americans took to the streets for Earth Day than for any event since the Japanese surrender ending World War II.

Philip Shabecoff would later call Earth Day "the day environmentalism in the United States began to emerge as a mass social movement." But it was something larger still. More than the civil rights movement's March on Washington in 1963, more than the antiwar moratorium in 1969, Earth Day proved the ultimate expression of liberal synergy. If environmentalism could awaken a dormant liberal like Richie Garrett, attract a conservative like his nephew Jack, and erect alliances with a president as disdainful of protest politics as Richard Nixon, then it could drive the American center significantly to the left.

Nowhere did the evidence of realignment appear more irrefutable than in the Senate race just then unfolding in New York State, a race that included Richie Garrett's political hero, Dick Ottinger.

• • •

One Sunday evening two months after Earth Day, as the candidates seeking the Democratic nomination for Senate clashed in a debate, Dick Ottinger found himself being pilloried for a statement he had once made about the Vietnam War. The offending comment was not, as might have been supposed, Ottinger's call for Lyndon Johnson to stop bombing North Vietnam and seek a negotiated settlement. Nor was it his endorsement of a Viet Cong role in forming a new government in South Vietnam, or even his warning that the size of the American military was threatening to transform the United States into a "national security state." No, what infuriated Ottinger's opponents was a 1965 speech in which he had criticized antiwar protesters.

"I don't know the speech," Ottinger responded, and one of his foes proceeded to open the 1965 edition of *The Congressional Record* to page 27,895. Indeed Ottinger had described a particular protest as "a shocking spectacle . . . demonstrating incredible ignorance about the situation in Vietnam," and gone on to say, "If these young demonstrators really want the fighting to end, they should take their placards and signs to Communist capitals." Rather than defend his words and portray himself as the enemy of all extremism, Ottinger complained, "It sounded simply out of context."

That exchange typified the campaign, one being fought so far to the left that the political center went unguarded. The seat at hand had belonged to Robert Kennedy until his assassination in 1968. Over the decades New York had sent to Washington such renowned liberals as Robert Wagner Sr., Herbert Lehman, and Jacob Javits. Within the Democratic Party, Ottinger faced Paul O'Dwyer, the architect of the antiwar New Democratic Coalition, and Theodore Sorensen, a speech-writer for John F. Kennedy and the director of Robert's presidential campaign. Whoever triumphed in the Democratic primary would confront the Republican incumbent, a born-again liberal named Charles Goodell. Appointed to serve out Kennedy's unexpired term, Goodell had thrown off his prior conservatism to condemn both President Nixon and the Vietnam War, even writing a book about dissidents with the inflammatory title *Political Prisoners in America*.

There was another candidate, William F. Buckley Jr.'s brother James, representing the Conservative Party. Any sensible politician or thoughtful journalist should have remembered that in another three-way Senate race just two years earlier Buckley had polled 1.1 million votes while spending only $115,000. In Crotonville, for instance, he had drawn nearly one-quarter of the vote against Javits and O'Dwyer. But for months after Buckley entered the 1970 campaign both the media and his potential opponents persisted in treating him as a sideshow, a protest candidate on the fringe, bereft of the money and organization a major party could supply.

Instead, the attention focused on Ottinger's victory in the Democratic primary, Goodell's successful pursuit of the Liberal Party endorsement, and the resulting pageant of left-wing one-upsmanship. Ottinger and Goodell espoused nearly identical positions, from decrying the use of Agent Orange in Vietnam to recommending diplomatic recognition of the People's Republic of China to reproving the "excessive" bail ordered for thirteen Black Panthers awaiting trial in New York. Straining to uncouple from his Siamese twin, Ottinger insisted he had opposed the Vietnam War first, at a time Goodell "was talking about bombing Haiphong Harbor and building and using lithium bombs."

Yet events suddenly favored a conservative. Barely one week after Earth Day, with its aura of liberal harmony, American forces invaded Cambodia, fissuring the home front as never before. During the subsequent wave of campus demonstrations across the country, National Guard troops shot dead four students at Kent State. National sympathies might well have attached to the antiwar movement had not its most radical elements chosen with their own violence to "bring the war home." In the late summer of 1970 a physicist at the University of Wisconsin died in the bombing of a military research facility. During the first ten months of 1970 police in New York City dealt with 8,700 bombings or bomb threats. Just two days before the Senate election, officers raided three "bomb factories" maintained by the Weathermen, an underground offshoot of the Students for a Democratic Society.

James Buckley prepared to collect the electoral benefits of popular revulsion at the violence. And his good fortune was no accident. The man directing his campaign, political consultant F. Clifton White, had been anticipating the backlash against liberalism for nearly a decade. Beginning in 1961, White launched and led a conservative revolt within the Republican Party, delivering the presidential nomination to Barry Goldwater in 1964. Four years later White managed Ronald Reagan's belated campaign for the presidency and very nearly snatched the GOP's nomination away from Richard Nixon.

Along the way, White paid special attention to cultivating estranged Democrats, particularly those with union cards and immigrant pasts. He pressed the Goldwater campaign to produce a half-hour commercial that would capitalize on such voters' fears of social disorder. Entitled *Choice,* the film juxtaposed scenes of race riots and street crime against those of children saluting the flag and lumberjacks clearing land, leaving no doubt as to which version of America was the fault of indulgent liberalism. As White wrote in a campaign memo to Goldwater:

THE BIG ISSUE . . . IS THE MORAL CRISIS IN AMERICA TODAY. It is made up of several components: crime, violence, riots (the backlash), juvenile delinquency, the breakdown of law and order, immorality and corruption in high places, the lack of moral leadership in government, narcotics, pornography—*it all adds up to the picture of a society in decay.* . . . This issue—morality—can be the [equivalent of the] "missile gap" of 1960. . . .

Every day the front pages of the nation's newspapers are filled with stories of crime and violence—ranging from rape to riots, from juvenile delinquency to embezzlement. We have, in fact, the built-in, national reservoir of hundreds of millions of dollars worth of publicity working for us.

Initially the approach seemed a monumental failure. Goldwater himself ordered *Choice* off the air as "nothing but a racist film." By most obvious measures, the 1964 election delivered a crushing blow to conservatism. But in the 1966 midterm elections, the Democrats lost forty-seven seats in the House of Representatives and Ronald Reagan swept into the governorship of California on a million-vote margin. Two years later the combined support for Richard Nixon and George Wallace left Hubert Humphrey with just 43 percent of the popular vote.

So when James Buckley first considered entering the 1970 Senate race, F. Clifton White commissioned an opinion poll from a consultant normally hired by Democrats. The results showed the party alienating its blue-collar voters on issues such as crime, patriotism, and campus protests. Throughout the race that followed, Buckley voiced unstinting support for the war and unceasing contempt for student demonstrators. The Buckley campaign targeted its advertising at ethnic voters, especially Catholics, buying time on television's *Dean Martin Show* and radio broadcasts of Notre Dame football games. For his symbol, the candidate adopted the American flag.

Only belatedly did the Ottinger camp recognize that Buckley could attract a sizable plurality of voters, that in a three-way race not even New York had enough liberals to go around. With this realization, Ottinger faced the conundrum that liberal Democrats increasingly would in the years ahead: How do you win the middle from the left? How do you run against your own record? During three terms in Congress, Ottinger had tried to characterize himself as a "social liberal and fiscal conservative." But the definition would not bear scrutiny. Most of the billions of dollars that Ottinger crowed about cutting from the federal budget had been earmarked for the military. While calling for "welfare reform," he objected to workfare. His own polling indicated that voters disagreed more strongly with his opposition to the death penalty than even with his stand on Vietnam.

The solution was to "sterilize me," as Ottinger himself later put it. In a strategy shaped with his campaign manager, Stephen Berger, and his media consultant, David Garth, Ottinger tried to occupy the electoral center by dodging controversial issues and direct confrontation. He avoided attacking Buckley for fear of legitimizing him and Goodell for fear of antagonizing potential voters. Even as Ottinger's campaign developed position papers on topics ranging from mass transit to health care, it stressed pragmatism in the slogan "Ottinger Delivers," broadcast as incessantly as several million dollars of family wealth would allow. So ubiquitous were the advertisements that a cartoon of a slumbering man in *The New Yorker* carried the punch line, "The following dream is a paid political dream brought to you by Citizens for Ottinger." More seriously, Tom Buckley wrote in *The New York Times* that Ottinger, "finding himself flanked by the Galahads, or Don Quixotes, of the far right and antiwar left, had been waging an extremely cautious middle-of-the-road campaign."

Environmentalism provided the single exception. A genuine issue and yet a safe one, it could establish Ottinger as an idealist without restricting his appeal to the left. With a constituency that stretched across lines of social class and political persuasion, the Hudson River Fishermen's Association set out to make the case. Bob Boyle spoke on Ottinger's behalf from the Audubon Society to the Junior League, from Vassar College to the American Museum of Natural History. The association paid to reprint and distribute an encomium to Ottinger from the outdoors reporter for an upstate newspaper. And Richie Garrett spent eight months writing letters to the editor, orating in Parker-Bale, and appearing in commercials. Long after the election, one of those commercials would persist for Richie as the proof of Ottinger's unrewarded decency.

It was a television spot, filmed very early in the primary campaign. Richie could recall the date easily enough—March 15, 1970—because his father had died the previous night. He had just taken his mother, Lizzie, to the hospital to claim the body before meeting Ottinger near the Penn Central maintenance shop. With a film crew following, the two men walked along the tracks, pointing together to the pipe that disgorged oil. Then they trod the banks of the Croton River, dyed black by the discharge. Although their own voices were not heard in the finished commercial, which was narrated by entomologist Dom Pirone, a viewer was meant to assume they were speaking about pollution.

Actually the men had been talking about Edward Garrett, and the mourning showed in the pouches under Richie's eyes and the furrows crossing his forehead. The congressman had met Edward only once or twice, fleetingly, and wanted to know something of his substance. Of all the stories Richie could possibly share, about six brothers with one suit in San Juan Hill or hiking to White Plains in search of work or the cellar party after Jack came home from the war, he reached for what felt most intimate and proprietary of all, the nicknames. Others might have

called his father Eddie Rock or Digger but only Richie knew him as
Zeke and Zig. "So long, Zig," Richie had whispered to him at the end.

"I realize what you're doing today isn't what you should be doing,"
Ottinger had said as they walked along the trestle. "I know where your
heart is."

"It's all right," Richie answered. "We have plenty of people there."

"If there's anything anyone in your family needs . . ."

Richie turned down the offer, and when Ottinger repeated it in a
condolence card he turned it down again. All that mattered to him was
the gesture itself.

Ottinger could hardly expect 7.9 million voters spread over 49,576
square miles to appreciate his humanity as Richie did. He was running
an electronic campaign, after all, one bent on proving he was not a
"fuzzy-minded do-gooder," as the candidate himself put it to an AFL-
CIO audience. But he never anticipated that the commercial might back-
fire, that at the time environmentalism seemed most inviolate it could
be generating a counteraction. That force expressed itself in two ways.
First, it declared environmentalism guilty by association of being part of
a larger liberal agenda of social revolution. Second, and more specifically, it framed environmental regulation not as the enemy of imper-
sonal, unloved big business but of blue-collar, industrial workers.

For both those reasons, organized labor maintained a chilly distance
from Ottinger. The state AFL-CIO withheld its endorsement of the Democrat until three days before the election, and the Westchester County
Building and Construction Trades Council backed him only with stated
misgivings. The deadlock in building the Storm King hydroelectric plant,
one of Ottinger's proudest achievements, was depriving the Hudson
Valley of 1,500 construction jobs. One of the council's members warned
Ottinger, "Those damn fish, they don't vote." The same argument
emerged more formally in the ongoing litigation against the Penn Central, another linchpin of Ottinger's record as an environmentalist. The
railroad went bankrupt in June 1970, and its chief attorney in the pollution case seized the occasion to pit ecology against economy:

> As plaintiff has chosen to cast the matter, all comes to a simple, irreduc-
> ible basic tenet: the cause of the Bald Eagle and the Herring Gull and
> the like must and should and shall have precedence in call upon the
> tenuous resources of the defendant rail carrier in bankruptcy, barely
> surviving in its desperate efforts . . . to maintain essential public trans-
> portation services needful for the economy of over one-quarter of
> these United States. I submit that the Orwellian order of priorities . . .
> is most illogical and captious.

Ultimately, the president of the state building-trades council endorsed Buckley. So did unions representing New York City's police officers, firefighters, and longshoremen. Since cops were forbidden by law to take part in political campaigns, the Buckley operation developed a mailing list of their wives. The candidate indulged his labor supporters by rarely mentioning his support for right-to-work legislation.

In Crotonville, precisely the type of community Ottinger needed to capture, Richie as his surrogate endured the blue-collar discontent. A local grocer, writing to the *Citizen Register,* labeled Richie a "red herring." Around the American Legion hall people dubbed him "Senator Clearwater." When he began to speak they cried, "Get off the soapbox, you phony bastard." There was, in all the gibes, a superficial humor, an aspect of deflating the lofty. Richie prided himself on answering in kind, informing the newspaper, for instance, that of all the species of herring he had ever found in the Hudson not one was red. But he knew a true rage was loose. He could hear it in a new kind of midnight phone call, not from informers tipping him off to pollution but from anonymous enemies who hissed, "Cut the shit out, you goddamn pinko."

Vulnerable as Dick Ottinger was, attacked alternately for being too liberal and not liberal enough, he entered October 1970 clinging to the lead. A poll in the *Daily News* gave him 35 percent of the vote to 28 for Buckley and 16 for Goodell, with 21 undecided. As Stephen Berger read the situation, if Ottinger could hold onto his traditional base among blacks, Jews, and liberals, and win just a smattering of "hard hats, ethnics, upstate conservatives" then he could reach the 40 percent threshold practically required to win.

Reality, however, refused to subscribe to plan. President Nixon declined to issue even a pro forma endorsement of Goodell, freeing Republicans to vote for Buckley. Spiro Agnew, the vice president, reviled Goodell as a "radical liberal" who had "strayed beyond the point of no return," "the Christine Jorgensen of the Republican Party." The Swedish transsexual demanded an apology, but Goodell owed Agnew thanks. Already Goodell had nurtured the image of a maverick, a man above mere partisan allegiance. Now he ranked as a certifiable liberal martyr, impaled alongside the "nattering nabobs of negativism," "pusillanimous pussyfooters," and other Agnewian demons.

With his consciously tepid campaign, Ottinger could hardly compete, especially in the romantic precincts of the left. *The New York Times* conferred its coveted endorsement on Goodell, citing his superior "leadership" in the liberal causes it admitted he had only recently taken up. The feminist leader Gloria Steinem patronized Ottinger with faint praise in *New York* magazine, the very almanac of trendiness. "Ottinger is that magical thing to reformers," she acknowledged. "He is Right on the Issues. That is, he has voted well or taken good public positions on everything from ecology to civil rights. Furthermore, he has an enormous capacity for hard work and an obvious will to win." The rub, then, was "character." In Steinem's view, Ottinger bore no small share of the blame for the protracted war in Vietnam. "I wonder where we'd be today," she approvingly quoted an unnamed antiwar leader as saying, "if Democrats like Ottinger had shown the kind of leadership against Johnson that Goodell has had the courage to show against his party's leader?" To that dubious argument Steinem added a second. Instead of spending $5 million of family money on his own campaign, Ottinger should have endowed other liberal candidates. He paid his campaign workers too much; he ran too many "slickly packaged" commercials.

The allegation of buying office had, in fact, dogged Ottinger from his very first race for Congress, when he circumvented campaign finance laws by funneling contributions from his relatives into twenty-two different committees. Certain liberals, clearly including Steinem, never forgave him for outspending his opponents in the Senate primary seven to one. Still, a historian would be hard-pressed to find a better example of the American left's capacity for self-destruction than in its sniping at Ottinger. Few observers doubted that, numerically speaking, he was the candidate most capable of defeating Buckley. Yet at the point in late October when Goodell was teetering on the verge of withdrawal, he gained enough support at Ottinger's expense to convince himself to remain in the race.

On October 25, only nine days before the election, the *Daily News* reflected the impact in its latest poll. James Buckley now led with 37 percent to 30 for Ottinger and 24 for Goodell, with only 9 percent left undecided. An opinion survey in the *Times* brought Ottinger news that was still worse. Of all the issues, the one that had surged in importance during the campaign was crime, arguably Buckley's strongest point and undeniably Ottinger's weakest.

In one final reversal of strategy, the Ottinger campaign tried to turn aggressive. Berger even insulted the candidate just before press conferences, hoping to kindle an anger for the public to see. But Ottinger, so convincing in personal encounters, lacked the bold emotions and physical presence that make for public charisma. Far from delivering blows, he spent the last days reeling from Buckley's, fending off charges he supported the Black Panthers and Students for a Democratic Society, all the "anarchists and barbarians pulling down a civilization they never could have constructed." For public consumption Berger predicted a narrow victory; privately he readied the flag of surrender.

In a turnout that approached three-quarters of all registered voters, a stunning figure outside a presidential election, Buckley won with a plurality of 39 percent, finishing two percentage points and 117,000 votes ahead of Ottinger. Goodell took precisely the 24 percent the *Daily News* had forecast. Predictably, many liberals ascribed Buckley's victory to the curious geometry of a three-way race, just as they would a decade later when Alfonse D'Amato defeated Jacob Javits and Elizabeth Holtzman for New York's other Senate seat. In both instances, these liberals were practicing dangerous self-delusion. Buckley virtually doubled his vote from 1968 to 1970; he attracted so much money he actually outspent Ottinger in the closing weeks. Most of all, his victory argued that the sort of conservative once considered unelectable for national office —Ronald Reagan, for instance—could annex enough of the electoral center to win. "I am," Buckley declared in victory, "the new politics."

In Crotonville, Richie Garrett spent the early evening of Election Day working at the dining-room table, updating records for the cemetery, mapping out a new section, and scheduling a few events for the fishermen's association. Then, as the returns began to come in, he repaired to the easy chair and television in the living room. He went to bed knowing Ottinger was trailing and awoke to hear confirmation of defeat on the radio. For a moment he remembered the sight of Ottinger stumping in Westchester late in the campaign, willing himself to work the crowd, his face limp and sallow. How many thousands of hands, Richie wondered, must he have shaken?

"They didn't quite listen," he told his wife, Gloria, and then he drove off to the cemetery. Perhaps, though, it was Richie and his hero who had not listened to the rumblings all around, the plate tectonics of political realignment. James Buckley carried Crotonville, exactly doubling his vote total from the 1968 election, while Dick Ottinger lost one-third of his support. And the phenomenon was hardly exclusive to Richie Garrett's corner of the world.

Across Westchester, in New Rochelle, Frank Trotta Sr. and his wife, Lorraine, had shown up at Trinity Episcopal Church at five-thirty in the morning, a half hour before the polls opened, to cast their precinct's first votes of the day. Both went to James Buckley. On the midnight shift that night, Lorraine picked up scraps of results from a radio in the switchboard operators' bathroom. Frank Jr., given special dispensation to stay up late on a school night, rushed to the local Conservative Party headquarters to celebrate.

One hundred forty miles upstate, Jack and Vilma Maeby disagreed yet again. Their son had just turned eighteen, and Vilma vowed that if he drew a low number in the draft lottery she would drag him to Canada herself. In the meantime, she went to Goodrich Elementary School and voted for Charles Goodell, the embodiment of her antiwar sentiments. Jack felt no less dreadful about sending his son off to Vietnam. But he could support the war if the United States would simply start fighting to win, and he loathed the student protesters he saw "performing" every night on the news. On his way to the Montgomery Ward warehouse, he stopped to vote for Buckley, and on CBS that night Walter Cronkite told him he had not been alone.

Along with the campaign, so ended fishing season for Richie Garrett. Autumn was chilling the Croton and Hudson Rivers, and soon the striped bass would descend to the bottom, lying motionless until spring. Some weekend soon, Richie would store his rods in the cellar and pull his boats onto high land. In a few weeks he could start hunting deer.

By the time the next St. Patrick's Day arrived, and Richie and Augie headed for their favorite spot, one part of his life had changed forever. Never again would Richie commit himself to the hurly-burly of politics, not even when Bob Boyle asked if he wanted to run for Dick Ottinger's old seat in Congress. "Not qualified," Richie answered. The next politician in the Garrett clan, Richie's nephew Tim Carey, was then three years out of the army, attending community college, and registered as a Democrat, at least for the moment.

Part Three

Counter-revolution

Chapter Twelve

Uncle Paulie's Porch
(Frank Trotta Jr.)

FOR MOST OF THE 1960S, THE DECADE WHEN FRANK TROTTA Jr. grew from childhood toward maturity, his favorite uncle lived just two doors down Birch Street on New Rochelle's South Side. Paul Trotta shared a tall frame house faced with asphalt shingles with eight relatives spread across three generations. More precisely, he shared a kitchen and office and workshop off the basement with his brothers, Dominic and Danny. All were bachelors. All were veterans of World War II. It showed.

Above a dartboard on one wall hung the Nazi helmet Paul had brought back from Germany. Cases of beer stood stacked in a corner; sodas and candy bars filled a refrigerator. The unmoving air smelled of wine fermenting in wooden casks and oil coating tools against rust. Just outside the basement door lay what the uncles called their porch, a concrete patio that opened onto Grandfather Giuseppe's tomato patch. Most of the day it belonged only to the brothers' dogs, Dukie and Bucky.

On summer nights Frank would drift to the porch after dinner, toss a tennis ball against the side of the house, and wait for his uncles to finish their meal. Danny was courtly but quiet. Dominic always had a gripe, about taxes or politics or how his finger still ached from when a radio fell on it during the war. But Uncle Paulie would offer Frank peanuts and a Coke, or pay him fifty cents to wash the new Dodge, or even take him to the Bronx Zoo.

Best of all, Paulie would settle onto a porch chair beside the boy and tell war stories, war stories the equal of anything on Frank's favorite television show, *Combat*. During the Battle of the Bulge he had driven supplies to the front with the famous Red Ball Express. At one point the Germans had trapped him and the troops he provisioned for three days. Liberated by American bombers, Paulie and the rest rolled toward Berlin, and it was during the furious pursuit of Hitler that his signature tale was set.

As Paulie conjured the scene for his rapt nephew, Dominic and Danny rolled their eyes and moaned, *"Stunad."* Literally this bit of dialect translated as "out of tune," but colloquially, as they intended, it meant, "He's like a broken record." Surely the brothers were bored after twenty years of hearing those same lines—"I mouthed off to the Jerries and they hit me with the gun butt," "I fired that BAR till it felt like my arms and legs were flying in the breeze." But perhaps they were jealous, too. Danny had operated radar in the Aleutians and Dominic had repaired equipment in the rear echelon with the Signal Corps; neither had a saga to compare with Paulie's, much less a Bronze Star and citation to prove it:

> While on a mission deep inside Germany, Corporal Trotta and several other drivers of a convoy were ambushed by a German patrol and taken prisoner. After a brief but vigorous battle a number of his comrades were wounded but Corporal Trotta maintained a cool head and sought a means of escape. Seizing an abandoned Browning Automatic Rifle when the guard of the German patrol momentarily relaxed his vigil, Corporal Trotta employed it on the German party and quickly disorganized the enemy control and led his comrades to freedom. The intrepidity, leadership and devotion to duty displayed by this courageous soldier set a sterling example for his comrades and reflect great credit upon himself and the armed forces.

Frank responded not only to the heroism but to the way Paulie wore it. Paulie never bothered much with the American Legion or the Veterans of Foreign Wars, never felt compelled to make a public display of his valor. Neither did he carry any psychic residue from the war, not shell shock or even bad dreams. The very day in 1945 he had burst through the front door in an Ike jacket and combat boots, he simply lit up a Camel and launched into a story for the benefit of a few nephews. From that afternoon to the evenings Frank spent in his thrall a generation later, Paulie had remained content to drive a delivery truck for Coca-Cola and know that a few moments on a roadside in Germany had defined his life.

Beneath the surface Paulie's military service conveyed an even more powerful message. On the eve of World War II the prospect of American intervention had split Italian immigrant communities bitterly. Taking arms against Nazi Germany meant taking arms against its fascist ally, Mussolini's Italy. When Mayor Fiorello La Guardia of New York condemned the dictator in 1941, he lost half the Italian vote in a reelection race. Even during the war families in New Rochelle sympathized sufficiently with the Italian prisoners of war confined at Fort Slocum, a base just offshore in Long Island Sound, to host them for dances and let them romance their daughters.

Paulie Trotta, though, had grown up in a household whose immigrant father forbade the children to speak his native tongue. "You're in America," he insisted. "Talk American." The very mention of Mussolini sent him into tirades about Satan. In joining the army with his brothers, Paulie had shown himself willing to die American.

It was a lesson not lost on his nephew. Frank's family had moved to Birch Street in 1962, when he was seven, and he was hearing Paulie's stories against the backdrop of a new war in Vietnam. Congress passed the Tonkin Gulf Resolution when Frank was nine; the Tet offensive came midway through his seventh-grade year in grammar school. In the aftermath of Tet, with antiwar protests growing, Frank measured the peace movement by his family's standard and found it not only cowardly but also disloyal.

Four of his uncles had served in World War II. Both Paulie and Seely, Frank's one maternal uncle, had earned decorations for their courage. All these men considered the Vietnam War to be as just as their own, different only in the specific ideology of its totalitarian enemy. On many warm nights Frank overheard his father and uncles talking on the sidewalk, incensed by the latest protest march to make the news. "This country's given 'em everything," went one refrain, "and they're giving nothing in return." Frank remembered those words on the day in 1969 when students walked out of New Rochelle High in an antiwar demonstration, shutting down the entire school. There was no idealism in refusing to fight, Frank believed, just fear.

Blessed Sacrament High, the parochial school that Frank entered in the fall of 1969, practiced a relatively passive sort of patriotism. The style hardly suited Frank. On the day of the Vietnam moratorium in October 1969 he wore an armband emblazoned with a flag and the slogan "These Colors Don't Run." He owned one necktie striped in red, white, and blue, another with the image of Uncle Sam. During a course in public speaking, he delivered a defense of the war as his final address. He even convinced the principal of Blessed Sacrament to allow him, rather than a paid custodian, to raise and lower the flag each day.

So consumed was Frank with Vietnam that his teachers sometimes assumed he thought of nothing else. A social studies instructor, himself a former marine, once assigned a term paper on "any American topic." Frank proposed the NFL. "The NLF isn't really American," the teacher responded. "It's part of what's going on in Vietnam. It's not appropriate for . . ." No, Frank interrupted, not the National Liberation Front, the National Football League.

That was one of the rare times Frank acted his age. As a teenager he longed for adulthood. He devoured the *Daily News* at breakfast and waited on the stoop every afternoon for the *Standard-Star* delivery boy. In addition to baseball cards, he collected political buttons and bumper stickers. After he volunteered to represent Richard Nixon in a mock presidential debate during eighth grade, he called the national campaign headquarters to request position papers and the texts of major speeches.

The counterculture never made much headway on Birch Street. While Manhattan celebrated itself as "Fun City," Frank's parents permitted him to make the half-hour trip there only twice in eighteen years, and one of those was for the Christmas show at Radio City. If Frank Sr. spotted anything resembling a hippie as he drove through New Rochelle, he rolled down the window and shouted, "Get a haircut, you son of a bitch." When the civil rights movement gave way to Black Power, he cried, "Whattaya want, you lousy bastards? First you wanna integrate. Now you wanna segregate. Make up your goddamn minds."

Lorraine was less abrasive but no less disturbed. The daughter of one of her phone company friends drank soda secretly laced with LSD at a party. Some of the new operators were hired directly from a drug rehabilitation program; another boasted of juggling three boyfriends and a husband. "I know what they like," the woman explained. "Just suck it like a lollipop." With her own modesty so besieged, Lorraine responded to Richard Nixon more for his achievements as parent than as president. In his daughters she saw proof that even in the liberated '60s children could grow up untainted by drugs, sex, or radicalism. In 1968 she sent Nixon a fan letter and a copy of *Life* magazine with his portrait on the cover; at reelection time four years later she submitted a campaign jingle.

> I'm a-fixin' to vote for Nixon
> He's the man for Uncle Sam
> For a vote well-spent for president
> Start a-fixin' to vote for Nixon

As the summer of 1970 unfolded, the summer after the American invasion of Cambodia and the shootings of four protesters at Kent State, Nixon decided to appropriate the antiwar movement's strategy of mass demonstration. He proclaimed July 4 "Honor America Day," and his staff assembled a "Super Salute to God and Country." From Bob Hope to Billy Graham, Johnny Cash to Kate Smith, entertainers and religious leaders signed on for the extravaganza. It would be held outside the Lincoln Memorial, reclaiming the ground occupied by so many antiwar rallies.

The idea catalyzed Frank. Here, at last, was a way to answer the peaceniks with more than silent forbearance or street-corner grumbling. Frank searched for a local celebration of Honor America Day that he could join. He called chapters of the Veterans of Foreign Wars, the American Legion, the Catholic War Veterans, and the Order of the Purple Heart, but not one had a plan. If anything was going to be done, Frank realized, he would have to do it.

He enlisted two classmates, Wayne Ross and John Connelly, who had stuck out as the other conservatives in a current events course. The three christened themselves Blessed Sacrament Students for America and resolved to hold a rally on July 4. With the date only weeks away, Frank acted with all the celerity he had brought in less politicized summers to exploring the South Side's abandoned railroad tunnels. He secured the parade permit, bouncing for hours from mayor to city manager to recreation director to police chief in pursuit of the requisite signatures. He pecked out press releases on a typewriter he had never even used for term papers. He enlisted as grand marshal the World War II hero who was New Rochelle's answer to Audie Murphy, and prevailed upon the Conservative Party's candidate for Congress to address the closing rally. Then he filled mailboxes for blocks around with a final appeal.

"The success of our parade depends on you," it pleaded. "We're counting on you. Don't let us down—please." Beneath a loopy signature, Frank had added in his inexpert typing, "Thanks A Million./."

• • •

At ten o'clock on the morning of Honor America Day, Billy Graham delivered his benediction in Washington. A mere ten thousand patriots were gathered before him, where thirty times as many protesters had thronged for the last Vietnam moratorium. Meanwhile in New Rochelle, Frank Trotta contemplated a flop of his own. The parade was supposed to be stepping off at ten sharp, but on the corner outside Blessed Sacrament Church he counted a paltry seventy-five marchers, sixty of whom he knew personally. Biting his nails, almost wishing for rain, he peered down the streets in all directions, only to find empty asphalt.

Frank understood from the Thanksgivings of his childhood how a parade ought to look and sound, all sirens and brass bands and prancing majorettes, with spectators three-deep elbowing for space along each curb. Why did his tribute to American soldiers threaten to be such a bust? He could not conveniently blame the weather, seventy-two degrees with sun burning through the overcast. And the tradesmen of the West End and the South Side, his logical constituency, could hardly afford to leave town for a holiday weekend. Maybe, Frank had to admit, people really were sick of the war. Maybe they didn't take a fifteen-year-old seriously. Worst of all, he worried, the answer was both.

Facing humiliation, Frank chose strategic delay. After ten or fifteen minutes the promised police escort appeared. So did the Republican candidate for mayor, a pleasant surprise. Then the "mobile unit" from a local radio station—nothing, in truth, but a station wagon equipped with a euphemism—pulled into view. Out emerged a reporter, Steve Osborne, barely above draft age himself, decisively opposed to the war, and officially on his day off. In the last few weeks Osborne had grown intrigued by Frank Trotta, this teenager of such preternatural maturity and conservatism.

All those who had heeded Frank's summons, out of solidarity or pity, now shuffled into formation. The police cruiser rolled onto Shea Place, the WVOX station wagon followed, and Frank Trotta's first foray into politics got under way. In khaki uniforms and white helmets, with belt buckles and tie clasps glinting in the sun, a color guard from the Veterans of Foreign Wars led the procession. Behind them paced the grand marshal and politicians, all formal in blue suits, and then in cardigans and flannels came various Trotta relatives, neighbors, and friends, three of them together bearing a flag the size of a tablecloth. A delegation from the American Legion, clad in dress blues and shouldering M-1 rifles, preceded children hoisting homemade banners. "Long May It Wave," declared one. "Peace Yes, Surrender Never!" vowed another. "I Won't Be Drafted," went Frank's contribution, carried by a surrogate, "I'm Joining." A half-dozen cars, headlights glowing and crepe paper trailing, brought up the rear. One of them, a Valiant with two flags affixed to the roof, carried Frank Trotta Sr.

His son, a stocky, dark-haired boy in a parochial school blazer and American flag tie, walking just behind the VFW contingent, was dreading every step. North on Maple, west on Main, and south on Weyman, Frank heard something worse than any heckling—the thick cottony silence of a muggy summer morning. He tried talking with Wayne Ross and John Connelly, his cohorts in Blessed Sacrament Students for America. He tried picking out landmarks like his cousin's liquor store and the telephone company building where his mother worked a switchboard. But always his eyes found the vacant curbs and the open sidewalks. When he saw the police blocking six lanes of the Boston Post Road, when he listened to the drivers pounding their horns in impatience, all because of this piddly little parade of his, he could only pray none recognized him as its organizer.

Nearing the end of their half-mile route, the marchers turned off Morgan Street and into D'Onofrio Park. As the setting for a patriotic rally it was appropriate in both obvious and subtle ways. It bore the surname of four brothers killed in World War II, and so honored soldierly sacrifice. Its baseball diamond and picnic grounds served the Irish and Italians of the South Side, the blue-collar ethnics Frank had most expected to reach. And situated downwind from the city dump and the dog pound, both particularly redolent in sultry July, D'Onofrio Park reminded those people exactly where they stood in the class hierarchy of New Rochelle, a hierarchy that was upending itself with the Vietnam War and the counterculture, growing more conservative at the bottom and more liberal at the top.

To Frank's shock and relief, more than one hundred people were awaiting the parade, filling the benches in an open-air pavilion. Eventually, as the marchers took seats, the crowd overflowed onto the surrounding grass. In this gathering, the men still shaved their sideburns and beards, and the women hemmed their skirts at the knee; here the only ponytail belonged to a girl in a Mickey Mouse shirt, clicking off snapshots with an Instamatic. The color guard and the dignitaries strode smartly onto a dais, actually two picnic tables shoved together and covered with cloth bunting; at its center stood a plywood podium Frank's father had nailed together and then painted in horizontal bands of red, white, and blue. When Wayne Ross rose to intone the Pledge of Allegiance, his blond head barely cleared it.

One of Frank's ringers, a cousin who was the town supervisor in nearby Pelham, played the emcee. The Conservative Party's candidate for mayor of New Rochelle spoke briefly. But the main attraction, and Frank's canniest coup, was Mike Coffey, a salesman running for Congress on the Conservative line. Coffey did not know Frank had also invited the incumbent, a liberal and patrician Republican in the Rockefeller mold, Ogden Reid. But while politicians of such impeccable antiwar credentials as George McGovern and Edmund Muskie had deemed it wise to endorse the Honor America rally in Washington, Reid snubbed the local equivalent and its precocious promoter. In an act of revenge, Frank added a keynote address to the event and offered it to Coffey. And Coffey knew better than to condescend. Only twenty-eight himself, not so much older than Frank, he realized the most energetic volunteers in his own campaign were teenagers turning more conservative than their parents. One of them, Roger Stone, would grow up to become one of the leading political consultants of the Reagan Revolution.

As his listeners hunched forward, elbows on knees, Coffey bashed Reid with his customary relish. On bill after bill Reid had voted against the Nixon administration. Why, he had even shared the podium at a local high school with William Kunstler, defense attorney for the Chicago Eight. For his own part, Coffey endorsed President Nixon's policy of "peace with honor." Then he spoke about oppression, not the oppression of ghetto blacks or Vietnamese peasants that the American left railed about, but the oppression in Communist lands. "We got the best system going on earth," Coffey proclaimed. "If you don't like it, leave it."

Few of conservatism's themes resonated more deeply with the children of immigrants, the people in D'Onofrio Park. Even a generation or two off the boat, collective memory told them what America had saved them from—starvation under British domination for the Irish, servitude to feudal landlords for the Italians, czarist pogroms for the Jews, and Stalinist terror for the Poles. The antiwar movement, with its strain of national self-hate, only drove them deeper into conservative arms. Even as Coffey was speaking in New Rochelle, a thousand Yippies were trying to disrupt the Honor America festivities in Washington. They lit joints in a marijuana "smoke-in," flourished the flag of North Vietnam, and bathed nude in the Reflecting Pool, retreating only when the police descended.

By noon, the crowd in D'Onofrio Park dispersed. Frank helped his father haul the podium to the family Valiant and they drove home. There Frank's mother, Lorraine, ironed his suit and tie, dry cleaning being a rare luxury. Two afternoons later the *Standard-Star* landed on the front porch, carrying a short article about the rally together with a picture of Frank, Wayne Ross, and John Connelly. Finally, after a two-week wait, the mail brought a developed roll of Super-8 film.

Frank threaded it through the projector that had been a gift from his parents and watched the parade, or at least five minutes of highlights. Some of them were dark, some of them were fuzzy, and some of them were mercilessly clear in capturing the desultory procession. Even as a fifteen-year-old mounting his first political event, Frank had aspired to be more than an amateur. One snippet, however, reminded him why he had made the effort. The bit of film showed a slender, balding man in a beige windbreaker first wiping his brow, then smiling a coy smile and turning shyly away. It was Uncle Paulie.

• • •

Several weeks after Honor America Day, Frank Trotta borrowed a suitcase from his parents and commenced his education in the intricacies of
campaign politics. He was bound sixty miles up the Long Island Sound
shoreline to the University of Bridgeport. For three days a few of its
classrooms and dormitories would host "TAR Camp," the training program of the Teenage Republicans. It was heady enough for Frank to be
spending a few nights away from home and family for the first time.
And staying on a college campus, even one more urban than ivied,
appealed to his precocity.

The only doubt Frank harbored about the venture was whether the
Republican Party was sufficiently conservative. He had joined the TARs
two years earlier largely because of admiration for Richard Nixon; the
Republicans he observed closer to home—Ogden Reid, Jacob Javits,
and Nelson Rockefeller—espoused virtually the same activist liberalism
and antiwar sentiments as most Democrats. Class resentments, too, colored Frank's scorn for them. When Reid held a reception for Republican
youth at his Westchester estate, Frank remained on the South Side,
marooned without a ride. It never occurred to the congressman, apparently, that some of his guests had two working parents sharing one car.

Soon enough, Frank would realize his fears about the Republicans
were misplaced. While the national party still gravitated toward the
political center, its youth programs supplied the shock troops of a right-
wing insurgency. There was, in fact, a certain parallel between the
Democratic and Republican Parties of the era, a mirror image between
the young legions of Barry Goldwater in 1964 and of George McGovern
eight years later. Hair length and ideology aside, in both instances the
most vigorous volunteers were also the purest idealists. As much as
Frank despised the New Left's goals, he envied its flamboyant rhetoric.
He and John Connelly, who already belonged to the National Rifle
Association, saluted each other with clenched fists and the slogan
"Power to the individual!" A few years later, during college, Frank produced buttons declaring, "Make Love, Not Laws."

One subtle distinction between the youth movement in each party,
however, lent the Republican version far greater impact over time. The
young people on the left flocked to a candidate—McGovern, Eugene
McCarthy, Robert Kennedy—far more than to a party. Indeed, their
assaults against the party organization arguably cost Hubert Humphrey
the presidency in 1968. After Kennedy was slain and McGovern was
battered into insignificance, and McCarthy slipped away from the national stage, many of their followers vanished, too.

On the Republican side, by contrast, young people joined the party apparatus itself and were cultivated over a period of years. Between them, the Republican youth programs—the TARs, the College Republicans, and the Young Republicans—spanned the ages from puberty to paunch. Rather than follow a single messianic figure, the young conservative activists learned how to operate a party, the better to seize its controls.

The stirrings had begun in the Eisenhower years, when the GOP appeared most unified behind its centrist leader. Two mavericks, F. Clifton White and William A. Rusher, alarmed that America was sliding toward socialism, assembled a conservative coalition in the Young Republican Federation. Their alliance brought together factions from the small-town Midwest, the booming suburbs of the West, and the segregated South. As importantly, the coalition left the moderate Northeast powerless for the first time in memory.

This transformation anticipated the evolution of the Republican Party as a whole. Rusher went on to become the publisher of William F. Buckley Jr.'s *National Review,* the most influential conservative magazine of the era, while White masterminded the Draft Goldwater movement. In creating a campaign organization, he eschewed GOP regulars to recruit heavily from the Young Republicans. The success of these tyros against a party establishment that favored Nelson Rockefeller served as a kind of creation myth for conservatives of Frank Trotta's age.

Along the way, not coincidentally, the Young Republicans refined a special talent for tormenting the party's liberal wing. "Bigoted young hellions," Senator Hugh Scott of Pennsylvania once called his antagonists. Rockefeller had feuded with conservatives in the federation since the late 1950s, when he purged White and Rusher from New York's delegation. Rumor had it that he refused to pay tuition for any New Yorkers to attend TAR Camp.

Judging from the 1970 session, the governor would have had sound reason. Frank's counselors amounted to the Pepsi Generation of the conservative movement. Roger Stone, who had nearly met Frank during Mike Coffey's race for Congress, would later hold leadership positions in the Reagan and Bush campaigns. Terry Dolan would direct the National Conservative Political Action Committee. Grover Joseph Rees would serve in the Reagan Justice Department and write extensively on legal issues for *National Review.*

Superficially, TAR Camp focused on strategy rather than ideology. Frank learned about the "diamond pattern"—a tactic of stationing shills throughout the auditorium during a debate so their applause would seem to the audience a groundswell. He learned about "spaghetti barricades"—sawhorses erected at an outdoor rally precisely so that trained volunteers could knock them down and surge toward the candidate in apparent spontaneity. He even learned about "rye-grass signs"—sprinkling seed on highway embankments so that it would spell a candidate's name when it germinated in the fall.

Outside the formal classes, a brash conservatism asserted itself. Decades later Frank would still remember Rees lecturing on a political philosophy distilled in the words on his lapel button: "Laissez Faire." Only seventeen, Rees had already completed his sophomore year at Yale and embraced a libertarian brand of conservatism. He spoke to the campers about Herbert Spencer's ideal of the "night watchman state," one committed to national defense and public safety but little else that might trammel personal freedom. Rees favored the war and opposed the draft, thought government should legalize drugs and stop paying welfare. He could make being a square seem downright rebellious.

One group of campers walked out during a speech by Lowell Weicker, a liberal Republican then running for his first term in the Senate. Stewart McKinney, a congressman of similar leanings from the bedroom suburbs of Fairfield County, was similarly boycotted. On the final night of TAR Camp, the counselors performed skits and parodies that skewered the liberal traitors of their own party far more than the Democrats of whom perfidy was expected. To the tune of the Beatles' "Yellow Submarine," they sang:

> We all live in a welfare state
> New York State, New York State
> We all share a socialist fate
> Socialist fate, socialist fate.

Onto the melody of "Old Man River" they grafted the words:

> Young John Lindsay
> He must know somethin'
> But he don't do nothin'
> He don't cut taxes
> He don't tow garbage
> And all his speeches
> Are empty verbage

The next afternoon Frank returned home, certain he had both a party and a place in it. If three days in TAR Camp had not quite prepared him to manage a campaign, they had certainly left him more savvy than the usual supernumerary. Possessed of both a belief system and a modicum of technique, he had only one question. "If I ever ran for office," he asked his parents, "would Grandpa vote for me?"

• • •

Frank meant his maternal grandfather, Silvio Burigo, and the chances were slender. Observing the evolution of his family, the lifelong Democrat could only howl of betrayal. "Ever since you got married," Silvio told Lorraine, "you're a Yankee fan and a Republican." She was not the only one breaking family tradition. As Frank formed his own political beliefs, he rejected the trade-union liberalism of his grandfather just as completely as he did the New Left. In the end, the inability of organized labor to hold the allegiance of a Frank Trotta damaged the Democratic coalition far more greatly than the failure of the antiwar movement or the counterculture to convert him.

This grandson and son of trade unionists, in fact, heard little but denunciations of organized labor. His father had once served as a shop steward and later helped organize a union in the Hartley Houses. By the late 1960s, however, Frank Sr. was fulminating against the rigid job classifications and work rules his own local had negotiated. The regulations meant that he, who performed all the sophisticated repairs of a mechanic, got paid $40 a month less than a mechanic because he was officially a janitor. The regulations meant that in a housing project rife with broken windows he could not buy and install glass himself, even though the glazier with the contract charged a 300 percent markup.

On her job, Lorraine fought against the organizing efforts of the Communications Workers of America. She preferred paying a dollar every month in dues to a quiescent company union than four or five times that to the CWA. There was more to lose in striking without any pay, she reasoned, than there was to gain in having a more aggressive union bargain on her behalf. Years later her fears were confirmed, when the CWA local went out for nine months and the Trottas lived on hot dogs.

Even Frank's aunt Mary Jane, without question the family liberal, hired a nonunion contractor in 1970 to expand her home in Danbury, Connecticut. Silvio was living there in retirement, and the decision rendered him apoplectic. Repeatedly he led Mary Jane through the half-finished rooms, pointing out flaws in the workmanship, both actual and imagined.

"Now, Dad," she said diplomatically, "not everybody is a perfectionist like you."

"Jesus Christ, goddamnit," he sputtered. "You're not getting what you paid for. These guys could care less about who they hire."

Some years later Lorraine had a confrontation of her own. She had by this time transferred from an operator's job to one clerking in the phone company's garage. Occasionally Silvio drove by to drop off corn and tomatoes from his garden. One particular day Lorraine was seething because a repairman, one of her favorites, was about to be released. Nobody had any problem with his ability or attendance. He just didn't want to join the union—in itself not a requirement—and on principle refused to authorize it to deduct dues from his paycheck.

"Daddy, I want to ask you a question," Lorraine began the instant Silvio entered the office. "Why does the union have the right to get you fired if you don't sign their card? It's not fair. It's not constitutional."

By now she was standing at her desk and shouting. Silvio had yet to move from the portal.

"Nitwit," he shot back. "Why should you get all the benefits if you don't pay the dues? When they go out on strike, it's for you, too."

"I don't care. It's wrong."

Turning to leave, Silvio pronounced, "You're hopeless."

Frank tried to separate the affection he felt for a grandfather with the disdain he felt for that grandfather's very ethos. At his most charitable, Frank saw unions as outmoded, a casualty of their own accomplishments. Now that the government enforced laws against child labor and sweatshop conditions, he figured, what purpose remained for a union? (To vote slavishly for Democrats, he answered himself.) More viscerally, Frank identified the whole of organized labor with Jimmy Hoffa, the thuggish and corrupt boss of the Teamsters, then serving a prison sentence for mail fraud and jury tampering.

Frank's beliefs were riddled with irony. The Teamsters, after all, broke from most of labor to endorse Richard Nixon for reelection, gaining Hoffa a presidential pardon. Unions in the building trades and law enforcement were increasingly moving to the right. There came a moment in the early 1970s when a Republican candidate for local office, for whom Frank was volunteering, won the backing of the local representing the Hartley Houses janitors. Frank was flummoxed. Why would any Republican want to be associated with a union?

In one integral way, though, Frank followed his grandfather's example. He understood how deep the divisions of social class cut in a nation that prided itself on being classless. The very first time he explored the North End, he registered not only such blatant symbols of affluence as backyard pools and tennis courts but the less obvious ones like the absence of sidewalks and streetlamps. And what the North End was to the South Side, New Rochelle High was to Blessed Sacrament. Frank competed against the public school's brightest in the WVOX *Quiz Bowl*, and after Blessed Sacrament had been thoroughly trounced, the New

Rochelle coach told Frank that he alone among his teammates was "worthy of being in this competition."

The words bruised Frank, but they did not shake him. It did not matter to him if the opposing coach judged him worthy, as if this guy were St. Peter guarding the gates of heaven. Of all the aphorisms in the Trotta household, Frank especially abided by the one that asked, "What do you care what other people think?" Few pieces of advice would better serve a teenager who had decided to join the Grand Old Party instead of the Woodstock Nation.

• • •

During Frank Trotta's freshman year at Blessed Sacrament, he had discovered the high school did not publish a newspaper. So, with typical alacrity, he launched one. Rather than satisfy himself with reporting on football games, club news, the senior musical, and other such staples of scholastic journalism, Frank also commented on the issues of the day. One of these was a bill, sponsored by an assemblyman from New Rochelle, to put New York's schools on a year-round schedule. Frank's craving for adulthood stopped short of relinquishing summer vacation, and his newspaper editorialized against the measure.

Not long after, in the late spring of 1970, Frank was walking down North Avenue when he recognized a face from a constituent newsletter. It belonged to Joe Pisani, the legislator who had put forward the bill. Frank introduced himself as a classmate of Pisani's oldest son and awaited a perfunctory parental query about school.

"I read your editorial," Pisani began instead. "I'd like to take it up with you sometime."

A wave of exhilaration rippled through Frank. For all the gravity in Pisani's voice, he could have been talking to a voter, a *grown-up*. Before continuing down the sidewalk, the legislator invited Frank to his law office a week later to continue the discussion.

When the day arrived Frank knew only enough to wear his Blessed Sacrament blazer, the sole formal jacket he owned. He had never seen an office except on television; his mother worked among the tangled wires of a switchboard, his father in a basement of cleaning supplies and spare parts. Here plaques and awards covered the walls—Legislator of the Year from the College Debating Association, Man of the Year from the New Rochelle Jaycees, Who's Who in American Politics. Pisani spoke to his secretary over an intercom, just like Perry Mason. A technological wonder called a mag-card typewriter, a precursor to the word processor, memorized and reproduced an entire sentence at one keystroke.

Summoning Frank to his desk, Pisani handed him a sheath of position papers, a department of education report, a copy of his bill, and a thick book of research on the virtues of twelve-month schooling. "I don't think you're well informed," he said. "You ought to read this. Let's discuss it after you're done."

Behind the bluster Pisani cared less about convincing his tender skeptic than reckoning his intellectual mettle. As the father of four children, he had attracted a fair number of their friends to his campaigns, and he trusted most with nothing more cerebral than hammering lawn signs into place. In these first brief encounters with Frank, though, Pisani had sensed an uncommon intensity, a quality he could only call "that look." From what he knew of Frank's background, he could see more than a bit of himself in the boy. The son of an immigrant bricklayer, Pisani had grown up on the South Side and become the first in his family to attend college—first Iona and then Fordham Law, both traditional rungs for Roman Catholics climbing from manual trades into politics or the civil service. It was not merely narcissism for him to imagine that Frank Trotta might well follow his trail.

Frank, too, sensed an immediate affinity. By any objective standard, Pisani's office was unexceptional. It boasted none of the mahogany paneling and Oriental rugs of a white-shoe Wall Street firm, none of the oil portraits of founding partners. Such opulence would have intimidated Frank, paralyzed him. In both physical and social terms, Joe Pisani occupied a niche lofty enough to impress Frank, yet not so lofty as to seem inaccessible. He had earned his position the only way Frank possibly could, through hard work and persistence, not family connections or inherited wealth.

That summer, the same pivotal summer of TAR Camp and Honor America Day, Frank dutifully plodded through the material about a twelve-month school year. He read it by lamplight in his bedroom and he read it by lantern during a backyard camp-out with his brother. It bored him. It did not change his mind. But he was fulfilling his part of the bargain. Or was it actually more of a dare?

If so, Pisani had a few more. Now that he knew Frank could think like a prodigy, he wanted to make sure he didn't behave like one. Arrogance was deadlier than ignorance for a politician seeking working-class votes. So in Pisani's Assembly campaign in the fall of 1970 he assigned Frank the grunt work, sending him to the train station at daybreak to press leaflets and shopping bags on hundreds of commuters. Not only did Frank perform the chore uncomplainingly, he never once overslept. For a fifteen-year-old male *Homo sapiens,* that practically defied the laws of biology.

Having survived hazing, Frank now joined the fraternity. In January 1971, Pisani awarded him a week-long internship in Albany, a position he usually reserved for a collegian. During the budget deliberations in late March, Frank returned for a second stint. What those weeks granted him was less instruction in the processes of government than immersion in the culture of government. Intellectually sophisticated as Frank was, he remained something of a hayseed, capable of being dazzled.

Everything in Albany glistened with novelty—the machine vending apples in the State Capitol lobby, the debate over a bill to legalize pigeon hunting, the carillon sounding from city hall, chiming Beethoven one day and the Mouseketeer theme the next. Sleeping in the Wellington Hotel, having breakfast in the Capitol cafeteria, and dining on Pisani's account at the Bleecker, Frank entered the orbit of legislator and lobbyist, bureau chief and chief of staff. If an elevator in the Capitol was operated by an attendant rather than a relay controller, it seemed quaint. If the legislature unplugged its official clock one minute before midnight on March 31, letting debate on the state budget proceed for weeks without violating the legal deadline for adopting one, then the pretense appeared harmlessly peculiar. So potent was Albany's potion that only years later would such practices strike Frank as emblems of the wasteful and inefficient government that he as a conservative sought to slay.

He regarded Pisani through the same charmed aura. In his early forties, brown hair silvering at the temples, Pisani stayed fit as the college rower he had been. On the floor of the Assembly, he could persuade or stemwind or call down hellfire and brimstone as the occasion demanded. A page whispered to Frank during one oration, "He's the best debater in this house." It was no secret that both Pisani and the party leadership envisioned him as a candidate for statewide office.

As public servant or private citizen, Pisani confounded the usual categories. He could discourse in classical Latin with his press secretary or chatter in peasant Italian with his father. He hunted deer and painted abstracts. One minute he might declare philosophy the ideal discipline for a politician and in the next recommend *Plunkitt of Tammany Hall,* a collection of lessons in the nitty-gritty of ward politics. He was a conservative who abhorred abortion, decried the state's tax rate, and in six consecutive years introduced a bill restoring the death penalty, only to have it vetoed by the governor each time. Yet he considered Teddy Roosevelt his political hero and built a liberal's record on consumer protection and children's rights. Years later Jack Kemp, the self-described "bleeding-heart conservative," would provide the nation with a sense of what Frank Trotta so admired in Joe Pisani.

Leaving Albany that spring, Frank told himself, This is where it's at. Through government you improved society and you improved yourself.

The affluent ranks of the radical left—"bred in at least modest comfort, housed now in universities," as the Students for a Democratic Society put it in the Port Huron Statement—enjoyed the luxury of rejecting membership in "the Establishment." An outsider in his own city by both social class and ethnicity, Frank Trotta aspired only to join it. And Joe Pisani offered proof that through politics all transformations were possible.

Meanwhile, Frank had to return to earth, otherwise known as New Rochelle. He owed Blessed Sacrament all the assignments he had missed while in Albany, no small responsibility for a boy who fretted whenever his average dipped below 95. Pisani delegated him various tasks in the home district, including supplying brochures on drug abuse to doctors, and soliciting donations of food for the annual banquet that benefited the legislative internship program.

Then, finally, the next major election year arrived. At the national level, 1972 offered the stark choice between Nixon and McGovern. Closer to home, Joe Pisani was running for a vacant seat in the State Senate. Personally, the race marked the latest stage in his ascent to statewide office; politically, it revealed even more clearly than did the presidential campaign how America was swinging toward conservatism. The Thirty-sixth District looked to be moderate enough: Its eight communities included New Rochelle, where liberal Jews and blacks formed a voting majority, as well as Mount Vernon and White Plains, both of which also had large minority populations. Yet the State Senate race was fought so far right-of-center that Pisani could not even command the Conservative Party's ballot line. That went to his Democratic opponent, John Passidomo, leaving Pisani to run newspaper advertisements featuring a photograph of himself and James Buckley, implying the senator's endorsement.

From Iona College to the Rye Golf Club, wherever Pisani and Passidomo debated, they spent most of their time agreeing. Crime was too high. Rockefeller wasted taxpayer money. The state had no business trying to build subsidized housing in New Rochelle. Pisani, however, could surpass the rote recitation of that creed. If he wasn't proposing state income-tax deductions for parents' costs in adopting children, then he was suggesting a new misdemeanor be created for reckless boating. Anyone could denounce the plan for low-income apartments; it took Pisani to offer his legal expertise free of charge to an elderly woman in a wheelchair who had been evicted from her tenement as part of land condemnation on the prospective site. Most cagily of all, Pisani forced Passidomo to concede that as a lifelong Democrat he felt obliged to "basically support the Democratic ticket," meaning George McGovern.

As Pisani's youth director, Frank put the lessons of TAR Camp into practice. He planted volunteers in the "diamond pattern" during a League of Women Voters debate. He sent them crashing through "spaghetti barricades" at the county Republican convention. He even invented a promotion that he later taught to TAR campers: Squeegees in hand, buckets at the ready, teenagers descended on cars parked near train stations and downtown stores throughout the district. "Your windshield has been cleaned by Youth for Pisani," read the flyer each left behind. "We hope you can now see your way clear to voting for Joe Pisani."

A virgin to drugs, a drinker only of his grandfather's wine, Frank imbibed the intoxicant that is a campaign. He dispatched all his homework during lunch and study hall, raced from Blessed Sacrament to a part-time job with the Chamber of Commerce, then worked from five until midnight for Pisani, cresting on coffee and adrenaline. Watching Frank recruit young people, organize the inherently disorganized, Pisani thought often of a line in his revered *Plunkitt* about how a fellow earns respect not speaking for himself but on behalf of a group.

The mayor of New Rochelle, Republican Frank Garito, had been noticing the same trait, too, ever since attending the patriotic parade more than two years earlier. Now he enlisted Frank into the most significant and glamorous event of the entire election season, an appearance by President Nixon. The president had selected a single day— Monday, October 23—to barnstorm through Westchester and Nassau Counties. These suburbs were essential to any Republican victory, and Nixon had taken them by surprisingly narrow margins in 1968. The plan called for him to fly into Westchester in the late morning and ride in a motorcade through eleven towns, New Rochelle among them, before helicoptering across Long Island Sound for a rally in the 16,000-seat Nassau Coliseum. In the context of an entire campaign, it was just one day among many. New Rochelle, though, had not known its like since the dreary Sunday morning in April 1945 when Franklin Roosevelt's funeral train pulled into the station.

While the rest of Blessed Sacrament's seniors anguished over the impending Scholastic Aptitude Test, Frank Trotta met regularly in city hall with advance men from the Committee to Re-elect the President. His role was to mobilize teenage volunteers who in turn would paper the city with posters and flyers promoting the motorcade. Humble as ever, Frank consented to wearing a shirt stuck with dozens of Nixon buttons to the train station, and limped home plucked and pricked. Mostly he listened, awestruck, to the exacting discussions of itinerary and security. How many minutes would the presidential limousine need to travel down Main Street and up North Avenue? What tall buildings along the route should have Secret Service agents on the rooftop? Where would protesters be most likely to gather? What intersections ought to have the biggest crowds?

All the rarefied air dizzied Frank. One day at Blessed Sacrament he cut class to attend yet another session with the advance men. Brother Walderman snagged him in the hall. It was bad enough that Brother Walderman was the dean of students, but Brother Walderman had an attitude. Greeted once as "Wally" by a shirtless student as a joke, he responded by hurling a crutch.

"What are you doing?" he asked Frank.

"Going to a meeting, coordinating the Nixon motorcade."

"That's an inappropriate reason to be out of class."

"This is a historic event," Frank nearly shouted.

"You have more important things to do," Brother Walderman answered, matching him decibel for decibel.

"Brother, you're wrong. I can't think of anything more important than this."

As echoes of confrontation lingered in the hall, Frank slunk back toward his class. Probably one of those liberal Democrats, he thought to himself. Ten or fifteen minutes later, with the corridor clear, he snuck away.

By the cool overcast morning of October 23, Frank knew the giddy sensation of completion. His reward would be watching the motorcade from the mayor's office—the equivalent, as he later put it, of "the corporate box at Yankee Stadium." Nixon landed at eleven o'clock and was due in New Rochelle at 1:50. All through the early afternoon the advance men around Frank followed his progress by walkie-talkie. So huge was the reception that the president was running fifteen minutes, thirty, an hour behind schedule.

Crowds thronged six-deep along Main Street and North Avenue, straining the rope barrier at the curb, climbing onto window ledges for a glimpse. Bunting hung in crescents and banners fought for space— "Hello Pat and Dick," "Together Again," "A Vote For Nixon Is A Vote For Peace." The operating engineers from Local 137 commandeered one corner, their hard hats painted gold for the occasion. Not everyone, of course, reveled similarly. The New Rochelle High School band voted not to march in the parade. Two dozen students from Mamaroneck wore white robes and clutched dolls splattered with red paint. "Why don't you go to Russia?" a woman shrieked at them. "Communists!" Atop the roof of city hall itself, beside the granite sculpture of an eagle, a Secret Service marksman crouched. Unknown to Frank, and virtually anyone else, the police had just arrested a young man whose car contained a sawed-off shotgun.

Meanwhile, children rode their bicycles down North Avenue, delirious to have open road and an audience. Then someone spotted a limousine and a cheer swelled. It contained only Governor Rockefeller and other state officials, and the ovation soured to sighs and boos. Several bands promenaded past, and still there was no sign of the president. Then, inside city hall, Frank Trotta noticed an advance man ushering the mayor downstairs and toward the street.

A limousine soon glided into view, and Frank could see Richard Nixon, beaming, waving, and flashing the V for victory sign. For weeks the *Standard-Star* had been running banner headlines above the syndicated articles by Woodward and Bernstein about how the White House had disrupted Senator Edmund Muskie's presidential campaign, part of the "dirty tricks" operation that would ultimately come under the umbrella of Watergate. But the people packing North Avenue roared in joy at the man in the paisley tie and herringbone topcoat, the wife in turtleneck and plaid jacket at his side. Perhaps, like Frank, they ascribed such attacks to the terminal bias of the liberal media.

Outside city hall the limousine slowed and halted. Roellen Garito, the mayor's ten-year-old daughter, presented the president a bouquet of Sweetheart roses, and he presented her a kiss on the cheek. Six other times during the motorcade, three in New Rochelle alone, President Nixon stopped the limousine and vaulted into the crowd to pump hands. Over the day some 350,000 spectators would salute him, an incumbent astride a landslide. Gaping at this pageant, Frank could only recall his own parade on Honor America Day. It had left him wondering if the "Silent Majority" really was silent, if not altogether mute. This outpouring shouted the answer.

After the limousine rolled around the bend in North Avenue and disappeared from sight, an advance man tapped Frank on the shoulder. "The president wanted me to give you this," he said, "and to thank you for all your help." He placed in Frank's palm a tie clasp, embossed with the signature of Richard M. Nixon and the presidential seal. The next morning Frank wore it to Blessed Sacrament with his red, white, and blue tie.

The afterglow faded quickly, though, because only two weeks remained in the State Senate campaign. Once deadlocked with Passidomo, Joe Pisani seemed to be opening a lead at last. He attracted endorsements that reflected the emerging conservative coalition, from taxpayers' groups to right-to-life activists to building-trades unions. The most powerful medium in the district, the Gannett Group's Westchester Rockland Newspapers, hailed his "excellent service in dealing with problems of government and caring for human needs and being very effective and successful in his efforts."

On Election Night, Frank manned telephone, adding machine, and walkie-talkie in Pisani's law office, transformed for several hours into campaign central. Pisani carried well over 60 percent in New Rochelle. He fought to a stalemate in Harrison, the town Passidomo served as supervisor. Pisani's margin of victory grew through the night to a resounding 17,000 votes and 16 percent. Only occasionally did Frank watch the presidential results on the office television. Nixon's triumph was a given.

Pisani thanked Frank and all his New Rochelle volunteers well before midnight, visited Republican headquarters elsewhere in the district, and then repaired to his home for the traditional all-night open house. Neighbors and relatives, poll watchers and envelope stuffers, mechanic and secretary and barber all whirled about in celebration. Pisani's father baked *pizza rustica* and his son's band played rock 'n' roll and at daybreak he himself cooked scrambled eggs for the entourage. Then Frank Trotta walked straight to school.

Politics did not completely overtake his life. He graduated as valedictorian, student council president, and Regents scholarship recipient, not the accomplishments of a distracted mind. Still, Frank's obsession was everywhere writ. In the yearbook, *Maple Leaves,* Pisani campaign buttons materialized gremlinlike in twenty-three different photographs. A picture of President Nixon during his New Rochelle visit appeared among the faculty portraits. Classmates wrote inscriptions such as "Mayor Trotta '76," "Good luck in your next presidency (Wash D.C.)," and "I'll see you in the White House." A wag named Robert Trangucci, who was apparently reading those Woodward and Bernstein stories that Frank tried to ignore, wrote, "Good luck in the presidential elections in 1984. When you run, I will bug the Democrats for you!"

For now, Frank had decided to attend the State University of New York at Albany, largely so that he could work part-time for Pisani in the legislature. But it was neither there nor in the classrooms where Frank would learn some of the most indelible lessons of the era.

• • •

By most academic measures, Frank enrolled in the state university primed to excel. While still in high school he had taken two semesters of college calculus. On a standardized test that SUNY administered, he placed out of an entire year's introductory courses. He was majoring in philosophy, under Joe Pisani's approving eyes, and honing his intellect by analyzing policy for the legislator. Why, then, did the campus feel so alien? Why did melancholy so often descend?

Those emotions had to do with leaving home, but not with any of the usual notions of homesickness. Birch Street and Blessed Sacrament, Uncle Paulie and Joe Pisani had all given Frank the assurance that he and his values belonged. He took Nixon's 1972 landslide victory as proof that the Silent Majority truly formed a majority. Now, removed from the womb of the South Side, he found himself in the minority, and not just any minority but one as minuscule and ridiculed as that of young conservative Republicans in the Watergate era. All through Frank's first year in Albany, the Nixon presidency was unraveling with revelations of political sabotage and executive obstruction. He could hardly walk down the hallway to his bathroom without passing some placard imploring, "Impeach Nixon. Mass Demonstration." Detested but feared on campuses when he was powerful, the wounded Nixon now attracted gleeful contempt. Students wore his jowly, swarthy caricature as a Halloween mask and gathered in bars over pitchers of beer to mock his televised speeches. Frank absorbed the scorn personally, for in Nixon the conservative, Nixon the foe of the media, even Nixon the homely underdog, he saw much of himself.

More than Watergate alone consigned Frank to the margins. As a young man pious and abstemious enough to have considered entering a religious order, he stood patently apart from his contemporaries. By the middle 1970s, the counterculture had lost interest in making revolution and instead gone commercial, becoming the favored lifestyle of American youth. Most colleges, for their part, had stopped bothering to police casual sex or recreational drug use or whatever else appeared to constitute young adulthood. Frank might prefer Jim Croce to Hot Tuna; he might leave his dormitory room when the marijuana joints flared; he might turn sleeplessly in his bed while a roommate made love with a girlfriend, not nearly as stealthily as they thought. But the discomfort and disapproval remained his alone, a formidable burden to bear. Ultimately even he invited his girlfriend for the night.

With the fissures in politics and culture came fissures in class. Compared to an Amherst or a Yale, SUNY-Albany served the unentitled; building the statewide university system, and particularly this sprawling modern campus, was one of Nelson Rockefeller's greatest acts of latter-day New Dealism. Frank's roommates, if liberal, knew nothing of limousines. Bob Franke was the child of a nurse and a public school principal, Frank Mendelson of an office manager and a gift-wrap salesman. Still, it occurred to Frank that those two always had a bit more money from home than he for a record or a dinner out. They could afford a room-and-board package including three meals each day, he a plan providing only breakfast and dinner. Lunch was usually an apple from the machine in the State Capitol, no longer such a marvel.

Frank had no complaint about working. Unbeknown for a time to his parents, he had worked afternoons all through high school, paying for supplies and the share of tuition his partial scholarship did not cover. He proudly subscribed to his father's formulation, "You can tell if somebody's honest by looking under their fingernails. If there's dirt, they're honest." Still, he could not help noticing that the students on full scholarship at Albany were not required to hold jobs; he often seemed to find them playing Frisbee on the quad. They got three daily meals for free. And a great many of them were minorities. This pattern, Frank could only surmise, was the doing of affirmative action.

How many of those students, Frank wondered, had graduated first in their class like him? Scored 1,315 on their SATs? Been named to *Who's Who in American High Schools?* In a college devoted to creating a meritocracy, why did his own merit languish unrewarded? Sure, Frank was receiving $250 annually from the Regents scholarship, but SUNY had added not one cent of its own. Frank arrived at an explanation: Something other than performance—race, poverty, whatever—dictated the decision.

There is little doubt that in the aftermath of the civil rights movement many colleges lavished far greater effort and resources on recruiting black students than working-class whites like Frank Trotta. Under pressure to admit more minorities, New York's City College, once renowned as the "Poor Man's Harvard," demolished its own rigorous and color-blind entrance standards. Frank's own family had seen in the discrimination case against Local 86 and the decline of the Hartley Houses evidence enough to convince them that certain blacks sought unearned advantages.

In fact, SUNY-Albany specifically refused to consider race as a factor in bestowing scholarships and financial aid. Its branch of the statewide Educational Opportunity Program did lower normal admissions requirements for several hundred students and offer them full tuition and room and board, but purely on the basis of family income. When the legislature enacted the program in 1968, Assemblyman Joe Pisani was among those who voted for it. In the 1973–74 academic year, Frank's first in Albany, a household of four like his own had to earn less than $7,150 annually to be eligible. As a practical matter, the disproportionate number of the program's beneficiaries were not white because a disproportionate number of the poorest New Yorkers were not white.

If Frank perceived the Educational Opportunity Program as an example of reverse discrimination—at his own expense—then his misapprehension had understandable roots. The campaigns in America for civil rights and affirmative action demanded that blacks be seen through the prism of race rather than class. In the extreme views of left and right, either blacks as a race possessed a unique moral claim to redress or they exploited their tragic history to seek favoritism from the state. For his own part, Frank believed liberal Democrats enticed blacks as a voting bloc to trade their ballots for largess, largess that would finally hobble them. All of these formulations, whatever their differences, shared the central assumption that blacks constituted a category apart. The pyramid of class in America somehow omitted them, and that absence encouraged people who hovered between the economic middle and the bottom to conceive of themselves as the nation's have-nots or left-outs in a scheme of social engineering and income redistribution.

The Trotta family occupied exactly that economic niche. Lorraine and Frank Sr. together earned barely $15,000 in the year Frank entered college. They had less money in the bank than they owed for aluminum siding. Yet the household income was too high for Frank to qualify for EOP or grants. The last thing he wanted was charity predicated on pity. He simply expected achievement, and achievement alone, to matter. And every time he passed the Frisbee game, every time he settled for an apple for lunch, he confronted the realization that it did not.

Geographically at least, Frank wrested himself from the campus. He took a leave of absence in the fall term of 1974 to manage Joe Pisani's reelection campaign, and when he returned to Albany he never again lived in a dormitory. But in changing address Frank could hardly escape the times, or the profound sense of isolation he endured amid them.

In the summer of 1975 he joined his old roommate Frank Mendelson and a third student in an apartment that cost each only $40 a month. Their building, 211 Sherman Street, teetered in the remnants of a German and Irish neighborhood called Cabbagetown, a district whose walk-ups and mom-and-pop stores were losing the battle against arson and abandonment. Plywood sheets filled windows and doors; porches weathered and sagged; garbage found its way even onto the tar rooftops. It seemed all too symbolic that a nearby tavern, the Shamrock, now showed on its marquee only SH M CK.

The students' house had asphalt shingles atop a wood frame, just like Paulie's on Birch Street, but it was every bit as disheveled as his was tidy. With the landlord dead and his estate in indifferent hands, the walls went unpainted, the front door never locked, and roaches infiltrated everything from an electric clock to a carton of Rice A Roni. Warmed only by a single space heater in winter, the place grew so stifling during the summer that Frank slept many nights on the couch in Pisani's office.

Frank Mendelson loved it. He had grown up in the North End of New Rochelle and never before lived anywhere so earthy. He drank beer on the stoop with his neighbors, as music poured from speakers set in someone's window. There was Mrs. Smith and her dog, Queenie, and the tall guy nicknamed Redwood who kept his future gravestone in his apartment, and Sylvia raising her three kids while her truckdriver husband served time for kiting checks coast to coast. The night the corset shop burned, Frank Mendelson joined the flock of spectators, experiencing the blaze less as the death rattle of a neighborhood than as an occasion for mutual support. Only years later would he realize that the locals he found so raffish and exotic wanted little more than to flee.

Frank Trotta had known that the moment he arrived. Nothing charmed him in the spectacle of children cadging beer from the neighborhood drunks, parents arguing in the street, and trash mounting on the ashes of the latest building to be torched. There was no romance in poverty, just poverty itself. He never learned the names or faces, much less the quirks and yarns, of his neighbors. Their mere presence goaded him to study, to work, to move away. Without an education, without the social mobility a college diploma would provide, he could easily enough imagine slipping into the quicksand of a Sherman Street.

The two Franks rarely spoke of all that separated them. They laughed together at *Monty Python,* downed the homemade dessert called Trotta's Treat, and found qualities to admire in each other. A psychology major of indefinite career plans, Frank Mendelson respected Frank Trotta's earnestness and dedication. Frank Trotta appreciated Frank Mendelson's compassion, the way he showed the neighborhood kids Charlie Chaplin movies, using a vacant lot for a theater and a brick wall for a screen. They even decided to share an apartment with two other students, though not on Sherman Street, in the following school year.

One day that fall the four roommates were settling the monthly expenses. From an empty pickling jar they pulled phone bills, receipts, and register tapes, in time-honored college tradition calculating who owed whom what down to the last penny. To cover his portion, Frank Mendelson produced a strip of blue paper, something like tickets for carnival rides. On closer inspection Frank Trotta realized they were food stamps.

As Frank Mendelson saw it, he deserved them. He had left his part-time job in a photo lab and stopped taking money from his family. Years later he could not recall exactly how he knew the procedure for obtaining food stamps. Perhaps, he said, he had learned how from a book by Abbie Hoffman.

Whenever Frank Trotta bought the groceries, he refused to even carry the food stamps, much less present them to a cashier. He had a job, two working parents, and a firm notion of who was poor. Poor were the orphans his mother supported through a club of switchboard operators called the Bell Babes. Poor were the children at the Indian school in North Dakota to which she sent a check every month. Frank Mendelson failed to meet any such definition of indigence. If a college student without any nefarious motives could compromise the welfare system so easily, Frank Trotta wondered, then how much could a real criminal pillage from it? This was not a new insight for him, just one reinforced in palpable form. Those food stamps symbolized liberalism's failure to him every bit as vividly as had the bike, fan, and typewriter his father lugged home from the Hartley Houses' garbage.

But in 1975, Frank felt impotent with the knowledge. What difference would it make, now that the country was veering once again to the left? Barely five years had passed since Honor America Day, just seven since Richard Nixon's election as president, and already conservatism seemed to Frank a spent force. After the midterm elections of 1974 the Democrats ruled the Senate by a three-fifths majority and the House of Representatives by two-thirds. A Democratic governor sat in Albany for the first time in sixteen years. Rarely in the century had fewer Americans identified themselves as being Republicans. To Frank, as to many others, the moment of defeat was obvious.

It fell on a Thursday evening, August 8, 1974, and he was hunched over the metal desk in Pisani headquarters in New Rochelle, lifting his eyes intermittently from a psychology textbook to a portable television set. Just nineteen, he was managing the reelection race, taking summer courses at Iona to clear the entire fall for politics. He checked the screen, still on a special report, *Presidential Crisis*. Then he gazed across Anderson Street to the storefront rented by Dick Ottinger, who was trying to win back his old congressional seat. There, Frank could only imagine, folks must be gloating. For months already, his own grandfather, Silvio, had been crowing, "I told you that your Tricky Dicky was no good."

The phone rang with Frank's mother reporting, "There's something going on in the White House." She spoke with an odd urgency, considering the entire world knew that at nine o'clock Richard Nixon was announcing his decision to resign from the presidency. Frank closed his book and on the blocks around him all human activity froze. A team of women fresh from a softball-league victory halted their celebration in the Beau Brummel, swiveling their barstools to face the TV. The local Republican Party chairman paced the back office of his clothing store. Thirty-one shoppers assembled before eleven floor models in the television department at Macy's. "It's like waiting," one said, "for the ball to hit the top on New Year's Eve."

Far from exulting, Frank grieved. He viewed Nixon's fall more like a coup than a triumph of constitutional process. It was the media's doing, the Congress's, John Dean's. Never would Frank tune in Dan Rather again. Only as time passed did Frank begin to blame Nixon himself. He could not forgive him, a lawyer, for subverting the law. And he could not forgive him for destroying conservatism's moment. It seemed appropriate somehow that Frank had watched the resignation speech alone, at a metal desk on a bare concrete floor, practically within earshot of the clucking Democrats. A minority of one on that warm August evening, he could hardly imagine how suddenly history might change course again, or how emblematic a role he and a few college friends might play in its redirection. By the time their revolution was over, Richard Nixon with his Soviet détente and wage-price controls would not even look like so much of a conservative.

Chapter Thirteen

The State Street Gang
(Leslie Maeby)

Leaning up on the toes of her Mary Janes, clutching a Styrofoam boater against the sudden wind, Leslie Maeby watched audacity descend in the form of a helicopter. As it touched down, a door flung open and a passenger leaped out and onto a parking lot in the Albany suburb of Colonie. Pivoting with an athlete's grace, he dashed toward a podium draped in bunting and a waiting crowd of two hundred. The man was Fred Field, a Republican candidate for State Assembly, and Leslie was one of his half-dozen "Field Girls," and both the chopper and cheerleaders demonstrated this would be no ordinary campaign.

In the forty-eight years leading up to the balmy afternoon of September 4, 1968, only twice had a Republican held any office that required defeating Dan O'Connell's Democratic machine. Republicans lost elections for the citywide positions in Albany; they lost elections for seats on the county board; they lost elections in districts for the state legislature and United States Congress, drawn so that the GOP's votes in suburbia were safely outnumbered three or four to one. At best, running as a Republican built character and career. If you played an especially spirited version of the sacrificial lamb, maybe Nelson Rockefeller would reward you with a sinecure as counsel or deputy director in the vast state-level bureaucracy he controlled.

Neither Fred Field nor Leslie Maeby intended to settle for any such consolation prize. Two years earlier a Republican, Dan Button, had upset a Democrat to capture a congressional seat, revealing the first signs of rust in the O'Connell apparatus. Now a slate of Republican candidates had banded together on the vow "Total Victory," the same slogan that appeared on scores of campaign buttons this day. Leslie saw the endeavor as even more than politics; it was mythology sprung to life, an epic struggle between good and evil. She envisioned Fred Field as St. George brandishing his broadsword against the dragon.

Leslie had fallen into the campaign accidentally enough, having been drafted from the ranks of the Pop Warner cheerleaders by Field's wife, Pat. For many of the other Field Girls, electioneering meant nothing more than trading one set of pom-poms for another. The candidate's own daughter, Linda, actively feared all the flesh-pressing; the tension of introducing herself to strangers raised blotches on her neck. Leslie, though, had been following politics ever since watching the Kennedy-Nixon debates at age seven, and she had overheard enough at the dinner table to assimilate her parents' contempt for the O'Connell machine. There was purpose in being a Field Girl. Only a few weeks earlier the headquarters had been a vacant store beneath the Wig Discount Center; now typewriters and telephones clattered and rang, and huge calendars charted every event until what the campaign flyers called "Field Day, Nov. 5." Besides, Leslie loved meeting people, and people loved meeting her. She had the budding beauty other girls might easily have envied—flowing brown hair, soulfully hooded eyes, a womanly figure—but also a genial nature that defanged jealousy.

Now Leslie wound through the crowd in the parking lot, clipboard in hand, recruiting volunteers for the campaign. She approached mothers in polka-dot dresses and men in charcoal business suits; she found the eyes behind the sunglasses and smiled in a way that made it miserly to refuse. With each name added to her list, she dispensed a lapel pin emblazoned "The Field Team."

At the podium, an emcee named Geoff Davis held forth, complimenting all the "sweethearts" and "great guys" in attendance. He was a celebrity in his own right, a onetime broadcaster for the Yankees now hosting a popular big-band radio show in Albany. Presently Davis gave way to an array of local, county, and statewide Republican officials, rising to the attorney general and Rockefeller surrogate, Louis Lefkowitz. So beloved was the governor by this audience that even his commissioner of taxation and finance drew hearty applause.

Then, as loudspeakers blared the sound of Barbra Streisand singing "People," Fred Field stepped to the microphone. At thirty-six he still had the looks of a lifeguard—muscular across the back, tanned on the face and forearms, blond hair just past crewcut length. Some in the crowd had known him since his days of football stardom in high school, others more recently from the Rotary Club or Little League or YMCA, and virtually all as a member of the Colonie Town Board for the past eight years. Only the several pens visible in his shirt pocket hinted at his full-time job as an efficiency expert at a steel plant.

None of these attributes, though, augured victory. While the 103rd District included Colonie, it counted the bulk of its voters in two Democratic strongholds, Albany's Arbor Hill ghetto and the factory town of Watervliet. Field faced a six-term incumbent, Harvey Lifset, whom even Republicans conceded to be a veritable statesman by the standards of the O'Connell machine. A paratrooper in World War II, Lifset had earned both a bachelor's degree from a respected private college and a *juris doctor* before embarking on a private legal practice. Since entering the Assembly, he had ascended to the chairmanship of its ways and means committee, one of the half-dozen most powerful positions in state government.

Scanning the crowd, Field fired what ammunition he had. "The 103rd Assembly District," he declared, "has been neglected for years because my opponent has gone down the line with the New York City bosses." To that standard bit of fear-mongering he added something far fresher. Lifset was earning $33,000 annually in what was officially a part-time position, and during the last session he had voted for a bill awarding legislators more generous pensions than those for other state workers. That act radiated the arrogance of entrenched power, which in Albany in 1968 meant the Democratic Party. The loudest ovation of the day, in fact, had gone earlier to the county Republican chairman, Joseph Frangella, for raising exactly that point. "He's a tired old man," Frangella said of Lifset. "He's thinking tired. Remember he voted himself a fat pension? Let's make sure he gets it. Put him into retirement."

Field's relative youth spoke to the audience. So did the campaign's populist theme song. Seen idealistically, the race against Lifset represented a principled revolt against corrupt bossism; viewed more cynically, it typified the battle for dominance between an old Democratic machine built on patronage and a new Republican one oriented around development. Either way, more stood at stake in the campaign than a single seat in the Assembly. In the 103rd District one could measure the shifting balance of power in America, the transfer of political might from city to suburb, some of the very forces only months away from electing Richard Nixon. And Leslie Maeby, just fifteen years old and beginning her sophomore year of high school, was in some small way both witnessing and participating in it all.

When Harvey Lifset learned of Field's opening rally, he cracked, "I guess I'll have to get my parachute out." Like most of O'Connell's candidates, he expected to win without exertion. "We don't run," went one of the boss's maxims. "We stand for election." Behind that rhetoric, so redolent of Parliament, O'Connell meant the machine would produce victory with its time-honored method of purchasing votes with jobs, services, and $5 bills. The individual candidate was almost irrelevant to his own election.

As the descendants of Democrats, many in the Republican camp intimately understood how daunting a task they faced. Field's maternal grandfather had served O'Connell as a committeeman and been rewarded with a post in the public library. His father, a menswear salesman, proudly waited on Albany's mayor, Erastus Corning. Robert Keating, Field's campaign manager, hailed from a still more illustrious bloodline. His great-uncle, and political mentor, was James Farley, Franklin Roosevelt's campaign manager in 1932 and 1936 and simultaneously the chairman of the Democratic National Committee. Even presidential candidates, Farley often told Keating, had to seek O'Connell's blessing, so ironclad was the boss's grip on tens of thousands of votes.

In his career as a journalist, Keating would see that clout for himself, and the spectacle would convert him into a Republican. For decades, O'Connell had cowed the two Albany newspapers, the *Times-Union* and the *Knickerbocker News,* by threatening to withdraw legal advertisements, a lucrative source of income. What few critical articles did appear had a mysterious way of vanishing from the files. But a new publisher, Gene Robb, arrived at the *Times-Union* in 1953, the same time Keating started as a police reporter, and seven years later the newspapers began operating under joint ownership, buttressing the finances of each. As exposés detailed vote-buying, bid-rigging, and sundry other scandals, O'Connell yanked legal advertising worth $250,000 per year. Undeterred, Robb and his executive editor, the future politician Dan Button, raked more muck. The boss, acting through his minions in the court system, had reporters and editors subpoenaed to testify before grand juries nineteen times during one twelve-month stretch in the early 1960s. It was no coincidence, then, that the media, so routinely accused of harboring a liberal, Democratic bias, produced in Albany the first Republican congressman in memory and the mastermind of Fred Field's campaign.

Keating and Field had been cogitating weekly for months prior to the September 4 rally. They raised $9,000 for the campaign, a fabulous amount for what looked to be a lost cause; the $500 they spent renting the helicopter was what most of Field's predecessors had used for an entire campaign. The investment landed him on all three local television newscasts, on radio stations across the dial, and in weekly and daily newspapers throughout the district. Already, Lifset was being out-flanked. A system of Republican committeemen, augmented by personal friends and the Field Girls, formed the counterorganization to O'Connell's legion of precinct captains and ward heelers.

The pace grew only more frenetic as the weeks passed. Camping out with the Boy Scouts, shelling clams at the police department picnic, parading with the volunteer firemen, shaking hands outside a sandpaper factory, Fred Field was ubiquitous. Four thousand dollars bought radio advertisements, with "People" playing in the background as a voice-over promised, "Fred Field will be there." In the appropriate section of the district, billboards boasted of Field, "Educated In Watervliet, Works In Watervliet, Cares About Watervliet."

Field did not lack an agenda so much as he did not need one. He was a liberal Republican in the Rockefeller tradition, endorsing activist government, especially in urban affairs. As a devout Catholic, he did oppose abortion, but the death penalty, too, and later in his career he would vote in favor of gay rights legislation. None of these stands mattered terribly much in 1968. Harvey Lifset, in his lassitude, elevated Field's energy and visibility into the most valuable qualities of all.

Keating flaunted them in a stunt called the "Field Blitz." Several nights each week, from Labor Day until Election Day, he selected a few blocks of the district. Into the sector rolled a converted laundry truck painted in the campaign colors of yellow and black and blasting appeals from rooftop speakers. Beside the vehicle strode Leslie and the rest of the Field Girls in their uniform of blue felt skirt, white blouse with Peter Pan collar, and suspenders striped like the flag. From split-level to Cape Cod to ranch house, they rang doorbells and insinuated themselves, reciting Field's own record and passing out the latest "white paper" attacking Lifset's.

Tremulous as ever, pining to play softball or hang out at the mall, Linda Field gladly allowed Leslie to walk point. The experience thrilled Leslie, compounding the excitement she had felt at the opening rally. Years later she would say that if she had joined a civil rights march at the same malleable moment in her life, she might well have dedicated herself to the movement. But the electricity of engagement, of collective action, first touched her on the Republican campaign trail and there her commitment would reside permanently.

Once Leslie had penetrated a household, Field in his trademark shirtsleeves loped up the sidewalk. He climbed a ladder to meet a voter nailing down shingles; he beseeched a shirtless man mowing the lawn; he convinced a mother in apron fresh from the stove. Swept up in the novelty, neighborhood kids poured into the street, surrounding the candidate with an escort of Sting Ray bikes. At evening's end, with Field back at headquarters and Leslie starting on her homework, Keating would walk to his master map of the district and drag a red marker over the latest streets blitzed.

On October 1, Field and the Field Girls opened a headquarters in Arbor Hill. There, in the poorest and blackest neighborhood of Albany, Field spoke of Lifset's state salary, state car, and state pension. "During our campaign," he declared, "we have found an astonishing number of people who don't know their assemblyman, have never seen him, have never heard from him, and have finally realized he has done nothing for their interests." He carried the message from tenement to boarding-house, to women in curlers and cotton housedresses, to men with crests of conked hair, to all those the O'Connell machine treated as its "deliverable darkies," to borrow the phrase that the columnist Mike Royko coined apropos of Chicago. Along the way, a photographer from the *Times-Union* noticed a hole on the sole of Field's right shoe. His shot of it, taken as the candidate walked the stairs of a battered row house, supplied the signature image of an underdog campaign.

Barely one month before Election Day, Harvey Lifset finally lurched into action, pressing for a debate. Claiming a scheduling conflict, Field stalled him, then negotiated the format down to a mere twenty minutes on the radio. Afterward, Lifset drew Keating aside and moaned, "You're making my life miserable." Over the next few weeks, reports reached the Field campaign that Lifset was actually going door-to-door. Surely that showed desperation, for as erudite an attorney as Lifset was and as skillful a tactician in the legislature, he was a dour, balding man of fifty-two utterly ill-suited for making ingratiating chitchat, much less a shameless plea for rescue. What was it, after all, that Dan O'Connell had told a thousand faithful at the Democrats' kickoff rally? The result would be "the usual."

Two days before this most unusual election, Keating called James Farley and predicted, "We're gonna win this thing." One night before the vote, Field volunteers by the hundreds hung flyers on 20,000 door-knobs. The morning of it, the *Times-Union* still gave Lifset a narrow lead.

Forty-five minutes after the polls closed, though, Fred Field knew he had won. Not only did he carry Colonie by an immense margin, he also took 30 percent of the vote in Arbor Hill. And most significantly for the national realignment under way, he captured Watervliet, which with its factories, mills, and arsenal was the very prototype of a blue-collar, white-ethnic community changing sides. The Republicans, in fact, fulfilled their promise of "Total Victory." Besides Field and Dan Button, who was reelected to Congress, GOP challengers took a seat apiece in the State Senate and the Assembly as well as the position of county attorney. The future novelist William Kennedy, then reporting for the *Times-Union* as Bill, wrote under the headline "A LAST HURRAH SOUNDS FOR AN OLD, WORN MACHINE":

> Could it be true?
> If it was true, then what did it mean?
> Nobody could say at 1 a.m., Wednesday, Nov. 6, 1968. It had all the makings of being as crucial a day as Nov. 8, 1921, had been, when the Democratic Party, sparked by a 1919 victory by the young ex-sailor, Daniel P. O'Connell, son of a South End saloonkeeper, had . . . made the first crack [in an earlier Republican machine].

Had Leslie Maeby been older than fifteen and been better acquainted with the grandfather she knew only as a restaurateur, she might have recognized something epochal in Fred Field's triumph. Dan O'Connell was, metaphorically, Joe Obrycki—or, rather more accurately, the boss Joe Obrycki wished he could have been. In its weariness, its corruption, its bigotry, its loss of utility, the O'Connell machine failed in 1968 for the same reason big-city Democratic organizations were starting to fail across the country. Some would be toppled by coalitions of liberals and blacks, others by Republican reformers; Baltimore's at various times fell to both. On that evening of November 5, Leslie never reached Field headquarters to celebrate; she and her parents watched Walter Cronkite well beyond midnight for the photo finish between Nixon and Humphrey. It was impossible for her to comprehend just how tightly the political and the familial had become intertwined, how closely the transformation in one lineage reflected that of a nation. All Leslie wanted to know was when the next campaign started.

• • •

In a less diplomatic household, a war surely would have raged for the political soul of Leslie Maeby. She was, after all, the daughter of a liberal Democrat and a conservative Republican, a mother who considered Jesus Christ the first socialist and a father who blamed Franklin Roosevelt for the welfare state. In deference to domestic tranquillity, Vilma and Jack Maeby avoided raising the innumerable issues that divided them. So geography more than ideology shaped the political identity of Leslie. Colonie was Republican so she became Republican—"a strong Republican," as she would later put it, "but almost by default."

In that one respect, that passivity, Leslie harked back to her grandfather more than to either parent. Joe Obrycki had joined the Democratic Party because it was the only party in Fell's Point, the only means of wielding power. Vilma and Jack, in turn, rebelled against such pragmatism, following their ideals to the opposite poles of the political spectrum. Now, a generation later, Leslie was reenacting it, albeit for a different party in a different place. How appropriate it seemed that when Leslie attended Joe's funeral in 1970, a mourner presented her with one of his palm cards from the 1939 election for Baltimore City Council.

Pragmatism by another name is flexibility, and the trait would serve Leslie well in the years ahead. She possessed talents more than passions, and when the Republican Party moved to the right she obligingly moved with it. Being a Republican was, to her, a profession, a profession that only secondarily enabled a worldview. "It's like if you decide to be a nurse when you're eighteen, and stay one for twenty years," she once put it. "It becomes who you are. How you read the paper. How you watch the news. Your whole outlook."

That evolution must have begun with a doting daughter's admiration for her father. Certainly, Jack never consciously taught Leslie his political beliefs; working fifteen-hour days at Montgomery Ward, he had little enough time to read the kids bedtime stories. Yet in a second-grade class whose teacher wore a Kennedy boater, Leslie supported Richard Nixon. Four years later she represented Barry Goldwater in a mock presidential debate. All went well enough until her opponent raised the subject of nuclear war. The fallout would settle on the grass, the cows would eat the grass, and then their milk would be radioactive. And then —this girl knew her audience—there would be no more milk-and-cookies time.

It was Vilma who discussed current events with Leslie on a regular basis. Together they digested daily papers from Albany and Baltimore, the evening news with Walter Cronkite, and the weekly compendium of *Time* magazine. Vilma made the issue of civil rights palpable for Leslie with stories of the Number 26 trolley in Baltimore, the black children who had to travel those extra forty-one blocks to high school. When the Chicago police did battle with antiwar protesters during the 1968 Democratic convention, both mother and daughter viewed the officers as villains—"the bad guys," as Leslie later said, "who're coming to beat you up and won't ask what you're doing." The Vietnam War existed for her less as a struggle against global Communism than a threat to draft her brother, Jack Jr. Leslie had been upset enough when a favorite chemistry teacher, the young one named Mr. Bennett who liked Simon and Garfunkel, disappeared one day for his induction physical.

Yet in this era of extremes, of being part of the solution or part of the problem with no neutral ground, Leslie sensed no pressure to choose. One thing, perhaps the only thing, Vilma and Jack agreed upon was Nelson Rockefeller's greatness. By claiming him as her own hero, too, Leslie resolved a divided political heritage. Rockefeller was a Republican who governed like a Democrat, building agencies and edifices on a New Deal scale, marrying grandiose gesture to common touch. He transformed the fairways of an elite country club into a campus for the state university, which Leslie herself would ultimately attend. He bulldozed a faltering neighborhood to erect the South Mall, a complex of government buildings inspired by the Dalai Lama's palace, and suburban families like Maebys flocked to its museum, plaza, and performing arts center. As Fred Field's example showed, local candidates cast themselves in Rockefeller's activist image and were rewarded with whopping majorities at the polls. In the shadow of Albany, if not in the evolving Sun Belt, Republicans campaigned on what government could do, not what it should undo.

Winning term after term, Rockefeller also represented constancy, order, permanence. These were virtues Leslie clung to in the maelstrom of the late 1960s. She inhabited an immediate world reassuring in its sameness. Not one of her friends had parents who were divorced. Her high school contained among its thousand students the barest sprinkling of blacks and Jews, a handful of Deadheads to pass for the counterculture, and an antiwar movement that consisted of one boy named McLaughlin. With its ball fields and tennis courts and indoor pool, its orchestra and computer club and performances of Shakespeare, Shaker High manifested the dream of suburban public education, and Leslie availed herself of all it could offer. She studied Russian, performed in school plays, competed on the synchronized swim team, and pawed the football sidelines in the brown fur of the team mascot, the bison. Her own idealism took the form of volunteering as a candy striper. Leslie savored the very predictability of her life, the comforting rhythms of day, week, and year—visiting relatives in Baltimore at Easter, renting a cabin with the Nicollas on Schroon Lake in the summer, eating franks and beans for dinner every Saturday because it was her father's favorite dish.

That sense of stability first trembled on the Sunday night of July 23, 1967. As usual, Leslie and her mother settled together in the family room to watch the *CBS Evening News*. All around them were gathered the modest pleasures of middle-class existence, the emblems of financial security—floral sofa and imitation-leather recliner, carpet woven tightly in a caramel shade, bookcases laden with school portraits of the children, color television in a handsome maple console.

On television that night, Harry Reasoner introduced the lead story. "In a hundred places," the voice of an unseen correspondent, John Hart, somberly intoned, "Detroit is afire." Barely twelve hours since the police had raided an after-hours club in the black ghetto, what would become the most destructive and lethal race riot in American history had consumed vast stretches of the city. The screen filled with an aerial shot of block after block spewing smoke and flame. In short order followed close-ups, cameos of desolation: fire vaulted from an apartment window; a brick lodged in a bus windshield cobwebbed by its impact. Then came what television news called a "compression shot," scores of charred and looted stores pressed by telephoto lens into a single frieze of chaos.

Through these images, Hart said little, as if the conflagration defied any powers of description. Finally he supplied a few details—one hundred blocks "under siege," a curfew declared, police protecting firefighters, National Guardsmen protecting police—and then he asked a middle-aged black man in a knit shirt and sunglasses who in particular was rioting. As the man prevaricated, a younger black pushed his way into the camera's range. "I'll tell you who's doin' it," he said in exultation. "We all is doin' it." The report culminated with Hart surrounded by guardsmen bearing rifles, a curtain of fire rippling behind them, sirens and gunshots piercing the air. "It looks," he concluded, "like a B-52 raid in Detroit."

Cushioned by hundreds of miles, Vilma viewed the riots with a historical and decidedly liberal perspective. "These people have been down and out so long," she told Leslie as they watched, "now it's coming out." Within a week, President Johnson appointed the National Commission on Civil Disorders, popularly known as the Kerner commission, to investigate the causes and suggest solutions. Its final report arrived at fundamentally the same conclusion as had Vilma, arguing that "white society is deeply implicated in the ghetto" and advocating "national action on an unprecedented scale" to provide inner-city blacks with better housing, education, and jobs. But nothing in Leslie's images of black protest, of the peaceful marchers who seemed the natural heirs of those dignified and long-suffering students on the Number 26 trolley, had prepared her for the destructive and self-destructive pageant of black rage. Regarding the ruins of Detroit, she could only think of the biblical Armageddon.

Just four nights later violence erupted much closer to home, in Albany itself. The trouble started in the midsummer twilight, as several hundred young blacks streaming from a community dance and a basketball game coalesced into a mob. For hours they coursed through the

Arbor Hill slum and the commercial streets downtown, setting fire to a furniture showroom and a liquor store, shattering windows in dozens of small businesses, from Solomon's Mens Wear to the Five Sisters Luncheonette to Bob Daubey's Home Billiard Tables and Supplies. A young white motorist, driving unawares into the havoc, took twenty stitches to close a gash from a brick. Flying glass cut six others, rioters and passersby both. By the time rainfall and one hundred helmeted police stilled the streets, forty-four boys and men had been arrested for inciting to riot.

By the standards of Detroit, of course, the turmoil in Albany barely merited mention, but through her father Leslie felt upheaved by genuine tremors. The Montgomery Ward building stood only a mile up Broadway from Arbor Hill, and between its retail store and distribution center contained more than $10 million of merchandise. The company posted security men on the roof with binoculars and sidearms, bracing for an invasion of looters. Rumors swirled that blacks by the carload—no, the busload—were flooding into Albany from Harlem or Philadelphia. Gangs were making Molotov cocktails, it was said, whites were being pummeled on the streets. Summoned to an emergency meeting the morning after the riot, Jack learned that Ward's warehouses all across the country were fortifying; the facility in Baltimore had even installed steel sheets over its ground-floor windows.

Indeed it was a time of terrible synchronicity. Even as 4,700 army paratroopers and 6,700 National Guard troops restored cold peace to Detroit, riots ignited in small cities across the country, from Waterbury, Connecticut, to Elgin, Illinois, to Tucson, Arizona. These were places that like Albany contained slight black populations and no history of turbulence, places that seemed to have exploded in mimicry. Amid Detroit, Albany, and all the rest sounded the threats of black leaders who had renounced the civil rights movement in favor of militant racial nationalism. Stokely Carmichael implored American blacks to mount a guerrilla war, Adam Clayton Powell called the riots "a necessary phase of the black revolution," and H. Rap Brown urged blacks in Washington to "get you some guns" and "burn this town down." "Violence is necessary," he went on, framing his most notorious aphorism, "it is as American as cherry pie."

In this week when Leslie Maeby turned fifteen, it seemed to her the entire nation was unraveling. Normally so effervescent, she now drifted into preoccupied silences. Sitting on her bed after dinner, she forgot even her sister's presence in the room. How was she supposed to get her diploma, choose a college, find a career? What was the point in planning a future? After 1967 came 1968, with the assassination of Martin

Luther King and more riots. Leslie learned over the high school intercom one June morning that Robert Kennedy had been slain. In the family room two months later, she watched aghast as police gassed and clubbed protesters during the Democratic convention, as a United States senator decried from the podium the "Gestapo tactics." Yet even when Leslie's momentary sympathies flew to the students, as they did in Chicago and again after the shootings at Kent State, her soul craved stability. That hunger let her hear the Republican cry for "law and order" not as a synonym for oppression or a code phrase for bigotry but as the only hope of preserving "some sort of civilization."

Calm returned to Albany, if not America, within days of the 1967 riot. Two or three years later, halfway by accident, Leslie discovered Arbor Hill for herself.

A bar named Mike's Log Cabin, indeed built of pine trunks like an Adirondack retreat, hunched incongruously beside a black barbershop and a soul-food restaurant on North Swan Street. For decades, teenagers had flocked there to drink beer illegally in what amounted to a rite of passage. Since the tavern served Hedrick's, the O'Connell machine's brew, its owners never feared losing their liquor license. Fred Field had drunk there as a high school student in the late 1940s. William Kennedy made a handful of visits over the years. By the early 1970s, Mike's was welcoming its second generation of underage drinkers, literally the sons and daughters of earlier customers. They gaped at the relics suspended from ceiling and walls—at the stuffed heads of moose and deer, the oxen yoke and wagon wheels, the cradle and bomb casing. They sidled alone to the mahogany bar or nuzzled with a date beside the gas fireplace or bellowed with the fellas in a booth, erecting pyramids from the bottles they emptied playing a drinking game called Thump. When someone dropped a quarter in the jukebox for Lou Rawls to sing "Natural Man," the wooden-plank floor creaked with wobbly dancers. If a police officer wandered in, it was rarely to check IDs. More likely he had come to enjoy a platter of clams and a draft on the house. The ward boss enjoyed the same deal.

Outside the doors of unchanging Mike's, however, time had visited Arbor Hill with a vengeance. Once the shared domain of a black elite descended from freedmen and of immigrant waves of Irish, Italians, and Poles, once the neighborhood where Jack and Vilma Maeby shopped for homemade kielbasa, Arbor Hill had degenerated by Leslie's time into a monochromatic slum. Like her, most of Mike's regulars then were offspring of the suburbs, students from Shaker, Colonie, and Christian Brothers High Schools who traveled into Arbor Hill four or six to a car for safety. Every time Leslie passed Albany Memorial Hospital, right on the border of Colonie and Arbor Hill, she rolled up the window and locked the door. From the newspapers alone, she knew of Arbor Hill as the site of murders, drug deals, and melees. Now she could observe firsthand the frame tenements, weatherbeaten and listing, the brick row houses with cracked windows and fissured masonry, the vast lots reduced to rubble, some for so long the ground had gone to seed. About four blocks up Clinton Avenue from Mike's, a curbside drug bazaar vended marijuana, heroin, and cocaine. While Mike's itself maintained immunity from street crime, courtesy of its largess to police and politician alike, occasionally a neighborhood kid would snatch the purse of a customer en route or steal the tape deck from a parked car or hover outside the front door with a baseball bat and lungful of threats.

By one reading of history, Arbor Hill's demise owed at least partly to Nelson Rockefeller, Leslie's paragon. The construction of his epic mall had uprooted some 1,500 blacks from the South End and sent them teeming into Arbor Hill, the only other integrated section of the city. As they arrived through the early and middle 1960s, landlords carved homes into boardinghouses, many of which in turn would be razed for housing projects capable of accepting only a fraction of the displaced.

But the case against Rockefeller relied on circumstantial evidence. Legally speaking, Arbor Hill belonged to Albany's Democratic machine, and it was the machine Leslie blamed for the menace, the torpor, and the decay. To her the salient difference between Colonie and Arbor Hill lay not between black and white or lower class and middle class but between Democratic government and Republican government. Limited as that conclusion was, it held more than a little truth. In 1963, well into the civil rights era, Dan O'Connell told a *Times-Union* reporter, "The only ones I want calling me 'Mister' are niggers and Jews." The city fathers never challenged the pervasive pattern of housing segregation, one occasionally enforced by arson, and regarded the community action programs of the War on Poverty as threats to their hegemony. Leslie had seen the results of this antipathy in Fred Field's 1968 campaign. A substantial minority of Arbor Hill's blacks, disgusted at having their Democratic loyalty assumed, risked retaliation by voting against the O'Connell machine.

Sometime during Leslie's senior year of high school, she visited Mike's Log Cabin for the last time. That was the norm for nearly all its precocious customers. Some went away to college, and not even those who stayed in Albany returned to a place so associated with a younger self. Besides, there was a bar down the street with rhythm-and-blues bands and a black clientele for collegians inclined to slumming.

In one way, though, Mike's Log Cabin never left Leslie. It afforded her an unforgettable view of Democratic failure, of entropy, bungling, and racism. So when she entered the State University of New York at Albany in the fall of 1971, a confirmed Republican, she considered herself not only on the side of law and order but also on the side of the angels.

• • •

Just before her first set of midterm exams, Leslie Maeby learned she would soon acquire that rarest of commodities for a collegiate freshman, a single room. Her roommate, newly affianced, intended to drop out of school immediately. The urgency arose, it seemed, from two small complications. The future groom was black, and the bride-to-be was already carrying his child

Behind a facade of good cheer, Leslie careered between censure and shock. All fall she had anxiously borne the boyfriend's weekend visits, dragging her sleeping bag onto the industrial carpet of an adjoining lounge. Rumor had it the student infirmary dispensed diaphragms and birth control pills. That was not precisely true, but the university did allow private gynecologists and Planned Parenthood counselors use of its facilities to meet patients and do so. With protection so proximate, Leslie could only wonder if this conception was accidental. She knew that her roommate's parents abhorred the black boyfriend—more so, perhaps, since he was not some exotic infatuation but a longtime steady with career prospects in radio. Had sperm and egg conspired to give Mom and Dad the finger?

It was the revolt against parental authority, or more precisely the absence of it, that most unnerved Leslie about college. Life without adults left her vertiginous. Gaining a single room, far from dispelling the discomfort, mutated it into new forms. No longer could Leslie rely on a roommate's presence as the acceptable excuse for dispatching a date at night's end. Now she had to say no, and then resist the pleading and sighing and eye-rolling disbelief. Meanwhile one woman or another in the dormitory was requesting Leslie's room for a tumble. If she didn't feel like a matron, she felt like a madam.

Leslie searched for a sanctuary and discovered one in the form of an anachronism. In the spring of 1972, during the ritual called Rush Week, she pledged the sorority Chi Sigma Theta. Even in its heyday, the Greek system had never dominated the Albany campus; instead of the fallen mansion of *Animal House* stereotype, each fraternity and sorority was accorded a section of dormitory space. And during a time when students experimented with off-campus communes or food cooperatives, ridi-

cule greeted a social institution redolent of chugging contests and home-
coming floats. Fewer than 700 students from an enrollment of 10,000
belonged to the seventeen fraternities and sororities during the 1971–72
academic year. In the following fall, the freshman handbook, which
listed organizations from the Sailing Club to the Young Socialist League,
left the section entitled "Greek Societies" conspicuously blank.

What struck others as hopelessly dated, and corny besides, beckoned Leslie as blessedly temperate. In Chi Sigma Theta, the sorority she
pledged, she found mirrors of herself, suburban children unashamed of
their upbringing, neither prissy nor prudish and yet keen about safe-
guarding a certain propriety. The "hell mother" who hazed Leslie came
from Colonie itself and demanded nothing more arduous of her than
serving breakfast in bed to several fraternity brothers. On the walls of
Chi Sigma Theta's common room in Ten Eyck Hall hung portraits of
each class of sisters, inured to trend in their V-neck black blouses. Below
the Day-Glo poster in a bedroom might repose a Raggedy Ann doll,
What was then called Women's Lib put off these young women with its
stridency, although later in life many would identify themselves as feminists and benefit from the movement in paycheck and promotion. For
the moment, Jacqueline Kennedy with her glamour and grace filled the
contours of role model, and the goal of marriage without career required
no apology. Every Thursday those sisters without beaux made for
O'Heaney's, the traditional Grecian mating ground, hoping to attract a
date for Saturday night.

Individual conservatism led inevitably to the ideological sort. As the
American left liked to put it, the personal was the political. For Leslie
Maeby and her sisters to drink Bud instead of smoking pot, to wear an
evening gown to a formal instead of a peasant dress to a rock concert
was to declare principles. Most members of Chi Sigma Theta never
espoused their beliefs any more explicitly, but several were already
working as pages in the State Capitol, making their presence all the
more comforting to Leslie. In pledging a sorority, in trying to do little
more than escape the dormitory's pressure to sleep with young men she
did not love, she had unwittingly advanced her political career.

The conduit between Chi Sigma Theta and the Republican Party,
between college and the rest of Leslie Maeby's life, was a twenty-two-
year-old alumna of both the university and the sorority, Cathy Bertini.
To call Bertini pixieish was to describe more than her physical dimensions. She could conjure things into being, things like an internship
in the State Capitol with a salary and academic credit, or a summer
job collecting tolls on the Thruway or doing maintenance in a state
park. Bertini held a title with the state Republican Party as director of

youth activities, and she had a credit card to charge dinners at the Bleecker. But ultimately her power resided in five Rolodexes, each the size of a modest wheel of Swiss, the product of nearly a decade in politics.

Bertini had passed out her first flyer at age thirteen in her father's campaign for town council in Cortland, New York. Unlike many of those young politicians she would mentor, she grew up in the bosom of the Republican Party. Cortland lies in a valley between Syracuse and Binghamton, distant in more than miles from such urban hubs. With its unduly wide Main Street flanked by Wiltze's department store and the Varsity malt shop, it evoked nothing so much as a midwestern county seat. Precisely such places had formed the backbone of Robert Taft's GOP, and it seemed no mere geographical coincidence that F. Clifton White had been raised nearby in Earlville.

For three summers in her teens, Cathy attended the TAR school held at Colgate, where White had taught political science. She established a TAR Club in her high school, and in an unforeseeable way helped establish her name. During her senior year Nelson Rockefeller was running for reelection and planned a campaign trip to Cortland. An advance man planning the event with Bertini's father explained that he wanted 2,000 people to greet the governor—at eleven in the morning on a workday in a town of just 19,000. "You've got to get real," the elder Bertini pleaded. The advance man was a Manhattan banker on leave; nothing was more real to him than issuing orders to underlings.

Then Cathy went to work. She convinced her high school principal, conveniently enough a Republican, to send the entire student body to hear Rockefeller speak as an educational experience. That morning she equipped several hundred classmates with placards, buttons, and bumper stickers. The advance man later called her father to marvel, "Where'd you get all those people?"

By the measure of the Republicans to come after her, Cathy positioned herself almost suspiciously in the middle of the road. She admired Rockefeller and advocated a vigorous government role in such areas as conservation and higher education. His campus for the Albany branch of SUNY rose in twenty-story towers around Cathy during her college years. It would seem only appropriate years later that her patron proved to be not Ronald Reagan, the true believer, but George Bush, a man expediently and inconclusively converted from the Connecticut moderation of his father to Sun Belt conservatism.

But it took a fellow Republican to draw such a distinction. Cathy went through college during the most traumatic years of protest—1968, 1969, 1970—and to most of her classmates she was simply the enemy.

She crossed picket lines to attend classes during a student strike after Kent State. A classmate who spotted her recruiting for the College Republicans bellowed, "You Nazi!" Even a boy named Greg from her hometown harangued her in the cafeteria line. Since Cathy knew him, she tried to explain. Yes, the system was flawed, deeply flawed, but she believed in it enough to want to improve it. "Yeah," Greg answered, unmoved, "but you're gonna grow up and get married and have children and stop doing all these things. You won't be around long enough to make a difference."

He guessed right only about her getting married. The summer soldiers, it could be argued, were really those like himself—all torn jeans, tie-dyed shirts, and brash slogans. In high school, as Greg should have remembered, Cathy had chosen an aphorism from Edmund Burke to appear under her yearbook portrait: "All that is necessary for the forces of evil to win the world is for enough good men to do nothing." In 1968, as Leslie was working as a Field Girl, Cathy organized the campus vote for Arnold Proskin, a Republican who won an upset victory as county attorney. Two years later, barely a college senior, she worked full-time on Rockefeller's reelection campaign. In victory speeches, candidates began to mention her name. And in September 1971, three months after earning her degree in political science, Cathy Bertini inherited the position of youth director from one of her own mentors.

Her domain was a converted attic on the fourth floor of a brick townhouse at 315 State Street, the headquarters of the state Republican Party. The party itself may have been flush, underwritten as it was by Rockefeller's millions, but this room evoked a white-elephant sale. Cathy worked at a metal desk so bulky and gray she dubbed it the "battleship." From the basement a volunteer dredged up discarded office equipment—file cabinets with scratches and dents, manual typewriters, a mimeograph, and a contraption called the A&M for imprinting envelopes. The same excavation uncovered a few Eisenhower buttons and a ticket stub from the 1946 state GOP convention, which instantly served as decorations on the red, white, and blue walls. Elsewhere the adornments changed by the campaign year. A bumper sticker in psychedelic shades for Jacob Javits would yield to a photograph of a newly paved state road with the slogan "Pothole Haters for Rockefeller," which in turn would give way to a poster of Richard Nixon with Wilt Chamberlain. Into this virtual clubhouse grown-ups rarely ventured; they communicated by intercom.

There was nothing puerile, however, about what Cathy Bertini did. The GOP headquarters literally stood amid political power in New York State, less than two blocks up the hill from the State Capitol, the legislative offices, and the major agencies. The venues most favored by politicians for cutting deals and leaking stories to the press, the Bleecker and the Lark Tavern, lay within five minutes' walk. The front window on the fourth floor looked across State Street into the office of Victor Condello, the highest-paid lobbyist in town, with clients of such national import as Mobil Oil and Montgomery Ward. An especially keen eye could spot the Assembly speaker or Senate majority leader stopping by for a cocktail beneath the chandelier.

To a collegiate Republican like Leslie, accustomed to stuffing envelopes and eating Hamburger Helper, Cathy herself qualified as an operator. She could recommend the faithful for internships and summer jobs; she could charge cocktails and steak dinners at the Bleecker. She planned the annual TAR Day held in Albany, enlisted counselors and teachers for TAR camps and schools, and marshaled volunteers for various election campaigns. Through these activities Cathy's protégés met congressmen and senators, the governor, and even the president. Days before the public, they knew which state commissioner was being forced to resign or where the next state convention was going to be held.

It came as no surprise, then, that the State Senate asked Cathy Bertini to become its first female page. She turned down the job but searched her sorority for a sister with the requisite composite of deference, responsibility, and beauty. That young woman, Barbara Stuart, wound up appearing on the front page of the *Daily News* and on a television game show. Suddenly the legislature wanted more women, and Cathy emerged as the patronage broker. From Chi Sigma Theta came Chris Ammirati, Laura Piening, and Jeanne Quinn, Leslie Maeby's "hell mother," and finally, in January 1973, Leslie herself.

Pages were so integral to the State Senate's doings that their stools filled gaps between the legislators' own chairs, like a sort of connective tissue. Not that the pages ever rested very long. On a given day Leslie might fetch lunch from the cafeteria for one senator or rent a tuxedo for another or hear Rockefeller himself deliver the State of the State address, to her satisfaction demanding life imprisonment for heroin dealers. As much as she conceived of herself as a veteran already, as determined as she was not to gape in starstruck awe, she never before had watched law being wrought.

The process, though, suffused her with something less than pride. The very first day of the session, the senators squandered hours picking their seats. Only three women served in the chamber—Carol Bellamy, Karen Burstein, and Mary Anne Krupsak—and Leslie overheard all the cracks on the days they wore pants. Most of all, Leslie discovered that the majority did not merely rule but reign. She had entered politics to defeat a dictatorship, the O'Connell machine. That her own party, the Republicans, controlled the State Senate made its tactics no more palatable to her. If the majority leader placed a single star next to any bill on the daily calendar, it would not be heard. During one floor debate she heard a Democrat open a speech, "My bill, which won't see the light of day. . . ." Sent on errands to the Legislative Office Building, Leslie discovered that the Republican senators enjoyed corner offices, suites with three or four rooms, while the typical Democrat settled for half the space and one-quarter the staff.

"You grow up learning we have this fair system and everybody has a voice," Leslie would say years later in retrospect. "You read *The Federalist Papers* and learn the government was set up so that even minorities would have a voice. Then you see it in action. You started to be skeptical. 'Why is it like this?' You started to realize the system is about power, not democracy. You had to learn the game, position yourself so you could make a difference, be influential. In Colonie, it was more idealistic. Then you realize that's not the way it is. 'Well, this is real life.' "

At the end of her first session in May 1973, at the age of only nineteen, Leslie weighed a choice between her conscience and her desires. She decided to remain in an imperfect, even corrupted profession rather than resign from public life with some abstract idealism intact. It was the same answer Cathy Bertini had given in the cafeteria line to her hometown critic. And with Bertini's intercession, Leslie rose rapidly through the echelons of the state party, serving in 1974 on its platform committee, organizing college voters in the gubernatorial race later that year, and attending the 1976 Republican National Convention as an at-large delegate. One night, as Jack and Vilma Maeby watched the television coverage, the camera lingered over Leslie during "The Star-Spangled Banner."

More and more, the constellation of young people around Bertini formed the personal and professional ensemble of Leslie's life. And it was through Bertini that she met Frank Trotta and Tim Carey. Bertini did not forge history; she facilitated it. Through the attic over which she presided, through the talent pool she assembled, through the opportunities she afforded, these three expatriates from the Democratic past, from ward clubhouse and union hall and ethnic ghetto, marched toward the Republican future.

Frank Trotta had encountered Bertini even before starting college. Early in 1973 he came to Albany for a dinner honoring the outstanding Young Republican in each State Senate district, and Bertini attended in her role as youth director for the state party. Soon after matriculating at

SUNY, he found himself periodically included among her entourage for meals at the Bleecker. The culinary comforts, though, meant less to him than did the psychic ones. Frank treasured the attic at 315 State Street as a touchstone of shared values in an alien time and place, the equivalent to what the North Italy Society or Local 86 union hall had been for his grandfather Silvio. Tim Carey had met Bertini in the spring of 1972 over the beer barrel at a Young Republicans fund-raiser. He was still a registered Democrat at the time, but a mutual friend of his and Bertini's brought him along as a known expert in tapping kegs, not to say draining them. Before long, Bertini steered him into a summer job in a state park and, as always exacting her price, had him serve as a volunteer security guard in a TAR school. Soon after, he changed his registration to Republican.

The circle around Cathy Bertini called themselves the State Street Gang. Some were liberals of the Javits strain, others conservatives in James Buckley's thrall. Predictably, feuds erupted along the fault lines of ideology, as those who were buddies on the fourth floor might well labor for competing candidates in a primary. Love affairs blossomed and wilted, between Tim Carey and Laura Piening, between Leslie Maeby and Paul Cardamone, her campaign manager in a failed race for the Albany County board. Frank Trotta ultimately married Laura's sister, Susan. Whatever the cleavages within, the State Street Gang survived in response to the antagonism without. Even with Richard Nixon in the White House, and exponentially more so with him extricated, these young Republicans lived estranged from their contemporaries. Many times in the 1974 campaign Leslie drove hours to some college campus to find only two or three students willing to meet her. When the alternative consisted of antiwar marchers, McGovern volunteers, and dabblers in casual sex and recreational drugs, the schisms between factions of the State Street Gang became as abstruse and irrelevant as those between the leftist sects of the Great Depression, each with its own table in the City College cafeteria.

In the Age of Aquarius, the dawn of the new era, the State Street Gang championed the status quo, or, more accurately, a vision of an even earlier America, one untainted by welfare-state liberalism and the rights revolution. The gang's members possessed both a majority's certitude that they spoke for all but the malcontented fringes of a nation and a minority's aggrievement, excited by their oddity within their own generation. The very intensity of their nostalgia, of what a critic would call their reactionaryism, paradoxically created the true revolution in American politics in the final decades of the twentieth century. And the State Street Gang formed its partisans, a more effective underground than the Weathermen with their explosives and communiqués ever came close to being. Like all effective guerrillas, they went unnoticed because they dressed so inconspicuously. Really, how could people that straight be that subversive?

Chapter Fourteen

Poor Snob
(Tim Carey)

O<small>N THE NIGHT OF</small> O<small>CTOBER</small> 20, 1967, <small>ONLY HOURS BEFORE</small> the antiwar movement would besiege the Pentagon, Specialist Fourth Class Tim Carey unrolled his sleeping bag across one of its corridors. Alongside the bedroll he placed his helmet, gas mask, M-14 rifle, .45-caliber pistol, ammunition pouch, and tear gas grenades. As far as Tim could see, his comrades in the 503rd Military Police Battalion similarly ensconced themselves, burying their eyes from the fluorescent lights and wriggling for comfort against the terrazzo floor. Only in the narrow pathway between their collective feet and the far wall could anyone walk, and just as sleep was descending a passing soldier bumped into a hopper used for loading tear gas. Seconds later an acrid fog suffused the air. Farther down the hallway, where the battalion gave way to other units, troops struggled upright and stumbled away, groping behind blinded eyes.

Amid the bedlam, with their nostrils and armpits burning, with tears and mucus streaming, Tim Carey and his buddies merely waited. After all the gas they had inhaled in training, they had grown immune, if not to its effects then to the panic and flight those effects conspired to cause. In just a few minutes, they realized, the worst would subside, leaving their skin tingling as if from after-shave. A few men simply pulled on their masks, rolled back into slumber, and snored through their charcoal filters until morning. The rest congratulated themselves on another test met. This was, after all, the 503rd, "Patton's Palace Guard" in World War II, veterans of the Dominican Republic intervention in 1965. Just four months earlier the battalion had packed its gear, taken its inoculations, and executed its wills in preparation for flying into the Middle East war. Only Israel's six-day victory canceled the trip.

For most of the past year, though, the 503rd had been drilling for duty in something closer to civil war, the race riots and political protests kindling across America. Hour by monotonous hour it practiced tactics that harked back in some cases to the Napoleonic campaigns—how to clear a street in a marching wedge; how to leave those being gassed a route of retreat; how to maintain an impassive face against constant provocation. When the battalion held maneuvers Tim got to play a hippie antagonist, donning granny glasses, buckskin jacket, and shoulder-length wig to stir revolution on the imitation corner of Oak and Broad. The 503rd made instructional films for police departments; it demonstrated techniques for the FBI. On this night a brigadier general, Carl C. Turner, visited the men in their hallway to shake hands. The next afternoon, the attorney general, Ramsey Clark, and the secretary of defense, Robert McNamara, would observe their performance from the windows of the Pentagon.

For all the gravity of the assignment, Tim knew only its rudiments. In a briefing, his commanding officer had told the men that an antiwar march was planned, with its terminus outside the Pentagon. There were rumors and threats of an attempt to storm the building. A character named Abbie Hoffman had even vowed to levitate it in an exorcism. "You have to hold your line," the commanding officer had said. "Don't let the people through. Make sure things don't get out of control." Beyond that, neither Tim nor anyone else in the battalion required direction. What was the point of all that training if not to render instruction unnecessary?

Not only did the impending protest seem vague to Tim, so did the larger movement that had organized it. He had never come any closer to antiwar activism than flashing peace signs during the 503rd's riot rehearsals. He was twenty years old, barely months beyond a job installing and repairing oil burners. Even after being drafted, he had never expected to serve, not with his 20/200 eyesight. On the morning he went to Fort Hamilton in Brooklyn for his induction physical, he fully expected to return home for dinner in Crotonville as a 4-F. Instead, he was riding a troop train to Fort Jackson, South Carolina, with only the clothes he was wearing. After basic training, when he was selected for the MPs, he asked a sergeant why. "For the motor pool," he was told. That made sense; Tim had been fixing cars since he was twelve, and no doubt the talent had shown on the army's aptitude test. But, no, he wasn't bound for changing the oil in jeeps. Soon he was policing Fort Bragg in North Carolina, dragging spouses to neutral corners in marital rows, peeling apart the bodies during brawls at the noncommissioned officers' club, and meanwhile being steeled to safeguard his nation against insurrection.

But if Tim and his comrades were supposed to hate their peers across the barricades, or at least to regard them as the enemy, the antipathy had not taken hold. What the men in the 503rd harbored was not fervent anti-Communism so much as a mixture of obligation and inevitability. You got drafted; you went; you went, if you were Tim Carey, just like your father and your uncles and your big brother had gone before you. The domino theory had nothing to do with it, and the idea of enlisting was preposterous, except under the sort of legal duress Michael Carey had known. Most of the MPs in the 503rd hailed from the Northeast, from places like Boston and Philadelphia and Long Island, and they exuded a cosmopolitan cynicism, at least compared to the faction of small-town southerners in the unit. Each kept a calendar with the days left in his hitch marked in descending order. It was called an "F.T.A.," literally the abbreviation for the recruiting slogan "Fun, Travel, Adventure," but more commonly for "Fuck the Army." One guy in the barracks, Eddie Katheder, a would-be folksinger, brought records by Tom Paxton, Bob Dylan, and Joan Baez. When the MPs shot pool in the dayroom, they brayed along with Phil Ochs on "Cops of the World." It drove the southerners crazy, almost as crazy as the sight of Eddie and his crowd smoking a joint.

Tim heard Ochs's song not as an anthem of dissidence, but as an acute comment on a war he saw as absurd rather than immoral. Nobody had even declared it a war. What was that phrase he remembered from studying Korea? "Police action." Was that what you called it when boys were dying and America still kept its biggest guns holstered? The only advice Michael had ever given Tim about the military was to stay in the pack, not call attention to yourself. That meant serving two years and then going home, maybe to take the exam for becoming a New York City cop. Or so Tim Carey thought on the evening of October 20, clucking at soldiers who couldn't handle a little tear gas, envisioning nothing more demanding the next day than glorified guard duty.

Across the Potomac, the leaders of the demonstration understood the import clearly. This event aspired to be the largest in the nation since 100,000 "doves" had massed in Manhattan six months earlier. As important, it marked the transformation of the antiwar movement from protest to resistance, Old Left to New. The sponsoring coalition, the National Mobilization Committee to End the War in Vietnam, consciously welcomed Maoist and Trotskyite sects alongside Quaker pacifists and the suburban bourgeoisie of SANE. From Jerry Rubin and David Dellinger to Dr. Benjamin Spock and the Reverend William Sloane Coffin, the leadership crossed lines of generation and tactics. Few observers could miss the symbolism that the rally preceding the march on the Pentagon would be conducted from the steps of the Lincoln Memorial, the very ground consecrated in August 1963 by Martin Luther King and the March on Washington.

Under the aquamarine skies of Indian summer, weather that normally would have brought touch football to the site, a crowd assembled in the tens of thousands. Some had arrived the previous day for a mass return of draft cards at the Department of Justice; some had lurched stiff-legged out of overnight buses just that morning, bag lunches in hand. They looked not like the hippie caricature Tim had portrayed but the college students they were, clad in tweed coats and flannel shirts and penny loafers, perhaps a paisley bandanna or a serape carried back from a Peace Corps stint. Like delegations to a mock convention, each group bore aloft its sign—"Princeton Seminary," "Ethical Culture School," "Rutgers Newark," "B.U. S.D.S." When Pete Seeger soared into the final harmony of "Wasn't That a Time," his listeners applauded earnestly enough for a hootenanny.

The largest banner of all, stretched taut behind the podium, declared in block letters tall as a hedge, "SUPPORT OUR GI'S . . . BRING THEM HOME NOW!" It was a message at least some of the organizers strained to convey, appreciating the precarious path their movement walked between patriotic dissent and wartime disloyalty. Yet even this rally, notable for its good manners above almost all else, frayed at the edges. From a homemade flagstaff, someone flew the Viet Cong colors. A placard proclaimed, "Avenge Che!" "Johnson Bullshit," offered another. From the stage, one performer led a sing-along that surely would have enraged the MPs languishing in a Pentagon corridor. "It takes a real man to say, 'I won't go,' " she caroled. "It takes a real man to say, 'No.' "

By the time the rally ended and the procession to the Pentagon commenced, the serene surface was blistering with confrontation. Among the protesters themselves, arguments erupted over whether to follow the rather circuitous permitted route or advance more directly, inviting a showdown with the authorities. For the moment, moderation prevailed. A gaggle of counterdemonstrators, saying they represented the Polish Freedom Fighters, Inc., brandished their own signs about the "Red Clergy" and "Jewish-Red Anarchy." "You're escaping," one shouted at a medical student. "No," the young man insisted, his voice cracking with nerves, "I will go to Vietnam after I graduate." To which the Pole chortled with a derision rich beyond words.

Meanwhile, Tim remained indoors and ignorant. It was Ramsey Clark and Robert McNamara who monitored the march's progress by radio and closed-circuit television. It was they who decided how to deploy the 10,000 men at their disposal. There were federal marshals, many hardened by duty in Montgomery, Alabama, and Oxford, Mississippi, during the civil rights crusade. There were troops from the Eighty-second Airborne, only months removed from service in the Detroit riot. There were Armored Cavalry and National Guardsmen and federal Park Police. Fifteen judges stood ready in Washington to conduct assembly-line arraignments, and 1,500 vacant jail cells had been reserved. Despite all the manpower and all the judicial machinery, the goal of the Johnson administration that day was to "act in a way which holds to the absolute minimum the possibility of bloodshed and injury [and] minimizes the need for arrest," as a planning memorandum put it. Any other outcome would qualify as a public opinion disaster, something a president already astride a divisive war could ill afford.

Shortly after one-thirty, Tim Carey and his companions in Company A of the 503rd were summoned into action. They marched out a basement door, up a flight of concrete steps, and aligned themselves at the front of a raised plaza overlooking a parking lot, where the march was officially to culminate. The full complement of MPs took the shape of an inverted U, cupping the colonnade of the Pentagon's Mall Entrance. Tim himself held a post in the front rank, the most likely scene of a collision with protesters. Before him ran only two ropes, pitched at the levels of knee and waist, the sort of restraint suited to a movie-house concession stand.

Those ropes formed part of the scheme for avoiding strife. So did the assignment of the 503rd. Dressed more like police than soldiers, they would present less provocation, it was thought. On orders, most had left their rifles inside the Pentagon and their pistols unloaded. The task of making arrests belonged to several hundred federal marshals who were situated twenty yards behind the front line, and were wearing business suits augmented by helmets and billy clubs. If all went well, if all subscribed to plan, their efforts would not be required, for the wall of imperturbable MPs would have convinced any protester to reconsider aggression. Perhaps none of the demonstrators would realize most of the MPs were just teenagers, as light as 135 pounds, and for all their training were virgins to genuine crowd control, much less on the scale of some 35,000.

Beneath his helmet and behind his baton, Tim showed a mask of

318 • T h e   I n h e r i t a n c e

pure opacity. Look straight ahead, he repeated to himself in the mantra
of drills. Don't answer. Talk out of the side of your mouth so only the
MP next to you can hear. Inwardly, however, the spectacle filled him
with awe. Never had he seen a larger crowd than the several thousand
who filled the bleachers when Ossining High played Sleepy Hollow in
the annual football rivalry. Even Scott Kessler, a more worldly comrade,
shared the sensation. He had spent a few New Year's Eves in Times
Square and this throng struck him as something vaster, for there were
no skyscrapers to interrupt the bodies.

For the moment, the mood indeed seemed celebratory. Pivoting his
eyes across the crowd, Tim spotted people drinking beer and smoking
marijuana. Farther down the formation of MPs, where they were carrying rifles, a girl placed daisies in muzzle after muzzle. From an unseen
stage drifted the choppy rhythms and nasal harmonies of a rock band
called the Fugs. Soon they halted in favor of the modal drone of multi-
tudes chanting "Ommmm" in their attempted exorcism. If it worked as
Abbie Hoffman had predicted, then any time now the Pentagon would
rise three hundred feet aloft, turn orange, and start spinning. And Tim,
eyes obediently forward, would miss the whole thing. He could only
think it was true what cynics said about these student protesters: They
didn't give a damn about politics, they just wanted an excuse to party.

Then he saw the first can fly toward his position. Tomato soup, he
noted as it lay dented on the ground; he had stocked plenty in his days
at Shopwell. Another missile soon followed, then a third. Anyone who
had bothered to lug a case of canned soup a mile and a half from the
Lincoln Memorial to the Pentagon, Tim realized, had arrived with assault
in mind. But his training forbade any response. He stood rigid as rocks
and soda bottles fell in squalls, as faces pressed so close to his own he
could feel the breath that carried temptations and taunts. "You're an
asshole . . . Come on over with us . . . Do you know what you stand for?
. . . Just lay down your gun." Two rows into the crowd, an unsleeved
arm rose, clasping a draft card that danced with flame. Another hand
lifted another card to it, as casually as bumming a light. Then there were
four, six, eight cards afire, mocking the conscripts mere feet away.

All around Tim swirled a cacophony. Demonstrators howled, "Hell
no, we won't go." Copters chopped the air. A platoon sergeant shouted
from behind, "Don't listen to 'em. Keep your place. Keep your space."
Then a captain took up the bullhorn: "A Company, hold your ground.
A Company. Nobody comes and nobody goes. Just hold your ground."
It sounded as much a plea as an order.

Tim never saw the first surge coming. Years later he could only
compare the experience to being at Belmar or Seaside, his favorite
places on the Jersey Shore, and getting toppled by an unexpected

breaker. "Leave us alone," he ordered fecklessly. "Get back." Protesters by the hundred were shredding the line. Some grabbed MPs by the chin strap, spinning them to the ground. Others yanked at the tear gas grenade secured in each man's utility belt. During the tussles many detonated and began spewing gas. The cloud billowed so thick even Tim lost his vision. He pulled on his mask, found no improvement, then tore it off. Bodies banged. Voices grunted. Marshals and sergeants backpedaled into the defense called a shrinking perimeter, leaving the forward MPs atomized and adrift in the human tide.

If Tim's life to this point had yielded a single truth, if all the drills had underscored a single tenet, it was to protect your own. Squinting into the banks of gas, tightening his fist around his baton, Tim cared nothing for Vietnam or Lyndon Johnson or the army or the Pentagon. He wanted only to find his comrades, Terry Sunkes and Joe Kelleher and the rest. He swung his club into chests and necks, each stroke of wood against bone sounding like a shattering dish. He attacked anything around him not wearing MP green. True to his training, he never lifted his weapon against any foe's skull. No, it was too easy to break a baton that way.

Only when reinforcements poured from the Pentagon, taking gun butt, nightstick, and combat boot to the protesters, did the battle line push safely in front of Tim. With his position now manned by fresh MPs, he staggered back toward the colonnade. Between gasps of breath he asked if everyone was all right. There was word one of the MPs had been injured, but nobody knew whom or how badly. Terry Sunkes, it turned out, had been knocked down and nearly trampled. Joe Kelleher had pushed Scott Kessler out of the path of a kick in the groin, and then Kessler had battered his attacker to the ground. Contained and incensed, the crowd bellowed in sarcasm, "Hold that line! Hold that line!"

Each side fired by bloodshed, the rage built for ninety more minutes. Then, at five-thirty, as day was resolving into dusk, a glory of auburn and lavender, the offensive was launched. A force of demonstrators, easily beyond a thousand, burst through the single line of MPs at the far edge of the perimeter. Immediately ahead lay a secondary entrance, marked simply "Corridor 7." Tim missed the moment of attack, occurring as it did fifty yards diagonally behind him. By the time he turned, he saw the protesters being driven back by the Sixth Armored Cavalry, 638 strong, which had been waiting in the very hallway breached. Bristling with rifles and bayonets, the unit rolled forward until it restored a defensible front. Then came the medics and the marshals, attending to many of the forty-five injuries and 667 arrests the demonstration would ultimately produce.

By midevening, only an encampment of two thousand marchers

remained, burning picket signs and barricades for heat. Tim Carey finally repaired to his hallway and his sleeping bag. Dramatic as the day had been, he shared no war stories with the 503rd. His silence was partly a function of professionalism; even handling a car accident or a bar fight at Fort Bragg, he hated to gossip about duty. More important, what he felt now exceeded anything that could be handily reduced to an anecdote. As he relived the experience of the last eight hours, he focused not so much on the soup cans or the exorcism or the blinding gas as on a single phrase borne on the wind. At one point early in the afternoon, the breeze had swiftly changed direction so that it carried sound especially clearly from the stage. Someone was speaking—the comedian Dick Gregory, Tim would later learn—about just who filled up the army. "Poor blacks," Tim was pretty sure he heard, and "dumb whites."

Maybe, Tim told himself now, those words were what had riled the crowd. Or maybe he was crediting Gregory too much. What had been riled, at least these few hours later, was within Tim. Until today, it had never fully struck him how different he was from those people across the ropes, most of them his own peers. He knew a handful of classmates back in Ossining who had gone to college or gotten married for the deferments or finagled a way into the National Guard to avoid combat. But those had seemed like individual decisions, not the pattern etched by privilege. And for young men like Tim who went into the service, basic training set out to destroy any such distinctions as social class. With his shaved head, olive uniform, and standard-issue glasses, Tim gazed into the latrine mirror some mornings unsure if he was seeing himself or the private behind him in line. Then, at Fort Bragg, only one distinction appeared—between the cops, of whom he was one, and the resentful soldiers they policed.

It took Dick Gregory calling Tim Carey dumb to smarten him up. Hardly anyone in his unit, now that he thought about it, had a college education. Even the officers corps, without enough degreed men from which to draw, was accepting high school graduates. Tim knew that college had plenty to do with class. The schools in Ossining rarely prepared a Crotonville kid to be anything loftier than a mechanic or clerk. College was for the wealthy of Chilmark and Briarcliff, for the middle class of The Hill. Tim hardly begrudged his contemporaries who took ivied sanctuary while he obediently marched, not when "I shoulda gone to college" was a standard barracks refrain. But he could barely contain the disbelief, the near hatred, that those fortunate sons should attack American soldiers, should attack *him,* for bearing the burden they shirked.

What Tim's viscera told him ultimately found confirmation in the emotionless realm of statistics. Eighty percent of American soldiers in Vietnam hailed from poor and working-class homes, calculates Christian G. Appy in his authoritative 1993 book *Working-Class War*. In profiling the four hundred men from Long Island killed in Vietnam, *Newsday* described the vast majority as having been the children of "blue collar or clerical workers, mailmen, factory workers, building tradesmen, and so on." Harvard's graduating class of 1970, in comparison, contained just two veterans among its nearly 1,200 men. This class schism held just as true for the world immediately around Tim Carey. All four sons in his family served during the Vietnam War, with two of them seeing combat and the eldest, Michael, being severely injured in an ambush. The one hundred households of Crotonville sent twenty-three sons into the armed forces during the Vietnam era, bettering the level of participation for America as a whole. With a population of about 24,000, Ossining lost thirteen young men, giving it a per capita death rate twice the nation's. Across the Croton River, in the more affluent and liberal community of Croton-on-Hudson, not a single boy perished. As Tim's mother, Edith, had shouted at the local draft board in 1972, when her youngest son was called, "You've already got three of mine. Go get one from somebody who hasn't given *any*."

Years would pass, of course, before Tim or anyone else discovered most of this data. As of October 21, 1967, some 18,000 Americans had died in Vietnam, less than one-third of the ultimate total, and both the war and its opposition were escalating rapidly. Within hours of the Pentagon protest, imitative rallies arose in Tokyo and Paris, Oslo and Berlin. Several days later a priest, Philip Berrigan, poured blood into the files of the Selective Service headquarters in Baltimore. The next month the Students for a Democratic Society sent a delegation to Hanoi. One of its members, Cathy Wilkerson, would ultimately join the Weathermen and plunge into hiding after a homemade bomb exploded in her father's Greenwich Village townhouse. Three of the principal organizers of the Pentagon rally—David Dellinger, Jerry Rubin, and Abbie Hoffman— would sit as defendants in the Chicago Eight trial. Norman Mailer, arrested at the Pentagon, would liken the demonstrators to Civil War heroes in *The Armies of the Night*. The day the Pentagon was stormed, as he saw it, was the day the American left threw off its "damnable mediocre middle," its "sterile heart." His friend Jimmy Breslin, writing the morning after in the *Washington Post,* found less to celebrate. After a rally of "taste and human respect" before the Lincoln Memorial, he argued, some three thousand "troublemakers . . . put a deep gash into the anti-war movement."

And into Tim Carey's psyche, it could be added. For years afterward, large crowds riddled him with fear. He turned down free tickets to football and baseball games. He went mute addressing a high school audience during the 1972 presidential campaign. Seized by cold sweats and nausea, he once retreated from an amusement park in the midst of a date. His nightmares of the Pentagon demonstration ceased only when he trained himself not to dream.

Eventually, he mastered his anxieties sufficiently to undertake an extremely public life. And the message that would animate it was also forged that day and night of October 21, 1967. Tim remembered not the peaceable mass but the abusive and violent fringe, the ones who taunted him, the ones he clubbed, the ones who returned to college dormitories while he returned to Fort Bragg. He had not yet heard the phrase "liberal elite." For the first time, however, he understood the concept and recognized its face.

• • •

Many afternoons for a period of Tim Carey's childhood, he joined his older brother Michael in a ritual called an alligator fight. The weapons were the chain-store shoes they wore to Catholic school, shoes so worn the soles flopped loose from the uppers, especially with a kick. Their daily contest done, Tim and Michael fetched the glue, slathered on a layer, and placed andirons atop each shoe while the adhesive dried. The next day at school, though, the boys' feet sweated and the seal came undone, and the cycle started anew. What might have ended it, a trip to Thom McAn, fell beyond the budget of Charlie and Edith Carey, raising seven children on the salary of a supermarket butcher.

Born in 1947, Tim formed part of the baby boom only chronologically. In a nation of growing affluence, his family and his neighborhood clung at the border between the working class and the working poor. Some homes in Crotonville lacked water meters and indoor toilets into the 1960s. From Tim's second year until his thirteenth, the Careys lived in a house rented from an aunt, with a furnace that heated only the top floor. All winter Edith carried her children's meals from the chilly kitchen to the bedrooms upstairs, and at night she laid unzipped coats over their blankets. Tim usually slept wearing his grandfather's hat.

Even as a boy, even in the cocoon of Crotonville, Tim realized how much he missed from the middle-class birthright. If he wanted a bicycle, he had to scavenge parts from the garbage dump and jerry-rig it himself. When kids chose sides for baseball games, he went unpicked until the end because he had no glove. Seeing a new movie meant rowing up the Croton River and trudging through the marshes to hunch beside a speaker in the back row of the Starlite Drive-In. "Timmy Two-Cent," others called him for dragging his wagon through Crotonville in search of deposit bottles. Better to be razzed, though, than to be broke. Most days Tim sold the homemade dessert in his bag lunch for spare change. He caddied on weekends at a country club. On Tim's fifteenth birthday, Edith presented him with the job Michael had just left stocking shelves in a pharmacy. Often Charlie Carey, wallet empty and pockets drained after paying the household expenses, had to borrow coffee money from Tim. Without his own car, Charlie drove to church many Sundays in the creaking Plymouth his teenaged son had bought for $25.

Parents like Edith, who had survived the Depression with its looming starvation and homelessness, certainly considered themselves comfortable now. There was money enough to pay tuition for the older boys at St. Augustine grammar school and to make donations to the Catholic school for the deaf that educated and boarded a daughter, Sharon. The dinner table usually bowed with full platters of meat loaf and beef stew and, every Friday, fried flounder.

More important, in compensation for a life of paycheck-to-paycheck subsistence, Crotonville wove a rich mesh of community. In the 1950s and 1960s, every bit as much as in the Depression, men spent their weekends building one another's homes like Amish farmers joining in a barn-raising. The American Legion post sponsored sports teams, held holiday parties, and showed Tom Mix westerns. Without any public park, the children created their own recreation program—fishing and swimming in the Croton, hiking along the aqueduct, pitching tents and building campfires in various backyards. After John F. Kennedy was slain, youngsters pooled the money they had earned doing chores and sent it in a shoebox as a donation to the presidential library. An embossed thank-you card arrived weeks later, bearing in place of a postage stamp the signature of Jacqueline Kennedy.

Tim received a more direct political education than most, courtesy of his grandmother Lizzie. From her he heard stories of Democratic leadership and compassion, stories that stretched from Al Smith to John Kennedy but centered on Franklin Delano Roosevelt and the Works Progress Administration, saviors of Mama Cypher and Edward Garrett. Sometimes Lizzie took Tim, as well as his uncle Richie, when she led the local candidates through Crotonville. Even in a social setting, drinking a 7&7 at the Parker-Bale bar or stopping at the Delmar after Mass, Lizzie showed Tim the mixture of charm and command that make for successful politics. On Election Day, Tim usually brought lunch and dinner to his mother as she served as a poll watcher in the American Legion hall. To see so festive a place turn solemn planted in Tim a reverence for democracy as profound as the one he felt for Charlie Parker and Clifford Bale, the symbols of wartime sacrifice. Or as he reminded himself on his errand, "No goofing off."

Only when Tim left the confines of Crotonville to attend public high school did he discover that outsiders had a rather different idea of the place. In the early 1960s, when Tim attended Ossining High, it separated students with chemical precision. Tracks one through five contained the college-prep pupils; six through ten belonged to those learning business subjects and anticipating at most a community-college degree; eleven through thirteen held the unfortunates pursuing what were euphemistically called general studies. This hierarchy supposedly reflected science and merit, specifically each incoming student's performance in earlier grades and on standardized tests. What it also happened to mirror was the class order of Ossining, an order that left the blacks from near Sing Sing and the white ethnics of Crotonville inhabiting the bottom.

By Edith Carey's recollection, Tim had scored into the 130s on an IQ test during elementary school. That made little difference to the social engineers of Ossining High. He came from Crotonville, and everyone knew what Crotonville kids were like—hot-rodders in black corduroy jackets, gum-smacking girls with peroxide-blonde bouffants, the lot of them smoking in the alley outside the cafeteria or a back booth at Kipp's drugstore. Tim got the curriculum all the boys from Crotonville got—wood shop, auto shop, metal shop, and print shop. His English courses barely grazed literature, while his mathematics classes never reached algebra, a subject that college-prep students took as early as eighth grade. The system preordained that Tim could not qualify for a diploma endorsed by the state Board of Regents, a necessity at that time for applying to college. More subtly, it kept him and his friends from spots in the student council or the National Honor Society or the Key Club or the senior play, all those measures of scholastic status. Under the yearbook photograph of Tim with his pomaded "D.A." there appeared not a single activity or membership; he listed his career goal as "oil burner man."

Among the faculty, only one teacher, Priscilla Larrabee, inveighed against tracking. "My God," she declared one day in the teachers' lounge, "what an injustice." To which a colleague replied, for the benefit of the entire room, "Listen to her again, crying."

For their part, the Crotonville students took perverse pride in living down to the lowest expectations. After the drab uniform and Baltimore Catechism of St. Augustine School, after the obedience enforced by Sister Florine and her ruler, Ossining High felt like parole. "Do as little as possible," remembered Jack Garrett Jr., Tim's cousin and closest friend, "and go as little as possible." Tim specialized in sneaking out of school and back into his home through the bedroom window; when his mother began working as a housekeeper, he convened poker games. To his father's heartbreak, he got thrown off the football team for smoking. The friends who signed Tim's yearbook inadvertently painted a portrait of rebellion and class resentment: "Remember all the drinking we did" . . . "Please stay out of trouble" . . . "Don't forget the time you taught Pizzirusso how to work a racket" . . . "I hope you get a good job in Crotonville so you can look down on [assistant principal] Palmer and the rest of the faculty." Virtually the only teacher or administrator to inscribe Tim's yearbook was Joseph Rauschkolb, the truant officer. "This four years," he wrote, "has been so long."

But within the stereotype of juvenile delinquency, as the idiom of the era had it, teenagers like Tim Carey abided by an almost chivalrous code. Crotonville esteemed solidarity and physical prowess among its young men. It was essential for a boy to defend himself by fist, especially a boy as slight and bespectacled as Tim had been early in childhood, and he obligingly battled the class bully in third grade. Taking risks mattered, too. Tim drag-raced on the Route 134 straightaway. He rode ice floes in the Croton River. Most famously among his friends, he dove into it from an eighty-foot cliff. The bruises from that belly flop covered his chest like medals. And they foretold the decorations he would earn in a real army.

• • •

On the afternoon of July 19, 1968, Tim Carey swung open the screen door of his house, free of the army at last. He shoved his dress greens far back in the closet, stuffed his club and helmet in a crate, and yanked off his combat boots in favor of the cowboy variety. He kept only his photo album within reach, as a safeguard against nostalgia, a reminder of what a taskmaster Uncle Sam had been. Tim wanted nothing more than to taste his mother's meat loaf, gulp a Bud at the Oasis, and acclimate himself again to the familiar contours of Crotonville. He joined his father and his uncles as a member of the Parker-Bale post. He bought a '56 station wagon, the sort of warhorse he had owned before being drafted. He found his buddy Pete Birrittella, back from his own stint as an MP in Germany, pumping gas again at the family Texaco.

Soon enough, though, Tim discovered that in his absence the social chaos of the '60s had crept into Crotonville. He was sitting on the wall outside Kromer's deli one day, part of the usual crowd doing the usual things—smoking cigarettes and drinking beer and ignoring the owner's cry, "Get outta here, you shit-asses!" Then a boy of about ten whom

Tim had never before seen shambled up the road and into view. He had olive skin, uncommon enough in a neighborhood of Irish and Germans, and it bore a patina of filth. Wordlessly he vanished into the store, and wordlessly he emerged and made for home, cradling a six-pack.

Over the next few weeks Tim intermittently saw others from the family repeat the trip—the mother, all bones and stringy hair; the father tanned in his sleeveless T-shirt; the daughter with huge brown eyes. "Hey, Bette Davis," the Kromer's regulars would call to her. She never responded. The family, Tim learned, was renting an apartment above Pop Graber's store, closed for several years by now. They were on welfare, the first people on welfare he had ever met. Officially the father neither lived in the household nor assisted it, except that he spent a lot of nights there and worked steadily as a landscaper. Tim spotted him many mornings driving off in a pickup truck, the payload spiked with rakes and hoes. Only the dimwit caseworker seemed not to notice.

To Tim, it was a real hoot. Two years of taking orders in the army had taught him to hate authority as much as any hippie did. He was living home for free, earning decent money on the Chevy assembly line in Tarrytown, flush enough not to worry what his tax dollars were buying. Good for them, he thought about the family. They're getting theirs.

With no steady girlfriend, Tim built his social life around several bars that offered unescorted women free admission. He found himself especially drawn to those a bit older than himself, in their mid-twenties, and it developed that quite a few were single mothers. Some divorced, some deserted, most were taking public assistance while working off the books as barmaids or waitresses. Flirtation with them had a certain Kafkaesque quality. "I'll call you," Tim promised one. "You can't," she answered. "I'm not allowed to have a phone." The craziest story came out of a bowling alley. A lady Tim knew faintly would mind the children of customers in return for free games. For some reason, the manager reported her barter as income, and she lost a portion of her monthly benefits.

These random encounters distressed Tim. The welfare system, he realized, punished people for working. It penalized them for saving. It turned the honest into cheaters. He could hardly blame the women he knew for learning the lesson well. Those wads of cash they never reported paid the baby-sitter, filled the gas tank, and took the kids to the movies. Wasn't the government supposed to help the people who wanted to help themselves? For the moment, Tim asked that question less in anger than profound confusion. One night he was watching a documentary about the New Deal on public television, and there appeared footage of Harry Hopkins testifying before Congress about the

WPA. He was stressing the importance of tying relief to work. That was the kind of aid Tim had heard about from his mother and grandmother, the kind that gave people not only money but also self-respect. How could it have evolved into a program that rewarded you only for sitting on your ass?

Tim had not snoozed away twenty years, after all, just served two in the military. Yet the modern world was rousing him as rudely as it had Rip Van Winkle. Welfare was only the first of the shocks.

The Ossining that Tim thought he knew had always tolerated gangs and rumbles, based on nothing larger than neighborhood bragging rights. The men's softball team from Parker-Bale competed regularly against an all-black squad sponsored by the Sportsmen's Club, and the players turned drinking buddies after the last out. Even the tracking system at Ossining High, so repugnant in most respects, thoroughly integrated Crotonville's white teenagers with their black peers. But suddenly Ossining was cracking open along the fault line of race, as Tim heard firsthand from his own younger brothers.

Chucky Carey, then a junior at Ossining High, had been sitting in bookkeeping class on the Friday afternoon of April 5, 1968, when black students began streaming down the hallway. As his teacher blocked the doorway, Chucky seized the chance to leap out a side window, grateful for any disturbance that allowed him to escape. Enraged by the assassination of Martin Luther King Jr. the previous night, the black students broke forty windows in the school before blocking traffic downtown for hours and beating one shopkeeper. More in terror than in honor, Ossining closed its schools, stores, and municipal offices on the day of King's funeral.

Less than one year later, on February 25, 1969, the smoldering acrimony flared into violence again. In a narrow hallway beside the school gym, a favorite spot for athletes of both races to loiter while cutting class, erstwhile teammates brawled. Peter Carey, a junior hurling haymakers in the middle, would remember it almost fondly decades later as "a good fight." Paradoxically, it was Chucky, wandering innocently into the maelstrom after having overslept, who wound up suspended. Twenty police officers finally quelled the violence, and a dozen patrolled the hallways for nearly a week afterward. According to the black version of events, a boy from Crotonville had instigated the fight by ordering a black cheerleader away from a water fountain with the words "Out of my way, nigger." In Peter Carey's recounting, the cause was uncertain but the effect was clear: Blacks were rampaging, and among the white students only those from Crotonville refused to be intimidated. Maligned for decades already, Crotonville now bore the scarlet letter of racism.

In response, two of Tim's uncles, Eddie Garrett and Roger Peterson, called up their softball pals at the Sportsmen's Club. Each side would bring some of its teenagers to Parker-Bale one night, it was agreed, and everyone would talk out the problems and get Ossining back to the way it was. From the very outset, tension ruled the room. The black students, fearing they would be ambushed, had come with hidden clubs, which the whites discovered when one rattled to the floor. Then a black teen told the whites, "You don't belong with the boys from The Hill." In his way, he was calling for an alliance based on class instead of race. But what Peter, Chucky, and their friends heard was another insult, another way of calling them scum, not good enough to make friends with the children of middle managers and insurance agents—not truly *white*. Its fragile dialogue ruptured, the meeting collapsed within minutes, never to be resumed. Five years later the most destructive riot ever struck the high school, injuring eighteen students, causing the suspension of twenty-seven, and for a week putting youths under a dusk-to-dawn curfew.

Tim Carey, still living at home during the 1969 confrontation, re-coiled with disgust. He harbored no illusions about black anger in America, not after his MP battalion had policed Washington during its 1968 riot. But it sickened him to watch the same destructiveness, the same hatred of whites, infecting his hometown. Ossining was not Wash-ington, a southern city when it came to subjugating its vast black popu-lation. Here blacks formed barely 10 percent of the population; here jobs in the prison and the factories sustained a stable black working class. What exactly was their gripe?

There was some history that Tim did not know that might have persuaded him that even in Ossining black aggrievement did not begin with Martin Luther King's assassination. As far back as 1940, black high school students had protested against the choice of the senior play, a drama about plantation life called *Lena Walters,* in which the only black roles were those of servants. The school responded by selecting a play with no black characters whatsoever. But Tim was seven years shy of being born in 1940, and during his childhood Crotonville was busy enough fighting prejudice against itself to pay much attention to anyone else's crusade. Reluctantly, Tim understood Ossining's upheavals as proof that blacks opposed King's method of nonviolence and goal of integration. Most important for the conservative he would become, he saw white liberals indulging the impulse of black nationalists toward a kind of *re*segregation, rewarding the rioters with programs and dollars earmarked for "equal opportunity."

It was a phrase that haunted Tim's own aspirations. No longer did he intend to settle for the billet of an oil burner man. He had taken an extension course in algebra during his army service and learned the *Uniform Code of Military Justice* well enough to become the barracks equivalent of a jailhouse lawyer. His new plan, joining the New York City police force, encouraged him to study criminal justice, and Westchester Community College offered open admissions to war veterans. Yet when Tim applied for the fall term of 1969, the admissions officer who was evaluating his high school transcript told him not to bother. He was destined to fail.

"Give me my shot," Tim insisted.

"You'll be wasting our time," the man replied, "and your own."

Working a midnight shift shipping cars and attending classes by day, Tim earned a 3.63 grade-point average. In May 1971, just before he graduated, he donned suit and tie for induction into the college's Key Society, its highest honor. While he hardly considered himself a scholar, he had discovered, as he later put it, "God gave me a talent, the talent to work harder, longer, smarter than people who are richer and more intelligent." He was "a C-plus in a D world."

So it affronted Tim's work ethic and resurrected yet again the class scorn of Ossining when the State University of New York at Albany refused to admit him. First he railed over the telephone that the university was ignoring his record at Westchester and that it had plenty of room for "equal opportunity" students—meaning those, overwhelmingly minorities, enrolled under the Educational Opportunity Program. Then he drove to Albany for a more calculated assault. SUNY was being unfair to veterans, he proclaimed to an admissions counselor, and surely New York's congressmen would be disturbed to hear about it. The counselor pleaded with Tim to calm down. The tirade spiraled on. Finally the man traded information for silence: Say you'll major in anthropology; that department still has openings.

Thus declared, Tim arrived for the fall semester of 1971. Admitted too late to receive a dormitory room or a meal plan, he spent his first months sleeping in his '67 Fairlane and eating at McDonald's. SUNY discomforted Tim in less obvious ways, too. His introductory classes consisted of several hundred students in a lecture hall with a professor off in the middle distance narrating a slide show. Unstimulated, Tim managed a 2.6 average. And the place was so young. It made for a poor enough match that his roommate was eighteen, six years his junior and untouched by the military. But he also had a rigidity that Tim could only associate with someone affluent enough never to have shared a bedroom, much less with three brothers. When Tim sauntered back from the bars after midnight, the roommate complained about being awakened; when Tim brought home female company, the roommate refused to leave. So Tim did as much of both as possible, and by Christmas vacation had driven his irritant into exile.

By coincidence, Tim found a subculture of soul mates just down the hall, in the common room ceded to an outfit called the Potter Club. Founded in 1931 in homage to Edward Eldred Potter, a collegian killed during World War I, the club had long attracted veterans as members. Many of them, older and stronger than their classmates, also competed in varsity sports. Like the fraternities it in many ways resembled, the Potter Club claimed an anthem, a handshake, and a ritual of hazing pledges by depositing them deep inside a cave. But it also boasted a tradition of racial and religious tolerance rare in the Greek system. The club Tim discovered counted among its members Jews, Italians, Irish, and Puerto Ricans. Many of them served as Big Brothers for the children in a local orphanage.

To the uninitiated, however, the Potter Club looked downright barbaric. With the arrogance of an occupying army, members covered the walls of their common room with barn wood and installed a wet bar. They screened porno movies, swilled overproof vodka, and literally swung from a chandelier. On Tim's twenty-sixth birthday, he downed a shot of tequila for every year. By its preponderance of veterans and athletes, by its preference for alcohol over drugs, the Potter Club subscribed to conservatism of a sort. More seriously, the club became a flashpoint for the racial tensions growing on campus as the Educational Opportunity Program brought SUNY-Albany large numbers of black students for the first time in its history. After a fight in a dining hall between several members and black students, a reputation for racism attached to the Potter Club. When its basketball team played an all-black squad for the intramural championship, spectators packed the arena in anticipation of bloodshed. That the Potter players, in defeat, honorably congratulated the black victors did little to rehabilitate their image.

For Tim Carey, the Potter Club was like Crotonville North, with a single, salient exception. Crotonville still obeyed Lizzie Garrett and voted Democratic. The Potter Club connected to the Republican Party through a member of both, George Van Riper. He played the same intermediary role for club members that his friend Cathy Bertini did for the sisters of Chi Sigma Theta, but he played it in a way suited to his gender. If Bertini offered entree to position and access to power, Van Riper held out the prospect of getting laid a lot. Superficially, he could hardly have looked more the nerd, this gangly, freckled farmer's son from a hamlet that had voted itself "dry." Appearances aside, "Rip" was a womanizer with a thirst for Boone's Farm and a pitch-perfect Nixon imitation. It was only typical that he drew Tim into Republican politics by asking him to tap the keg at a fund-raiser in return for drinking all night for free.

A kinship between Van Riper and Tim arose instantly. In the summer of 1972, the two shared an apartment off campus, with Tim repairing cars at curbside to pay his share of the rent while Van Riper buttoned down for a job in the State Assembly. Those occupations typified their symbiosis. Van Riper taught Tim a painstaking approach to politics, whether building a coalition to pass legislation or preparing an auditorium for a campaigning candidate, right down to placing a water glass beside the podium. "Politics is a huge chessboard," he preached. "Every move is important." For his part, Tim showed Van Riper a liberating disrespect for money and title. Nelson Rockefeller maintained an entourage called the Governor's Club, composed of the most generous contributors to his campaigns, and Van Riper once wangled an invitation to one of its cocktail parties for himself and Tim. "Whatta I wanna be with those people for?" Tim answered. In tribute, Van Riper christened him a "poor snob."

As the emblem of the Silent Majority, Richard Nixon excited no similar contempt in Tim, and in the fall of 1972 he gladly took a job recruiting young volunteers for the president's reelection campaign. Assigned every college in a three-county area, he gave precedence to several all-female institutions. Van Riper instructed him in a rating system said to have been pioneered by a Republican operative in the South named Lee Atwater. Tim would set up his table in a student center or cafeteria, and as any young woman stepped forward to sign up he would hand her one of three pens—black for the plain, red for the attractive, and green for the irresistible. Later in the evening Tim would hold a pizza and beer party for all the volunteers, and, just coincidentally, would have a critical need to confer privately with the greens.

As if being paid to drink and date was not lucrative enough, Tim received a victory bonus from the Nixon campaign. Along with Van Riper and another cohort, he spent it on a vacation in St. Croix, his first trip off the American mainland. A few months after returning, he and Van Riper received invitations through Cathy Bertini to a reception at the White House. With Tim's '67 Fairlane parked amid the limousines, they strode in frilly rented tuxedos right past the receiving line and toward the shrimp bowl. Only after seeing it replenished did Tim realize the social convention was to shake hands with the president before gobbling his appetizers. As a string quartet played, these Potter Club hellions conversed with astronauts, senators, and cabinet officers. At one point they gazed across the Rose Garden to the Washington Monument.

"Take a long look," Tim said wistfully. "We'll probably never see this again."

Soon after, with Van Riper passed out drunk in the rear seat, Tim drove back to Albany. The night did seem fantastical, slightly surreal. He had not followed ideology into the Nixon campaign as much as coincidence and financial necessity. The same could be said of his attitude toward politics as a whole. He still planned to become a cop.

After completing his political science degree in late 1973, he entered a management-training program with the Pinkerton guard company. Very quickly he decided the instructors knew less about security work than he did after two years with the 503rd. Worse, he had gotten the job through his fiancée, Laura Piening, and now their engagement had unraveled. The son of a mother who prayed openly to St. Jude, the patron of lost causes, Tim felt no hesitancy about appealing to the divine. "What do You want me to do?" he found himself often asking. "What am I supposed to do?"

The sacred answer arrived in the profane form of George Van Riper. He hired Tim to work as an advance man for Jacob Javits during the senator's 1974 reelection campaign. So liberal was Javits that the more conservative members of the State Street Gang presented Tim with a pink shirt. He muttered something about its being salmon, and saving the country from Ramsey Clark. Javits had only visited Cuba, after all, while his Democratic opponent had been to Hanoi. It was true, though: As much as Tim savored the proximity to a United States senator and admired Javits's rise from poverty on the Lower East Side, he could not pretend at passion. Javits was part of the Rockefeller crowd, the insiders, the big spenders.

During the spring term of 1973, Tim had interned with Perry Duryea, the speaker of the Assembly and Rockefeller's chief antagonist within the state Republican Party. Duryea was the kind of politician who impressed Tim. For all the power of his position, he remained an underdog, an outsider by dint of his conservatism. Tim had never forgotten the day he was sitting in Duryea's outer office when several leatherbound volumes arrived from the governor. These contained an artist's renderings of the proposed sports complex that was Rockefeller's latest version of public works as personal monument. "I don't even wanna see it," Duryea had barked in defiance. "Send it back." That Duryea himself was a millionaire did not matter to Tim. In that moment, one "poor snob" thought he recognized another, and through him the possibility that you could be a Republican and a rebel.

• • •

Nearing his thirtieth birthday, with its connotations of stability and career, Tim Carey trod a path of obstinate independence. As three of his friends from the State Street Gang rose through the Republican apparatus to direct statewide parties—Van Riper in Kansas, Karl Ottosen in Pennsylvania, and Ed Lurie in New York—Tim refused to become "anybody's boy," as he dismissively put it. After the Javits race in 1974, he returned to Ossining to tend bar at Izzy's, a shot-and-a-beer joint near the railroad tracks. When he signed on to his next campaign, for a congressional candidate in the Binghamton area named Bill Harter in 1976, it was not as a hired hand of the party but as a freelance consultant, a small-scale version of F. Clifton White. Instead of implementing strategy, Tim made it. He worked directly with a pollster and a media consultant, both of whom he had helped to select. He managed the money; he supervised the advertising; he forged alliances in county seats far from Ossining or Albany, alliances that would prove vital in elections to come. After Harter's defeat, amid a presidential election shadowed by Watergate, Tim went back to bartending. The woman he began courting and ultimately married, Alida Burns, was a single mother scrambling to support two children as a waitress. Instead of a dowry, she brought to wedlock her debts.

From this duality in Tim's life, this cycle of immersion and withdrawal from the electoral wars, a purpose emerged. Crotonville formed his grounding wire, his conduit to the ordinary voter. No matter what the putative professionals claimed about a resurgence of liberalism, waving opinion polls and touting "generational politics," Tim knew otherwise from Izzy's. Beneath the usual chatter about the Yankees or the Rangers, he sensed an undertow of discontent among the regulars, the prison guards and tradesmen and wire-mill workers. They groused about the race riots in Ossining and those stupid "Whip Inflation Now" buttons and the ignominy of that last American helicopter lifting off from Saigon. Most of them were Democrats, but Tim called them "small-c conservatives," which was to say, future converts for him.

That future improbably arrived with a telephone call in January 1978. The chairman of the state Republican Party, Bernard Kilbourn, asked Tim to consider working for a man he had never heard of in an obscure and pointless job. The man was Lewis E. Lehrman. The job was scheduling hearings around the state for a committee drafting the party platform. For the preceding twenty years, the era of Nelson Rockefeller, few political rituals had proven emptier. Whatever the panel heard and whatever it wrote, three truths overrode all else. The candidate was Rockefeller. The platform was Rockefeller. The money was Rockefeller, if not his own then his family's.

Now, however, an entire liberal dynasty was tottering. Rockefeller had doubly departed, first leaving Albany in 1974 to become Gerald Ford's vice president and then being replaced by Senator Bob Dole on the 1976 ticket. His chosen successor as governor, Malcolm Wilson, lost in his first election. Jacob Javits, a senator since 1956, and Louis Lefkowitz, the state attorney general since 1957, were aging toward defeat and retirement, respectively. The logical heirs to the Rockefeller tradition, former mayor John Lindsay and Congressman Ogden Reid, had already deserted to the Democratic Party. Without Rockefeller as the banker of last resort, the state party had staggered out of the mid-1970s $800,000 in debt.

To Lewis Lehrman, newly installed as chairman of the platform committee, this vacuum of money and power spelled opportunity. And as Tim Carey snooped around the state, filling in the biography behind the name, he started to realize why. Only thirty-eight years old, Lehrman had built a fortune in the vicinity of $20 million as president of the Rite-Aid discount pharmacy chain. Between assuming the position in 1969 and resigning it in 1977, he had expanded a modest family business from 69 stores to 648, driving annual sales from $47 million to $455 million. Moreover, Lehrman could think as well as buy his way into a position of political influence. An award-winning scholar at Yale and Harvard, he espoused free-market economics in such liberal magazines as *New Times* and *Harper's* as a way of "assaulting the citadel head-on." (He wrote under the nom de plume of A. Gallatin, after the Treasury secretary in Thomas Jefferson's cabinet, an exponent of free trade and sound money.) Lehrman's wealth had purchased a Manhattan apartment from Richard Nixon and endowed a conservative think tank. Indeed, his political roots resided in New York State's Conservative Party. When its senator, James Buckley, ran for reelection in 1976 as the candidate of the Republican Party, too, Lehrman followed him into it as a fund-raiser and adviser. Even after Buckley's loss to Daniel Patrick Moynihan, Lehrman put some of his capital and much of his persuasion into balancing the state GOP's books.

His goals for the party went far beyond solvency or an orderly transfer of power. What was needed was a populist uprising with a manifesto to match. Lehrman planned to create both the same way he had created the Rite-Aid network, by driving to cities and towns and paying attention to Main Street. As a retailer, he had never rented a storefront until he stood outside it at noon, three, and five, counting foot traffic with a hand-held clicker. As a politician, he intended to listen to those walkers talk. If his intuition was right, they wanted lower taxes, less government, and a crackdown on crime. And in a party rebuilt from below and realigned to the right, Lewis Lehrman himself might well figure as a candidate for governor four years hence.

There was just one problem. Lehrman knew virtually nothing about the political landscape of upstate New York. That was where Tim Carey fit in. He understood the system without being its captive. By this time, he had worked from Montauk to Buffalo in races for president, senator, and representative, as well as in two dozen different campaigns for the state legislature. Yet he had also tended bar, built cars, pumped gas, painted houses, and washed dishes—hardly the résumé of what Lehrman disparaged as the "professional political class." If anything, it was the Ivy Leaguer with his eight-figure net worth and fondness for fox hunts who needed to prove his substance to the "poor snob." Still, the warrior in Tim craved another campaign, and the platform committee was the closest thing to one in the political off-season. During the first days of 1978 he reported to Lehrman's office in Manhattan for an introductory interview.

The meeting lasted five hours and eradicated any preconceptions Tim might have held. What he noticed about Lehrman was not aristocracy but its absence, the difference between a man born into money and a man who earned it. This multimillionaire executive used a stark dining-room table for a desk. The leather on his briefcase was cracking with age. His fedora had a hole in the brim. When Lehrman spoke of hailing from the *"Babbitt* country" of Harrisburg, Pennsylvania, he meant it as a compliment to a place he associated with the values of thrift, discipline, and hard work. In Tim, meanwhile, Lehrman found someone ineffably familiar. There was a kind of guy Lehrman had often hired to run a Rite Aid store—usually Irish or Polish or Hungarian, a decent athlete with a sense of humor and a big family, ambitious enough to aspire to management, unaffected enough to unload a delivery truck himself. Tim exuded those qualities, plus some college polish and political savvy. Although he remained too fond of public works and the construction jobs they provided for Lehrman's taste, Tim could inform him, with authority, that the statewide party was a hollow husk. Only one county leader, Joseph Margiotta on Long Island, commanded an organization worthy of respect. The rest, Rockefeller holdovers, stood at the head of empty divisions. Not that ideas and money alone would vanquish them. "Nobody gives power," Tim warned Lehrman in closing. "You have to take it."

For the next six months, until the state Republican convention in June, Tim arranged sixty hearings designed to do just that. From Staten Island to Plattsburgh to Jamestown, he booked Elks clubhouses and American Legion halls, and scheduled appearances for Lehrman on talk shows, with editorial boards, and before Rotary Club luncheons. Lehrman had selected a platform committee that deliberately ranged from banker to plant manager, senator to fruit grower, college president to car dealer, and coincidentally included Frank Trotta as president of the College Republicans. He charged Tim with soliciting a comparable spectrum of witnesses. To the predictable parade of Republican officials Tim added Democrats and independents; among the usual Chamber of Commerce burghers and League of Women Voters biddies he mixed farmers, entrepreneurs, senior citizens from subsidized projects, and antagonists in the debates over abortion and gun control. From those dissonant voices Lehrman construed confirmation of his own beliefs. Here were citizens outraged at tax rates and welfare costs, fearful to shop downtown amid the trash and the crime. Here were town councils and county boards groaning under the burden of mandates from Albany and Washington. Tim heard almost none of it. During the testimonies he prowled the hallways for a pay phone, confirming speakers and alerting media in the caravan's next stop.

What Tim listened to was the voice of Lew Lehrman. Each evening, after the microphones had been unplugged and the cassette tapes re-wound, he drove the chairman several hours toward the following day's destination. Lehrman shed his suit coat, unlaced his black shoes, and flipped on the dome light. Leveling his briefcase across his lap as a desktop, he moved through the daily pile of paperwork, sheet by sheet. Those pages worth keeping returned to the briefcase and the rest tumbled onto the backseat, their last stop before a motel garbage can. When Lehrman had finished, and nothing lay ahead but highway and time, he convened class for Tim, with all the scholarship and presence that had once won him a Carnegie Foundation fellowship in teaching.

"What would you do," Lehrman asked one night, "if you were walking down the street and saw a $50 bill on the sidewalk?"

Tim lifted his eyes from the road, gazed quizzically across the seat, and spoke tentatively.

"I'd bend over and pick it up."

"Okay," Lehrman went on. "Would anybody else?"

"Anybody would."

"Even though bending over requires effort?"

Tim nodded.

"Now suppose you're going to be taxed at 50, 60, 70 percent on the income you make by the effort of bending over?" Lehrman asked, his voice gathering momentum. "Would you do it?"

"Definitely not."

"If you knew the tax rate would go from 70 down to 20, would you bend over more often?"

"Seventy to 20," Tim blurted. "Of course!"

The point of the parable, Lehrman explained, was incentives. Yes, human beings were products of religion and culture and class and nationality, all forces Tim comprehended. But they answered, too, to economics. Any tax, any law, any regulation exacted a price, whether clear or covert. And every individual considered that price in his behavior. Did you bend down or did you keep walking?

During the years he had opened Rite-Aid stores across twenty states, Lehrman told Tim, he always hired local contractors. Invariably some carpenter or painter would ask to be paid at least partly in cash. Although Lehrman refused, he hardly deemed these men criminals. They simply calibrated the taxes they owed against the public services they expected to get and pocketed the difference. It was the government, the predatory government, turning the decent corrupt.

The words struck Tim with the force of epiphany. He thought of his old girlfriends, worse off working than on welfare. He thought of the tradesmen in Crotonville, bartering carpentry for plumbing, a paint job for a used car. He thought, most of all, of his father. Well into middle age, his back ruined by years as a butcher, Charlie Carey had gone into business for himself with several taxis. One afternoon in the mid-1970s, Tim walked into the living room to find him chatting with a self-employed friend. The man was telling Charlie something about "how to handle the cash," meaning how to cheat on his income tax. Charlie's eyes sharpened with attention, and he asked his friend about one particular trick, "Now, how do you do that?" In that moment Tim had felt something between pity and shame that this man—husband and father, veteran of a world war, worker since his teens—could be tempted by a few hundred dollars to break the law. Now, through the lens of Lehrman's theories, he saw his father almost heroically, defending his wallet against the state.

Tim never shared the memory with Lew Lehrman. He had a less naked way of letting the teacher appreciate that the pupil had learned. One morning he was walking Lehrman into a meeting with the editorial board of an upstate newspaper. Spying a penny on the floor, he stooped to collect it. "See," he said as he straightened, "when it's money, I pick it up."

Off the road, too, the tutorial proceeded. Lehrman devoured information in a way that reminded Tim of the brilliant robot in the B movie *Johnny Five*. In turn Lehrman deluged his protégé with editorials from the *Wall Street Journal* and articles from *Commentary* and the *National Review*, all in all the short course in conservative philosophy on issues ranging from affirmative action to the Panama Canal treaties, the gold standard to the Middle East. More important for Tim, who learned best by observation, Lehrman's eponymous think tank attracted the emerging brain trust of the New Right.

There was Jude Wanniski, an alumnus of the *Journal*'s editorial page, and Irving Kristol of *The Public Interest,* a leader of those once-liberal Jews dubbed neoconservatives. Jeffrey Bell, a speechwriter in Ronald Reagan's campaign for the 1976 Republican presidential nomination, would soon conquer New Jersey's veteran liberal senator, Clifford Case, in a primary election. Jack Kemp, a quarterback turned congressman, was the most fervent advocate of tax cuts in Washington.

All of these men, and the intellectual legitimacy they embodied, descended ultimately from William F. Buckley Jr. and the *National Review.* The man and the magazine did for conservative ideology what F. Clifton White and the Draft Goldwater movement had done for conservative organization—prepare it to dominate the Republican Party. And in entering the hothouse of the Lehrman Institute, Tim Carey was being drawn into the broad sweep of political history, much as Frank Trotta had been in attending TAR Camp.

Buckley had launched *National Review* in the midst of the moderate Eisenhower years, at a time when the literary critic Lionel Trilling insisted that liberalism was America's "sole intellectual tradition" and conservatism nothing more than a miscellany of "irritable mental gestures which seem to resemble ideas." Buckley consciously modeled *National Review* on two magazines of the left, *The Nation* and *The New Republic,* which in the 1920s and 1930s had articulated the intellectual precepts of the New Deal.

From the very first issue, *National Review* strove to create a single coherent philosophy from the three prevailing strands of conservatism —anti-Communism, religious morality, and free-market economics. As vitally, Buckley rejected any alliance with the anti-Semitic and conspiratorial elements of the right, particularly the John Birch Society. The attacks on what he called "crackpot alley" ultimately opened space in the conservative coalition for such Jewish thinkers as Kristol, Midge Decter, and Norman Podhoretz.

National Review's early circulation, less than 20,000, belied its influence. The magazine reached the handful who would eventually reach the millions—a Georgetown student named Patrick Buchanan, for instance, and an actor turned corporate spokesman, Ronald Reagan. L. Brent Bozell, Buckley's colleague and brother-in-law, ghost-wrote Barry Goldwater's 1960 book, *The Conscience of a Conservative,* which went on to sell 3.5 million copies. And Buckley himself rose to celebrity. As syndicated columnist, television host, cover subject in *Time,* and best-selling author of travelogues, mysteries, and memoirs, he exuded a wit, charm, and erudition that popularized conservatism in the mass market.

The pundits at the Lehrman Institute all abided by the trinity Buckley had framed. They considered the Soviet Union an "evil empire," as Ronald Reagan would later put it, and they blamed the welfare state for social chaos. Most of all, they believed in the magic bullet of tax reduction. It would achieve, they argued, two vital goals—enlarging the economy and shrinking the government. As far back as 1974, Kemp had introduced legislation seeking tax cuts under the revealing rubric of the Jobs Creation Act. Now, four years later, he and Senator William Roth of Delaware were preparing a bill to reduce personal income-tax rates by one-third over three years and to index tax brackets to inflation. "If you tax something, you get less of it," Kemp once said, in a phrase Tim could just as easily have heard from Lehrman. "If you subsidize something, you get more of it. In America, we tax growth, investment, employment, savings, and productivity. We subsidize nonworking, consumption, welfare, and debt."

In a speech written for Reagan in the 1976 race, Bell had attacked "the belief that government, particularly the federal government, has the answer to our ills." He continued, "This collectivist, centralized approach, whatever name or party label it wears, has created our economic problems." The solution, he argued, was to pare $90 billion from the federal budget by transferring many welfare-state programs to the states.

The antitax orthodoxy of Lehrman, Kemp, and Bell rested extensively on the scholarship of the economist Arthur Laffer. His theories did nothing less than repudiate the New Deal, replacing the Keynesian prescription of deficit spending with "supply-side" invigoration. As Washington raised tax rates, Laffer held, private industry had less reason to expand and thus create jobs. Only by lowering rates would the economy revive and flourish, so much so that total tax revenues would actually increase. Laffer invoked the example of President Kennedy's 1963 tax cut: Instead of costing the government $89 billion over the next five years, as expected, it generated a windfall of $54 billion. The graph that showed this phenomenon quickly became known as the Laffer curve. More than once, Lehrman sketched it for Tim on a notepad or napkin.

In liberal and even moderate company, such ideas were treated as seriously as alchemy. Bell's "$90 Billion Speech," as it was routinely ridiculed, hobbled the Reagan campaign in 1976. Both the Jobs Creation Act of 1974 and the Kemp-Roth bill of 1978 went down to defeat. Democrats depicted supply-side economics as the latest Republican version of feeding the poor with leavings from the rich. Their very phrase of attack, "trickle-down," harked back to William Jennings Bryan.

What Tim Carey heard, though, was simplicity itself. The people he knew who worked hardest were those who worked for themselves— his friend Ken Peterson hanging wallpaper, his cousin Wally Bale doing construction, even his father with the taxis. Lowering taxes would make everybody a bit more of his own boss. Tim understood that a role existed for government, even big government, in bringing dreams to fruition. His own ascent would have been impossible without the state university, his family's survival without the WPA. But all the rhetoric he absorbed about excessive and intrusive government found expression in an amusement park, Rye Playland. Tim had no problem with the place, except that it was run by Westchester County. With Coney Island, Great Adventure, and Seaside Heights all around, the New York area was hardly suffering from a shortage of amusement parks. So why was the public sector competing with the private and spending $3 million a year to do it? If Westchester County plowed his taxes into Rye Playland, then God alone knew where Albany and Washington were dumping them. It could only force a healthy reckoning for the bureaucrats to live on less of his money.

In cultivating Tim Carey, Lewis Lehrman captured more than one heart and mind. The conservative populism he envisioned could not by definition be imposed from above. Those below had to choose to embrace it. Cerebrally, Lehrman had convinced himself long ago that the working and middle classes should abandon their sentimental attachment to the party of Franklin Roosevelt and the New Deal. But thinking so was different from seeing the evidence in the person of Tim Carey of Crotonville. Behind Tim, Lehrman imagined every manager he had ever hired for a Rite Aid store, multiplied by the millions into an army of revolution.

It seemed to Lehrman no coincidence that just as his platform committee was assaying the discontent in New York, the very heartland of liberalism, citizens across the continent were acting on it. On June 6, 1978, two weeks before the platform would be formally unveiled, California voters overwhelmingly approved Proposition 13, the opening salvo in the so-called taxpayers' revolt. The measure restricted property-tax rates to one percent of actual value, less than half the average, and forbade communities to try raising the levies to compensate for the lost income. Equally significant was the way Proposition 13 divided the electorate, stranding blacks and public employees on the losing side. So swiftly had the political climate changed that opponents of Proposition 13 longed for a second chance at Proposition 1, a more moderate curb on property taxes defeated five years earlier. Its advocate had been the governor, Ronald Reagan.

In that spirit of rebellion, Lewis Lehrman addressed the state Republican convention. He spoke of "conquest" and "civil war" and "the basic order of battle." "Albany and Washington," he proclaimed, "have become the source of our oppressors." Quoting John Marshall, one of the first chief justices of the Supreme Court, he declared, "The power to tax is the power to destroy."

Standing along the rear wall of the ballroom, behind the delegates and the press, Tim Carey beamed. Partly he was appreciating his own handiwork—the committee banner above the dais, the sound system tuned to ideal resonance, the water glass within Lehrman's easy reach, just as George Van Riper had shown him years ago. Mostly he was admiring his mentor and waiting for the ignorant or skeptical to understand why. "This guy," Tim had told a few reporters already, "is for real."

The policies Lehrman espoused from the podium—reducing taxes, restoring the death penalty, easing state and federal mandates on local government—sounded less than revolutionary. But they, like their architect, were the product of an intellectual ferment liberals had long and mistakenly believed the right wing could not possibly possess. Now Lehrman was teaching the whole audience what he had taught Tim in the car. Incentives and disincentives, money in a word, governed behavior. The lawless committed crimes because, with punishment so lax, crime paid. The lazy went on welfare because, with benefits so high, welfare paid. The industrious fled the state because, with taxes so onerous, flight paid. "Our economic crisis," Lehrman concluded, "has become a moral crisis."

Nothing in the eight single-spaced pages of Lehrman's address affected Tim more than that sentence. It decoded his own life. He was playing by the rules in a society that had changed them. Couldn't he have screamed as loudly as any black about the bigotry of Ossining? Hadn't he dreaded war as much as those college kids taunting him at the Pentagon? Couldn't he have tended bar off the books at Izzy's? He was still "Timmy Two-Cent," expecting pennies on the bottle, a fair reward for a fair effort. Welfare and affirmative action and the overlaying income taxes of county, state, and nation denied it to him. Lehrman's fusion of social conservatism and economic liberty promised its restoration.

After the convention approved the platform, a number of the younger delegates launched into a version of "Rock of Ages" that went back to TAR Camp. "Rockefeller's not for me," they sang with severity

342 • The Inheritance

befitting a dirge. "He is not the GOP." Not only was Lehrman burying Rockefeller, the New Dealer manqué, but also Eisenhower and Nixon, accommodationists at heart. This platform challenged even the Ronald Reagan of 1976, who had distanced himself from Jeffrey Bell's "$90 Billion Speech" and sworn to select a liberal as his running mate.

For precisely such reasons, it struck at least one reporter, Francis X. Clines of *The New York Times,* as prophetic that the Republicans were sharing their hotel with an association of funeral directors. Indeed, the Republican ticket for state office largely failed in a fall election shaped elsewhere by a backlash against Jimmy Carter and the Democratic Party. Perry Duryea, the legislator Tim had long admired, lost the governor's race to Hugh Carey by 273,000 votes, or about 6 percent. Among Duryea's three running mates, only the centrist Edward Regan triumphed, winning the position of comptroller. By one interpretation, the people had repudiated Lehrman's platform. By another, they had not quite caught up to it yet.

• • •

During his basic training in the army, Tim Carey had drilled in a tactic called drawing fire. A commander would order it when he suspected the enemy was hiding nearby, but did not know exactly where or in what numbers. One platoon would separate from its larger company, deliberately break cover, and lure the other side into action. Vital as drawing fire was to battlefield victory, it was a duty for which Tim could never imagine volunteering.

Yet he thought of it often in the waning days of August 1980, as he weighed an offer to direct the presidential campaign of Ronald Reagan in metropolitan New York. Tim recognized he had been recruited for reasons having more to do with diplomacy than talent. He held strong, personal ties to leaders in both the Conservative and Republican Parties, which needed to suspend their usual feud for the campaign. Beyond that, he had the reputation of being a "sound mechanic," as he put it, someone who would execute orders. Hardly anyone in the Reagan campaign expected to carry New York State or to win more than a pittance of the city's vast vote. All they asked of Tim was to make some noise without spending much money, maybe scare Jimmy Carter into shifting time and resources there from Ohio or Pennsylvania, the states Reagan truly sought.

The prospect left Tim less than exuberant. He had responded profoundly to Reagan from the first time he had heard him speak, at a Conservative Party banquet in October 1975. To remain free for some role in this campaign, he had forfeited the opportunity to manage Alfonse D'Amato's race against Jacob Javits and Elizabeth Holtzman for the Senate, letting his State Street Gang companion, Karl Ottosen, pluck that plum. Now the offer had arrived, with a job description of noble failure. But Lew Lehrman, his mentor, pressed him to say yes. Proximity to Ronald Reagan, he reasoned, would only propel Tim's career and his education in conservatism. And Lehrman, like few others, believed Tim could do more than draw fire.

Now Tim set about proving it, both to his prospective superiors and to himself. He never doubted that Carter was vulnerable with middle-class voters on the basis of inflation alone. Tim had bought his own home recently with a mortgage of 14 percent. It was a tract house in a development favored by the nurses and clerks of a nearby Veterans Administration hospital. Around the neighborhood, in the pages of the *Pennysaver,* and on the bulletin board of the supermarket, Tim could reckon disgruntlement in the notices of boats for sale. These were not yachts, but runabouts for weekend fishing, docked in the driveway because a marina cost too much. When a cop or a bus driver or a building superintendent had to sell his Boston Whaler, and probably the trailer with it, he was losing a simple luxury it had taken years of scrimping to acquire. While that wasn't exactly poverty, it sure was downward mobility.

Apostate that he was, Tim believed the same frustrations could yield a Republican vote in New York City. Based on his experiences there in several Assembly races and Duryea's gubernatorial campaign, he carved the city in two. Instantly he surrendered the liberal strongholds, some affluent and white like Brooklyn Heights, Riverdale, and the Upper West Side, and others poor and black like Bedford-Stuyvesant and Jamaica. The potential vote for Reagan resided at their edges, in the sections of Brooklyn and Queens that Tim called green belts. Verdant only in comparison to the slums nearby, these were districts of bungalows and duplexes, rent-controlled apartments and middle-income co-ops. They housed Irish and Italians and Greeks and Jews who taught school, fought fires, built houses, drove buses, owned groceries. In their lives if not in their faces, Tim might have recognized them in Crotonville or served them beer in Izzy's.

For nearly twenty years these people had been grating under the activist liberalism in which their city specialized. Their shared history was one of desperate exodus from former neighborhoods turning blacker and more treacherous. Resettling in many cases mere blocks from those ruins, they feared nothing more than a repeat, and saw portents of it in various liberal initiatives. Some 90 percent of white Catholics voted against a 1966 proposal to appoint a civilian review board over the predominantly white police department. The following year, the traditional alliance between blacks and Jews in the city ruptured, as black parents and a largely Jewish teaching force clashed in a vicious and vitriolic struggle over control of public schools in one Brooklyn district. Middle-class whites in Forest Hills marched for two years in the early 1970s against a city plan to erect subsidized housing. At roughly the same time Italians and Jews in Canarsie alternately occupied and boycotted schools to block the placement of thirty-one black children from the adjacent slum of Brownsville. In a city thus traumatized, the entire borough of Staten Island had turned Republican by the 1972 presidential election. Yet Staten Island engaged Tim's interest less than the neighborhoods that had not yet changed parties, if only he could find them.

Without computers, pollsters, staff, and money, he launched into a microscopic examination of voting patterns in the green belts. He started by selecting about two dozen Assembly districts, each one small enough to be nearly homogeneous. Then he chose several elections to study. Gerald Ford in 1976 provided the profile of a disaster, Perry Duryea in 1978 an average of sorts, and Edward Regan in the same year a model of victory. Tim culled returns from the state and city election boards and sifted through thousands of the "buff cards" each voter must sign at the polling place, thus determining the turnout by party registration. Then he punched the numbers into a pocket calculator and deciphered the black digits for his answer. Sure enough, there were places where Edward Regan had doubled Ford in percentage and outdrawn Duryea in raw votes. It happened in the Italian enclaves of Bay Ridge and Carroll Gardens in Brooklyn. It happened in the Queens neighborhoods of Richmond Hill, South Ozone Park, and Queens Village, all hovering on the verge of racial change. Every Democrat who had split his ticket for Regan had shown that, given the right candidate, he could surmount the psychological hurdle of voting for a Republican.

To those areas Tim added such Jewish sections as Borough Park in Brooklyn and Forest Hills in Queens, where a single strand of foreign policy mattered more than welfare, quotas, or crime. Despite Jimmy Carter's role in negotiating the Camp David peace treaty between Israel and Egypt, many Jews accused him of favoring Arab interests in the Middle East. First the president's United Nations ambassador, Andrew Young, was revealed to have met secretly with representatives of the Palestine Liberation Organization. More recently, in March 1980, the United States had voted in the United Nations to condemn Israel for erecting settlements in territory seized during the 1967 war, and no amount of blaming it on a "communications error" could repair the damage.

Finally Tim transmuted his research into a series of color-coded maps, identifying the places where Democratic fealty was fraying. He intended to rip it loose with phone calls and flyers and volunteers ringing doorbells. All that supposed, of course, he was hired for the job. Armed with his calculator and maps, Tim presented himself to George Clark, at age thirty-nine the state director of Reagan's campaign and a renegade of the first rank.

The child of New Deal Democrats, Clark had first broken with his heritage in 1969, joining in the insurgency of a conservative Republican, John Marchi, against Mayor Lindsay. Three years later he supplanted an ineffectual moderate as the Republican Party chairman in Brooklyn and immediately declared war on Nelson Rockefeller. First he led a mutiny against the governor's scheme to have Robert Wagner Jr., mayor as a Democrat from 1953 to 1965, run in 1973 on the Republican line. "When the hell did they let you out of the sandbox?" Rockefeller shouted at his young antagonist during one meeting. Then, in 1976, Clark dared to mount a campaign for Ronald Reagan in the New York primary. All delegates in the state officially ran uncommitted, meaning in practice that Rockefeller could deliver them as a bloc to Gerald Ford. But with scrupulous organizing in his own borough, Clark managed to elect fourteen delegates pledged to Reagan, and against tremendous pressure at the national convention they and he refused to compromise. So grateful was Reagan that two years later, with Clark's county organization in disarray, he flew east to headline a fund-raising dinner.

Like Tim, Clark drew his ideology from his life outside politics. He had attended parochial schools and St. John's University during a period when Francis Cardinal Spellman imprinted a conservative Catholicism on the New York archdiocese. Still devoted to the church as an adult, Clark served on the St. Edmund's parish council and coached the St. Columba Little League team. His profession, too, contributed to an abiding sense of caution and propriety. The Clark family owned a real-estate agency that dated back to 1871 and had earned its longevity by not overreaching. From its base in the neighborhood of Gravesend, Clark Realty specialized in the single-family homes and small shops of working-class ethnics. These people did not speculate in property; they poured a lifetime's savings into that corner bakery or brick duplex, and anything that threatened the value amounted to bank robbery.

It was at age eight, accompanying his father to appraise several buildings, that Clark first encountered the underside of the New Deal. At one apartment house he noticed four or five names listed beneath the same doorbell. The reason, his father explained, was that the tenant was collecting welfare under every alias. In his twenties, Clark heard how the Lindsay administration was actually paying bonuses to realtors who had located housing for welfare clients. He understood what the Manhattan bureaucrats never did: The slumlords who were being rewarded for their supposed enlightenment were actually jamming poor blacks into fragile neighborhoods to foment white flight and their own bonanza. Trying to revive a county Republican Party that "had a reputation for going down like the *Titanic* every Election Day," as one political reporter put it, Clark found in welfare one of his most potent selling points. "Never have so few paid so much for so many to ask for more," he liked to joke. Another bitter crack went, "The Democrats are the party of the people . . . with their hands out."

Managing the family agency himself by the late 1970s, Clark watched inflation confound his modest clientele. Mortgages had climbed so high he had to personally intercede with a bank to gain one customer the favorable rate of 19.5 percent. "We're gonna wait," many would-be buyers told him. "Things have gotta get better after we get this Carter guy out." Just after eight on many mornings, Clark shopped at a supermarket in the lower-middle-class neighborhood of Sheepshead Bay. It was an hour when the store belonged to pensioners, mostly Italians and Jews, and often they asked the six-foot-one Clark to reach the high shelves. "Can you believe the price of tomatoes?" Clark would typically say, as he placed the can in the cart. "Since Carter became president," one grandmother groused. To which an old man within earshot added, "And look what he's doing to the rest of the world."

When Tim finished presenting his theory of the green belts, Clark asked no questions. Tim doubted he had understood or much cared. The state director hired him instead on trust and instinct. That was fine with Tim. If anything, he preferred being left alone to having a nosy boss. Or at least he did until he discovered exactly how alone he was being left.

Shortly after Labor Day, Tim reported to Reagan headquarters in midtown Manhattan. A limestone townhouse next to the "21" Club, appointed with marble and mahogany, it gave a first impression of plutocracy. The illusion vanished just one flight above the lobby. Ceilings cracked with water damage. Soot collected on sills. The single elevator, so quaint with its accordion grating, required convalescence between trips. Distrusting it, Tim climbed the stairs to his third-floor office, a former maid's room overlooking an air shaft. "Unfurnished gloom," one visitor wrote of the building, "like a Charles Addams drawing."

Whatever money the national campaign saved on interior decoration, it certainly did not spend on supplies. The New York staff regularly ran out of flyers, buttons, bumper stickers, and postage. The leader of a committee devoted to "Democrats for Reagan" drew his own signs with oaktag and felt-tip marker, as if the presidency at stake in this election were a student council's. In his fashion, Tim settled on a military metaphor. It was one thing to be ordered to draw fire, but he felt like a grunt left behind at Corregidor facing the Japanese as MacArthur cruised to safety in Australia.

To win the green belts for Reagan, Tim possessed no tool more advanced or expensive than a telephone. He commanded about one hundred for the entire city, split among seven locations, and dialed by an ever-changing force of volunteers. With such imperfect means, Tim intended to reach 540,000 voters in selected Assembly districts of Brooklyn and Queens, a mixture of registered Republicans, independents, and ethnic Democrats. First, in late September and early October, he wanted to learn whom they favored among Reagan, Carter, and the independent candidate John Anderson. Those who chose Reagan or called themselves undecided would receive literature and possibly a personal visit. Then, in the final three days of the campaign, Tim insisted that a follow-up call be placed to every single one.

Elemental as the plan sounded, it was bedeviled from within and without. For reasons Tim could only ascribe to patronage, Clark's home borough of Brooklyn enjoyed three phone banks. The wife of the Bronx County Republican chairman managed the operation there for a sweet salary. The national campaign staff, meanwhile, wondered why Tim bothered to call Democrats, and in the outer boroughs of all places. They wanted impact in Manhattan, where the media might notice. Most of all, the received wisdom discounted the type of shoe-leather strategy Tim had designed. Pundits, professors, and media consultants all agreed: Parties were dead, canvassing no longer mattered, and candidates won with polls and commercials.

Tim loved nothing better than proving them wrong. The first round of phone calls revealed 60 percent favorable ratings for Reagan among ethnic Democrats, equaling his goal. Even the number of undecided voters cheered Tim. From experience he knew they would fall three to one against an incumbent. The predictions of a low turnout also played to his favor. Let the other side stay home and mope about the lousy choices; Tim Carey would nag and drag his people to the polls. He ordered the Manhattan phone bank to start calling Queens instead, doubling his capacity there. At one point in October the national campaign asked Tim to arrange a photo opportunity for Nancy Reagan with a supporter in Manhattan. "Ain't nobody in Manhattan supporting us," he replied. "I been calling Queens." In a compromise, Reagan visited volunteers at a phone bank in Brooklyn, where to Tim's horror all the working-class women showed up in fur coats.

That fiasco aside, the national campaign underscored Tim's efforts by consistently presenting Ronald Reagan as the true heir to Franklin Roosevelt. In delivering his acceptance speech to the Republican convention that summer, Reagan had quoted from FDR's first inaugural address. His rallies appropriated the Democratic anthem, "Happy Days Are Here Again." He spoke to longshoremen in Buffalo and a "Save Our Steel" rally in Steubenville, Ohio; he stumped through Milwaukee and Pittsburgh, Cleveland and Kokomo, Akron and Flint, Youngstown and Bayonne. During campaign stops in New York and Pennsylvania on the same day in early October, Reagan introduced himself as a "New Deal Democrat" in the tradition of "such great Democrats" as Kennedy and Truman. A quarter-million union households received a campaign brochure reminding them of Reagan's background in organized labor. "He led the Screen Actors Guild in its first strike and he won it!" the pamphlet bragged. "Elect the former union president, President."

What Reagan offered—a 30 percent income-tax cut over three years and a $195 billion reduction of the federal budget over five—completely contravened the New Deal formula of "tax and tax and spend and spend," as Harry Hopkins had put it so famously. But with double-digit inflation gripping the nation and unemployment rates reaching as high in parts of the industrial belt, Reagan could fairly usurp the usual Democratic role of fighting for the little guy. He managed even to transform the misstatements that hampered his campaign into stirring pieces of political theater. Just after Labor Day, for instance, the Reagan campaign had arranged to have the candidate attend a barbecue in suburban Detroit with construction and factory workers, about half of them jobless. As Reagan recounted the event in later speeches, the host spontaneously "invited me to come into his backyard for hot dogs and he invited in some of his friends and neighbors, all of them unemployed." Similarly, Reagan told a luncheon of Teamsters union members in late August that lives like their own had "been shattered by a new Depression—the Carter Depression." The national unemployment rate then registered 7.6 percent, far below the official figure for a depression, and Reagan issued an adroit correction. What truly measured depression, he said, was not an economist's numbers but an ordinary person's misery. Over the weeks he refined this notion into the refrain "A recession is when your neighbor loses his job. A depression is when you lose yours. And recovery is when Jimmy Carter loses his."

Reagan also revised his own record. It was true enough he had entered politics as a New Deal Democrat, stayed in the party until 1962, and served as a union officer. But he selectively disowned more recent positions that antagonized labor. He retracted his prior stand that unions be governed by antitrust laws. No longer did he blame the Occupational Safety and Health Administration for unduly impinging on management. Normally the defender of private enterprise, he called for restricting Japanese auto imports and assailed Carter for dedicating a nonunion steel mill.

Most important in New York City, which was just five years past the brink of bankruptcy, Reagan reversed himself on the issue of federal aid. The city was presently seeking $900 million in federal guarantees of municipal bonds, having already received $750 million in similar guarantees and $2.3 billion in direct loans. While the Carter campaign virtually wallpapered subway cars with posters of the president signing past loan-guarantee legislation, Reagan had said in 1978 he prayed nightly for Washington not to rescue New York. But since New York had not defaulted, he now averred, the system clearly worked. Mayor Edward I. Koch himself briefed Reagan on city finances on October 17, and the import of that meeting far surpassed the fiduciary. Koch qualified as a genuine hero in the green belts, both for steering the city back to solvency and "standing up" to "black militants," as the phrases inevitably went. During the campaign season itself Koch was pressing ahead with the shutdown of a city hospital in Harlem against massive protests and accusations of racism. Simply by hosting Reagan, George Clark believed, Koch effectively endorsed him.

The feeble economy and the Iranian hostage crisis afforded Jimmy Carter few options in his campaign. Relentlessly he raised the specter of Reagan as troglodyte. "American[s] might be separated" by a Reagan victory, he warned in a speech on October 4. "Black from white, Jew from Christian, North from South, rural from urban." Evoking Lyndon Johnson's broadsides against Barry Goldwater, he warned an audience on October 19 that electing Reagan would push America closer to the "nuclear precipice." It was to Carter's apocalyptic rhetoric, as much as to a specific point about Medicare, that Reagan unleashed his rehearsed retort in their sole debate: "There you go again."

For all that, most polls found the race deadlocked. A joint survey by CBS and *The New York Times* in the third week of October put Carter ahead of Reagan 39 percent to 38, with 9 for Anderson, and 13 undecided. As late as election eve, the *Times*-CBS poll gave Reagan a lead of just one percentage point, 44 to 43, and the Gallup survey placed the challenger's advantage at three points, 46 to 43, within the margin of error for a dead heat. More to the point for Tim, a *Times*-CBS survey of the local vote in mid-October reported a comfortable lead for Carter statewide and a two-to-one hold on the city. If the high technology was right, the green belts strategy was bound for failure.

"Did you see the latest?" an assistant fretfully asked George Clark late in the campaign.

"The latest what?" he countered. "Save me the paper 'cause I'm going fishing and need to wrap fish. There's a secret vote out there."

Instead of opinion polls Clark had consulted an oracle whom he knew only as Mr. Safran. An elderly Jew who still spoke English with Yiddish inflections, he owned a tile and linoleum store in Sheepshead Bay and lived across the street from Clark in the adjacent neighborhood of Marine Park. One morning, as each man was putting out the garbage, Safran walked gingerly toward his neighbor.

"I vant you should know I'm voting for Ronald Reagan," he confessed. "It's the first time I vote for a Republican."

"Mr. Safran, you made my day," Clark exulted.

Then he lifted a Reagan button off his lapel and offered it. Safran threw up his hands as if warding off an acid attack.

"I vould't vant anyone should know."

On the morning of November 4, Election Day, Tim entered campaign headquarters to find the lobby thick with volunteers. These were not the idealists who had been toiling in the boroughs for two months, the college kids from St. John's and Hofstra, the bricklayers and hairdressers. The late arrivals subscribed to that Manhattan species, the opportunists. Lured by the scent of victory, they had begun migrating to the tumbledown townhouse after the debate one week earlier. Their numbers increased by the day, and this morning a few even appeared résumé in hand. Tim considered them an augury.

He nudged through the crowd and climbed the stairs to his garret. The phone banks needed to pump 89,000 calls into the green belts within the day. On the fourth floor, he checked that the Manhattan operation was dialing Queens as ordered. Then he drove to the Queens headquarters and one of the Brooklyn installations, ensuring that every phone stayed in perpetual use.

By three in the afternoon, Tim returned to Manhattan and waited for the trickle of intelligence. The national campaign privately predicted victory, he learned, but the pattern in New York remained a maddening mystery. In the final consequence of a bargain-basement campaign, he could not afford to hire enough poll watchers to report back on the vote. Where were people turning out? In what numbers? By what registration? After months of plotting for this day, Tim felt proprietary as a parent about the "identifiables," as he termed the potential Reagan voters. For what little he knew of them as afternoon darkened into night, every last one could have overslept.

A celebration built around wine, Brie, and a large-screen television in a renovated conference room on the second floor. Tim eschewed it. He hunched forward in a folding chair one flight above, sipping a beer and peering into a portable with aluminum foil on its antenna. His wife, Alida, perched beside him. Around them clustered the rest of the ultimate insiders—George Clark, volunteer director Charlie Freeman, and the state party chairman, Bernard Kilbourn. At 7:02 P.M., NBC declared Reagan the winner in Florida. It gave him Ohio at 7:31 and Connecticut at exactly eight. The polls in New York closed at nine and only moments afterward the network projected Reagan winning the state. Suddenly the floor rocked with bodies leaping in triumph. Tim swallowed Alida into an embrace. "Now can I have my husband back?" she chided. Then, damn it if Jimmy Carter didn't ruin their night. At 9:50 P.M. eastern standard time, he conceded. All Tim's adrenaline, months in building, drained away.

Clark and the rest descended to the second floor to meet the media. Tim lingered briefly at the fringes, then repaired upstairs alone. He switched from channel to channel, searching futilely for results from the city. He phoned D'Amato headquarters, trying to reach his old friend Karl Ottosen, the campaign manager. Again, he had no luck. Feeling hungry at last, he went down to the party room. It yawned before him as empty as Times Square five minutes after the ball falls.

Only the next morning did Tim discover how much he had accomplished. Jimmy Carter had taken New York City by barely 300,000 votes, less than half his margin over Gerald Ford four years earlier. In parts of Brooklyn, the outcome had swung even more dramatically. George Clark's home Assembly district, which Carter had won by 9,000 votes in 1976, awarded Reagan a bulge of 6,000. A nearby district in the heavily Jewish neighborhoods of Sheepshead Bay and Brighton Beach, which had gone three to one for Carter last time, begrudged him a 2 percent plurality. And in Queens, which Tim had deluged with phone calls, Reagan carried 45 percent of the vote, just three points behind Carter.

A debate instantly commenced over what the Reagan victory meant. Not much, went one line of reasoning. Despite capturing forty-four states and 489 electoral votes, Reagan finished with just 51 percent of the popular vote. The third-party candidacy of John Anderson, while not costing Carter the election, had certainly deprived him of states like New York. "The biggest perception Reagan had going for him," said John Sears, who managed the early stages of the Republican's campaign, "was that he wasn't Jimmy Carter." Robert Teeter, one of Reagan's pollsters, opined, "Ideology is not very important to most voters."

Yet by being elected, no matter how, Ronald Reagan had immediately shifted the political center to the right. A man dismissed not many years earlier as too extreme to be electable, he had drawn one-quarter of Democratic voters. He pried loose from the New Deal coalition 51 percent of the Catholic vote, 44 percent of the union vote, and 39 percent of the Jewish vote. The Reagan landslide returned Republicans to control of the Senate for the first time in twenty-six years and toppled such liberals as George McGovern, Birch Bayh, Frank Church, and John Culver. Alfonse D'Amato, barely known outside the Long Island town of Hempstead months earlier, defeated Javits and Holtzman for a Senate seat.

Before long, political experts spoke of a distinctive phenomenon, Reagan Democrats, and located their epicenter in Macomb County, Michigan, an area of suburban Detroit thick with white-ethnic, union-ized factory workers. It became a station of the cross for journalists and pollsters, attracted from Manhattan and Washington by the vox populi. Tim could have saved them the gas. Reagan Democrats thrived, too, in Astoria and Midwood, Sunnyside and Canarsie, those green belts in liberalism's backyard.

Chapter Fifteen

Enchantment and Its Opposite
(Frank Trotta Jr.)

P ERCHED ON GRAY LEATHER STOOLS IN A NEW ROCHELLE BAR, Tim Carey and Frank Trotta lifted their beers in wary reunion. For all the convictions they shared, they had been drifting apart since their college days with the State Street Gang. Tim had pitched headlong into state-wide and national politics, while Frank, torn between the sirens of idealism and upward mobility, had trod through law school and into the stability of a large Manhattan firm. Until this late afternoon in June 1981, they had not seen each other since a state Republican convention three years earlier. Only during the stretch of mid-January when both their birthdays fell did they speak socially. And precisely because it was not January when Tim had telephoned and invited him out for drinks, Frank puzzled over the genuine agenda.

Several rounds into the stilted chitchat, Tim provided the answer with a question. Was Joe Pisani going to run for governor next year? Privately, Frank thought so, but for Tim's ears he pleaded uncertainty. He still considered the state senator his mentor, a figure deserving of loyalty, and he had only suspicions about which opponent Tim truly represented. Once comrades, they parted more like a couple ending a blind date, all promises and no plans about getting together again.

It never occurred to Frank that Tim was probing not Joe Pisani's availability but his own, and for no less an endeavor than extending the Reagan Revolution. After the 1980 landslide Tim had returned to the employ of Lewis Lehrman. Nominally, he directed security for Lehrman the executive; unofficially, he was assembling a staff for Lehrman the undeclared candidate for governor. In Frank Trotta, Tim perceived the ideal campaign counsel, conversant in both election law and political logic, capable of being no mere lawyer but a sage.

Several weeks after their meeting, with Pisani still undecided, Tim contacted Frank once more. "Come on down and see our office," he said, "and see Lew again." On the philosophy of never closing a door ahead of himself, Frank made an appointment.

When the day arrived the men spoke for only five minutes, time enough for Lehrman to remember what he had appreciated in Frank as a member of the 1978 platform committee. He was bright, serious, circumspect, and, thank God, not intellectual, a word that translated to Lehrman as all talk, no action. Youth itself argued in Frank's favor. Lehrman had expanded Rite Aid's network of discount drugstores during his own twenties, when he was footloose enough to travel by motorcycle. For one reason alone Lehrman hesitated to offer the job. He wondered whether Frank Trotta, so sensible, would actually step off the partnership track for the longest of long shots, a candidate opposed by the party hierarchy and unknown to the electorate.

"Are you enjoying your work?" Lehrman asked, testing.

"I'm learning a lot," Frank replied inscrutably.

What he was learning, besides the intricacies of writing briefs and searching cases on Lexis, were the varieties of discomfort at Weil, Gotshal & Manges. In an office attired by Barneys and Paul Stuart, Frank dressed in discounts from Syms. While the other attorneys savored life in Manhattan, he still lived in his hometown. So ruthless was the competition for advancement that certain associates withdrew books their colleagues needed from the law library. Or they turned off the office lights of those who went home earliest, the better for the partners to notice. Leaving one evening to treat his girlfriend to a Broadway musical for her birthday, Frank draped a suit coat over his chair as camouflage.

The firm put Frank's political expertise into lobbying. The exchange of governmental acts for personal favors sickened him. One prominent state legislator even prevailed upon Frank to play the intermediary with his mistress, once calling at two in the morning to learn her whereabouts. A senior partner pressed him into service as a poll watcher for the Assembly speaker, Stanley Steingut, who personified the liberal Democratic politics Frank most detested. In a private mutiny, he decorated his office wall with a framed invitation to the Reagan inaugural.

He knew, though, he had not earned the honor. He had voted for Reagan, but all the while worrying that Reagan was too conservative to win. What little spare time he had for volunteering that fall went into a few local races in New Rochelle. At the very moment Jimmy Carter conceded, Frank was consoling a grocer named Rocco, who had been defeated for a seat on the city council. Only when a voice elsewhere in the election night party shouted, "Can you believe we won the Senate?" did the force of history shake Frank from his parochialism. All the analyses he read in the succeeding weeks centered on the concept of Reagan Democrats. These were the tradesmen and unskilled laborers he had grown up among on the South Side, Frank realized, the ones who had marched in his Honor America parade. For all his political acumen, he had slept through the earthquake in his midst.

Now came Lew Lehrman dangling that rarest form of grace, a second chance. After drafting the state Republican platform in 1978, itself a harbinger of "Reaganomics," Lehrman had mounted, indeed created, another bully pulpit as an economic adviser to the state party. He produced lucid and persuasive reports on topics ranging from casino gambling to public transportation to property-tax relief, each analyzed through the lens of incentives. It seemed logical enough, then, that Lehrman assisted the Reagan transition team and contended for the position of Treasury secretary. What was surprising, though, was his subsequent disappointment with the administration. The fury of activity in Reagan's first months as president—when at his behest Congress cut income taxes by 25 percent over three years and pared $35.2 billion, or about 5 percent, from federal spending for 1982—struck Lehrman as being piecemeal and diffuse. Restoring a beleaguered economy required a simultaneous effort to cut taxes, balance the budget, reduce the scope of government, and stabilize the currency. Short of returning to the gold standard, Lehrman believed he could execute just such a master stroke as governor of New York.

His ideology made the most personal kind of sense to Frank. Whenever liberals claimed tax relief would benefit only the wealthy, he recalled one of the few family vacations of his childhood. Money was so tight the Trottas could not leave for Montreal until his parents received their income-tax refunds, and every day that summer Frank waited for the letter carrier. As for meddlesome government, he was becoming acquainted as a lobbyist with its infinite variety. He dealt with agencies in Albany that protected wetlands and registered unclaimed property; he met with lawmakers intent on regulating commerce from fine-art auctions to sidewalk peddlers hawking Gucci knockoffs. Each week New York City published an entire newspaper devoted to the latest municipal laws and regulations, which it was Frank's miserable duty to read.

Yet when Tim finally offered him the position of campaign counsel, over drinks one evening in September, Frank temporized. With two lawyer friends he "ran the hypotheticals," as the jargon had it, arraying the pros and cons of joining the campaign. All their calculation came down to the same old standoff between security and passion. Then Frank went to his fiancée, Susan Piening. She was more liberal than he, supporting abortion rights and voting in 1980 for John Anderson, and she considered much of politics a bore. But she knew Frank's blue moods, with their distracted silences and terse answers, and she had noticed many as his frustration grew at Weil, Gotshal & Manges. Take the job, she told him, it'll make you happy.

It made him that and more. There was no small measure of the Old Testament prophet in Lehrman, a mixture of personal magnetism and ideological purity that spoke eloquently to conservatives of Frank's generation. Much of the State Street Gang ultimately joined the staff—Karl Ottosen as campaign manager, Leslie Maeby as scheduling director, Paul Cardamone as upstate coordinator, and Tim as field coordinator. George Van Riper flew in from Kansas, where he directed the state party, for a week of strategy sessions. Lehrman recruited his press secretary, John Buckley, from a job covering politics and rock 'n' roll for an alternative newspaper. The research director, Dick Behn, a former journalist and teacher, liked to quote Jefferson about a little revolution now and then being a good thing.

Lehrman often called his candidacy an "enterprise," and Frank appreciated all the term connoted. He had seen enough rich men wave their wallets to receive nominations, only to turn niggardly during the campaign. He had worked in enough storefronts, slept in enough cars, and cadged enough food and drink for rallies to find nothing romantic in politics on the cheap. Lehrman augmented his youthful staff by hiring the media consultant Roger Ailes and the pollster Richard Wirthlin, experts associated, respectively, with Richard Nixon and Ronald Reagan. The campaign boasted the latest technology—portable faxes for field operatives to communicate with headquarters; an Apple II Plus computer with spreadsheet software for tracking delegates; and three Lanier word processors for producing fund-raising letters in unprecedented volume.

The question was how to transmute deep pockets into victory. At the point Frank joined the campaign staff in November 1981, Lehrman registered single digits in the polls. The Republican organization scorned him as a maverick outside its command, all but formally endorsing the candidacy of Edward V. Regan, the state comptroller. More to the point, the organization dominated both stages of the nominating process, the state convention in June and the primary election in September. Even were Lehrman by some miracle to capture the nomination, his Democratic foe looked to be Mayor Edward I. Koch, a national figure at the crest of his popularity. "The guy's gonna lose," a veteran Republican warned Frank. "You're burning your bridges."

Lehrman envisioned a "campaign of ideas," and he needed money beyond his own to vault those ideas over the party mandarins to the voting public. So Frank plunged instantly into the laws governing campaign finance. How much could a person give? What about someone from out of state? Outside the country? A corporation? A child? Once he missed the last train to New Rochelle and slept on the office floor. He attended his father's seventieth birthday party wearing a beeper, and indeed was summoned away, dividing the family equally between the incensed and the impressed.

Still Lehrman fought with him in the very first week. In drafting guidelines for donors, Frank treated loans as contributions, subjecting them to strict statutory limits. Lehrman insisted a loan was really an advance, a gray area. The law says a loan is a contribution, Frank said, and a candidate for governor has to live by the letter of the law. Lehrman strode away, leaving Frank so rattled he walked around the block to settle himself. When he reentered the office, half expecting a pink slip, he instead found Lehrman chuckling. "Well," he said, "if you're that adamant about it."

Having proven his prudence and backbone alike, Frank graduated to greater assignments. Foremost among them was overseeing Lehrman's announcement, an event that had to present the dark horse as viable and the millionaire as folksy. The plan called for Lehrman to declare his candidacy among the morning commuters in Grand Central Terminal, ride the train to White Plains while being interviewed by a major political reporter, and then fly to Albany and Buffalo for appearances in time for the evening newscasts. Frank retained a long-range weather forecaster to choose the ideal day. With Roger Ailes, he tested campaign placards to see which shade would look best on television. His father even constructed a scale model of Grand Central, which Frank used to guide Lehrman through every step in advance. On the morning of January 11, 1982, with the first stages completed and the plane for Albany awaiting, Lehrman turned to Frank and issued his ultimate compliment: "It was like a Rite Aid operation."

He spoke too soon. Meteorologist to the contrary, January 11 turned into a day of blizzards along Lake Erie and below-zero cold everywhere north of the Bronx. With the Buffalo airport smothered by two feet of snow, the campaign plane wound up grounded in Albany. When Lehrman reached the state's second-largest city the next morning, John Buckley and Tim Carey had to shovel a path into the building where he was to speak. Television and newspapers alike lavished more attention on the weather than on the new candidate for governor, with *The New York Times* consigning his announcement to page B7. Frank could hardly blame himself for nature's caprice, but neither could he escape the consequences: Lew Lehrman was still, as his foes gloated, "Lew Who?"

Six months lay ahead until the convention, and the campaign needed to pursue two strategies, intensely and at once. It deluged the general public with radio and television commercials, introducing Lehrman as the force behind Rite-Aid's growth, just the guy to bring jobs to New York. Meanwhile it courted delegates one by one, beginning with those Lehrman had met in his travels with the platform committee. The message to Edward Regan in all this activity was that Lew Lehrman would not quit, whatever the cost. Or as the candidate himself privately put it, "The reason I'm going to win is that I have balls and the other guys don't."

Indeed, Regan abandoned the race midway through March. Between Lehrman and the nomination remained several lesser adversaries and the scrutiny that a sudden front-runner receives. As a conservative populist, a candidate seeking votes in the middle and working classes, Lehrman depended on being perceived as a self-made man rather than a rich one. Thus his commercials stressed Rite-Aid as his pedigree, not Yale or Harvard, and seized upon the emblem of his red suspenders, so baldly unfashionable. In the rural counties upstate, Lehrman often drove to events in a pickup truck.

The task of confronting the issue more directly fell in large measure on Frank. No law required a candidate to reveal personal finances, he told Lehrman, but political wisdom recommended it. He buried himself with Lehrman's accountants for days, studying tax returns as thick as novels. Frank's own Form 1040 usually ran to three pages. He had felt almost embarrassed to earn the grand sum of $25,000 in his first year at Weil, Gotshal & Manges, and here was a man with an annual income in seven figures and a net worth of $24,827,339. What struck Frank most, though, was how much Lehrman had paid in taxes, nearly $2.5 million over the previous five years.

From that insight grew a strategy, more the brainchild of Dick Behn than of Frank himself. Who better to champion the taxpayer than the champion taxpayer? John Buckley crafted a press release on Lehrman's financial condition, trumpeting his tax payments in the first paragraph. A chart listed every dollar the candidate had paid since 1977—to Washington, Albany, and city hall; on income and real estate and stock transfers. All this information went to reporters in mid-April, the height of tax season, and was accompanied by a statement from Lehrman.

> When I talk about New York State taxes, I know what I'm talking about. I've paid them ... I chose to run for Governor because there are too many New Yorkers who can't afford New York State income taxes, retired New Yorkers who can't afford the property taxes, and young New Yorkers who don't have jobs because taxes have driven jobs and business elsewhere.

Meanwhile Frank girded for the convention. Lehrman had been quietly accumulating delegates since Edward Regan's withdrawal, probably enough to win a ballot line but not to avoid a civil war. From State Senator Roy Goodman, a liberal cut from John Lindsay's cloth, to Nassau County chairman Joseph Margiotta, boss of a conservative machine, virtually every party leader of consequence still opposed Lehrman. For the first time Frank realized a depressing truth of politics. The great divide fell not between left and right, but inside and outside. "The permanent government," Lehrman called his foes. Dick Behn, too, had a phrase for them: "the incumbecrats."

Appreciating the enemy as never before, Frank prepared with a vigilance bordering on paranoia. He studied the layout of the convention hotel, a square-block behemoth in Manhattan, and booked the Lehrman crew into quarters on an elevator bank adjacent to the ballroom. He placed the campaign headquarters in a suite that was accessible by stairway, should the elevators fail or grow suspiciously busy. Every floor captain received a baseball cap to be readily visible. Remembering his uncle Paulie's tales of the Navajo code talkers in World War II, Frank equipped two Chinese-American staffers with walkie-talkies to pass instructions between suite and ballroom in a patois they called "Chinglish."

June 17, the day the convention was scheduled to vote, dawned well. A poll by the *New York Post,* a tabloid that had shamelessly boosted the Koch candidacy, rated Lehrman the Republican most capable of defeating him. A cadre of campaign workers, Frank among them, slipped a copy under the door of all four hundred delegates. For all that, Lehrman took barely 26 percent on the convention's first ballot, leaving three opponents within six points of him. The second ballot barely changed. Then Guy Parisi went looking for Frank Trotta.

They had known each other for roughly a decade, since meeting as Young Republicans and teaching at a TAR school together. When Parisi's political career stalled in his home borough of Brooklyn, it was Frank who suggested moving into Westchester. The advice proved so wise that these days Parisi played right hand to the county chairman, Anthony Colavita. And Colavita controlled one of the largest blocs of delegates in the convention. All were pledged to a state assemblyman, James Emery, whose campaign Colavita chaired, and for months Frank had been trying futilely to pry a few loose. Just the previous night he had bought Parisi a drink and said, "The door's open."

Now Parisi located Frank on the fringes of the convention floor. "Tony's ready to come on board," he said. "We need to talk. In private." The chairman and the candidate, each accompanied by his cornerman, met five minutes later in the anteroom between a banquet kitchen and a service elevator. As waiters rattled past with serving carts and janitors lugged away sacks of trash, diplomacy proceeded.

"I'd like you to consider Jim Emery for lieutenant governor," Colavita said.

"I won't rule it out," Lehrman answered.

"And I'd like to be state chairman."

"I won't rule it out."

Before the next round of voting, Emery withdrew. Another challenger, Richard Rosenbaum, instantly followed. Lehrman won 69 percent of the third ballot. Once the pariah of the state party, he stood now as its official designee for governor.

"The Kampaign Kids," one reporter dubbed Lehrman's staff. Another wrote of their "almost bellicose zeal," while a third quoted a political foe grousing, "The junta took over." From that day a sign on Karl Ottosen's door announced, "Junta Headquarters." As for Lehrman, he sent a note to Frank Trotta's mother.

Dear Lorraine:

Many thanks for the telegram. You may not have had any doubts, but I think Frank may have had one or two. I wish you could have been at the convention to see General Trotta in action. He put together a wonderful battle plan and deployed his troops perfectly.

By Friday, he even smiled.

Three months later, in the primary election, Lehrman easily dispatched his last Republican opponent, a former United States attorney, Paul Curran. The Democratic voters, meanwhile, delivered Lehrman a gift. Ed Koch, the favorite, the folk hero, the latter-day La Guardia, lost to Mario Cuomo, entitled but obscure as the lieutenant governor. A fly in the ointment, Frank had thought of him. Nothing more.

Almost alone in the Lehrman camp, Tim Carey cursed the outcome. As a self-described "street politician," he had been watching Cuomo assemble a statewide organization over the years. Sifting through local newspapers, squinting at articles an inch or two long, Tim now observed the effects. Here a county chairman endorsed Cuomo, there a union organizer did, somewhere else it was a minister—all of them with proven records of delivering votes. The AFL-CIO and the New York Federation of Teachers were lending their rank and file to the type of phone banks that Tim had utilized so fruitfully in 1980.

"This election," Cuomo declared the morning after the primary, "will be a referendum on Reaganomics."

As such, it put Lehrman instantly and uncharacteristically on the defensive. Elected to rescue America from economic distress, Reagan was presiding over the worst recession in forty years. Unemployment stood at 9.8 percent, having risen 2.2 percent in the past year, and 10.8 million people were jobless. In McKeesport, Pennsylvania, the sort of steel town where Reagan had campaigned so effectively in 1980, hundreds of idled workers marched against him, carrying a coffin labeled "American Dream." A Congress cowed by the president one year earlier overturned his veto of a $14.2 billion supplementary spending bill. Among the scores of Republicans to defect on the issue was Senator Alfonse D'Amato.

In the industrial cities of New York, layoffs mounted throughout October—330 from Bethlehem Steel in Lackawanna, 499 from General Motors in Tonawanda, 100 from Adirondack Steel in Watervliet. The total number of jobless statewide, 686,000, surpassed the populations of Albany, Buffalo, and Syracuse combined. New York State had fewer positions in manufacturing than at any time since the Great Depression.

Three weeks before the election Reagan went on national television to ask Americans for "the courage to see it through," to "stay the course." No words more shook the Lehrman campaign. Its candidate was trying to run as an agent of change, to paint Cuomo as the heir to a failed order, and now Reagan was making the newcomer sound like the incumbent. Several times in the days after the speech, Frank heard Lehrman grumbling out its phrases, jawline tight and chin jutting in exasperation.

Privately, Lehrman blamed the recession on Paul Volcker. As chairman of the Federal Reserve, Volcker had stanched the money supply to tame the raging inflation of the Carter years. Of course, a tailspin had followed. With interest rates above 20 percent, who could afford to buy a car or a house? The solution was not less Reaganomics, Lehrman believed, but more Reaganomics, purer Reaganomics, the master stroke. The challenge was how to offer the program without uttering its name.

Frank himself recognized a different dilemma. Mario Cuomo was Italian. So were thousands of the conservative Democrats whose votes Lehrman desperately needed. When Cuomo told stories of his immigrant parents and their neighborhood grocery, he touched collective memory. He had made his political reputation in the early 1970s as the attorney who stopped the city from demolishing sixty-nine homes in the Italian enclave of Corona, Queens, to clear land for a new high school. Mediating a volatile dispute about subsidized housing in the nearby neighborhood of Forest Hills, he demonstrated sensitivity rare for a liberal to the middle class's anxieties about crime and racial upheaval. Now, within reach of being the first Italian-American ever elected governor in New York, he stirred an emotion deeper than partisan loyalty. It was the communal pride that Irish Catholics had felt when Al Smith ran for the same office in 1918 and that Jews had known when Herbert Lehman did in 1932.

Never did the phenomenon become clearer to Frank than on the Saturday afternoon in September when he accompanied Lehrman into Manhattan for the Feast of San Gennaro. The event celebrated sentimentality as much as Catholicism, drawing back the children and grandchildren of Little Italy from their suburban diaspora. They thronged Mulberry Street by the hundreds of thousands, devouring *zeppole* and sausages, swaying to Neapolitan ballads, and pinning dollar bills on the massive shrine to the patron saint. Since the days of Tammany Hall the festival had been a politician's paradise, a setting so crowded and jovial any candidate could expect to be swarmed over, if only by accident.

As Lehrman picked his way through the multitude, shaking hands, Frank fretted. He remembered seeing Alfonse D'Amato campaign during San Gennaro two years earlier, the crowd all but crushing him alive. Nobody threw a bear hug around Lehrman. Not enough cried in that familiar way, "Hey, Lew." Surely these people recognized Lehrman in his red suspenders, the image from hundreds of commercials. And surely, Frank believed, they shared his beliefs—lowering taxes, restoring the death penalty, halting state payment for abortions. But they were treating Lehrman like a neighbor, not one of the family.

"We've got to show," Dick Behn cracked a few days later, "that Lew is really the Italian in the race."

To capture the swing vote of white ethnics, Lehrman spent money on the scale of Rockefeller, topping $10 million by mid-October. It showed most obviously in commercials stressing jobs and crime. Less visibly, but more important, it paid for the most sophisticated version of direct mail in any American campaign. The Lehrman operation could tailor letters by ethnic group and party affiliation literally house by house. One version, printed on paper with a kelly green border, said, "Irish-Americans realize just how liberal Mario Cuomo is." The Jewish model warned, "Mario Cuomo favors quotas and therefore reverse discrimination."

These expensive efforts invited a backlash, and got it when Cuomo chose the slogan "Experience Money Can't Buy." During a televised debate, as Cuomo exceeded the time limit in answering a question, Lehrman extracted a gold pocket watch from his pants and thrust it toward the Democrat. Cuomo halted in midsentence and said, "That's a *very* expensive watch, Lew."

But ideas as much as money characterized the Lehrman campaign. Since the primary race he had been writing and releasing position papers of startling range and detail—eight single-spaced pages on Long Island's water problems, sixteen on small-business development, seven on welfare reform, seventeen on the judicial system. He devoted no less than fifty to an economic plan for the state, oriented around a 40 percent cut in its income tax. The proposal earned front-page attention in *The New York Times* and prompted Cuomo into answering with his own blueprint, forty-six pages in length.

Sixteen points behind on October 8, Lehrman drew virtually even two weeks later. The Republican leaders who had fought against him at the convention and the primary, who had maintained a disapproving distance since then, began campaigning actively on his behalf. From Long Island, one state legislator called Leslie Maeby to say, "You might've picked the right horse."

Frank himself watched the drama in the form of daily tracking polls. A few thousand votes, even hundreds, he realized, might well determine victory. As campaign counsel, he could do maddeningly little about it. So much of his time went into routine duties, whether preparing disclosure forms or negotiating contracts with vendors. Twice he filed complaints about the Cuomo campaign with the state Board of Elections, and twice the media accorded his charges the space of a modest obituary. But there was one possible way Frank could help tip the election.

Beginning in September, with Lehrman already nominated by the Republican and Conservative Parties, Frank had set about gaining him a third line designed to lure independents. He gathered nominating petitions, trained dozens of volunteers, and struggled to fulfill the byzantine requirements of state law: 20,000 total signatures, with at least one hundred apiece from seventeen different congressional districts. Several nights Frank himself carried clipboard and pen from house to house. In the end, he landed Lehrman on the ballot with the Statewide Independent Party. Then, to dissuade Cuomo's campaign from photocopying the petitions for a legal challenge, he commissioned his father to build a single binder for the five-foot stack, all held fast by the hinge from a mousetrap.

Through each twist of the campaign, Frank's admiration for Lehrman grew, and for a very particular reason. All his life, it seemed to Frank, the educated had disparaged his ideas. He still remembered Brother Smith at Blessed Sacrament, incensed that he supported the Vietnam War, saying, "Your father probably reads the *Daily News.*" Then there was the professor of criminal justice at SUNY who ignored Frank when he suggested that not everyone in prison was there because of poverty.

Well, nobody mocked Lew Lehrman's brain. He had—what was that word Frank remembered from Latin?—*gravitas.* Mario Cuomo might speak about St. Augustine and Teilhard de Chardin, two wellsprings of his Catholic liberalism, but Lehrman could discourse every bit as eloquently on Jacques Rueff and Jean-Baptiste Say, the founts of his free-market ethos. Even *The New York Times,* to Frank the house organ of the liberal establishment, acknowledged, "Whatever else turns out to be true of New York's 1982 campaign for governor, it will have been a contest between two powerful, searching intellects."

Then, two weeks shy of Election Day, Frank and several other insiders noticed something strange in the tracking polls. Having drawn to a deadlock with Cuomo only days earlier, Lehrman was suddenly faltering. About the same time Tim Carey started receiving calls from his field operatives upstate, from Binghamton and Rochester and a dozen other cities. Where were Lew's commercials? Why wasn't he on radio and TV anymore? What was going on? Karl Ottosen, the campaign manager, demanded an answer from the company hired to buy airtime for the advertisements. There were no open slots left, he was told. The more conspiratorial minds in the Lehrman campaign imagined Cuomo's hand at work. No evidence supported that theory, but after the election the company did repay $300,000 under threat of a lawsuit. Meanwhile Ottosen approached a competing outfit. No problem, they said, how much do you want to spend?

On the Friday morning of October 22, four days after the commercials had mysteriously disappeared, Lehrman trailed Cuomo by ten points. The entire campaign staff and several dozen volunteers assembled in Manhattan to address the crisis. Under direction from Frank, Tim, and Ottosen, they split into ten pairs and roared off in rented cars for television stations in every corner of the state. Each team carried a tape of Lehrman commercials and a check for the time being booked by the new agency; each operated under orders to arrive by five o'clock, speed limit be damned. Once the station offices closed for the weekend, Lehrman would forfeit two more days of exposure, and with it, in effect, the election. Every car beat the deadline.

All told, Lehrman poured $850,000 into television during the final stretch of the campaign, leading a Buffalo reporter to pronounce the onslaught the "Lew Lehrman Film Festival." The direct-mail operation churned out 8 million letters. With the national unemployment rate by now above 10 percent, Lehrman for the first time publicly criticized his party and his president.

On the morning of Election Day, November 2, 1982, Leslie Maeby finished scheduling a victory tour for Lehrman, which would follow the same itinerary as had his announcement caravan. Tim Carey stopped into a military surplus store to buy rank insignias for the campaign staff. Frank Trotta, a careful lawyer to the end, prepared a motion requesting that the state supreme court impound every voting machine.

By seven o'clock that evening, however, Lehrman learned from confidential exit polls that he would lose. As early as nine, he offered to concede in person to Cuomo. Rebuffed, he let the tally continue for hours. Frank remained ignorant and anxious. Suit coat off, vest unbuttoned, and tie slackened, he stood in the ballroom of the Sheraton New York in Manhattan. He studied a television monitor mounted on the wall, saw Cuomo building a lead, then turned his eyes toward the carpet. He was twenty-seven, and his hair fell across his forehead in the same boyish way it had twelve years earlier on the morning of the Honor America parade. When the counting was over, Cuomo had won by 181,000 votes from more than 5 million cast. The Statewide Independent Party, Frank's project, had drawn only 15,933.

On the morning after a sleepless night, Frank and Susan trudged from the hotel toward Lehrman headquarters. It seemed impossible that on his first visit there, some fourteen months earlier, he had gotten lost. Now his feet could find 641 Lexington by homing instinct. At the front door, he and Susan kissed and parted. A trained midwife, she was starting a new job that day, leaving a municipal hospital for a private one. Frank knew only what was ending. He crossed the floor toward his office. Fantails of paper covered the desks. Cigarette butts bobbed in cups of stale coffee. For once, the place didn't look much like an enterprise. Frank wondered how he was going to support a family now. Maybe he never should have left Weil, Gotshal & Manges. Maybe conservatism in New York was a lost cause.

Lehrman answered one question that day, announcing he would

keep his staff on the payroll until year's end. Classy, thought Frank. Plenty of campaigns cut off salaries in October, pleading noble poverty. Yet the very decency of Lehrman's gesture made him ache. For the past year, he had reunited with the State Street Gang in the service of a leader he esteemed and an ideology he embraced. It was that rarest of endeavors, politics without compromise. Now, like a romantic recovering from a great, failed love affair, Frank understood he would never again experience quite the same passion. In truth, he had only begun his descent from enchantment to its opposite.

• • •

At six o'clock on the morning of December 1, 1983, nearly thirteen months after Lew Lehrman's defeat, the phone rang in Frank Trotta's bedroom. "Turn on 'VOX," blurted his mother, Lorraine, referring to the local radio station. Frank did. It was his wife's birthday, and every year Lorraine had the disc jockey play "Longer" by Dan Fogelberg, one of Susan's favorite songs. This time, though, Frank heard no music, only a man saying gravely, "I expect to be indicted." He recognized the voice instantly as that of Joe Pisani. For seven years Frank had heard the rumors, followed the investigations, and even been questioned once himself. But rarely had the notion of Pisani as corrupt impressed him as being anything other than a partisan form of character assassination. It was Pisani who had discovered the political talent in Frank as a high school freshman, trusted him as a teenager to manage a campaign, hired him as a collegian to review legislation. After passing the bar examination Frank had even sworn in Pisani for a fourth term. Now, though, the senator was predicting that the federal government would charge him with income-tax evasion. Abruptly Frank remembered himself at age three or four, watching a newscast about several department-store Santas filing for unemployment after Christmas. It was the day his first illusion died.

Frank woke Susan, tugged on a sweatsuit, and fetched the *Times* from his doorstep. As he peeled through its pages, searching in vain for more information, he dialed Dick Behn, as wise a political mind as he knew. It seemed inevitable to Frank that the media would be calling him for comment; he was widely known as a Pisani protégé and currently chaired the Republican Party in New Rochelle. What should he say? With Behn, he shaped a statement meant to split the difference between demonstrating loyalty to a mentor and protecting his own credibility. When the first reporter called, Frank supplied the deft double entendre, "I can't believe Joe Pisani would do those sorts of things."

As Pisani had forecast, the United States attorney in Manhattan indicted him that very day. The thirty counts went beyond tax evasion to mail fraud and embezzlement, and they cumulatively accused the senator of purloining $83,000. Some of the money had come from campaign contributions, some from his law partnership, and some from the Temporary State Commission on Child Welfare, which he headed. In that last position, the indictment held, Pisani had given a no-show job to an acquaintance, Thomas Mallon, as a covert way of purchasing his summer bungalow for the commission's secretary, Kathryn Godfrey. The indictment delicately described her as being "a close friend of the defendant."

"A vendetta," Pisani said of the charges. "A patchwork of rubbish, garbage, and nonsense." Frank had listened to similar words from him before. For a long time he had believed them. He prayed he still could.

Twice during the late 1970s grand juries of the state supreme court had investigated Pisani, first in relation to alleged Medicaid fraud by a political ally and then for alleged misuse of state funds by the senator himself. Neither panel ever issued an indictment, and Pisani brazenly dismissed the inquiries as part of a "witch-hunt" launched by Democratic rivals. Frank's own brush with prosecutors led him to agree.

It started one afternoon in late 1978 with a message on Frank's desk at Weil, Gotshal & Manges. An investigator with the second of the grand juries wanted to talk about Pisani. Frank closed his office door and returned the call. With all the composure he could muster, Frank set a meeting for the following week. Hanging up, he felt the tremors. Here he was, a first-year associate, mere months beyond the bar exam. Had anybody else seen the message? What if he got subpoenaed? What would the firm think? Frank willed himself to the chamber of a senior partner and explained the situation. "Tell them everything you know," the partner advised. "Be truthful." He paused and added, "And if you need a lawyer, let us know."

On the appointed day Frank delivered himself punctually to a state office building in Lower Manhattan. There two investigators waited behind a steel desk in a room too long between paint jobs. "If you cooperate," one said by way of greeting, "you have nothing to worry about."

The pair started with questions about Frank's tenure on Pisani's staff. What was his title? What services did he render? As the investigators realized he had worked in Albany, not the district office in New Rochelle, they dove excitedly into files. Who was on the payroll of the child welfare commission? Who was a friend of Pisani's? Who was put there by the majority leader? Did anybody ever do campaign work on state time?

Frank dreaded the next moment. Surely the investigators would press him to name names. He knew one, a guy who split time between Albany and New Rochelle. Frank had seen him drive Pisani to political events and recruit volunteers to hang campaign posters. That was so petty, so common. Was the state so fanatical to hang Pisani that it would destroy some gofer in the process? Frank ordered his eyes to stay level, his voice to hold steady. Only his fingers, as cold as if bloodless, disobeyed. But the question never came.

One investigator walked Frank to the elevator. "We didn't think you were forthcoming enough," he said. "You're not off the hook yet." Reddening with temper, Frank thought, There's nothing to be on the hook about.

Indeed he heard no more of the controversy for nearly three years, until October 4, 1981. Frank awoke that Sunday morning to a front-page article about Pisani in the *Standard-Star*. With the state senator then running for county executive, the newspaper had undertaken its own examination of his career. Frank poured himself coffee, sank into a kitchen chair, and skimmed the first few paragraphs. In a perfunctory way, the story described the Pisani he knew, the architect of compassionate legislation on child-welfare issues. Mostly it recounted the charges that Pisani had larded the commission's payroll with friends and flunkies.

By practiced habit, Frank launched into a defense. Anyone could be investigated; that meant nothing. Why couldn't the media let go of Pisani? Nobody had ever proven he'd done anything wrong.

Then Frank turned to the inside pages, where the story continued, and a photograph arrested him. It showed a white clapboard cottage with a stone chimney and lace curtains in the window. The bungalow was owned by Joseph Mallon, who, the article said, had earned about $22,000 from the child-welfare commission in the late 1970s. Officially he had helped Pisani write a book about children's issues that went inexplicably unpublished. As for the home, the article described it as a "summer retreat for commission members," among them Joe Pisani and Kathryn Godfrey. It even quoted a neighbor as saying Mallon had sold the place for $17,000 at roughly the same time he was working for Pisani. Curiously, the sale was never recorded, but the bills for property tax, telephone service, and utilities started being sent to Godfrey.

These blows caught Frank unguarded. He had never heard of Joseph Mallon. He had never heard of the bungalow. He had never heard Pisani describe Kathryn Godfrey as anything more than a high school classmate now working as the commission's secretary. Frank had known Pisani for eleven years, been his aide and protégé and surrogate son. He had chosen classes on his advice, shared hotel rooms on the road, paid respects together at the same wakes. If this stuff was going on, he asked himself, how could I have missed it?

Except that he had not. Scouring his memory, Frank recalled an occasion in 1976 when he was serving on Pisani's legislative staff and reviewing a financial disclosure form. In the column for "campaign disbursements" there appeared a wedding present for an associate. Not yet an attorney, Frank had assumed that under the general wording of state law the expense was legitimate. Now he wondered. Frank also remembered a Friday afternoon in 1974 when he caught a ride with Pisani from Albany to New Rochelle for the weekend. Before they got on the Thruway, Pisani placed a few calls from his apartment. "I'll call you later," Frank overheard him saying at one point. "I love you." Then Pisani phoned his wife. All these years later the memory meshed with the photograph of the bungalow.

For the first time Frank turned his sympathy away from Pisani. Maybe it was the senator's family that needed defending. In all the races Frank had worked, back to 1972, he had watched Joan Pisani uncomplainingly organize volunteers and plan fund-raisers for her husband. Frank had gone through four years of Blessed Sacrament with one of Pisani's sons, and his younger brother Joseph had been a classmate of another Pisani boy. Of the two Pisani daughters, Frank thought instantly of Teresa. The campaign poster in 1974 showed the senator kissing her, a toddler in a pinafore. Above the image floated the words "Please vote for my Daddy."

Fighting back his misgivings, Frank did exactly that in November 1981. Pisani, in fact, ran a remarkably strong second to the favored incumbent. The following fall he won reelection for his sixth term in the State Senate. Absorbed as Frank was then by Lew Lehrman's campaign, he rarely thought of Pisani. Shortly after the election, Lehrman hired Frank permanently to represent him, as well as several conservative political action committees and a lobby that advocated for Ronald Reagan's agenda. Lehrman was someone with a worldview, a philosophy, not merely a hodgepodge of interests and angles. And he understood that a public figure had to remain, as he often put it, "cleaner than Caesar's wife."

With the indictment in December 1983, Frank was yanked back inside Pisani's circle, at least emotionally. The thirty counts against the senator closely echoed the allegations in the *Standard-Star* article about misuse of state funds, and additionally charged him with defrauding his law partners of $18,000, embezzling $14,000 from a widow who was his client, and evading $32,191 in income tax. Worse still, the government added nine more counts in February 1984, accusing Pisani of obstructing the federal investigation. As for how Pisani spent the money, the list assembled by prosecutors included Caribbean vacations with Godfrey, investments in a professional boxer, a wedding ring and athletic club dues for a son, and a trip to Europe to watch that son compete in a rowing championship.

Frank could not ascribe all thirty-nine counts to a political grudge, not when the United States attorney was a Republican, Rudolph Giuliani. But neither could he presume Pisani guilty of more than philandering, repugnant though that was. For nearly eight years now, ceaselessly hounded by the media and the state, Pisani had continued to excel as a senator. His name belonged to legislation that reformed the foster-care system, created a new class of bonds to finance urban redevelopment, and held the hearing-aid industry to quality standards. Even when Frank disagreed with Pisani on certain issues, often finding him too moderate, he admired the senator's energy and commitment. This was not an evil man. But was he an innocent one?

A jury began weighing that question on Monday, April 30, 1984, when arguments opened in *United States* v. *Pisani.* Frank intended to attend the trial as soon as his duties for Lehrman took him to New York. Until he could see the proceedings for himself, he refused to read most of the press coverage, just as he had avoided it during Watergate. Once again a hero of Frank's was falling, and once again blaming the Democrats and the liberal media could not explain away everything. So he chose willful ignorance over the anguishing dissonance between head and heart.

On the last day of the first week of testimony, Frank was conducting some business for Lehrman near New York's City Hall. The United States Court House loomed just across Centre Street. In midafternoon, during a pause between thunderstorms, Frank climbed the seventeen granite steps to the bronze door, strode across the marble floor of the lobby, and ascended by elevator to Courtroom 1105.

There the grandiose gave way to the mundane. Orange carpet ran rumpled across the floor. An air conditioner tilted precariously out a window frame. In six rows of oaken benches, many with nicks, gouges, and screw holes, sat no more than a half-dozen reporters and spectators. Not even that breed of recreational trial-goer sensed much entertainment in the plight of Joe Pisani. Hearing someone arrive, the senator turned to spot Frank, and gave him a nod and a smile.

"I don't believe so," a witness was saying to the federal prosecutor as Frank settled into his seat. "I don't believe it was recorded anywhere."

Instantly Frank recognized the slight, bespectacled man as one of Pisani's law partners. He was testifying about "partnership returns," "trust funds," and "escrow accounts." While Frank understood the definition of each term well enough, he could not divine how they bore on the trial. Presently the prosecutor ended his questioning, and Pisani's attorney, Robert Kasanof, launched into the cross-examination. Most of it turned on the minutiae of "finder's fees" and the "basic partnership agreement." But then, in phrasing a question, Kasanof referred to the prosecutor as "the United States Attorney." The judge, David Edelstein, interrupted to state for the record that Rudolph Giuliani was not in the courtroom.

"I certainly didn't mean Mr. Giuliani," Kasanof said. "I am sorry."

"Why don't you say what you mean?" Edelstein shot back.

"Because it is three-fifteen Friday afternoon," Kasanof replied, "and I am a little off the mark."

"Do you suggest I adjourn at approximately three-fifteen?"

Hearing the sarcasm, Frank felt confirmed in his fears. The judge was out to get Joe Pisani. Sure enough, a few minutes later Edelstein cut off Kasanof in the middle of a question: Had federal attorneys leaked advance word of the indictment against Pisani to the law firm's senior partner? Every subsequent time Kasanof tried to ask it, the prosecutor objected and the judge sustained. In the scope of an entire trial, these exchanges meant little, but for Frank, given the aperture of thirty minutes, they awakened dormant outrage. This wasn't justice; this was an inquisition. Or so he wished, against all knowledge, to believe.

Just past three-thirty, Edelstein granted a recess. Pisani rose from his chair and turned to the door. Then he walked back to Frank and threw an arm paternally across his shoulders.

"How's it going?" Frank asked.

"They're throwing everything they have at me."

Pisani withdrew his arm and walked toward the hallway, searching for Kasanof. Frank took the elevator back down to the lobby and headed for the subway to Grand Central. He never returned to Courtroom 1105.

After three more weeks of testimony and four days of deliberation, the jury found Pisani not guilty of eleven counts and guilty of eighteen —one of embezzling from the widow; four each of income-tax evasion and false filing; and nine of mail fraud, which largely concerned the undocumented use of campaign funds for personal purposes. The jury remained deadlocked on ten more counts, but federal prosecutors decided not to pursue a retrial. As it was, Pisani faced more than eighty years in prison. Two months to the day after receiving the convictions, Judge Edelstein sentenced Pisani to four years in prison and a $69,000 fine.

Grieved as Frank was by the verdict, he could find no reason to

372 • The Inheritance

dispute it. "It's a shame," he told a reporter, once again selecting a phrase for its shadings of meaning. He had not appealed to the judge for leniency with Pisani—even as monsignors and rabbis, social workers and music teachers, adoptive parents and union officials all wrote such letters—and yet he shivered at the image of him in jail. All Frank could think of was the time in first grade he had visited his uncle Dom, the night watchman in city hall. Dom was giving him a tour of the building, showing off some renovations, and they ended up in the basement, where the police department kept a holding cell. As a gag, Dom offered to lock him inside. Frank recoiled. What scared him most was not the bars but the exposed toilet behind them, emblem of a life stripped of dignity.

For the immediate future, Pisani remained free on bail as he appealed the convictions. Frank meanwhile fathomed the wreckage. Pisani had resigned his Senate seat, to avoid the ignominy of ouster, and surrendered his license to practice law, thus sparing himself disbarment. After thirty-two years of marriage, his wife, Joan, was suing for divorce and laying claim to two family homes. Several of Pisani's children, Frank heard, refused to speak to him. Even among the core of Pisani supporters, a peculiar form of condemnation arose. They might profess his innocence of the charges; they could even tolerate him cheating on his wife; but what absolutely infuriated them, they told Frank, was that Joe Pisani had fallen in love with a black.

In September 1985, Pisani won a qualified vindication. The federal court of appeals upheld only one of the eighteen convictions, that of embezzlement. The court ordered a retrial on eight counts related to tax evasion, and it reversed the nine convictions for misuse of campaign contributions. Pisani had clearly put the money to personal use, the court noted, but no law at the time expressly forbade it. Under a statute passed since then, the court observed pointedly, "we would not hesitate to affirm his conviction."

Rather than stand trial again, Pisani pleaded guilty on July 2, 1986, to one count apiece of income-tax evasion and filing false returns on nearly $35,000 he had taken from his campaign chest. Later that month, on the day he was sentenced to one year in prison, Pisani uttered his first public words of contrition:

> I don't want to give this court any impression about fudging or walking away or trying to explain away in some cheap way my plea. I received money that should have been reported and I didn't report it. I committed a crime for which I am very sorry. As a result of doing that, I stand before you today. I have lost everything. I spent my entire life, from

the day I got out of high school, building and working for a success and now it is all shattered. And I am not saying that anybody should throw any flowers or cry for me. I did stupid things. . . .

I paid. And the greatest amount of payment for what I have done is the thoughts I have in my mind and my heart that I let my friends down, I let my kids down, I let those that love me down. And that is not going to go away.

Those words came too late for Frank Trotta. It was not in his nature to hate, or to howl of betrayal, and yet something had broken inside. He would correspond with Pisani in prison. He would write on his behalf for reinstatement to the bar. He could not, however, unknow what he knew. For years, Susan had told him, "You're too good for politics." Now, reluctantly, he began to believe her. For the first time since his early teens, since arguing about the school calendar with a classmate's father named Joe Pisani, he was investing his faith outside the flawed realm of humanity.

• • •

In the spring of 1985, during the period Pisani was waging his appeal, Lew Lehrman called Frank Trotta. Instead of inquiring as usual about the status of a contract or invoice, Lehrman began bluntly, "I don't want you to read about this in the papers. . . ." Before Frank could imagine what cabinet office his boss was taking, Lehrman finished the sentence: ". . . but I am converting to the Roman Catholic faith."

Born and raised a Jew and married to an Episcopalian, Lehrman had first gravitated toward Catholicism more as a philosophy than a religion. He took a course in Early Church Doctrines at Yale and in other classes discovered the writings of St. Thomas Aquinas. Even as Lehrman ended his formal education, building careers with Rite Aid and in politics, he never stopped studying Thomist thought and seeking in religion a truth unavailable in the secular world. Eventually, the intellectual attraction engendered a spiritual one.

Frank knew nothing of the pilgrimage, except that he had been embarking on one of his own in the opposite direction. During his sophomore year of college he had fallen away from the church. He could not tolerate the hypocrisy of sleeping with his girlfriend on Saturday night and on Sunday morning worshiping a God who demanded abstinence; it was truer to live as a lapsed Catholic than the "cafeteria" sort. Some guilt still lapped at him during Lent, and he might give up ice cream or beer and even attend a few services, but after Easter he withdrew once more. Months passed between the family events that re-

374 • T h e   I n h e r i t a n c e

quired Frank's presence at Mass; years unfurled without him submitting
for confession. He and Susan, a nonobservant Lutheran, had even
turned to a Presbyterian to wed them.

"Which one of you is divorced?" the minister had asked in a premarital counseling session.

"Neither," they replied.

"Then why," he cried in bafflement, "are you here?"

That was an especially trenchant question on the Sunday morning
of April 14, 1985, as Frank took a seat in the St. Thomas More Church in
Manhattan to watch Lehrman adopt the very faith he himself had abdicated. The Mass of Conversion incorporates four of the seven sacra-
ments—baptism, communion, confirmation, and the blessing of
marriage. Frank saw the anointments and heard the prayers with an odd
sense of detachment, as if a time-lapse film of his own life were flick-
ering across the altar. Only when the priest offered Lehrman the Eucha-
rist, the body and blood Frank considered himself unworthy of sharing,
did pangs prick him in the spot where conscience and memory cross.

More out of impulse than reason, Frank ventured back into church,
attending Mass the next two Sundays. Still, he neither confessed nor
took communion, and as he joined the congregation in responsive read-
ings he was speaking by reflex instead of piety. Then, leaving the five
o'clock service on April 28, he learned from Susan that his uncle Seely
had died.

During the funeral Mass several days later, Frank again stayed in his
pew during communion. This time he felt harrowed by the distance he
had created with his own disobedience. He longed for the host, the
wine, and the redemption they symbolized. He yearned for the cleans-
ing of confession, and the catharsis of penance. For in some ways he
blamed himself for Seely's death.

Seely had been serving as the deputy fire chief of New Rochelle
when the top position opened. He finished first on the qualifying examination. The mayor supported him and so did Frank, who for the past
few years had chaired the city's Republican Party. But the appointment
went to a deputy with less experience, a lower score on the civil-service
test, and not coincidentally, more allies in city hall. One week after
being spurned, Seely suffered a fatal heart attack.

With his corpse lay whatever shreds of respect Frank still held for
politics. Through three years as municipal chairman, years that coin-
cided with Pisani's fall, Frank had grown to view corruption as the
condition of electoral life. Some of it was as picayune as patronage and
nepotism, some of it as egregious as eliciting kickbacks from contractors. Frank kept a file labeled "New Rochelle Crap." At one point he

presented himself to the Federal Bureau of Investigation with a proposal to wear a wire. The agency declined him, but one of the figures Frank suspected of criminal behavior would plead guilty in 1991 to perjury and obstruction of justice.

As if Frank required any more incentive to reclaim his faith, he received it several weeks after Seely's funeral. Frank's brother Joseph announced his wife was pregnant with the family's first grandchild, and he asked Frank to become the godfather. From his years in parochial school Frank understood what that meant: Above all else, he bore the responsibility for educating his godchild in Catholicism.

At eleven-thirty one morning the following week, Frank stepped inside Blessed Sacrament, the church of his childhood. There he had received first communion, uttered his first confession, and been confirmed. There the funeral Mass had been celebrated for his beloved uncle Paulie. In a broader sense, too, Blessed Sacrament breathed history. As the seat of the first Catholic parish in Westchester County, it boasted a granite spire, vaulted ceiling, and mahogany baldachino arching behind the altar. All the grandeur bespoke the sacrifice of its founders, Irish immigrants toiling as laborers and maids, strivers not unlike Frank's own forebears.

He moved toward an anteroom off the foyer. Once the chamber where ushers dressed, it had become after the Second Vatican Council the "room for reconciliation," an alternative to the confessional box. A small sign indicated the name of the priest waiting within, and Frank flinched in disappointment. From what he had seen the past few Sundays, this priest seemed a throwback to the liberal sixties, all folk guitars and felt banners. But too much had brought Frank to this juncture. He opened the door, dropped to the kneeler, and spoke through the linen partition.

"Bless me, Father," he said, "for I have sinned. It has been eleven years since my last confession."

"What caused you to come back?"

Frank told him of Seely's funeral, and of the example Lehrman had set in converting.

"Of course I don't expect you to remember all the sins of eleven years," the priest said, so he asked specifically about murder, theft, and abortion.

"No, Father," Frank answered. But he listed many others. Anger. Lying. Premarital sex. Taking the Lord's name in vain. And, of course, all the years without communion. The roster finished, Frank awaited reproach. Surely, he thought, the priest would demand a penance more onerous than a few Our Fathers and Hail Marys. He was not some kid, captive to whims and hormones; he was an adult who had flouted God with all his mature faculties.

"Do you know how to say the Rosary?" the priest asked simply.

"Yes, Father."

"Please say the Rosary once in reparation." Frank would comply later, outside the room. For now, the priest intoned, "God, the Father of Mercies, through the death and resurrection of His Son, has reconciled the world to Himself, and sent the Holy Spirit among us for the forgiveness of sin; through the ministry of the church, may God give you pardon and peace, and I absolve you from your sins in the name of the Father, and of the Son, and of the Holy Spirit, amen." Then he added, "Stay close to the church."

Frank basked in those words. He walked up the side aisle of the sanctuary and paused at a rear pew to genuflect. Others might adore the organ music and heightened ritual of the Sunday service, but Frank had always favored weekday Mass with its spirit of contemplation. He remembered back to his freshman year at Blessed Sacrament High, when he and his mother worshiped together every school day at the eight o'clock Mass. It had always calmed his nerves about homework and tests.

Now the priest stood at the altar and said, "In the name of the Father, and of the Son, and of the Holy Spirit."

Frank parted his lips to answer, "Amen."

He quivered three times during that Mass—first in begging forgiveness for his sins, then in watching the priest consecrate the wafers, and finally in receiving communion for the first time since his lapse, the first time since politics had replaced Catholicism as his faith. The priest held in his left hand the ciborium, a vessel containing the sanctified hosts. With his right, he removed one and placed it in Frank's palm. It tasted strongly of semolina, like the uncooked pasta he had often snacked on as a boy. It tasted like home.

When the Mass ended, Frank strolled outside into the afternoon light. In troughs before the church blossomed flowers that the monsignor himself had planted. Along the side, in the grotto to the Blessed Mother, azaleas, wisteria, and lilies bloomed. From the parochial school playground, alive with soccer at recess, sounded squeals of glee. This was spring, after all, the season of rebirth.

In his own, Frank did not forget the political world he had inhabited. But he engaged it only selectively. He turned down offers to work in the congressional campaign of Joseph DioGuardi in 1986 and the presidential candidacy of Jack Kemp two years later. He resigned a position as deputy counsel to the state Republican Party. When the local

GOP ousted him as chairman in a revolt against reform, he absorbed the rejection with equanimity, even relief. He reserved himself for the battles a purist could fight without apology.

With skills honed in campaigns of far greater import, he assisted a candidate for municipal judge. Then, true to his standards, he refused a judicial appointment as victory's reward. He drew the charters and served as the attorney for a triumvirate of conservative organizations in New York State—the Empire Foundation think tank, a lobby called CHANGE-New York, and the Political Action Committee to Kick Out Unresponsive Politicians, known to Frank's satisfaction as PACK-UP.

The defining moment arrived in February 1990, when the American Bar Association took up the issue of abortion. A resolution being considered by the group's governing body, the House of Delegates, essentially endorsed the Supreme Court ruling in *Roe* v. *Wade* legalizing abortion. Besides its symbolism, the measure carried practical consequences: Its adoption would allow the association to file amicus briefs in two abortion cases then pending before the high court.

In nearly twelve years as an ABA member, Frank had chafed often at its politics. The association leaned left by reflex, it seemed to him, whether the issue was an arms buildup against the Soviet Union, the nomination of Robert Bork to the Supreme Court, or proposed legislation to outlaw desecration of the American flag. Frank especially recalled the debate on a resolution calling for the federal government to hire more legal-aid attorneys. Why did everyone worry so much about the criminals? he had thought. Didn't the victims have rights, too? Without floor privileges at that convention, Frank had seethed silently. But he realized he was too politically ambitious to attack liberalism among its believers.

This time, on the abortion issue, Frank enjoyed no excuse. He held speaking rights as a member of the ABA's Board of Governors. But the body he represented there, the Young Lawyers Division, had already endorsed the pro-abortion resolution. If Frank publicly opposed it, he had been warned, the division might censure him. And he knew that a more intimate constituency of one, his wife, disagreed with his absolutism. Susan could never conceive of having an abortion herself, yet she could never forget the family story about a grandmother who had died from a bungled illegal abortion.

The morning of the debate Frank attended Mass. Then, before the national press, television cameras, and nearly five hundred lawyers, the young man who had never addressed a gathering larger than the auditorium full of parents at Blessed Sacrament High's graduation soared into oratory. It was February 12, Abraham Lincoln's birthday, and

Frank spoke of abortion through the metaphor of slavery, one he had often heard Lew Lehrman employ. He spent fewer words on the Supreme Court's ruling in *Roe* v. *Wade* than on its Dred Scott decision a century earlier. The Chief Justice of that era, Frank reminded his audience, had pronounced the black slave "a being of an inferior order" who had "no rights which we were bound to respect."

"The Abolitionists," Frank continued, "knew that blacks were human and thus entitled by every law: natural, divine, human, and humane to live and to live free. These Americans rejected the surface appeal of the pro-choice argument: Let each define 'life' and 'liberty' for himself or herself. Lincoln said that with some the word 'liberty' may mean for each person to do as he pleases with himself. While with others the same word may mean for people to do as they please with others. Lincoln and the Abolitionists knew that no one has the right to dispose of an innocent person's life and liberty."

It did not matter to Frank that the resolution ultimately passed by a margin of better than two to one. It did not matter that no candidate of his had ever lost an election that badly. Nothing in twenty years of Republican causes, with the single exception of the Lehrman campaign, filled him with as much pride and purpose as that speech. Even John Cardinal O'Connor, the archbishop of New York, wrote to him in gratitude. Then, at a later ABA convention, Frank confounded those who appraised him as a predictable right-winger by speaking in favor of an antidiscrimination measure that included gays and lesbians. The church condemned the sin, he argued, but never the sinner. Yes, there was something bracing, something elevating, about being impolitic at last. If life's just about who's gonna win, Frank could tell himself now, I should be at the racetrack, betting on horses.

• • •

Midway through the afternoon of May 1, 1992, one of Frank Trotta's colleagues in Lew Lehrman's Connecticut office phoned a bank in Manhattan to order a wire transfer. "We're closing," the bank employee told him. Two days earlier, a jury in California had acquitted four police officers of beating a black motorist named Rodney King, an episode captured on videotape. Los Angeles had exploded into the worst riots in modern American history, and now New York was girding for its own cataclysm. Already rumors swirled that looters had invaded Macy's, that Penn Station had locked its doors.

Frank called Susan at her job in a Bronx hospital; he called the day-care center that took care of their three-year-old, Matthew, and the baby-sitter at home with their toddler, Anselee; he called his mother, who had heard on WVOX that blacks were marching in protest along North Avenue, shattering windows as they went. Frank lived on North Avenue, less than a mile from downtown. He drove home immediately, following a circuitous route to avoid the demonstrators' path.

On the shady slope where his turn-of-the-century colonial rested, quietude reigned. Frank watched the television for a time, until the footage of Los Angeles upset Matthew. Only the next morning did he learn exactly how close the turbulence had come. First his brother Joseph phoned to recount what he had heard on his police scanner—fires and tear gas and cops summoned from other towns. Then, when Frank lifted the *Standard-Star* from his doorstep, his gaze fell on the photograph of several police barricaded behind their patrol car. About seventy teenagers had rampaged for three hours, smashing windows in forty stores and setting fire to two trucks and a restaurant.

For several years Frank had been thinking about moving away from New Rochelle. This settled the issue. The politics in town were foul, the New York State taxes were too high, and lately crime had crept virtually to the Trotta doorstep. Thieves had broken into both family cars and the garage. A rapist had struck half a block away, a carjacker in the parking lot of a neighborhood restaurant. And now New Rochelle, that paradigm of integration, had produced a riot.

Frank could afford to choose his destination carefully. He was within months of completing a master's degree in business administration at Columbia University. Lew Lehrman had paid the tuition, the better to prepare Frank for his current assignment handling legal and administrative affairs for the investment business. Frank was earning enough to afford an upscale neighborhood and even owned a few stocks in his retirement plan. For the son of a janitor and a switchboard operator, he had achieved at least the financial version of the American Dream. The next address for Frank Trotta and family would be Greenwich, Connecticut.

Still, Frank was not leaving just a house or a city. He was leaving history. New Rochelle was Uncle Paulie on the porch, telling war stories. It was his mother taking him to Mass on school mornings, and his father lugging home a bicycle or typewriter from Hartley Houses. It was washing windshields with Youth for Pisani, recruiting neighbors for the Honor America parade. It was Silvio Burigo, progenitor of a political line his grandson had redirected and then abandoned.

Frank had seen Silvio for the last time in February 1978. The patriarch was living then with his daughter Mary Jane in the house expanded to his consternation by a nonunion crew. Haggard from liver cancer and chemotherapy, he wore pajamas most days and rarely rose from a brown tweed recliner. He watched television more than he talked. Within several weeks he would be dead.

But Silvio did speak to Frank that day. He recalled the period in the early 1950s when he was trying desperately to get his sister Onelia out of Italy. She had left America decades earlier with Silvio's widowed mother, and the country would not grant her reentry. Silvio sought help from a plumbing contractor, Ray McGovern, who had gone into politics and risen to the office of state comptroller. McGovern won Onelia a visa, and with it Silvio's vote in every election to come. McGovern was a Republican. After all the times Silvio had chided Frank about working for "them," he strained now for conciliation. "I always vote," he said, "for the man."

Those were words worth remembering one Sunday in the spring of 1992. The phone rang in Frank's kitchen with a voice from the past, that of a senior partner from Weil, Gotshal & Manges. "How'd you like to be Ross Perot's election lawyer in New York," he asked, "get him on the ballot?" Respectfully as the green associate he once had been, Frank declined. The partner insisted, "Money's no object with this guy."

It was understandable that the partner had made the overture. Not only did Frank possess talent and experience at election law, he had also grown every bit as disgusted with career politicians as had those middle-class mutineers soon to be dubbed Perotistas. The difference was that Frank nurtured no illusions about their hero. No, somebody who had gotten rich on contracts from Medicaid was not about to dismantle the welfare state. And Perot favored the right to abortion. Frank liked Perot just the way he had met him, as the swashbuckling executive in the book *On Wings of Eagles*, as a character.

The partner, though, was right about one thing. Money was no object. Not all the billions in a Texas fortune could lure Frank Trotta ever again into idolatry.

Chapter Sixteen

Incumbent Protection
(Leslie Maeby)

LESLIE MAEBY DROVE INTO QUEENS ONE MORNING IN JANUARY 1984 equipped with the address of a state senator named Martin Knorr and the assignment of saving him from extinction. She stopped briefly in the reception area of his district office, the part the public saw. Then she cracked open the door to his private anteroom, a place only intimates were entrusted to enter. Gazing upon the dishevelment and smelling the stale air, Leslie soon understood why. She picked her way down a jagged path between file cabinets, storage cartons, and loose folders, her steps stirring the dust. Here sat a desk heaped with papers, there a threadbare sofa, where Knorr slept frequently. All that was missing was the man himself.

Leslie met him about a week later in Albany in the company of an aide. Knorr was tall and rumpled, and he clasped a cigarette in a trembling hand. The aide did most of the talking, occasionally turning to say, "Right, Marty?" Knorr answered in a robust voice, always saying, "Right," and always saying it a few seconds too late. Leslie kept thinking of a forty-five record being played at thirty-three.

She had other numbers in mind, too. The Republican Party held a majority of thirty-five seats to twenty-six in the New York State Senate. The Democrats ruled the Assembly, and Mario Cuomo reigned as governor, and with a swing of just a few seats the next November the GOP would be reduced from opposition to irrelevancy. So the party had hired Leslie to perform "incumbent protection" for eight senators from New York City and Long Island. Nobody, it was clear to her, needed more protecting than Martin Knorr.

For most of his nineteen years in the State Senate he had proven invulnerable. He represented a district carefully gerrymandered to enclose the conservative Catholic neighborhoods of Maspeth, Ridgewood, and South Ozone Park within a curious hourglass shape. Knowing the landscape, Knorr delivered on issues and image alike. He stridently opposed low-income housing, legalized abortion, and busing to integrate schools; he visited the first-aid squads and senior citizens' centers, and offered public comfort to the grieving parents of two toddlers killed in a Christmastime fire. For lack of a viable Democratic alternative, labor unions endorsed him, and, in recognition of his personal rectitude, so did the reformers of the Citizens Union.

By now, though, Knorr was seventy-eight years old and both personally and politically infirm. He had been reelected two years earlier by a margin of just 3 percent against an opponent who happened to be a half century younger and the son of the incumbent Queens district attorney. A rematch loomed, and with it the question not only of whether Knorr would win but whether he would survive.

He had not spoken on the floor of the State Senate for five years, by some accountings, and he often appeared to doze through debates. The committee he had most recently chaired spent nearly $100,000 annually while rarely convening, much less acting. "Slothful, somnambulant, and ineffective," pronounced an advocacy group that studied the panel. Knorr did not even live in the modest row house he claimed as his legal address, Newsday discovered, but rather in a stucco home draped with ivy, miles away from his working-class district.

As Leslie quickly came to realize, Knorr required a staff member to buy his clothes, send out his dry cleaning, and remind him to shower. His dentures occasionally fell out. Then there was his tendency to overindulge in what he called "bloody Scotch." After a formal banquet held by the Albany press corps one recent year, Knorr had first passed out in a hotel ballroom, then awakened to urinate on a wall, and finally toppled into unconsciousness trying to punch a reporter who was steering him into a taxi.

In a genuine democracy, Martin Knorr might well have been ousted long before Leslie appeared. But he served in the New York State legislature, which was really a dictatorship of the incumbents. Every two years New York's voters walked through the ritual of casting ballots for competing candidates, but in no state of the union was the result of legislative elections so preordained. The success rate for an incumbent in New York hovered high in the nineties; by one critic's reckoning, a sitting legislator was more likely to be indicted than defeated. In 1988 two who were actually under indictment for campaign law violations would easily win another term.

The state legislature annually earmarked upwards of $100 million in taxpayers' dollars for perpetuating itself. The money paid for radio and television studios, reserved for the use of legislators alone, that produced talk shows and sound bites for local stations. It paid for mailing newsletters thick with each legislator's accomplishments to the constituents back home. It paid for so-called member items, grants every incumbent bestowed without bidding, supervision, or accountability on community groups of his own choosing. In passing the 1984 state budget, for instance, the 211 legislators voted themselves a record-breaking $40 million in member items. There was $80,000 for the Sleepy Hollow Boxing Club, $40,000 for a Holocaust study center, and $25,000 for the Bassmaster Classic, the "Super Bowl of Bass Fishing." Public money, in sum, underwrote a political machine.

This particular machine recognized no distinction between Republican and Democrat, liberal and conservative. Rather, it entrenched a division of partisan power, in which Democrats controlled the Assembly and Republicans the Senate. Political action committees, in turn, directed an overwhelming amount of their campaign contributions to each chamber's majority, further compounding the advantages of incumbency. Principles and ideology faltered before the oldest rule of the racetrack: Never bet on losers.

Leslie knew the system well enough. For several years after graduating from college in 1975, she had worked for State Senator John Dunne, rising from legislative aide to chief of staff. Dunne had held office since 1965, and not simply because the public approved. Leslie remembered the radio feeds, the newsletters, the grants to this museum and that Little League. At first, she had regarded the system as proof of "how unfair things were," an even grander version of the inequities in office space and staff size she had observed while working as a page. Then she saw what happened when one dared to defy the established order.

In 1977, Dunne sought the Republican nomination for executive in Nassau County, which meant opposing the candidate selected by the party boss, Joseph Margiotta. Leslie resigned her legislative job to help direct the campaign. In the week leading up to the primary, she worked forty-eight hours without sleep to produce 20,000 postcards urging a vote for Dunne. The mail went mysteriously undelivered until after

Election Day. One of Margiotta's district leaders later bragged to Leslie that the machine had pressured several postmasters to sit on it. Not only did the machine defeat Dunne, but it also blacklisted Leslie within the state party. She was refused a job in Perry Duryea's campaign for governor in 1978. Tim Carey interceded to find her a position scheduling Edward Regan, the candidate for comptroller on Duryea's ticket. On her first morning she was fired.

For three months that summer and fall Leslie backpacked through Europe. Not in a decade, not since becoming a Field Girl at the age of fifteen, had she so removed herself from the electoral wars. It was an anguished withdrawal. Her sense of being capable, and more than that of being worthy, had always rested in politics. Why am I being punished? she asked herself. I'm a nobody. This is so unfair. All the thoughts led to one other: Do I really want to do this with my life?

Yet as Leslie wandered from cathedral to museum, youth hostel to pension, every stray copy of the *International Herald Tribune* tempted her with its headlines. Midterm elections in Congress approached; the governor's mansion in Albany was being contested. She flew home in time for Election Day, voted the Republican line, and honored John Dunne's importuning to rejoin his legislative staff. With distance, she could even rationalize Margiotta. Sure, he pulled that stunt with the mail. Sure, he forced every county employee to kick back one percent of his salary to the machine. But he must have provided low taxes and good government. Why else would his people keep winning? Leslie Maeby had made her peace with incumbency as practiced in the state of New York. It would prove a useful truce for the assignment of re-electing Martin Knorr.

In those early weeks of January 1984, Leslie studied Knorr's prior race against Tom Santucci. The two men had spent nearly equal amounts of money, a dire sign for any incumbent. In the pages of neighborhood newspapers, stocked with press releases from politicians seizing credit for anything from furnace inspections to flu shots, Knorr rarely rated a mention. He did not keep a press secretary on staff, unlike John Dunne and a good many other legislators. More incredible to Leslie, Knorr had not even bothered sending out newsletters. He was still coasting on reputation, name recognition, and loyal turnout from senior citizens. "It's like the Kennedy name," insisted the chairwoman of the Queens Republican Party. "Even if the body was dead, they'd still go down the line and vote for Marty Knorr."

That proposition was near an empirical test. One meeting with Knorr and one glimpse of his back room had convinced Leslie he was best hidden. Her polling showed that voters actually considered the senator's age an attribute—provided, of course, that they associated it with experience, not senility. Even as the de facto campaign manager, Leslie would see Knorr only a half-dozen times in the ten months until the election. Her strategy required the perquisites of incumbency, not the incumbent himself.

Early on, Leslie compiled the name of every voter in the district from 1982 and checked it against the birth dates in registration records. All those older than sixty, logically the core of Knorr's support, went onto a master list. Then Leslie wrote a letter in the senator's name about his advocacy for the elderly, a typical bit of political propaganda in the guise of constituent service. Every person on the roster received it, at state expense.

Over the coming months Leslie produced the four newsletters Knorr was entitled to mail annually to all 100,000 households in his district. Other letters followed, each one nominally about some legislative issue. Leslie sent them bulk rate rather than first class, for at the lower price the legislature paid for greater volume. By campaign's end, she would later estimate, the incumbency machine had deluged Knorr's district with nearly one million pieces of mail.

And at Leslie's behest it did more than that. In March she pleaded Knorr's case before aides to Warren Anderson. As majority leader in the State Senate, Anderson controlled the money for member items each Republican senator received. Traditionally, the most senior legislators enjoyed the greatest largess, and few were inclined to forfeit a dollar. "That's crazy," Leslie argued at the meeting. "If we're going to use this to political advantage, we need them for the marginal guys."

Fortunately for Leslie, Anderson's chief counsel lived just outside Knorr's district and recognized how precarious the incumbent's perch was. Knorr's share of member items doubled quickly, and Leslie set about salting them throughout the district. She rewarded centers serving the elderly, always a reliable source of voters, and associations of merchants, each with a store window for a Knorr poster. Some $85,000 went to a local charity, Polonians Organized to Minister to Our Communities, which prominently assisted the ill, the elderly, and recent immigrants.

The Republican leadership in Albany also manufactured an image of vigor for Knorr. During the late spring, for instance, the State Senate took up a thoroughly innocuous bill requiring gas stations with more than four pumps to provide an air pump for tires. With Warren Anderson's sanction, it bore the name of Martin Knorr as sponsor. The same thing happened with legislation giving war veterans in New York City a property-tax deduction, mandating compensation for crime victims, revoking the license of any driver repeatedly caught running red lights —more than a hundred measures in all.

For Leslie's purposes, it hardly mattered that many of these bills never escaped from committee or fell to defeat on the floor. They supplied the grist for her newsletters and press releases. And each one bore a photograph of Knorr showing an almost elegant gentleman, with lips pursed, eyes attentive, gray hair swept back from the temples in a Clark Gable way. Leslie called the portrait, at least a decade old, "Marty's kindergarten picture."

When the legislative session concluded in early July, Leslie doubled her commitment to Knorr's race to two days per week. She dispatched him selectively to audiences that would not mind, that indeed might not even notice, his doddering manner. One week the event might be a barbecue for hospitalized veterans, another the grand opening of an agency serving the homebound elderly. As fall and the peak campaign season neared, she coaxed Knorr through the taping of several radio spots. None exceeded thirty seconds; the senator mumbled and stumbled with a longer text. Even so, he required six or eight takes to manage an acceptable reading. Once again, the state picked up the tab for these purported exercises in "public service."

However unsavory Leslie's methods were, they at least fell clearly within the law. The same could not be said for Tom Santucci's campaign. All along, Leslie suspected the Democrat was receiving covert aid from his father, the borough's district attorney. Only years after the election did a state commission reveal just how right she was. It found that forty-eight employees of John Santucci had manned phone banks, bought tickets to fund-raisers, and otherwise assisted in the son's race, often bowing to pressure to show themselves to be "team players." The commission decided the activity stopped short of being blatantly criminal. But it assailed the ethics of such "volunteer" efforts, quoting one of the district attorney's bureau chiefs:

> The tragedy was, from my perspective, I had a lot of young, fire-in-the-belly assistant district attorneys right out of law school, who really wanted to get out there and do a job, and act like professionals. Then they were exposed to this kind of thing. It caused terrible morale problems. I think they stopped seeing themselves as upholders of the law.

In the fall of 1984, however, Leslie Maeby had only rumors and hunches. Neither helped her with the problem at hand, which was that Tom Santucci was mounting a visible and energetic challenge. He had sharpened his political skills as a district leader at the age of nineteen. By his early twenties, fresh from law school, he was serving as the legislative counsel to a Democratic assemblyman. And he had nearly defeated Knorr once already.

Santucci opened two headquarters in the district. He proposed programs to raise teachers' salaries and rescue elderly homeowners from foreclosure. Shrewdly straddling the political middle, he endorsed both the death penalty and legal abortion. Most of all, Santucci reminded the voters he was twenty-five years old. "We need dynamic young leadership," his advertisements declared. His typical campaign day started at seven in the morning and wound through church, subway station, and supermarket for fourteen hours. Shaking hands along Liberty Avenue, the main shopping street in the district, Santucci was quick to strip off his suit coat and sling it over a shoulder in the time-honored style of Bobby Kennedy.

Leslie answered back with the slogan for Knorr, "He Has What the Others Don't. Experience!" One campaign flyer depicted a child named "Young Tommy Santucci" being led along by Daddy. Advertisements listed every community group that had ever seen fit to honor Knorr, from the Blinded War Veterans to the Italian Executives of America. When Knorr refused a televised interview, an aide ennobled the dodge by explaining, "He's not a man to toot his own horn." Every time Tom Santucci pressed for a debate, Leslie sent a surrogate in the senator's place.

Except, that is, for the night the Glendale Property Owners Association held a forum. Knorr stood before a crowd of sixty, holding index cards listing his achievements, many of them the doing of Leslie and the party leadership. Trudging through the unfamiliar litany, he lost his place and read the same card three times. Finally, an aide tapped Knorr on the sleeve, and he compliantly thanked the group, took his seat, and shut up. For precisely such a moment, Santucci had brought along a city council member, Arthur Katzman, himself a septuagenarian of undiminished temper. "You senile old bastard," he shouted at Knorr. "You don't even know your own bills."

In this presidential year, it was true, Knorr could grab the coattails of Ronald Reagan. But Santucci enjoyed the relative advantage of running on a ticket led not by Jimmy Carter but by Walter Mondale, a candidate endorsed early and prominently by organized labor, a major force in the Senate district. Better still, Mondale's running mate, Geraldine Ferraro, represented the area in Congress. Shortly after the first presidential debate, when Reagan at times appeared aged and confused, Santucci's polling showed him drawing even with Knorr.

The incumbency machine, however, ground relentlessly along. Never in Knorr's career had so much money in member items flowed into the district. "Before you ran," the leader of a merchants' association confided to Santucci, "we got $2,000. This year, we got $25,000." A freshman senator in the Democratic minority would never wield such amounts. As if voters needed a reminder, the Polish community group to which Knorr had steered $85,000 gave away cheese, butter, milk, and flour to some 1,500 residents in the weeks just before Election Day.

The Republican State Senate Campaign Committee, the repository of political action committee money, poured about $125,000 into Knorr's race, roughly doubling the amount Santucci spent; measured another way, for every quarter-page advertisement Santucci bought, Knorr could afford one twice the size. Every household in the district received ten different Knorr mailings, some underwritten by the state and others the party, and many of them in full color on glossy paper.

Improbable as it might have seemed to outsiders, the state AFL-CIO awarded the rigidly conservative Knorr both its formal endorsement and scores of volunteers for phone banks and an Election Day get-out-the-vote operation. "Let's face it," said Victor Gotbaum, the executive director of a particularly liberal union representing public employees. "When you have a State Senate controlled by Republicans, it's only natural that you should support a GOP incumbent who's been good to you."

By the morning of November 6, Election Day, Leslie Maeby could exhale. There were enough drivers to convey all the senior citizens to the polls. Union volunteers with walkie-talkies monitored the turnout. Ronald Reagan had righted himself in the second presidential debate and was routing Mondale even more thoroughly than he had Carter. Yes, it was safe enough even for Martin Knorr to be permitted a few public appearances.

When the counting ended, Knorr had taken 43,487 votes to Santucci's 40,779, matching the 3 percent margin he had achieved two years earlier. The other seven candidates for State Senate under Leslie's aegis all triumphed as well, and the Republican Party held control of the chamber, as it had for all but one year since Pearl Harbor.

"You elected a dead man," Tim Carey chided Leslie. He spoke at least partly in admiration, for it had required all her talents to elect Martin Knorr despite Martin Knorr. Now that he was back in office, she could begin grooming a younger and healthier successor, local Conservative Party leader Serphin Maltese. Indeed Maltese would win the Senate seat in 1988, after the Republican Party ordered Knorr into retirement.

Eventually, the system of incumbency protection would provoke a populist backlash in the form of a movement for term limits. The crusade focused largely on Congress, the most visible of arenas. But even as entrenched as members of the House of Representatives were, they did not equal the staying power of New York's state legislators. In 1990 the reelection rate for incumbents would reach an astonishing 98.9 percent.

For her part, Leslie bore no regrets. Running the Knorr campaign had left her with the queasy stomach of compromise, but not the stricken conscience of sin. The race had supplied that sensation of accomplishment, of professionalism, her reason for being in politics. You know what you're doing, she thought. You put together a plan. And it works. And what if the Democrats had actually captured the State Senate, the last bulwark of Republican restraint? Just imagine the taxes.

• • •

One morning in September 1989, Leslie Maeby started a new job in an old place. She was the finance director for the state Republican Party, working in the same townhouse whose attic had once harbored the State Street Gang. Her office, in fact, occupied the same room on the fourth floor that had belonged to Cathy Bertini, the sorority sister who had recruited Leslie into the College Republicans.

Leslie felt satisfaction in the symmetry. Her life in politics had pointed to this moment. At the age of thirty-six she had just completed four years as an executive assistant to the state comptroller, Edward Regan. She had learned the state's budgeting system, with all its maddening quirks, and had even helped draft a report condemning Albany for delaying grants promised to nonprofit groups simply to improve its own cash flow.

She had also learned that Regan lacked the requisite campaign chest and political instincts to evict Mario Cuomo as governor. Lew Lehrman had withdrawn from politics by this time. Jack Kemp was ensconced in George Bush's cabinet. Alfonse D'Amato showed no signs of wanting to relinquish his Senate seat for a risky run against Cuomo in November 1990. The prevailing wisdom held that Cuomo was unbeatable, having won reelection in 1986 with a record-setting vote total. New York State, the orthodoxy went, had gone untouched by the Reagan Revolution.

Leslie refused to believe it. So did multimillionaire J. Patrick Barrett, the chairman of Avis. Having sealed a political alliance by contributing $100,000 to Bush's 1988 presidential campaign, Barrett had recently assumed the chairmanship of the state party. His mission was to install a Republican as governor for the first time since 1974. Leslie believed that Barrett himself—conservative, likable, and fabulously rich—would make a formidable candidate. That was why, after all these years, she was walking again toward 315 State Street.

It took a practiced eye to recognize the place. Scaffolds scrambled vinelike up the face of the building. A fog of mortar dust, set loose during repointing, drifted through the autumn air. Inside the townhouse, pipes clanged and fresh paint gleamed. Negotiating her way up a staircase covered with drop cloths, Leslie peered into the second-floor kitchen, a fugue of decorator tile, hardwood cabinets, and new appliances. Resuming the climb to her office, she passed one of Barrett's assistants.

"What do you want done?" he asked. Carpet? Or a varnished wood floor? What about her bathroom? All the others were being rehabbed.

"There's no reason," Leslie answered. "The office is fine."

She spoke not out of sentiment for the hangout of her college years but a sense of fiscal caution, if not outright alarm. Leslie had already studied the books of the state party. Just four months earlier it had reaped more than $1 million from a fund-raising dinner featuring President Bush. The whole windfall, supposedly meant for unseating Cuomo, had already been spent. And the books offered no clear explanation how.

To Leslie, if to nobody else, this was the worst time to be giving 315 State Street a fashion makeover. She wondered why her own salary was $65,000, at least a third too high. Everyone understood that access to power, not a weekly paycheck, was the real compensation in a political job. Barrett had tripled the state party's full-time staff to a dozen, a level it had not achieved since Nelson Rockefeller and his fortune had retired from government in 1976. Who exactly was going to pay for this spending spree?

Soon the answer emerged: Leslie was, at least indirectly. Several superiors began demanding that she schedule another fund-raiser, preferably in November and for $1,000 a plate. Experience told Leslie to resist. Neither of the two choices for headliner, Richard Nixon or Henry Kissinger, was available for the chosen date. More important, the same core group of donors was simply not going to subscribe to another top-dollar event just five months since the last one. The pressure from above mounted. Leslie dutifully prepared invitations to 3,500 supporters. Normally, such an appeal would draw upwards of 300 takers. This time a mere 50 said yes. Leslie canceled the fund-raiser and posted a $10,000 debit for the cost of the misbegotten mailing.

Leslie lugged her misgivings home to her husband, John Cashin. Now a reinsurance broker, John had met her a decade earlier when both worked for the same state senator. John appreciated Leslie's political skills—self-assurance, an ebullient spirit, the willingness to type a letter or answer the phone or meet constituents, regardless of her own title. But the one talent that he knew fell outside her temperament was selling.

In his twenties, though, John had excelled at it, meeting his quota five straight years for IBM. He taught Leslie the same "structured sales call" he had once practiced so expertly; they rehearsed all the stages from "establishing rapport" to "the close," the moment when Leslie could tell her quarry, "So I can count on you for . . ." and name a number unflinchingly. At home, coming from the man she loved, this formula had the sound of a solution. In the real world, Leslie faced obstacles besides her own touch of timidity.

The election year of 1990 arrived with the state party effectively broke and without a candidate. Reluctant to try another fund-raising dinner, Leslie devoted three months to cultivating what was called a "major donor group," composed of people willing to contribute $25,000 apiece toward a war chest against Cuomo. She sifted through hundreds of names of past donors to Republican campaigns; she considered friends and business associates of both Barrett and Joseph Fogg, a managing director of the Morgan Stanley investment bank, who was serving as finance committee chairman. Finally, in March, she convened the fifty likeliest prospects in a Morgan Stanley conference room for a "dog-and-pony show." A political consultant analyzed Cuomo's weaknesses; Fogg schmoozed and stroked; Barrett set the example by pledging his share. By evening's end, Leslie had fifteen takers, a total of $325,000.

Two months later it was all gone. "You should see these bills," Leslie's assistant would say as she reviewed the staff's expense reports. Thousands upon thousands of dollars vanished into cellular phones, luxury hotels, and room service, all of it categorized under the catchall of "party-building." Yes, Barrett had deep pockets, but so had Lew Lehrman in 1982, and he had never hesitated to upbraid Leslie for purchasing too much wine and cheese for a campaign reception. He might have been tyrannical, she realized in retrospect, but at least he wasn't naive.

Ultimately the spending exceeded even Barrett's willingness to cover shortfalls from his own pocket. Meanwhile a fund-raiser with Henry Kissinger barely broke even. Two rounds of layoffs decimated the party staff. Paychecks very nearly bounced. The renovation of 315 State Street halted with the plumbing unconnected in one bathroom and the line of new paint just grazing the third-floor landing.

Despite the vast sum the Republican Party had squandered in the preceding year, the party could not even show a candidate for governor. As of May 1990, the month that ended with the nominating convention, no fewer than nineteen men had already rejected Barrett's offer. At first, Leslie had joked about the "candidate-of-the-week." Recruitment was somebody else's department. Lately, though, she was finding that even the most generous benefactors refused to contribute to a leaderless ticket.

As the search for a candidate grew desperate, Leslie left Albany for four days to attend a campaign finance school operated by the Republican National Committee. Her instructors there emphasized that raising money for a candidate was like selling shares in a business. People were making an investment in a product. Investment. Product. Investment. Product. Nothing in her months as finance director depressed Leslie more than those words. She had no product. Not even a Martin Knorr. You could at least fool people with a figurehead.

Leslie did not fear losing to Cuomo in November. She had been part of losing campaigns plenty of times before, but the party had at least mustered a candidate. Pride pulled her in contrary directions. Quitting on the brink of election season could damage her reputation. Then again, so might staying associated with a fiasco. She had already endured exile once in her career.

At home, John measured Leslie's disturbance by her placidity. Most Mays they gardened together or rode bikes through the country. This one found Leslie preoccupied and phlegmatic. "Why don't you quit?" John asked. "I'm not a quitter," she replied. "You're not the breadwinner," he reassured her, "so you can afford to have principles." Those words clung. The next time Leslie stepped into 315 State Street it was to give notice.

As a favor, she agreed to work through the convention. True to form, the state party wasted what little money it had left booking single rooms, not the customary double, for staff members. Then, on May 31, Leslie finally learned whom the party planned to nominate for governor: Pierre Rinfret. After twenty-one years in Republican politics in New York, working on campaigns for Lew Lehrman, Alfonse D'Amato, and innumerable others, she could not place the name.

A joke quickly coursed through the ballroom. Q: Where'd Pierre Rinfret come from? A: Roy Goodman's Rolodex. Humor hewed closely to truth. Roy Goodman, a state senator who unofficially led the party's liberal wing, had discovered Rinfret in the address book of a mutual friend. Rinfret was a decorated World War II veteran who became rich as an economics consultant; his personal fortune, estimated at $14 million, offered a ready source of campaign funds for a state party near bankruptcy. But Rinfret had never run for any elective office or established himself as a backstage power. The positions that endeared him to Goodman, notably outspoken support of abortion rights, divided the convention. Far from practicing the art of political persuasion to unite a fractured party, Rinfret earned such adjectives in the press as "combative" and "obstreperous." In Leslie's judgment, Rinfret boasted only one qualification for the nomination—his willingness to accept it.

That fall she voted for Herbert London, the Conservative Party candidate for governor. So many other Republicans similarly deserted that Rinfret barely avoided the disgrace of finishing third. Mario Cuomo rode back into office atop a thirty-two point cushion. Not since the era of Al Smith had the state's Republican Party been so humbled.

Regarding the wreckage, Leslie considered one especially troubling theory. It held that the Republican hierarchy, or at least part of it, had wanted Cuomo to win. By this line of reasoning, the party's legislative leadership, especially in the State Senate, stood to lose both prominence and clout under a Republican governor. He, not they, would speak for the party in Albany. Yesterday's power brokers would be tomorrow's errand boys. Leslie had seen proof enough of the hypothesis back in 1982, when the party establishment fought for months against Lew Lehrman. When she thought of her own decades of toil, she could only wonder, If this is what it was all for . . .

That thought implied a question, and the question begged an answer. Leslie provided it four months after the election. Having already resigned from the state GOP, she retired from politics altogether.

• • •

A few blocks east of White Plains Road in the Bronx, east of the El station and the Greek diner and the rap record store, east of the apartment blocks crowded with immigrants from Russia and the Caribbean, unrolled a campus oddly evocative of New England. A wrought-iron fence circumscribed its seventeen acres, upon which rose seventeen buildings of Georgian design, their bricks red and their dormers white.

This was a private, residential school, and it touched the senses in the way such a place does, with the rattle of alarm clocks in the dormitories and the aroma of bacon frying in the cafeteria. It also moved to some rhythms quite its own. Early on a school morning, when the buses of certain day students disgorged, the halls would sound lightly with the skittering of canes across tile; the blind pupils were finding their way to class. On Friday afternoons, as the academic week ended, shouts and shrieks occasionally echoed down those same corridors; some of the boarders were protesting against being returned for the weekend to homes riven by drugs, violence, and neglect.

The New York Institute for Special Education was a refuge from the metropolitan bustle, and from families and other schools that had failed. And for Leslie Maeby, it was a refuge from politics. In March 1991 she accepted the position of director of development and public relations for several thousand dollars less than the Republican Party had been paying her. She was to perform many of the tasks she had for various candidates—raising money, writing newsletters, seeking favorable coverage in the media. Here, though, virtue elevated effort.

The institute served about five hundred children, ranging in age from six months to twenty-one years, all united by a struggle to enter the mainstream. Many were blind and virtually all lagged severely in development owing to a welter of emotional and physiological woes. They had come on referrals from schools and hospitals; they had come from poverty, single-parent homes, crack mothers. To the institute fell the task of preparing the very youngest to enter public school in time for kindergarten, and educating the rest toward college or an occupation, as well as the ability to live independently.

Leslie steeped herself in the spectrum of classes and activities. She watched the toddlers of the "Readiness Program" graduate with diplomas, mortarboards, and teddy bears. She saw blind students learn how to operate braille computers and catch the Fordham Road bus. She followed the student council, the basketball team, and the production of *The Wizard of Oz*. Nobody on the faculty, she realized, was there in search of a member item or a political appointment or a summer job for their kid. It's so real, Leslie thought. It's life and death.

She filled the newsletter with stories of hope and possibility, with snapshots bound to soften the hardest heart. When blind children from the institute's summer camp went with sighted chaperones to a Yankees game, Leslie landed a column about it in *The New York Times*. Meanwhile she set about raising $1 million per year, an ambitious goal for the institute. She replaced the drawer of index cards that contained fund-raising records with a computerized database. To the annual appeal, a letter that varied year to year only in its date and paper color, Leslie added campaigns for bequests, corporate matching grants, gifts of stock, and even life-insurance benefits. These donations, she felt certain, would not be squandered on room-service meals and cellular phones.

Over the weekends Leslie brought John tale after tale of the schoolchildren. "So what do you want to do," he asked at one point, "adopt one?" Both knew it was a joke. John had three children from his first marriage, and only once or twice had the institute permitted a staff member to serve as even a temporary foster parent to a pupil. Still, the comment attested to Leslie's commitment; her mother made the same observation. It was quite a change from their usual sparring about whether Alfonse D'Amato was a sleaze.

The job gave John and Leslie more than conversation. For most of their six years of marriage he had worked in Manhattan and lived in a co-op in Brooklyn while she, based in Albany, had occupied a house 150 miles upstate. During Leslie's tenure with the state party, John had enrolled in a master's degree program at New York University partly to fill the empty evenings. Finally they could subscribe to the New York Philharmonic, cook meals from *Gourmet* magazine, and attend golf school in the Catskills. Politics had often obscured the sentimentalist in Leslie; now she could read aloud to John from *The Bridges of Madison County*, weeping as she went.

Leslie entered the election year of 1992 unattached to a candidate or a cause. In a nation of angry and cynical voters, she had earned the right to disaffection by harsh experience. George Bush was hardly the man to relieve her malaise. Trawling once through the institute's files, Leslie had discovered a thank-you note Bush had written after a visit during his term as ambassador to the United Nations. That gesture summed up Bush's career, it seemed to Leslie. The presidency was his reward for a lifetime of favors delivered and thank-you notes sent. No wonder he left her so unmoved.

Only a few vestiges of her former life lingered. She donated money to Alfonse D'Amato and raised it for Serphin Maltese, the heir to Martin Knorr's seat. When Ross Perot launched his third-party candidacy, Leslie sent away for information from his front group, United We Stand America, as if to size up the opposition. Still, nothing in these spasms of involvement led Leslie to doubt the wisdom of her essential withdrawal from politics. Then Tim Carey invited her to volunteer in the primary election for a seat in the State Senate.

It seemed, at first glance, a curious use of her talents in a year with a president, a senator, and all thirty-one representatives on the New York ballot. But the candidate was George E. Pataki, an old friend of Tim's and a rising star on the right.

The son of a Hungarian immigrant who farmed, delivered mail, and bottled gin, Pataki had grown up in the depleted factory city of Peekskill, where his best friend was a black teammate on the high school basketball squad. He had won an academic scholarship to Yale, where he flummoxed his classmates by supporting Barry Goldwater in 1964, and gone on to excel at Columbia University Law School. Better still to Leslie, a woman soured on the political establishment, Pataki had made a career of shocking the complacent. First, in 1981, he had overthrown a Democratic machine to be elected mayor of Peekskill, and once in office he had revived the economy of a city that before his election had been almost unable to pay its police officers. Then, in 1984, he had toppled a sitting Democrat to capture a place in the State Assembly. This year, after four terms in the Assembly, he was running against one of his own party's incumbents for the Republican nomination in a State Senate district.

Once a mentor to Pataki, Mary Goodhue now symbolized that combination the New Right particularly loathed—old money and liberal ideas. She also had the unfortunate habit of taking her grandchildren to Florida during the legislature's budget debates. PACK-UP, the conservative political action committee that Frank Trotta represented, had specifically targeted her for defeat, contributing both money and research to the Pataki campaign.

Tim Carey had studied a decade's worth of election results in Goodhue's district to predict a turnout of 16,000 voters in the primary and to identify the 8,900 Pataki needed to be assured of victory. Some could be reached with shoe leather at clambakes and church festivals; others could be persuaded by letters to local newspapers and a televised debate. But Tim needed money, too—$7,000 for each batch of direct mail, $8,000 for a week's worth of radio spots, a total of $185,000 before primary day in mid-September. And that was why he needed Leslie Maeby.

One day in the early spring she reported to Pataki headquarters. It was a damp basement in downtown Peekskill, a room with a folding table and a fitful printer and file cabinets in three mismatched colors. Index cards and stationery spilled from their trays. Empty soda bottles collected in cardboard trays. Only a single placard, stenciled with the words "Another Family for Bush," reminded the occupants that any campaign except their own was under way.

Leslie gave over early mornings, late nights, and so many weekends that she began to joke about divorce. The old skills returned, undiminished by a season of idleness. Leslie drafted fund-raising letters, arranged house parties, and each day called another ten prospective contributors. When a ballroom had to be decorated for a cocktail reception, she inflated balloons with the practiced efficiency of a nurse diapering newborns. Greeting the guests, she spotted a vaguely familiar judge walking through the door, riffled through a mental Rolodex as he strode down the hall, and welcomed him seconds later with a "Henry, how *are* you?" that sounded both familiar and sincere.

The morning of the primary brought two new accoutrements to the basement, a jar of Tums and a box of Especol. "For NAUSEA," its label explained. Leslie soldiered through the earliest hours of voting, visiting precincts in Croton, and scavenging data and rumor from poll watchers. Then she drove to the Bronx to shepherd a *Newsday* reporter through the school. That done, she roared back toward Peekskill to work the phones. She sat before the picture window in a donor's den, oblivious to the tableau of the Hudson Highlands at sunset, tapping out phone numbers with the eraser end of a pencil. "My name's Leslie and I'm calling for George Pataki," she said time after time, always patient, always perky. She turned around the pencil to scrawl notes on her call list—"Left message," "Already voted"—and she counted it as praise when one woman shrieked, "You've called me ten times in the last two days!" Only Leslie's spare hand, rolling and kneading two rubber bands, betrayed her tension.

Nearly five hours later, just shy of eleven o'clock, that same hand lifted a beer in celebration. George Pataki had won, coming within six votes of Tim Carey's goal. Toward one in the morning, Leslie tore a corner off a sandwich. It was the first food she had eaten all day.

The general election made for an anticlimax. At the same time Pataki was predictably routing his Democratic opponent, George Bush was losing the White House to Bill Clinton. Leslie's husband, John, arrived at the Pataki victory party with a kiss and the latest tally of electoral votes, 175 to 28. By the time he returned from the bar with Budweisers for them, the margin had widened to 238 to 46. In this unaccustomed moment of defeat, the voices around Leslie vented resentment and hate.

"We can rename our country the United States of Media," said a Pataki volunteer. "I never saw the media beat the drum for one candidate like this."

Then the first, minuscule results from New York State appeared, with Clinton taking 85 percent.

"It's Israel calling up," muttered a graying man in a football jacket, "and telling the Jews how to vote."

The only conspiracy Leslie recognized was the one in her own family. In 1988 her mother had finally cast a presidential vote for a Republican. This year, repelled by the Christian right's prominence in the GOP, she supported Bill Clinton. So did Leslie's sister, a young widow with a toddler and no health insurance from her job. The Democrats were promising medical coverage for every citizen.

Not that Leslie interpreted the election as evidence that liberalism was making a comeback. The problem with George Bush, as she saw it, was not that he was too conservative for America but not conservative enough. A bumper sticker popular with the right wing summed up her analysis: "George, you promised . . . no new taxes."

Leslie had to admit it; Bill Clinton had co-opted the Republican Party's issues—crime, welfare, tax relief, and reverse discrimination. On the road to the Democratic nomination, Clinton had rebuked Jesse Jackson and executed a brain-damaged murderer, promised to cut taxes for the middle class and to end "welfare as we know it." In his acceptance speech he had rejected the tax-and-spend prescriptions of the New Deal, Fair Deal, and Great Society. "A mainstream American campaign," Leslie called it with begrudging admiration.

At nearly eleven, George Pataki strode into the victory party smiling and showing thumbs-up. The grousing stopped and the applause grew, rhythmic and joyous. The disc jockey played "Glory Days" by Bruce Springsteen, the same star Ronald Reagan had sought to embrace years earlier. With his gangly limbs, rumpled suit, and self-deprecating smile, Pataki resembled in all exterior ways New Jersey Senator Bill Bradley. Indeed, Leslie envisioned him as a senator or a governor.

But she did not expect to make the journey. This one campaign, this one taste, had sated her. When Pataki offered her a job in Albany after the election, she turned him down. Been there, she thought, done that.

Ending her second year with the institute, however, Leslie fidgeted with disquiet. She longed for the jolt of win-or-lose pressure. Some afternoons, it seemed, hours passed without footsteps in the hall. Plans existed for the school to launch an international program, expand the summer camp, and rehabilitate campus buildings, many of them seventy years old. But the board of trustees, Leslie was coming to believe, did not share her own vision of aggressive fund-raising. Was this just another campaign that did not want to win?

During those months of uncertainty, in June 1993, Leslie drove to Peekskill for lunch with George Pataki and Tim Carey. Partly the three were considering Pataki's next move; mostly they were celebrating Tim's new job. Just a few weeks earlier he had accepted a position as regional field representative for the Republican National Committee. He would oversee major campaigns in New York, New Jersey, Pennsylvania, Maryland, Delaware, and West Virginia. Already he had immersed himself in Rudolph Giuliani's bid to unseat David Dinkins as mayor of New York and Christine Todd Whitman's challenge to Jim Florio, the governor of New Jersey.

In some ways, as Tim himself concurred, he was an unlikely man for the job. He had dealt with the party's field representatives while running various campaigns, and considered them, especially during the Bush administration, a bunch of rich kids with expense accounts. Sure, he had wanted the money they could funnel from the national committee, but not the advice that accompanied it. A typical conversation began with Tim asking, "And how many fucking elections have you won?"

But in the months after Bush's defeat, conservatives within the party had ousted his appointed chairman, Rich Bond. In his place stood a Reagan man from Mississippi, Haley Barbour; and the executive director he installed, Scott Reed, knew Tim through their mutual patron, Jack Kemp. "Haley's looking for adults," Reed had told Tim by way of recruitment. "He's looking for people with expertise. He's looking for people who win." Given approval from Reed and Barbour to retain a few private clients and the seat on the Westchester County Board he had held since 1984, Tim had assented.

Now Leslie and Pataki peppered him with questions. What's the job like? How much traveling is there? What's the license? Translated from political jargon, that meant what was the assignment, the goal? The answer, ultimately, was electing a Republican president in 1996.

Something stirred in Leslie. She had never worked in a presidential race, never been closer to one than trying futilely to place Bob Dole on the ballot for the New York primary in 1988. Suddenly her career felt unfinished, incomplete. Not that she expressed any of these longings. Her old friend, after all, already had the job.

"Well, you know," Tim said casually, "they're still looking for somebody in New England."

"What do you think about me?" Leslie ventured.

"You'd be wonderful." He paused. "But why'd you want to do it?"

Then she explained the appeal of a presidential campaign. That night she brought the conundrum to John. The position would demand travel almost every week; she would probably have to move back to the house upstate. If the conservative version of family values implied patriarchy, then perhaps John was a closet liberal, at least on one matter. "I'd rather lose the convenience and companionship temporarily," he told Leslie, "for the sake of having you fulfilled in your career."

The next morning Leslie formally applied for the post. Hired within a week, she divided her time between the party and the institute before leaving the latter entirely in August. Most of the important races in New England loomed in 1994, so during the final weeks of the 1993 campaign Leslie was free to assist Tim in New York and New Jersey. Christine Todd Whitman defied the pollsters to defeat Jim Florio with a relentless attack on his tax increases and her own promise of cuts. Rudolph Giuliani, meanwhile, became the first Republican mayor of New York in twenty-four years.

The granddaughter of a ward heeler in a Democratic machine, the blood of the blood of Joseph Obrycki, Leslie Maeby had helped resuscitate a defeated Republican Party. It entered the midyear elections of 1994 with a plausible chance of seizing a majority in the Senate and gaining numerous seats, if not actual control, in the House of Representatives. In her territory alone, Leslie would be working five races for the Senate and twenty-four for the House. Looking further ahead, however, to 1996 and the battle for the White House, she still had converts to make within her own clan.

Midway through the afternoon of January 13, 1994, Leslie's mother, Vilma, drove out on errands. Another driver ran a stop sign and slammed into her car. For eight hours she lay unconscious in a nearby hospital. When Vilma finally awakened, a doctor began determining if she had suffered any brain damage. What's your name? he asked, and Vilma answered correctly. What's the date? he asked, and she got it right. Who's the president? From her bed, Vilma gazed at the doctor, struggled to focus her vision, and said with relief, "A Democrat."

Chapter Seventeen

Red Suspenders
(Tim Carey)

N EARLY SIX HOURS LAY AHEAD UNTIL THE POLLS OPENED, BUT by a strict reading of the clock Election Day of 1994 had begun. The Crystal Bay restaurant in Peekskill, the scene several hours earlier of a tumultuous rally, had emptied and stilled. Gone were the chants, the cheers, and the toasts. In their wake, the last few logs in the fireplace crackled. A train whistle sounded from the old New York Central tracks, a few hundred yards to the east. Turning along a bend in the Hudson, on whose banks the restaurant rested, a barge loosed its horn, less in a blast than a sigh.

Only one table held diners past midnight, and at it Tim Carey joined the man he intended to elect governor before the day ended. He had waited twenty years for a Republican to reclaim the Albany mansion, a conquest that had escaped even the Reagan Revolution. Through those decades Tim had married and fathered two sons; he had gained thirty pounds and lost hair at the temples; he had buried both the grandmother who had introduced him to politics, Lizzie Garrett, and the college friend who had led him into the Republican Party, George Van Riper, killed in an airplane crash at thirty-five. Others from the State Street Gang had retired from the battlements, whether in weariness, disillusionment, or satisfaction with a prominent patronage appointment.

In the years since college, though, Tim had gradually come to know George Pataki. They had met in 1977, when Tim was asked to provide the young lawyer with free instruction on reviving the Republican Party in Peekskill. Four years later, when Pataki ran for mayor of the city, Tim lent some expertise on campaign flyers. These days Tim liked to tell reporters, "The moment I met him, I knew he would be governor." In truth, he had sensed in Pataki intelligence and potential, potential in need of development. Tim went on to advise Pataki in four successful races for State Assembly and had shaped the strategy for his upset of an incumbent state senator, Mary Goodhue, in the 1992 primary. He did advance work when Pataki chaired the state party's platform committee, the same launching pad Lewis Lehrman had used for his own political career.

All those efforts anticipated a night in this same restaurant in the fall of 1993. Tim was running a fund-raiser for his own candidacy for the Westchester County Board. He had arranged for the guest speaker to be William Powers, installed by Alfonse D'Amato as chairman of the state party after the Pierre Rinfret disaster. At one point Powers placed himself beside Tim at the bar. "What do you think," the chairman asked, "about running your guy for governor?" Tim kissed him on the cheek.

Now, a year later, Tim played an important and official role in the Pataki campaign as a field representative for the Republican National Committee. But he occupied this table as a friend and colleague of far longer standing. In the other half-dozen chairs sat men and women who had known Pataki since grade school, high school, or his earliest bids for office. Among them, Pataki could freely indulge his habit of picking food off others' plates; at six feet five he had reach to spare. The owner of the restaurant, familiar with that appetite, replenished the table regularly with boiled shrimp and raw oysters and grilled steaks and steamed lobsters. "I think I killed George Pataki," the restaurateur would tell his wife a few hours later. "No human can eat so much food."

After a month of twenty-hour days Tim and the rest were giddy with exhaustion. They laughed about the first time Pataki had run for mayor and was preparing for a debate to be broadcast on cable television. He rehearsed one night before a friend's video camera and looked so catatonic on the playback that one running mate cried, "Where's the kitchen? I wanna get a knife and commit suicide." There were war stories, too, from the Assembly and Senate campaigns. And Pataki insisted that Chuck Palombini, a local Republican leader and a friend since 1980, tell the story of his honeymoon. The first time Pataki had heard it, he was still laughing hours later in his sleep. On this retelling, the entire table roared. "Ask my wife," Palombini said in conclusion. "She'll tell you it's all true."

Neither Tim nor anyone else spoke of the election about to commence. The prospect of defeat hovered, unacknowledged. It took Pataki himself to address it elliptically. "I've made a thousand new friends during the campaign," he said, "who I'll never hear from again if I lose. So it's only fitting to be here with the ones who'll stay my friends, regardless."

The stakes, of course, went exponentially beyond the social. Nationwide, voters would select all 435 members of the House of Representatives, thirty-five senators, and thirty-six governors. More than usual, the incumbent president faced a backlash in the midterm elections. In a handful of major races in 1993, the year after Bill Clinton's illusory landslide in electoral votes, the Democratic Party had lost the mayoralties of New York and Los Angeles, the governorship of New Jersey, a Senate seat long held by Lloyd Bentsen in Texas, and a House seat in Kentucky that had belonged to the party for 129 consecutive years. Then, during the summer of 1994, Clinton had abandoned his effort to push a national health insurance program through Congress. The issue once at the core of his appeal to the middle class had been transformed by Republicans and conservative Democrats into the albatross of liberalism, bureaucracy, and "big government." One of the Democratic Party's own leading strategists was encouraging candidates to distance themselves from the president.

Such an approach became impossible on September 27, the day Congressman Newt Gingrich unveiled the "Contract With America." A ten-point platform signed by every Republican candidate for the House, it reiterated many tenets of the Reagan era, calling for tax cuts, welfare reform, and a balanced-budget amendment. President Clinton seized on the contract to escalate the midterm campaign into a national clash of philosophies. November 8, 1994, would see a contest between orthodoxies—a Democratic liberalism that Clinton had largely adopted and a Reagan conservatism that the president plainly believed voters had rejected in electing him.

Perhaps no race in the nation more distilled the larger conflict than the one pitting Mario Cuomo against George Pataki. "Since Cuomo is the aging poster boy of contemporary American liberalism and since New York is its center," posited William Kristol, a prominent Republican theorist, "a defeat of Cuomo would have national significance." Both parties reacted accordingly. Senator Bob Dole, the front-runner for the Republican presidential nomination in 1996, headlined two fund-raisers that reaped $2.2 million for Pataki. Jack Kemp barnstormed with him in the waning days of the campaign. Vice President Albert Gore and Hillary Rodham Clinton both raised money for Cuomo, while the president himself made four appearances with the governor, eliciting upwards of $4 million. From the pulpit of a Harlem church Clinton hailed Cuomo as "the heart you must not lose," and from the dais of a Manhattan banquet he termed him "a national treasure." But it was Cuomo, so renowned an orator, who framed the essential phrase. "They're watching you, New York," he told an audience in the campaign's final week, "to see where you think the country should go."

Tim Carey thought it was time to go home and get some sleep. He stepped away from his shellfish and Bud Lite, and lifted his suit coat off the chairback. The others soon rose and followed, scattering into the parking lot. Once home, Tim did not bother checking the fax or computer in his basement office. Any crisis would have to wait until morning. On the wall of that silent room hung a sign that offered a clue to his seeming tranquillity. Even as he stood within hours of realizing his dream, of affecting history itself, he kept gallows humor and self-mockery close at hand. "Politicians and drunks," the sign read, "not permitted on premises."

• • •

Back in 1990, when Mario Cuomo had appeared most invincible, Tim Carey had begun assaying his infirmity. That fall, as Cuomo was gliding above Pierre Rinfret and Herbert London without granting them so much as a debate, as he was reinforcing his stature as the Democrat who could have the presidential nomination for the asking, Tim turned his own attentions to an obscure race for a seat in the State Senate. A Republican newcomer, William Larkin, was challenging a Democratic incumbent in a district anchored by the Democratic stronghold of Newburgh, a blue-collar city with a large minority population. So certain was the state GOP of defeat that with two weeks left in the campaign it withdrew both money and staff from the race. Hired by Larkin as a private consultant, Tim partly agreed. There was no point in running against an incumbent senator, not in a state with an incumbency machine. So he ran Larkin against the governor, author of the budget and thus of the tax rate. "Vote for me" went the slogan Tim helped design for the campaign, "and together we'll send Mario Cuomo a message he'll never forget."

On Election Day, Larkin shocked the sitting Democrat, winning by 16 percent. To Tim's mind, the upset revealed the depth of discontent among those voters he called "small-c conservatives," the ones who reminded him of his mother and brothers. Even in Cuomo's own triumph, Tim saw the timbers beneath the throne rotting. Yes, Cuomo had dispatched his two foes handily, but in the four years since that last election his share of the vote had plummeted from 65 percent to 53. If Cuomo could barely gather a majority against enfeebled opposition, Tim believed, then he was just waiting to be toppled by a more formidable foe.

The task of locating such a figure belonged to others, most prominently Alfonse D'Amato and William Powers. Once Tim accepted his position with the Republican National Committee in 1993, he was bound to neutrality in New York State's nominating process. Instead, he began developing strategy any candidate could adopt. Certainly, he found evidence in the defeats of David Dinkins in New York City and Jim Florio in New Jersey of how vulnerable Democrats were to being pigeonholed as tax-and-spend liberals. But it was in a race even less visible than William Larkin's that Tim tested the technique with which he intended to oust Mario Cuomo.

One day in March 1994 a state senator in Delaware unexpectedly died. He was a black Democrat in a section of Wilmington dominated by black Democrats and he had held the seat for thirty years. A special election was scheduled for the following month, and the man's son and namesake promptly declared his candidacy for the unexpired term. It seemed no more than a formality that a woman who administered a local apartment complex also entered the contest, for she was a Republican. "I have this race," the state Republican Party chairman told Tim. "Everybody says we can't win." Few words more thrilled the contrarian in Tim. He dove into the campaign, and he enlisted with him William Powers's son Jason, the resident computer genius of the Republican National Committee. Just six months earlier Jason Powers had designed the computer model for Rudolph Giuliani's successful mayoral race in New York City.

In an active, vigorous democracy, Tim could hardly have expected to overcome the Democratic advantage in registration in this Wilmington district—or, more to the point for Pataki, in New York State. But in the America of 1994, a nation profoundly disaffected with its political system, Tim could win by driving a minority into action. When he paused to think about it, the American ambivalence both disturbed and confounded him. His Irish forebears had died seeking political freedom. During the apartheid era in South Africa he had admired a black resistance movement that was willing to perish or endure prison in its quest for the ballot. In his populist fashion he favored same-day voter registration, a program most conservatives opposed as a tool for big-city machines to enlarge the Democratic vote. And yet, if citizens insisted on taking democracy for granted, their lassitude worked to Tim's professional advantage.

He and Jason Powers set about identifying the effective majority in a disinterested electorate. Drawing on the results in past elections, they separated the district's voters into camps of Republicans, Democrats, and independents. Then they subdivided each group into "primes," who voted even in primaries, and "non-primes," who stayed home until the general election. In a broad sense, Tim was making the same type of analysis he had fourteen years earlier for the Reagan campaign in New York City. The difference, however, was that computers had replaced pocket calculators. Back then, he could break down data to units no smaller than an election district, which generally contained about three hundred voters; now he could pinpoint his quarry house by house, apartment by apartment, person by person. Within weeks of taking on the campaign, Tim knew the name, address, and phone number of all two thousand voters whose ballots he needed.

The only other question was how to convince these potential voters to participate. Reason, facts, and calm persuasion left "non-primes" unmoved. They required what Tim called an "emotional trigger." His usual choices—high taxes and big government—fit miserably in a district of people paying few if any taxes and relying on the public sector for jobs or welfare. So he devised a slogan that stirred the collective black memory of disenfranchisement and powerlessness. "The Democrats are counting on you *not* to vote," said the telephone message Tim aimed at his core audience. "They keep a list of nonvoters and *you're on it.*"

Literally speaking, Tim maintained such a list, too; he was counting on the Democratic "non-primes" to sit home. Which they obligingly did. Less than one-quarter of the electorate voted. The Republican candidate captured the vacant seat with the ballots of just 12 percent of the registered voters.

Even a gubernatorial race in New York, Tim theorized, would not unfold so differently. Seven in ten registered voters had flocked to the polls when Mario Cuomo faced Lewis Lehrman in 1982. The turnout had slipped steadily in the governor's next two campaigns, and in 1994, Tim reckoned, it would rest barely above half. Disgust and disenchantment were his allies, provided they contained a streak of rage against incumbents that could be tapped selectively. The campaign, as it developed, more than sufficed. If Lehrman versus Cuomo had elevated politics to a Shavian plane of intellectual swordplay, then Pataki versus Cuomo reduced it to democracy as scripted by David Mamet—coarse, brutal, and blunt. "This," one Democratic consultant predicted, "is going to be the mother of all political food fights."

With their own candidate clinging to an approval rating of 32 percent in September, a drop of forty-five points in just over six years, the Democrats aimed their campaign against the one statewide politician nearly as unpopular, Alfonse D'Amato. Not only did the Republican senator deliver the nomination to Pataki in May 1994, but he surrounded the candidate with his own confederates. D'Amato's chief fund-raiser, communications director, and media consultant all assumed comparable positions in the Pataki campaign. Nearly half of the contributors to Pataki, *The New York Times* discovered, had previously donated money to D'Amato. The senator himself paid $400,000 worth of Pataki's campaign bills with the surplus from his 1992 reelection race until a court ruled the practice illegal. During a fund-raising dinner for Pataki one July night, a press photographer snapped a shot of D'Amato leading the candidate literally by the hand. Barely two months later the Cuomo campaign featured the picture in a television advertisement. "George Pataki?" asked the voice-over. "Maybe we should just call him Al!"

Fair or not, the attacks bore a logic. George Pataki made an elusive target as a state legislator hardly known outside his district. The most serious attack on him, levied by the *Village Voice,* charged that the same real-estate developers whom Pataki had attracted to Peekskill while mayor gave him lucrative legal business once he left office. Still, there was nothing illegal in his actions. They simply typified the classic symbiosis of development and Republican politics in suburbia.

Alfonse D'Amato, however, provided nothing if not a bull's-eye. He had learned his trade in the Nassau County machine, apprenticing to its leader, Joseph Margiotta, a man eventually convicted of extorting $500,000 in insurance kickbacks for his political allies. Even as a senator with undeniable talents for constituent service (hence his nickname "Senator Pothole") and political theater (buying crack undercover), D'Amato had skirted the edges of impropriety. The Senate ethics committee probed him in the early 1990s on four separate matters, two each involving his relationship with corporate campaign donors and his role in securing grants from the Department of Housing and Urban Development. Overall, the committee found "insufficient credible evidence" of ethical violations by D'Amato, but it noted that several key witnesses in one of the HUD allegations had taken the Fifth Amendment to avoid testifying. It also termed the senator negligent for not realizing his own brother was lobbying him on behalf of a defense contractor.

For all that, D'Amato was a three-time winner in races for the Senate. He had even escaped defeat in 1992, as Bill Clinton won New York, with a withering assault on his opponent as being "hopelessly liberal." Arthur Finkelstein, the media consultant responsible for that slogan, shaped a similar bludgeon for television commercials against Cuomo: "Too liberal for too long." Pataki put it similarly in appearances around the state, reciting the refrain "It's Mario Cuomo's fault." As for his own positions, Pataki focused on three core issues—reducing taxes, restoring the death penalty, and replacing welfare with workfare. His plan for reforming state government ran a mere four pages, a fraction of the length that Lehrman had devoted to numerous lesser topics in his 1982 position papers. This time around, as one Republican strategist remarked, the platform devolved to "ABC—Anyone But Cuomo."

The incumbent governor complied by mounting a campaign notable for its hypocrisy. A man who had vetoed death-penalty legislation annually, Cuomo abruptly proposed putting the issue to a statewide referendum. Several months after introducing a budget that trimmed various taxes, but not the state income tax, Cuomo floated the idea of cutting that, too. He suggested the state purchase the private Long Island Lighting Company for $9 billion. There was no precedent in the nation for a state to undertake so expensive an acquisition, but there were, of course, several hundred thousand voters on Long Island with an interest in lower utility rates. Throughout the campaign Cuomo refused to debate Pataki unless a raft of minor-party candidates were included to muddle the confrontation.

As a result, the ABC formula worked. Pataki held leads ranging from four to ten points in various polls conducted from June through mid-October. He raised millions of dollars more than Cuomo did. Then, on October 24, came what Tim Carey in the parlance of nuclear war called a "megaton hit." Rudolph Giuliani, the Republican mayor of New York, whom Tim among many others in the Pataki camp had helped to elect, endorsed Mario Cuomo. Giuliani then joined the governor on several campaign swings, proclaiming that a vote for Pataki would leave New York with "a government of D'Amato, for D'Amato, and by D'Amato." Within days Cuomo pulled ahead in most of the major polls.

He might have remained there had Giuliani not released a municipal budget ten days before the election. It called for the state to compensate the city for various programs that were otherwise facing retrenchment or demise. Albany was to provide $12 million for services to the mentally retarded, $8 million for alcoholism and drug-abuse therapy, $19 million for ambulance coverage, $140 million for subway passes for school-children, and on and on into the hundreds of millions of dollars. Finkelstein dubbed it simply, "The Deal." Pataki drummed away at the theme, exciting the traditional contempt upstate New Yorkers harbored for Gotham. In trying to deliver victory to Mario Cuomo, Rudolph Giuliani had instead offered Tim Carey an "emotional trigger."

All through the campaign, from June until Election Day, Tim and Jason Powers had been applying the lessons of Wilmington to New York State. They fed the Republican National Committee's computers a diet of census data, voter registration records, and the results of such prior elections as Cuomo's in 1990 and Giuliani's in 1993. When Powers had finished "massaging the numbers," as the jargon had it, there emerged not only an overall model of the "prime" independents and "non-prime" Republicans who represented the swing vote required for a Pataki victory but a roster of every single one of them. The information fit onto eighteen CD-ROM discs light and tidy enough for Powers to carry in a shoulder bag. This was the digital era's answer to a drawer full of handwritten index cards, yet the purpose remained unchanged: getting out the vote.

The ballot on November 8 might list the candidates for governor as George Pataki and Mario Cuomo, but at street level the election hurled Tim Carey against Bill Lynch. A union organizer turned political operative, Lynch had led David Dinkins to election in 1989 as New York City's first black mayor. It was his mission now to produce the largest black vote ever for Cuomo, especially in the disheartened slums of New York City. The Pataki campaign, in turn, depended upon Tim to flush out those independents and Republicans upstate and in the suburbs who normally would skip all but a presidential election. Tim authorized 823,000 phone calls to prospective voters in the five days before November 8, and he was prepared to order several hundred thousand more on Election Day itself. In this battle for the indolent, the indifferent, and the unmotivated lay the key to triumph.

• • •

At ten-thirty on the morning of Election Day, Tim Carey sauntered into the Lorenz Hart Suite of the New York Hilton, the Pataki "war room." He had slept until eight o'clock, later than he had in two months, and still managed to vote before nine. Obsessed as always with turnout, he noted that seventy-four citizens had preceded him, a fine sign in an election district of six hundred thirty. He wore an oxford shirt, paisley tie, and gray suit. Removing his coat as he entered the room, he revealed a pair of bold red suspenders. "Wearing red on Election Day," he announced to the half-dozen men around him, "comes from making Democrats bleed."

The suspenders also happened to have been the symbol of Lew Lehrman twelve years earlier. Beneath Tim's unflappable exterior that election still roiled his conscience. He recited the margin of defeat like an oath of vengeance: 178,000 votes. We lost by 178,000 votes. So many times since 1982 he had replayed his own actions, studied his own naiveté and mistakes, foremost among them depending on the party establishment to deliver victory. Now, in the Pataki campaign, Tim's trust barely exceeded the bounds of the war room.

He surveyed the oblong space. Along a bank of smoked windows, two computer terminals flanked a laser printer. Three telephones rested atop an adjacent table. A map of the state, divided into Assembly districts, covered one wall. A blackboard across the room carried the single message "Just Win Baby." The early shift had arrived at six, precisely when the polls opened, and since then had drained four thermal flasks of coffee. Platters of pastries lay untouched. In his briefcase, William Powers carried a bottle of Maalox.

Beneath a plume of cigarette smoke, his son Jason loaded programs into a computer. Throughout the day, as poll watchers reported, he would enter the actual turnout for both parties against the model for a Pataki victory. From those numbers Tim could intuit the course of voting and order additional phone calls to prospective supporters. Exit polls did not matter to him. An exit poll was predicated on the pattern of a previous election. If Tim inspired enough swing voters, he would shatter the pattern.

"What do we project for the city?" Tim asked Jason Powers.

"Forty-one point four."

"Ooh," Tim cooed, satisfied. The Board of Elections, he knew, had predicted a higher turnout. He reached for a sheet reporting the results of phone calls made since November 4. They showed support for Pataki among the "non-prime" in several key counties reaching nearly 75 percent. Tim nodded in approval. Finally he glanced at a political insiders' newsletter, *Hot Line,* freshly arrived from Washington. "IS CUOMO UP BY 13 OR 4?" read the headline. "POLLS DIFFER."

It was all conjecture for now. For the moment, perhaps the first moment in months, Tim faced no pressing task. He talked about how Leslie Maeby, working for the Republican National Committee in New England, expected to pick up a Senate seat and two in the House just from Maine. He passed along the committee's latest prediction for the Senate, which had the Republican Party taking eight seats, more than enough for a majority.

"How about North?" someone asked.

"Ollie's in trouble," Tim replied.

"And California?"

"Feinstein can still lose."

Tim looked back more than forward. A stout, goateed man named Garry Axenfeld had come from Florida to spend Election Day in the war room. He had managed Perry Duryea's race for governor in 1978 while Tim was directing scheduling and advance. Only at the remove of sixteen years and atop a $14.5 million campaign chest with Pataki did that cash-poor campaign qualify as quaint.

"He kept a goddamn on-fire B-57 going with his credit card," Tim proclaimed, throwing one arm around Axenfeld. "Airports wouldn't let us land, we owed so much money for gas."

"God, that was an experience and a half," Axenfeld added.

"And I was smoking then. Duryea had me up to three packs a day."

Anecdote by anecdote, they painted the past. They remembered the day William Powers first talked about running this unknown from Hempstead, Alfonse D'Amato, against the unbeatable Javits. They recalled the time buys that never got made for Lehrman. Only the voice of unimpressed youth interrupted the reverie.

"Timmy ever tell you he did the advance when Jesus walked on water?" chided Will Powers, Jason's brother. "He did press on the wheel, too, when it was invented."

Laughter rang out, the kind of laughter Tim had heard so often in army barracks and Izzy's bar and Crotonville. "Giving shit," was what this kind of affectionate ridicule was called. It beat back vanity, tempered pride, and contributed, in Tim, to a worldview he called "optimistic pessimism." He associated the spirit with Irish Catholicism, but it had served him well in politics, too, ensuring that confidence never swelled into arrogance.

Some people in the war room, especially State Senator Guy Velella, were eager to claim victory already, and more than that to gloat. As if abiding some warrior code, Tim always told his children that he never hated any foe.

"What time do we go to the Sheraton to laugh at him?" Vellela asked, meaning a defeated Cuomo. "That's what I wanna know."

"You got it wrong," Tim said at first, joking along. *"He* comes to *us."*

"I just wanna laugh at him."

"Be magnanimous," Tim said now. "Be Roman."

"What I want to be," Axenfeld added, "is minister of revenge."

Then, abruptly, the bravado subsided. These were not young soldiers, after all, bragging of valor while still on the troop ship. As Republicans of a certain age in a particular state, they had experienced both loss and humiliation. As conservatives, they had known alienation even during the Rockefeller heyday. It was 11:35 A.M., too early to celebrate anything but the arrival of a fresh supply of coffee.

The room, jocular no more, hummed with purpose. Velella dialed for results in the Bronx. Tim lifted a phone to each ear, checking the situation in his other states. Someone phoned upstate for the weather forecast, always an indicator of Republican turnout. Someone recommended judges to an election lawyer, should the campaign seek to have ballots impounded. Only Axenfeld, here as an alumnus, was left to pace the carpet.

Then William Powers yanked the receiver away from his ear and shouted, "Albany is goin' historic. Beyond presidential."

Silence descended. No city outside New York generated Democratic votes with the industry Albany did. The O'Connell machine, shrunken but undestroyed, could eradicate the margin it took the Republicans several entire counties to accumulate. Powers got back on the phone for more details.

"Colonie," he said, repeating aloud scraps of the field report he was hearing. "Bethlehem."

"Albany County," Tim reassured the room. "Our Albany."

Velella meanwhile cupped a hand over the mouthpiece of his phone.

"My Woodlawn Irish are comin' out heavy," he called to Tim. "Whose are they?"

"Not ours," Tim answered. "We didn't do anything for them. I wanted to. Arthur said no."

Thus intelligence found its way to the Lorenz Hart Suite. It flowed from poll watchers and district leaders. It filtered through the faxes and laptops of a dozen researchers installed next door. Each dribble of data slid instantly under the microscope. Blacks and Hispanics were voting in low numbers in the Bronx. That was good. CNN reported a high turnout by minorities. That was bad. Eighteen percent of the registered voters in upstate Monroe County had cast ballots by noon. That was bad. No, that was good. The county included Rochester, home city of B. Thomas Golisano, the independent candidate endorsed by H. Ross Perot. Tim had launched a special phone operation there branding a vote for him a waste.

Nearing one o'clock the voting day had almost reached its halfway point. Curious and proprietary about his own region of Westchester, Tim called his wife, Alida, at the Peekskill campaign headquarters. Pataki would win by four points, she gushed. Exit polls showed it. She had just overheard the results from a television crew shooting footage. Now she wanted to drive home and search through Prodigy, the on-line service to which the family subscribed, for other reports of impending triumph.

"Don't tell me about any CompuServe product," Tim answered, so irritated he confused Prodigy with its competitor. "You wanna do something useful? Get some people and go out and see how many voted so far. Let us know what the turnout is. We gotta get the vote out here, babe. Screw CompuServe."

• • •

Thirty miles and forty minutes after leaving the war room for lunch, Tim Carey pulled off the highway to Crotonville and into Pete Birrittella's gas station. From a service bay, Birrittella lifted a meaty, oil-streaked arm in greeting and called hoarsely to Tim that he would follow once he washed up. Comrades for a quarter century, since going off to boot camp together, the pair ate together every Election Day. Not the Pataki race, not seventy-five other campaigns across seven states, would deprive Tim of this ritual, this pilgrimage. And he was not about to ask the war room's permission.

The restaurant Tim chose was called the Briars, and it courted two types of customers. For families, it maintained a dining room of hanging plants, coach lamps, and floral curtains. For construction crews, softball teams, and other such tribes, it kept a bar festooned with football pennants, a deer's head, and the peaked hat from a Canadian Mountie. With the barstools filled by men in work boots and painter's caps, Tim and his old friend settled into a table just behind and ordered their favorite, baked clams.

"You gonna win?" Birrittella asked simply.

"We're gonna win," Tim answered. "Forty-eight to forty-four." Then, suddenly, his tone turned wishful. "By God, my third chance at governor. Oughta get one. Just one."

He tried not to talk about politics. Lunch with Birrittella was supposed to be the antidote to politics. They remembered that great vacation years ago in Acapulco. They grumbled about the Giants' loss last night. They joked about their mutual friend Max who got a license plate labeled MAXED OUT. Said it was for what his wife did to the credit cards.

Still, Tim drifted out of the banter to eavesdrop on the conversation at the next table. There sat four retirees, all in baggy sweatshirts and shoes with Velcro straps, and from their midst the word kept wafting: "Cuomo . . . Cuomo . . . Cuomo." Tim glanced to the television set pinioned high in one corner, from which CNN blinked in inscrutable silence. When the waitress returned, Birrittella ordered a second Scotch and Tim stayed with coffee, decaf no less. He did not intend to drink until much later, until he knew if it would be in celebration or sorrow.

"I like this stuff about how Reagan has Alzheimer's disease," Birrittella said, his gruff voice jarring Tim back to the moment. "He had that eight years ago."

"That's why he was such an effective president," Tim cracked in return.

Then the beeper on Tim's belt sounded, and his home number scrolled across the tiny screen. He repaired to a pay phone to call Alida. As promised, she had checked the local turnout—35 percent, high for the early afternoon. When the waitress appeared a moment later with a shot of anisette, the gift of a friend at the bar, Tim let her deposit it in his cup. "Just what I needed," he called to his benefactor. A sip later he added, "You vote yet?"

Just past three Birrittella grabbed the check and Tim headed ten miles northwest to pick up Alida. The beeper summoned him again, this time to call the private line into the war room.

"Where are you?" William Powers shouted over the car phone.

"In Westchester," Tim answered without flinching.

"I thought you went out to have lunch."

"I did." He paused like a comic. "In Westchester."

It was the wrong joke. Powers had barely left headquarters for days. He had not even joined Pataki on the final day's airborne tour of the state. Anger rose from the receiver like fumes.

"I thought you meant *around the corner!*"

Tim turned into his driveway and loped toward the front door. Across the street a neighbor was mowing the lawn. Tim bellowed over the engine, "Vote yet?"

Inside Alida zipped up her dress. Thanks to Rudolph Giuliani, it was easier to choose clothes. His endorsement of Cuomo had so infuriated her that she cleaned every closet in the house. On her way to the bathroom to apply her makeup, she passed a framed collection of snapshots from the Lehrman campaign. "I can't believe it," she said to Tim. "Twelve years have revolved."

He did not hear. He had already seized the kitchen phone. Someone in the war room told him a tracking poll had Pataki leading by one percent. Tim pretended enthusiasm for the sake of his listener, then turned brusque commander. "Tell me where the votes are and I'll tell you how we're doing," he said. "Is Harlem at 40 percent? Then I'm worried. Is Cortlandt at 40 percent? Then that's good." In the absence of such answers, he ordered $10,000 worth of phone calls to voters upstate.

Unruffled as Tim seemed in the kitchen, amid the crockery and cabinets, he felt awed by the technology at his disposal. In Lehrman's campaign, a single Apple with spreadsheet software had rated as the state of the political art. Now, computer programs initially developed for telemarketing had relegated 1982 to prehistory. Within minutes of Tim's order, Jason Powers would send rosters of names and telephone numbers by modem to the Atlanta data center of a company, Campaign Tel. Computer operators there would load the information into a software program called Small Wonder and transship segments of the voter lists to offices in several midwestern cities. Instead of ward heelers knocking on tenement doors and volunteers from a union local dialing from a card table in a converted storefront, personal computers a thousand miles from New York would begin placing calls at the unprecedented pace of 250 per hour. And each time someone answered, an employee chosen largely for vocal timbre would introduce himself and intone the message Tim himself had devised: "New York has suffered enough. We can't have another four years. Vote for change. Vote for George Pataki for governor."

At 3:42, twelve minutes behind a schedule only he seemed to know, Tim led Alida to the car. It was a four-wheel-drive, the replacement for an Olds Cutlass that he had retired after eight years and 170,000 miles. To save money, he had bought a dealer demonstration model that had already logged 5,000 miles of test drives. In five months Tim had added nearly 11,000 more, all in pursuit of Republican victory.

As the Chevy roared south through Westchester, Alida calibrated Tim's tension by his quiet. Normally, she marveled at his ability to shut off work the minute he arrived home, to ask about the boys or the bills or the plans for the weekend, and to listen intently as she answered. On a drive like this, they would usually search the radio for oldies, maybe sing along with James Taylor on "Fire and Rain." Just now, though, a talk show prattled away uninterrupted. After sixteen years of marriage and a multitude of campaigns, Alida knew Tim was thinking only of the checklist of duties branded on his brain.

"You all right, dear?" she asked finally.

"I'm havin' a heart attack."

"Insurance paid up?"

By now they had reached the Bronx. The car phone rang with William Powers demanding, "Are you still in Westchester?" Swerving through traffic, bounding pothole to pothole, the four-wheel-drive rattled on its chassis.

"I hate driving in New York with you," Alida said.

"Put on your seat belt," Tim replied dryly.

"It's on."

"Then put on your crash helmet."

They crossed the East River, elbowed down FDR Drive, and then, four blocks from the Hilton and the war room, wallowed to a halt. A fire at Saks Fifth Avenue had frozen traffic. Reaching for his car phone, Tim noticed a light pulsing in alarm. The battery was dying.

Still, he managed a conference call with Jason Powers and Steve Goldberg, the president of Campaign Tel, who was mired in the same traffic. The reports on turnout remained vague, maddeningly vague. Pataki was strong where he had expected to be strong, weak where he had expected to be weak, and, in other words, entirely capable of losing.

"We gotta pump it up," Powers said.

"Where?" Tim asked.

"Everywhere. We've only done 200,000. We need 200,000 more."

The Chevy squirmed through a gap and reached the corner of Park Avenue, practically within sight of the hotel.

"You know those parts of the city?" Tim asked. "Those twenty-six districts?" These were the green belts he had discovered for Ronald Reagan in 1980. "Do those first."

"Soon as you get in," Powers promised.

Tim watched the light ahead turn red. A stalled bus blockaded the intersection. Horns shrieked. Engines rumbled. Exhaust rose.

"Don't wait for me," he insisted.

With the last power in the car phone, Tim called the Republican National Committee. By now, five o'clock, the afternoon exit polls had arrived. Ann Richards, the incumbent Democratic governor of Texas, trailed George W. Bush, son of the defeated president. Rick Santorum and Thomas Ridge, Tim's candidates for senator and governor in Pennsylvania, respectively, both held leads. Oliver North and Charles Robb stood deadlocked, 44 percent apiece. And so, with exactly the same numbers, did Mario Cuomo and George Pataki.

• • •

At six o'clock on Election Night, with the last twilight drained from the sky, the smoked windows of the war room acted as mirrors on the bustle within. They reflected figures pacing across the carpet, hunching over keyboards, and cocking ear to telephone. They reflected Tim Carey and Jason Powers debating how best to utilize the final 200,000 calls. Direction was not the issue. Both men agreed on targeting the green belts of New York and sections of Long Island and Westchester, the places where Tim had found the Republican organization most deficient in 1982. But now, with three hours left until the polls closed, Powers wondered about changing the script.

" 'Now more than ever,' " he suggested.

"No," Tim answered. "It's gotta be against Cuomo. Jason, you gotta go for the emotional trigger."

That had worked so well for Christine Todd Whitman a year earlier.

Just remind people about Jim Florio's tax increases, remind them again and again and again. Like Pataki, Whitman had offered only a sketchy vow of tax relief by way of alternative. The polls in New Jersey, like those in New York today, had granted the incumbent Democrat a secure lead. The polls had not counted on Tim's telephonic onslaught, the high-tech and high-price equivalent of the precinct captain of yore, dragging every last barfly, peddler, and maiden aunt personally into the voting booth. "Get mad. Get even," went the slogan Tim had devised. "Get out and vote Republican."

The primacy Tim placed in getting out the vote was almost a running joke in the Pataki campaign. Just a few days earlier he had joined the inner circle of strategists for a meeting with Arthur Finkelstein, the media consultant. Finkelstein believed in television, in mass persuasion, and he was describing the final blitz of Pataki commercials. Tim raised the subject of phones. Sure, Finkelstein said, if there was money left over. Phones don't hurt. Tim made sure to tell Steve Goldberg that one. Phones don't hurt.

For the moment, as the Small Wonder software did its work, Tim retreated from the war room into William Powers's adjoining room. Several other campaign workers had already flopped onto the two beds. Tim sank deeply into a padded chair, legs outstretched and arms limp. On a console television, the guests sparred on CNN's *Crossfire*. It was eight o'clock, still an hour before the polls would close in New York. For an instant, Tim's eyelids drooped toward sleep.

"It's up to God now," he said to Sandy Treadwell, a vice-chairman of the state GOP. "Nothing we can do."

"We better win," Treadwell replied. "If we don't, we're all dead tomorrow."

"This is America, Sandy. They don't kill you. They just treat you like shit."

Treadwell passed Tim the remote control for the television.

"Get that thing away from me," Tim protested, tossing it onto the bed. "Give it to someone more stable."

A volunteer commenced cruising the networks. The evidence elsewhere gave cause for optimism. At eight-thirty, CNN reported the Democrats had lost both Senate seats from Tennessee and one apiece in Maine, Ohio, and Oklahoma. With two more seats, the Republicans would take control of the Senate for the first time since 1986.

"When does Al call the first meeting of the Banking Committee?" someone asked.

"Tonight, if I know him," Tim replied.

In a room populated by political experts, everyone understood the shorthand. Alfonse D'Amato, as the ranking Republican, stood to become chairman of the committee with power to investigate the Clintons' role in the Whitewater land deal. As if to exorcise the demons of every inquiry mounted by a Democratic Congress, from Watergate to Iran-Contra, several people took up the chant, "Subpoena power! Subpoena power!"

The racket attracted John Sweeney, the executive director of the state party. Much as his tasseled loafers and Italian-cut suit obscured it, he was the son of a union officer in the factory city of Troy.

"Forty-five minutes, we take back the fuckin' mansion," he shouted, covering Treadwell with pretend punches.

That reminded Tim of something. At a Pataki appearance in Albany several days earlier, a fistfight had erupted between his supporters and a Cuomo delegation. Was it true Sweeney himself had joined in?

"Yeah, I was poppin' people," he said. "Classic Mick. Went to a rally and a hockey game broke out."

He gave Tim a high five, then glanced at the television. Congressman Joseph Kennedy was being interviewed about his uncle Edward's victory in Massachusetts. At least one of the legendary liberals had escaped with his seat.

"Fuck you," Sweeney snarled, leaning toward the screen. He swiveled to face Tim, as if a fellow Irishman would especially understand. "I hate them lace-curtain motherfuckers."

Sweeney left to take a call in the war room. A pollster from one of the New York television stations was on the line. Meanwhile a researcher arrived with reports of the Republican turnout—75 percent in Suffolk County, 95 in Saratoga. "If we get that," Tim said, "we win." But it sounded almost too good, especially that Saratoga number. Were some district leaders bragging? Had the researcher transcribed the number wrong? Tim checked his watch, a basic Casio. It read 8:58. Soon enough he would be able to winnow truth from hype.

"Stop making your calls," he ordered Steve Goldberg, who had just arrived to await the results. "I know you, you'll be callin' till nine-fifteen."

"Pay up," Goldberg said, laughing.

Sweeney bolted back into the room. The station was abandoning its exit poll. The turnout upstate had destroyed the model. Just as Tim had planned.

He doubled over in the chair like a man stricken by appendicitis. Then he unfolded and exploded, back arching, veins rising, fists shooting toward the ceiling.

"We did it," he shouted. "Yes! We did it again!"

Finally, in a voice meant for his doubters, all the people who had told him he couldn't do it or was doing it all wrong, from the teachers at Ossining to the counselors at SUNY to the consultants who thought polls and television won elections, he cried, "Phones. Don't. Hurt."

As Tim called the Republican National Committee with the news, the numbers mounted. At ten o'clock, with a quarter of the precincts reporting and about one million votes counted, Pataki led by 40,000. Thirty-five minutes later, with nearly half the results tallied, he had doubled the margin. By 10:50, ABC declared Pataki the victor. Tim hugged Jason Powers and John Sweeney, but refused a congratulatory toast, saying, "Let's get back to work."

The resolution did not last long. Someone switched the television to NBC just in time for its first report that the Republicans were taking control of the House of Representatives. When the counting ended, they would have gained fifty-three seats there—including those of Thomas Foley, the Speaker, and Dan Rostenkowski, chairman of the Ways and Means Committee—as well as nine in the Senate, twelve governorships, and the mastery of fifteen state legislatures. The GOP would control Congress for the first time in forty years, the first time since Tim was seven years old and heard his grandmother bless the memory of Franklin Roosevelt. Around him now shrieks chorused and palms slapped. From the television, turned back to ABC, the columnist George F. Will hailed the election as "Reagan's third victory." Yet Tim could conjure neither word nor gesture for events so dramatic. He had anticipated the upheaval among senators and governors. But he had never expected to see a Republican majority in the House, not in his lifetime. All through the fall, as Newt Gingrich was issuing such a prophecy, Tim had thought, That's delusional. Hell, he'd bet against it in the Republican National Committee's office pool.

Now he strode out of the war room and toward life in the majority. He rode down to the lobby, crossed to another elevator bank, and ascended forty-five floors to the penthouse suite, the perch of the governor-elect. Along the way, it seemed, he passed every one of those thousand friends Pataki had said would disappear if he lost. He nearly collided in a hallway with Curtis Sliwa, clad in his Guardian Angels outfit from combat boots to red beret. Across the carpet, the comic Jackie Mason chattered in Yiddish to a Hasid wearing a Pataki bumper sticker on his black coat. Only after Tim cleared security to enter Pataki's bedroom itself did he spot the familiar faces from dinner or breakfast or whatever it was at the Crystal Bay, so long ago now it hardly seemed part of the same day.

Five minutes before midnight Mario Cuomo conceded. Once he did,

Tim and the rest descended to the grand ballroom, where the public celebration was building to a raucous crescendo. Tim lingered in the wings of the dais, as the emcee introduced John Sweeney and Sandy Treadwell. The entourage onstage had already grown three-deep. Tim usually hid from the spotlight on Election Night; he could think of only two exceptions, one of those in valiant defeat with Lew Lehrman. What mattered was that he knew what he had accomplished. And as a man who called himself an "optimistic pessimist," he realized pride had a way of playing boomerang. A year ago Tim could easily have joined Rudolph Giuliani on the podium instead of watching the victory speech in anonymity among the crowd. These days it helped not to be too closely linked with the mayor many Republicans called "Benedict Giuliani" and "Rudy the Rat."

"Timmy," the emcee called.

Tim hesitated.

"Tim," the emcee implored, waving for him.

He had known George Pataki for seventeen years. He had waited twenty to see a Republican elected governor. He embodied almost ninety of family history in America, a lineage that traced back to the day a young widow from Liverpool had scrambled down the gangplank to Ellis Island. Not so many blocks from here that woman had settled with her family, including the young girl destined to become Tim's grandmother, Lizzie Garrett. Not so many blocks from here, in the presidential campaign of 1928, a grown and married Lizzie had heard the street-corner shills of Tammany Hall stemwind for Al Smith. And she had pinned a campaign button on her daughter Edith, who believed for a long time thereafter that to be Irish and Catholic was to be Democratic. Now the band in the ballroom was playing "Revolution." Tim Carey stepped onto the stage.

Briefly, he found a niche in the front row beside Treadwell and Sweeney. He peered into the crowd, searching in vain for Alida. They had missed each other somehow in the penthouse suite and would not meet again, as it happened, until three o'clock in an elevator. Then William Powers strutted onto the stage, and soon after Alfonse D'Amato swaggered to the microphone, thrusting both thumbs skyward. Tim receded into the second line, then the third, like the shy kid in a class picture.

"You wanted change," D'Amato declared to the howling crowd. "You have it. Our next governor, George Pataki."

Before claiming his prize Pataki introduced his family. He thanked his running mates and the leaders of the Republican and Conservative Parties. "And three other guys," he then said. "You probably don't know them, but I do, and they mean a lot to me." He spoke of Mike Finnegan, a friend from Peekskill who had served as campaign counsel. And Kieran Mahoney, a political consultant. And Arthur Finkelstein. By now, Tim had nearly vanished from view, and soon he would disappear altogether. For just one final, fleeting moment, he shone through the mass—a patch of sweaty forehead, the glint of photoflash against eyeglasses. With that dab of light, that stroke, a part of history paused, at least until Sean and Brian Carey, just edging into their teens, still smitten with X-Men comics and Sega Genesis games, grew old enough to shoulder the family tradition of trying to change the world.

Afterword

"The era of big government is over," Bill Clinton declared in his State of the Union speech on January 23, 1996. Whether he truly believed his own thesis or was merely offering it as an election-year expedient, he was acknowledging the profound political transformation wrought by conservative Republicans. So drastically have politicians from Goldwater to Reagan to Gingrich shifted the electoral center to the right that in both of Clinton's presidential campaigns the Democrat has sought to appropriate traditionally Republican issues and rhetoric.

Try as he might to position himself as the "Comeback Kid," Clinton in 1996 only superficially resembles Harry Truman in 1948, another embattled incumbent beset by a hostile Congress. Truman conceded nothing to his adversaries; he won by wrapping himself in the New Deal and sparing no vitriol in prosecuting class warfare. In contrast, Clinton's State of the Union address bore the imprints of a Republican consultant, Dick Morris, and a speechwriter closely tied to Morris, Dan Baer. As a president forced by electoral logic to accommodate his enemies, Clinton brings to mind Dwight Eisenhower or Richard Nixon. They made peace with such staples of the welfare state as Social Security, public housing, environmental regulation, and affirmative action; Clinton preaches the conservative gospel on crime, tax cuts, family values, and welfare reform. Just as Eisenhower's victories proved that "We are all New Dealers today," as the historian Arthur M. Schlesinger Jr. wrote in the 1950s, a Clinton reelection in 1996 would demonstrate the mass appeal of conservatism.

This historic realignment has depended extensively, even dispropor-tionately, on families like those of Tim Carey, Leslie Maeby, and Frank Trotta—Catholics with Democratic pasts. A study of the 1994 election by the Ancient Order of Hibernians, an Irish-American group, shows that Catholics accounted for nearly one-third of the total vote while constitut-ing less than one-quarter of the population. And for the first time since the era of Al Smith, Catholics cast the majority of their congressional ballots for Republicans. The Catholic exodus from the New Deal coalition, first made manifest when Ronald Reagan took a majority of the Catholic vote in the 1980 presidential race, has now reshaped Congress.

Three generations after the *Irish World* depicted Herbert Hoover as John Bull, conflating the GOP with the WASP, the prototypical conserva-tive candidate in traditionally Democratic states like New York is a Cath-olic with immigrant, blue-collar roots. George E. Pataki, New York's governor, fits the profile precisely, as do the two running mates who won with him, Attorney General Dennis Vacco and Lieutenant Governor Betsy McCaughey. Even McCaughey's 1995 wedding is a measure of the political upheaval in America: Her husband, millionaire investment banker Wilbur Ross, is a Democrat; McCaughey, the barber's daughter from Pittsburgh, is a Republican.

Tim Carey and Leslie Maeby, who both worked for the Republican National Committee in the GOP's 1994 sweep, have since taken posi-tions in the Pataki administration—Tim serving as a liaison between the governor and local politicians, Leslie screening candidates for patronage appointments. Elected by a slender margin and forced to contend with a Democratic majority in the State Assembly, Pataki has nonetheless forced swift change upon the state that once virtually defined welfare-state liberalism. In his first year in office, Pataki persuaded the legislature to cut both the budget and taxes, and to tighten eligibility for welfare while providing incentives for recipients to hold jobs. He signed a bill restoring the death penalty, a measure that his Democratic predecessors Hugh Carey and Mario Cuomo had vetoed annually.

With Cuomo gone from the national stage, the New Deal tradition has lost its most eloquent voice and perhaps its only contemporary hero. It is true that Bill Clinton continues to support increasing the minimum wage and raising federal spending on education, to cite just two exam-ples of his residual liberalism. And it is true that he has not capitulated to the Republican Congress in its extreme approaches to reducing or ending various social programs. He has benefited from an opposition so unwilling to compromise, so insistent on not simply besting the president but emasculating him, that it has, to invert an adage, seized defeat from the jaws of victory.

Still, no one should construe Clinton's belated show of backbone as a resurgence of liberalism. Consider what he has already ceded to the Republican Congress. Newt Gingrich, not the president, has established the political agenda for the nation since assuming power as Speaker of the House on January 4, 1995. In the first ninety-three days of his term, Gingrich pushed through thirty-one bills, including nine of the ten provisions in the "Contract With America." Although only two of the contract's bills have become law, Gingrich has dramatically altered the political debate. Suddenly it is plausible that Washington will disown Aid to Families with Dependent Children, a welfare program that for all of its notoriety is a direct link to Franklin Delano Roosevelt and the New Deal. The system of price supports for farmers, another legacy of the New Deal, may well be eliminated. Not even Medicare, a middle-class entitlement backed by a powerful lobby of retirees, enjoys immunity from budget cuts.

On several issues in particular, President Clinton has bent far in Gingrich's direction. In September 1995, the president effectively endorsed a welfare-reform bill in the Senate that ended AFDC as a federal program. Two of the president's top aides, Leon E. Panetta and Rahm I. Emanuel, slapped high fives to celebrate the passage of what Senator Edward M. Kennedy called "legislative child abuse." A month after the vote Clinton confided to the audience at a fund-raiser in Houston that he had raised taxes "too much" in his first budget. "He keeps conceding these things," Senator Daniel Patrick Moynihan said in exasperation. "He doesn't understand that he's conceding the principles." Over the past year Clinton has proposed four different budgets to Congress, each moving nearer to Republican demands for a document that simultaneously cuts taxes, shrinks social programs, and closes the federal deficit within seven years.

In Congress, too, the evidence of conservatism's impact abounds, and not simply in the Republican Party's current control of both houses. Thirty years ago, when Moynihan wrote his report on the collapse of black families, liberals branded him a racist and foreclosed discussion of the very subject of black illegitimacy. By 1995, this same Moynihan, ertswhile pariah of the left, cast one of only twelve votes against the Senate's welfare-reform bill. Nearly three-quarters of Democratic senators, including the minority leader, Tom Daschle of South Dakota, and such prominent liberals as Barbara Boxer and Dianne Feinstein of California, joined the GOP in an overwhelming majority.

For another example, one need only recall the Senate Judiciary

Committee's bitter and electrifying hearings in 1991 on the appointment of Clarence Thomas to the Supreme Court. Two Republican senators on the committee, Arlen Specter of Pennsylvania and Alan K. Simpson of Wyoming, were furiously denounced by liberals for their interrogation of Anita Hill, the law professor who had accused Thomas of sexual harassment. Just four years later Specter entered the race for the Republican nomination for president as the only candidate willing to defy the Christian right on such issues as abortion rights and school prayer. By default, yesterday's sexist creep was reincarnated as today's liberal darling. When the acerbic and combative Simpson announced his retirement, the Washington media saluted him as part of a vanishing breed of pragmatic moderates.

Certainly, the ground that presently passes for the congressional middle is emptying fast. As of this writing, thirty-eight members of the House and thirteen senators have announced their retirement, a historical record. The ranks of the departing include such moderates as Bill Bradley of New Jersey, Nancy Landon Kassebaum of Kansas, William S. Cohen of Maine, and Howell T. Heflin of Alabama. This exodus, however, has a clear partisan tilt. Of the forty-nine seats being vacated, thirty-three belong to Democrats. At lower levels of government, a similar hemorrhage has been proceeding since Bill Clinton took office. Nearly 150 Democratic officeholders, from state legislators to judges to mayors, sheriffs, and constables, have switched party.

Even in possession of the White House, then, the Democratic Party acts as a minority in retreat. As Jason DeParle wrote in *The New York Times*, President Clinton has been reduced to fighting "a rear-guard action simply to preserve victories won a generation ago." In an essay entitled "What Became of My Democrats?" the investment banker Felix Rohatyn answered the question thusly:

> . . . it has become a kinder, gentler version of the Republican Party. It no longer stands for a clear set of principles. . . . The Democrats were once a party of ideas—a role now pre-empted by Republicans. I disagree with many of the Republicans' ideas and much of the ideology. But political power will go to the party with ideas.

Political power, to put it another way, is now the Republican Party's to lose. And, ironically, it shows signs of doing exactly that by repeating the mistakes of its antagonists. The GOP climbed back from its humiliation in 1964 largely because the Democratic Party abdicated the center, tying its fortunes to the antiwar movement and the identity politics of feminists and racial minorities. Yet it is now the Republicans, especially the freshman and sophomore members of the House, who appear to be similarly misreading their mandate, allowing Bill Clinton to occupy the middle of the road.

An aphorism attributed to the political consultant Arthur Finkelstein sums up the Republican Party's metamorphosis: "In 1964, I was a Goldwater Republican and everyone called me a loony. In 1995, I was a Goldwater Republican and everyone called me a liberal." The same could be said for Bob Dole, and, in fact, was being said by his opponents for the Republican nomination for president. The skew in the party has left Dole simultaneously protecting his right flank in a primary season dominated by conservative voters and trying to preserve a route back into the center for the general election. This is not simply a temporal problem. Dole's contortions reflect the Republican Party's complicated relationship with the Christian right, the most controversial element in the GOP coalition because of its insistent focus on such social issues as abortion, gay rights, and school prayer.

Again, one cannot miss drawing a parallel to the opposition. Since 1968, Democratic candidates have faced an essential dilemma. In running for Congress and especially in pursuing the presidential nomination, a candidate depends on mobilizing blacks, liberals, or organized labor—the foot soldiers who ring doorbells, man phone banks, and always vote. In presidential elections, though, Democrats suffer from the appearance of being the captive of precisely those special interests. The Christian right, by dint of its passion and organization, presents the Republican Party with the identical conundrum: Can't win with 'em; can't win without 'em.

The conservative movement's weakness for absolutism has already deprived it of several legislative victories. The Republican majority in Congress refused to compromise with the president, even on exceedingly favorable terms, to pass bills reforming welfare and balancing the federal budget. Insisting upon unconditional surrender, the House Republicans twice forced vast portions of the federal government to close rather than pass basic bills on appropriations and the national debt limit. "Shut it down," the most zealous Republicans cried. Yet surely, the Americans who wanted "less government" had never imagined that national parks from the Grand Canyon to the Statue of Liberty might be padlocked in the process.

That miscalculation by the Republicans indicates a larger problem: The party is both the beneficiary and the prisoner of its own rhetoric. In the most memorable phrase of his first inaugural address, Ronald Reagan declared, "Government is not the solution. Government is the problem." Uncoupled from Reagan's person, from his optimism and geniality, the premise has hardened from a skepticism of government into a demonization of government. The moderate American voter may well loathe the tax man, social worker, and GS-18 bureaucrat in the abstract, but he is hardly inclined to physically attack one, or to support those who do.

Yet the ideology of government-as-enemy found its purest expression in the bombing of the federal building in Oklahoma City on April 19, 1995. And while most of the country mourned the 169 victims, some of them children from a day-care center, the most radical Republicans in Congress answered with the same sort of indulgent double-talk that left-wing Democrats had often spouted after race riots and campus violence: Yes, of course, it's a terrible tragedy. But you must understand . . . Under Republican pressure, Congress launched hearings into the FBI's assault on the Branch Davidian compound in Texas, an event embedded in the radical right's martyrology. Two House members, Helen Chenoweth of Idaho and Steve Stockman of Texas, have maintained especially close ties to the militia movement. Even as estimable a figure as the Reverend Pat Robertson—telecommunications executive, former presidential candidate, and Yale Law School graduate—has devoted an entire book to unveiling the conspiratorial forces behind the New World Order.

Thus the conservative movement, at a time of its greatest triumph, faces the same challenge that it did during its wilderness years: How far to the right can a coalition extend without falling off the edge? Can the Republican Party of 1996 maintain its majority in Congress, to say nothing of capturing the White House, while making the single issue of abortion a loyalty test? Dare it court or even accept support from those who participate in or apologize for the armed paranoia of the militia movement?

During the late 1950s and early 1960s, William F. Buckley Jr. campaigned from the pages of *National Review* against the John Birch Society and its founder, Robert Welch. No matter how much the conservative movement gained in commitment from the Birchers, he argued, it lost more in credibility by being associated with those who swore Dwight Eisenhower was a Russian agent. When a reader criticized Buckley for attacking fellow conservatives and giving comfort to the liberal enemy, he responded in a letter that Newt Gingrich, Bob Dole, and Haley Barbour would be wise to remember:

> It was precisely my desire to *strengthen* the ranks of conservatism that led me to publish the editorial. Our movement has got to govern. It has got to expand by bringing into our ranks those people who are,

at the moment, on our immediate left—the moderate, wishy-washy conservatives: the Nixonites . . . I am talking . . . about 20 to 30 million people . . . If they are being asked to join a movement whose leadership believes the drivel of Robert Welch, they will pass by crackpot alley, and will not pause until they feel the warm embrace of those way over on the other side, the Liberals.

Put another way, the Republican Party need not worry about losing the votes of Tim Carey and Leslie Maeby, diehards both. It can assume that Frank Trotta, while disenchanted with the profession of politics, is not about to undergo a conversion experience and begin supporting Democrats. The ability of the Republican Party to win the presidency and hold Congress in 1996 depends less on the vanguard than on the stragglers in the rear, people like Leslie's mother, Vilma, and Tim's mother, Edith. Both lifelong Democrats, the women voted, however begrudgingly, for George Bush in 1988. Four years later, they reverted to habit and helped elect Bill Clinton.

Vilma Maeby and Edith Carey serve as reminders that even after thirty years of growing conservatism the American electorate suffers from a divided soul, an unreconciled heritage. One part of the national psyche, hearing Roosevelt, thinks of government as the WPA; another part, hearing Reagan, thinks of it as welfare. One part votes for less government and lower taxes; another part objects to losing any government program except welfare. What looks like gridlock in Washington may be an accurate representation of the countervailing forces within voters themselves. The budget deficit is nothing but a measure in red ink of the American desire for both social programs *and* lower taxes.

It is conventional to understand modern conservatism as a response to liberalism's failures and excesses. Yet the success of the left, too, enabled the right. Ronald Reagan, in his famous speech on behalf of Barry Goldwater in 1964, appropriated his climactic line about a "rendezvous with destiny" from Franklin Roosevelt. Newt Gingrich, addressing the House on his first day as Speaker, saluted liberal Democrats for having ended racial segregation. Thanks to liberal victories in the past, Social Security and civil rights, once targets for conservatives, nestle easily in the American mainstream. And the welfare state, with its superhighways and insured mortgages, built Colonie, emblem of Republican suburbia.

If any force will resolve the contradictions of that divided soul, it will be time itself. An eighteen-year-old, eligible to vote this November for the first time, has seen Ronald Reagan and Newt Gingrich dominate the political arena. A thirty-year-old was born after the Kennedy presidency and the March on Washington. A fifty-year-old associates government with the Vietnam War and Watergate. The generation that includes Vilma Maeby and Edith Carey is entering its elderliness. And when that generation passes, so will the collective memory of the New Deal, the wellspring for decades of activist liberalism.

S.G.F.
February 8, 1996

Bibliography

Books, Magazine Articles, and Scholarly Publications

Adams, Mildred. "Story of 'The Sidewalks of New York,' " *The New York Times Magazine*, September 9, 1928.

Allen, William H. *Al Smith's Tammany Hall: Champion Political Vampire* (New York: Institute for Public Service, 1928).

Alpen, Sara, et al., eds. *The Challenge of Feminist Biography: Writing the Lives of Modern American Women* (Urbana: University of Illinois Press, 1992).

Alsop, Stewart. "Left-wing Joe Pewism," *Newsweek*, October 25, 1971.

Anderson, John F., and Fred Blumenthal. *The Kefauver Story* (New York: Dial, 1956).

Appy, Christian G. *Working-Class War: American Combat Soldiers and Vietnam* (Chapel Hill: University of North Carolina Press, 1993).

Argersinger, Jo Ann E. "Baltimore: The Depression Years." Ph.D. dissertation, George Washington University, 1980.

———. *Toward a New Deal in Baltimore: People and Government in the Great Depression* (Chapel Hill: University of North Carolina Press, 1988).

Avrich, Paul. *The Haymarket Tragedy* (Princeton: Princeton University Press, 1984).

Baker, Russell. *Growing Up* (New York: Congdon & Weed, 1982).

Barnard, Eunice Fuller. "Governor Smith's 'Kitchen Cabinet,' " *The New York Times Magazine*, September 23, 1928.

Barrett, Wayne. "The Dark Prince of Peekskill," *Village Voice*, October 18, 1994.

Behn, Richard. "The Future of the Republican Party," *Empire State Report*, April 1977.

————, and Frank Trotta, eds. *Finishing First: A Campaign Manual* (New York: Committee to Make New York #1 Again, 1983).

Bellush, Jewel, and Dick Netzer. *Urban Politics New York Style* (Armonk, N.Y.: Sharpe, 1990).

Blakely, Jeffrey A., and John D. Northrip. *World War II Structures at Fort Chaffee, Arkansas* (Little Rock: U.S. Army Corps of Engineers, 1991).

Bloch, Herman D. "Craft Unions and the Negro in Historical Perspective," *The Journal of Negro History,* vol. 43, no. 1. January 1958.

Bloxom, Marguerite D. *Pickaxe and Pencil: References for the Study of the WPA* (Washington, D.C.: Library of Congress, 1982).

Bowly, Devereux, Jr. *The Poorhouse: Subsidized Housing in Chicago, 1895–1976* (Carbondale, Ill.: Southern Illinois University Press, 1978).

Bowman, John. S., ed. *The Vietnam War: An Almanac* (New York: World Almanac Publishing, 1985).

Boyle, Robert H. *The Hudson River: A Natural and Unnatural History* (New York: Norton, 1979).

————. "A Stink of Dead Stripers," *Sports Illustrated,* April 26, 1965.

————. "My Struggle to Help the President," *Sports Illustrated,* February 16, 1970.

Boyle, T. Coraghessan. *World's End* (New York: Viking Penguin, 1987).

Breihan, John R. "Between Munich and Pearl Harbor: The Glenn L. Martin Aircraft Company Gears Up for War, 1938–1941," *Maryland Historical Magazine,* vol. 88, no. 4, Winter 1993.

Brinkley, Alan. "When Mandates Collide." *The New Yorker.* January 29, 1996.

————. *Voices of Protest: Huey Long, Father Coughlin, and the Great Depression* (New York: Knopf, 1982).

Buckley, Tom. "Ottinger: Study of a Quiet Candidate," *The New York Times Magazine,* October 25, 1970.

Burke, Thomas E. "Hungry Men Can't Reason," *Journeymen Plumbers and Steam Fitters Journal,* April 1930.

————. "Labor and the Nation Hard at Work on NRA," *Journeymen Plumbers and Steam Fitters Journal,* September 1933.

Cabrini Extension Area: Portrait of a Chicago Slum (Chicago: Chicago Housing Authority, 1951).

Cannon, Lou. *Reagan* (New York: Putnam's, 1982).

Caro, Robert A. *The Power Broker: Robert Moses and the Fall of New York* (New York: Knopf, 1974).

Church, Stanley. "Foresight in Housing," *The Club Candle,* January 1949.

Cochran, Bert. *Labor and Communism: The Conflict That Shaped American Unions* (Princeton: Princeton University Press, 1977).

Cohen, Jonathan M. "My Word Is My Bond: The Rise and Demise of James H. (Jack) Pollack, Baltimore Boss." Senior thesis, Johns Hopkins University, 1993.

Coleman, Terry. *Passage to America: A History of Emigrants from Great Britain and Ireland to America in the Mid-Nineteenth Century* (London: Hutchison, 1972).

Coleman, Vernon T., Jr. "Labor Power and Social Equality: UAW Politics and Black Workers, 1960–1980." Ph.D. dissertation, UCLA, 1984.

Comprehensive Plan and Program of Public Improvements for the Village and the Town of Ossining, N.Y. (New York: Technical Advisory Corporation, 1930).

Conklin, Paul K. *The New Deal* (New York: Crowell, 1967).

Coontz, Stephanie. *The Way We Never Were: American Families and the Nostalgia Trap* (New York: Basic Books, 1992).

Corrsin, Stephen. "Polish Archival and Manuscript Sources for the Study of the Migration to America," *East European Quarterly,* vol. 17, September 1983.

Corry, John. "The Many-Sided Mr. Meany," *Harper's,* March 1970.

Coughlin, Charles E. *Father Coughlin's Radio Sermons: October 1930–April 1931, Complete* (Baltimore: Knox and O'Leary, 1931).

The Creation of a Forum Program: The New Rochelle Public Library Sponsors a Series of Housing Forums, April–May 1974. May 22, 1947.

Cronin, James M., ed. *Historical Development of Westchester County,* vols. 1 and 2 (White Plains: Westchester County Emergency Work Bureau, 1939).

Cultural Resource Assessment: Naval Submarine Base, Groton, Connecticut (Philadelphia: Northern Division, Naval Facilities Engineering Command, 1992).

D'Alesandro, Thomas L., Jr. *Tommy's Tapes.* (Baltimore: 1976).

DeParle, Jason. "Rant, Listen, Exploit, Learn, Scare, Help, Manipulate, Lead." *The New York Times Magazine.* January 28, 1996.

de Toledano, Ralph. "Joe Rauh's Counterattack," *National Review,* December 20, 1974.

Denfield, D. Colt. "How World War II Bases Were Built Fast—and Good!" *Journal of the Council on America's Military Past,* vol. 18, no. 1, April 1991.

Devane, Brother Austin D. "History of the New Rochelle. Public Schools, 1795–1952." Ph.D. dissertation, Columbia University, 1953.

Devlin, Gerard M. *Silent Wings: The Saga of the U.S. Army and Marine Combat Glider Pilots During World War II* (New York: St. Martin's Press, 1985).

DiPietro, Joseph A. *The History of the Italians of New Rochelle.* New Rochelle: Self-published, 1988.

Dodson, Dan W. *Crisis in the Public Schools: Racial Segregation, Northern Style* (New York: Council for American Unity, 1965).

"Down to the Wire," *Newsweek,* November 2, 1964.

Duberman, Martin Bauml. *Paul Robeson* (New York: Knopf, 1988).

Dubofsky, Melvyn. *The State and Labor in Modern America* (Chapel Hill: University of North Carolina Press, 1994).

Edsall, Thomas Byrne, and Mary D. Edsall. *Chain Reaction: The Impact of Race, Rights, and Taxes on American Politics* (New York: Norton, 1991).

Ehrenreich, Barbara. *Fear of Falling: The Inner Life of the Middle Class* (New York: Pantheon, 1989).

Erie, Steven P. *Rainbow's End: Irish-Americans and the Dilemmas of Urban Machine Politics, 1840–1985* (Berkeley: University of California Press, 1988).

Ethnicity in the Baltimore City Council. University of Baltimore Archives, Local Research Paper Collection, n.d.

Evening the Odds: The Need to Restrict Unfair Incumbent Advantage. New York State Commission on Government Integrity, 1989.

Fanelli, Elizabeth B. "Veterans' Emergency Housing," *The Club Candle,* May 1947.

Farley, John E, "Suburbanization and Central City Crime Rates: New Evidence and a Reinterpretation," *American Journal of Sociology,* vol. 93, no. 3, November 1987.

Fee, Elizabeth, Linda Shopes, and Linda Zeidman, eds. *The Baltimore Book: New Views of Local History* (Philadelphia: Temple University Press, 1991).

Fink, Gary M., ed. *Labor Unions* (Westport, Ct.: Greenwood, 1977).

Flynn, Edward J. *You're the Boss: The Practice of American Politics* (New York: Viking, 1947).

Fontenay, Charles L. *Estes Kefauver: A Biography* (Knoxville: University of Tennessee, 1980).

Ford, Reverend Fred Bennett. "The Housing Authority Goes to Work," *The Club Candle,* April 1941.

Fotheringham, Allan, "Nominating a Hero for 1987," *Maclean's,* January 19, 1987.

Fraser, Steven. *Labor Will Rule: Sidney Hillman and the Rise of American Labor* (New York: Free Press, 1991).

Freeman, Joshua B. *In Transit: The Transport Workers Union in New York City, 1933–1966* (New York: Oxford University Press, 1989).

Fry, Monroe. "Baltimore's Mermaids," *Esquire,* March 1956.

Gallatin, A. "Carter's Economic War Against Free Trade," *New Times,* July 22, 1977.

———. "The Great Food Disaster," *New Times,* December 9, 1977.

———. "Up, Up and Away: The U.S. Debt," *New Times,* December 27, 1977.

Garrett, Oliver H.P. "Profiles: A Certain Person," *The New Yorker,* October 9, 1926.

Germond, Jack W., and Jules Witcover. *Blue Smoke and Mirrors: How Reagan Won and Why Carter Lost the Election of 1980* (New York: Viking, 1981).

"A Giant Step—or a Springtime Skip," *Newsweek,* May 4, 1970.

Gillon, Steven M. *Politics and Vision: The ADA and American Liberalism, 1947–1985* (New York: Oxford University Press, 1987).

Glazer, Nathan, and Daniel P. Moynihan. *Beyond the Melting Pot: The Negroes, Puerto Ricans, Jews, Italians, and Irish of New York City,* 2nd ed. (Cambridge: MIT Press, 1970).

Goldberg, Arthur J. *AFL-CIO: Labor United* (New York: McGraw-Hill, 1956).

Goodman, Walter. *The Committee: The Extraordinary Career of the House Committee on Un-American Activities* (New York: Farrar, Straus & Giroux, 1968).

Gorman, Joseph Bruce. *Kefauver: A Political Biography* (New York: Oxford University Press, 1971).

Goulden, Joseph C. *Meany* (New York: Atheneum, 1972).

Graham, Otis L., Jr., and Meghan Robinson Wander. *Franklin D. Roosevelt, His Life and Times: An Encyclopedic View* (Boston: G. K. Hall, 1985).

Greene, Suzanne Ellery. *An Illustrated History of Baltimore* (Woodland Hills, CA: Windsor Publications, 1980).

Handlin, Oscar. *Al Smith and His America* (Boston: Atlantic Monthly Press, 1958).

Hartley, Robert R. "The Housing Problem in New Rochelle," *The Club Candle,* May 1944.

Hearings Before the Special Committee to Investigate Organized Crime in Interstate Commerce, United States Senate, Part 17 (Washington, D.C.: U.S. Government Printing Office, 1951).

Hill, Herbert. "The New York City Terminal Market Controversy: A Case Study in Race, Labor, and Power," *Humanities in Society,* vol. 6, no. 4, Fall 1983.

Hirsch, Arnold R. *Making the Second Ghetto: Race and Housing in Chicago, 1940–1960* (Cambridge: Cambridge University Press, 1983).

Hodgson, Godfrey. *America in Our Time* (Garden City, N.Y.: Doubleday, 1976).

Hofstadter, Richard. *The Age of Reform: From Bryan to F.D.R.* (New York: Knopf, 1955).

Hoge, Cecil C., Jr. *The First Hundred Years Are the Toughest: What We Can Learn from the Century of Competition Between Sears and Wards* (Berkeley: Ten Speed Press, 1988).

Hollowak, Thomas L. *Baltimore's Polish Language Newspapers: Historical & Genealogical Abstracts, 1891–1925* (Baltimore: Historyk Press, 1992).

———. *Faith, Work, and Struggle: A History of Baltimore Polonia* (Baltimore: Holy Cross Polish National Catholic Church, 1988).

———. "The Rise of Independency Among Baltimore's Roman Catholics." Master's thesis, University of Maryland, 1990.

Hunley, Kathleen Purcell. "From Minority to Majority: A Study of the Democratic Party in Lackawanna County, 1920–1950." Ph.D. dissertation, Lehigh University, 1981.

Hyde, Francis E. *Cunard and the North Atlantic, 1840–1973: A History of Shipping and Financial Management* (London: Macmillan, 1975).

Inventory: An Appraisal of the Results of the Works Progress Administration (Washington, D.C.: U.S. Government Printing Office, 1938).

Jackson, Kenneth T. *Crabgrass Frontier: The Suburbanization of the United States* (New York: Oxford University Press, 1985).

Jacobs, Bradford. *Thimbleriggers: The Law* v. *Governor Marvin Mandel* (Baltimore: Johns Hopkins University Press, 1984).

Judis, John B. "The End of Conservatism," *New Republic,* August 31, 1992.

———. *William F. Buckley, Jr.: Patron Saint of the Conservatives* (New York: Simon & Schuster, 1988).

Kaiser, Charles. *1968 in America: Music, Politics, Chaos, Counterculture, and the Shaping of a Generation* (New York: Weidenfeld & Nicolson, 1988).

Katzman, David M. *Seven Days a Week: Women and Domestic Service in Industrializing America* (London: Oxford University Press, 1978).

Kefauver, Estes. *Crime in America* (Garden City, N.Y.: Doubleday, 1951).

Kennedy, William. *O Albany! Improbable City of Political Wizards, Fearless Ethnics, Spectacular Aristocrats, Splendid Nobodies, and Underrated Scoundrels* (New York: Viking Penguin, 1983).

Kent, Frank R. *The Great Game of Politics* (Garden City, N.Y.: Doubleday, Doran, 1928).

Kessner, Thomas. *Fiorello H. La Guardia and the Making of Modern New York* (New York: McGraw-Hill, 1989).

Kimberley, Charles M. "The Depression in Maryland: The Failure of Voluntarism," *Maryland Historical Magazine,* vol. 70, no. 2, Summer 1975.

Klinkenborg, Verlyn. *The Last Fine Time* (New York: Knopf, 1991).

Kramer, Michael. "All-Star Family Feud," *New York,* June 7, 1982.

———. "Who Is This Guy Lew Lehrman?" *New York,* April 5, 1982.

Ladd, Everett Carll. *American Political Parties: Social Change and Political Response* (New York: Norton, 1970).

———. *Ideology in America: Change and Response in a City, a Suburb, and a Small Town* (Ithaca: Cornell University Press, 1969).

Liddell Hart, B. H. *History of the Second World War* (New York: Putnam, 1971).

Lowden, John L. *Silent Wings at War: Combat Gliders in World War II* (Washington, D.C.: Smithsonian Institution Press, 1992).

Lubell, Samuel. *The Future of American Politics* (New York: Harper & Brothers, 1951).

Lyons, Eugene. "Our New Privileged Class," *American Legion,* September 1951.

Mailer, Norman. *The Armies of the Night: History as a Novel, The Novel as History* (New York: New American Library, 1968).

Mangione, Jerre, and Ben Morreale. *La Storia: Five Centuries of the Italian American Experience* (New York: HarperCollins, 1992).

Markiewicz, Frank. "Baltimore's Polish Colony," *Baltimore Municipal Journal,* September 5, 1929.

McCullough, David. *Truman* (New York: Simon & Schuster, 1992).

McDonald, Marci. "A Crusader's Lonely Fight," *Maclean's,* March 24, 1986.

McDougall, Harold A. *Black Baltimore: A New Theory of Community* (Philadelphia: Temple University Press, 1993).

McElvaine, Robert S. *Mario Cuomo: A Biography* (New York: Scribner, 1988).

McNickle, Chris. *To Be Mayor of New York: Ethnic Politics in the City* (New York: Columbia University Press, 1993).

Miller, James. *"Democracy Is in the Streets": From Port Huron to the Siege of Chicago* (New York: Simon & Schuster, 1987).

Miller, James Nathan. "America the (Formerly) Beautiful," *Reader's Digest,* February 1969.

Mills, Nicolaus. *Like a Holy Crusade: Mississippi 1964—The Turning of the Civil Rights Movement in America* (Chicago: Dees, 1992).

Mitz, Rick. *The Great TV Sitcom Book* (New York: Marek, 1980).

Morgan, Dan. *Rising in the West: The True Story of an "Okie" Family in Search of the American Dream* (New York: Knopf, 1992).

Morrow, Ralph. "The 'Why' of New Rochelle's Model Home Projects," *The Club Candle,* October 1937.

Mullen, William. "The Road to Hell: For Cabrini-Green, It Was Paved with Good Intentions," *Chicago Tribune Magazine,* March 31, 1985.

Neal, Frank. *Sectarian Violence: The Liverpool Experience, 1819–1914; An Aspect of Anglo-Irish History* (Manchester, U.K.: Manchester University Press, 1988).

New York Legislative Record and Index: Regular Session (Albany: Legislative Index Company, 1984).

Orsi, Robert Anthony. *The Madonna of 115th Street: Faith and Community in Italian Harlem, 1880–1950* (New Haven: Yale University Press, 1985).

Perry, Elisabeth. "Why Suffrage for American Women Was Not Enough," *History Today,* September 1993.

Perry, Elisabeth Israels. *Belle Moskowitz: Feminine Politics and the Exercise of Power in the Age of Al Smith* (New York: Oxford University Press, 1987).

Phillips, Kevin P. *The Emerging Republican Majority* (New Rochelle: Arlington House, 1969).

Pilling, Ron. "Removing Formstone & Other Indignities," *The Old-House Journal,* September 1982.

Pocket Data Book Supplement, 1955 (Washington, D.C.: Office of the Comptroller, Department of the Army, 1955).

Polenberg, Richard. *War and Society: The United States, 1941–1945* (Philadelphia: Lippincott, 1972).

Proceedings of the Board of Supervisors of Westchester County, Sessions of 1930–1932 (Mount Vernon, N.Y.: Freybourg).

Proceedings of the Board of Supervisors of Westchester County, Sessions of 1933–1935 (White Plains, N.Y.: Artcraft).

Proceedings of the First Annual Convention, United Association of Journeymen Plumbers, Gas Fitters, Steam Fitters and Steam Fitters' Helpers of the United States and Canada. Pittsburgh: July 28–August 1, 1890.

Proceedings of the First Convention, United Association of Journeymen Plumbers, Gas Fitters, Steam Fitters and Steam Fitters' Helpers of the United States and Canada. Washington, D.C.: October 7–11, 1889.

Rauh, Joseph L., Jr. "Filibuster Forever," *The New Republic,* February 4, 1967.

———. "The McCarthy Era Is Over," *U.S. News & World Report,* August 26, 1955.

Redevelopment of Blighted Residential Areas in Baltimore: Conditions of Blight, Some Remedies and Their Relative Costs. Baltimore Commission on City Plan, 1945.

Reinberg, Linda. *In the Field: The Language of the Vietnam War* (New York: Facts on File, 1991).

Report of the National Advisory Commission on Civil Disorders (New York: Bantam, 1968).

Report of the Westchester County Park Commission. (Albany: Lyon, 1924).

———. (New York: Frederick T. Hitchcock, 1925).

———. (New York: Rand McNally, 1926).

Rieder, Jonathan. *Canarsie: The Jews and Italians of Brooklyn Against Liberalism* (Cambridge: Harvard University Press, 1985).

Rifkin, Bernard, and Susan Rifkin. *American Labor Sourcebook* (New York: McGraw-Hill, 1979).

Ritter, Kurt, and David Henry. *Ronald Reagan: The Great Communicator* (Westport, Ct.: Greenwood, 1992).

Roche, John Patrick. "Social Factors Affecting Cultural, National and Religious Ethnicity: A Study of Suburban Italian-Americans," *Ethnic Groups,* vol. 6, no. 1. Spring 1984.

Roth, Philip. *The Facts: A Novelist's Autobiography* (New York: Farrar, Straus & Giroux, 1988).

Rukert, Norman C. *The Fells Point Story* (Baltimore: Bodine, 1976).

Rusher, William A. "F. Clifton White, RIP: Tribute to the Late Republican Party Leader," *National Review,* February 1, 1993.

———. *The Rise of the Right* (New York: Morrow, 1984).

Sack, Kevin. "The Great Incumbency Machine," *The New York Times Magazine,* September 27, 1992.

Scheips, Paul J., and M. Warner Stark. *Use of Troops in Civil Disturbances Since World War II, Supplement II* (Washington, D.C.: Center for Military History, 1969).

Schlesinger, Arthur M., Jr. *A Thousand Days: John F. Kennedy in the White House* (Boston: Houghton Mifflin, 1965).

———. *The Vital Center: The Politics of Freedom* (Boston: Houghton Mifflin, 1949).

———. "Which Road for the Democrats?" *The Reporter,* January 20, 1953.

———, ed. *History of American Presidential Elections*, vols. I–IV (New York: Chelsea House, 1971).

Schlesinger, Stephen C., and Steven Kinzer. *Bitter Fruit: The Untold Story of the American Coup in Guatemala* (Garden City, N.Y.: Doubleday, 1982).

Schuyler, Montgomery. "Study of a New York Suburb, New Rochelle," *Architectural Record*, April 1909.

Schwartz, Jordan A. *The New Dealers: Power Politics in the Age of Roosevelt* (New York: Knopf, 1993).

Serrin, William. *Homestead: The Glory and Tragedy of an American Steel Town* (New York: Times Books, 1992).

Shabecoff, Philip. *A Fierce Green Fire: The American Environmental Movement* (New York: Hill and Wang, 1993).

Shoumatoff, Alex. *Westchester: Portrait of a County* (New York: Coward, McCann & Geoghegan, 1979).

Skogan, Wesley G. "The Changing Distribution of Big-City Crime: A Multi-City Time-Series Analysis," *Urban Affairs Quarterly*, vol. 13, no. 1, September 1977.

Sleeper, Jim. *The Closest of Strangers: Liberalism and the Politics of Race in New York* (New York: Norton, 1990).

Slovak, Jeffrey S. "City Spending, Suburban Demands and Fiscal Exploitation: A Replication and Extension," *Social Forces*, vol. 64, no. 1, September 1985.

Some Physical and Population Characteristics of Baltimore: An Analysis and Graphic Presentation of Factors to Guide in Sound City Planning and in Dealing with the Menace of Urban Blight. Baltimore: Commission on Governmental Efficiency and Economy, 1943.

Starr, Blaze. *Blaze Starr: My Life as Told to Huey Perry* (New York: Praeger, 1974).

Statistical Abstract of the United States, 1959 (Washington, D.C.: U.S. Department of Commerce, 1959).

Steinem, Gloria. "Misgivings About Ottinger," *New York*, September 21, 1970.

Stern, Robert A.M., Gregory Gilmartin, and John Montague Massengale. *New York 1900: Metropolitan Architecture and Urbanism, 1890–1915* (New York: Rizzoli, 1983).

———. *New York 1930: Architecture and Urbanism Between the Two World Wars* (New York: Rizzoli, 1987).

Stolarik, M. Mark. *Forgotten Doors: The Other Ports of Entry to the United States* (Philadelphia: Balch Institute Press, 1988).

A Survey of Attitudes Toward Government Assisted Moderate and Low Income Housing in Westchester County, New York, vol. II (Bronxville: Quayle, 1972).

Talbot, Allan R. *Power Along the Hudson: The Storm King Case and the Birth of Environmentalism* (New York: Dutton, 1972).

Thomas, William I., and Florian Znaniecki. *The Polish Peasant in Europe and America* (Urbana: University of Illinois Press, 1984).

Tricarico, Donald. "The 'New' Italian-American Ethnicity," *The Journal of Ethnic Studies*, vol. 12, Fall 1984.

Tucker, William. "Environmentalism and the Leisure Class," *Harper's*, December 1977.

Tuttle, William M., Jr. *Daddy's Gone to War: The Second World War in the Lives of America's Children* (New York: Oxford University Press, 1993).

U.S. Department of Commerce. *Age of Foreign-Born White Population by Country of Birth* (Washington, D.C.: U.S. Government Printing Office, 1932).

Unit History: 503d Military Police Battalion, 1967 Supplement (Fort Bragg, N.C.: Department of the Army, 1967).

Viorst, Milton. *Fire in the Streets: America in the 1960s* (New York: Simon & Schuster, 1969).

Waldinger, Roger, and Thomas Bailey. "The Continuing Significance of Race: Racial Conflict and Racial Discrimination in Construction," *Politics and Society*, vol. 19, no. 3, September 1991.

Watkins, T. H. *Righteous Pilgrim: The Life and Times of Harold L. Ickes, 1874–1952* (New York: Holt, 1990).

Webber, Michael John. "The Material Bases of the Democratic Party: Class and Campaign Finance in the 1930's." Ph.D. dissertation, University of California at Santa Cruz, 1990.

Weiss, Robert J. "'We Want Jobs': The History of Affirmative Action." Ph.D. dissertation, New York University, 1985.

Weissman, Ginny, and Coyne Steven Sanders. *The Dick Van Dyke Show: Anatomy of a Classic* (New York: St. Martin's, 1983).

White, F. Clifton, and William J. Gill. *Suite 3505: The Story of the Draft Goldwater Movement* (New Rochelle: Arlington House, 1967).

————. *Why Reagan Won: A Narrative History of the Conservative Movement, 1964–1981* (Chicago: Regnery Gateway, 1981).

————, with Jerome Tuccille. *Politics as a Noble Calling: The Memoirs of F. Clifton White* (Ottawa, Ill.: Jameson, 1995).

White, Theodore H. *The Making of the President 1964* (New York: Atheneum, 1965).

Wordock, John. "Where the Trail Didn't Go: Poverty, the Press, and the 1992 Presidential Campaign." Master's thesis, Columbia University Graduate School of Journalism, 1993.

WPA Guide to New York City (New York: Random House, 1939).

Wtulich, Josephine, ed. *Writing Home: Immigrants in Brazil and the United States, 1890–1891* (Boulder: East European Monographs, 1986).

Zaroulis, Nancy, and Gerald Sullivan. *Who Spoke Up? American Protest Against the War in Vietnam 1963–1975* (Garden City, N.Y.: Doubleday, 1984).

Collected and Uncollected Papers

Administration and Organization—Baltimore City, 1933–1961. Series VI Newspaper Clippings. Commission on Governmental Efficiency and Economy. University of Baltimore Archives.

Annual Reports, 1928–1935. Westchester County Department of Child Welfare. Westchester County Archives, Elmsford, N.Y.

Blight and Redevelopment, 1934–1955. Series VI Newspaper Clippings. Commission on Governmental Efficiency and Economy. University of Baltimore Archives.

General Correspondence. Civil Works Administration, New York State. National Archives, Washington, D.C.

General Correspondence. Local 86, United Association of Journeymen and Apprentices of the Plumbing and Pipe Fitting Industry in the United States and Canada. Mamaroneck, N.Y.

General Correspondence. Public Works Administration, New York State. National Archives, Washington, D.C.

General Correspondence. Works Progress Administration, New York State. National Archives, Washington, D.C.

Minutes, 1946–1969. Parker-Bale Post 1597, American Legion, Ossining, N.Y.

Minutes, 1931–1968. Polish-American Democratic Club of the Second Ward, Baltimore.

Press Clippings, 1924–1926. Westchester County Parks Commission. Westchester County Archives, Elmsford, N.Y.

Rauh, Joseph L., Jr. *Papers.* Library of Congress, Washington, D.C.

Sewing Rooms. Works Progress Administration, New York State. National Archives, Washington, D.C.

Triangle Shirtwaist Factory Fire. Robert F. Wagner Labor Archives. New York University, New York.

White, F. Clifton. *Papers.* John M. Ashbrook Center for Public Affairs, Ashland, Ohio.

Newspapers

Baltimore News American
Baltimore News Post
Baltimore Sun
Chicago Tribune
Citizen Register (Ossining, N.Y.)
Citizen Sentinel (Ossining, N.Y.)
Day (New London, Ct.)
East Baltimore Guide
Gaelic-American (New York)
Irish World (New York)
Jednosc Polonia (Baltimore)
Knickerbocker News (Albany)
New York *Daily News*
New York *Newsday*
New York Post
New York Times
Queens Ledger (Queens, N.Y.)
Ridgewood Times (Queens, N.Y.)
Standard-Star (New Rochelle, N.Y.)
Times-Union (Albany)
Townsman (Colonie, N.Y.)
Wall Street Journal
Washington Post

Oral Histories

Cone, Harold J. Groton Public Library.
Fritsch, Robert and Muriel, Ossining Historical Society.
Maher, Helen. Ossining Historical Society.
Naar, Flora Gee. Ossining Historical Society.
Perkins, Frances. Columbia University Oral History Collection, New York.
Peterson, Roger and Helen. Ossining Historical Society.
Rauh, Joseph L. Civil Rights Documentation Project, Washington, D.C.

————. John F. Kennedy Library, Boston.
————. State Historical Society of Wisconsin, Madison.
White, F. Clifton. John M. Ashbrook Center for Public Affairs, Ashland, Ohio.

Video Sources

CBS Evening News, report on Detroit riot, July 23, 1967.
CBS Evening News, report on Earth Day, April 22, 1970.
CBS Network, unedited "B-roll" of Earth Day, April 22, 1970.
Inside Albany, WMHT, Schenectady, report on Knorr-Santucci race, October 19, 1984.
NBC Network, unedited "B-roll" of antiwar march on the Pentagon, October 21 and 22, 1967.

Acknowledgments

Three days ago, my son Aaron turned four years old. Listening to him sing the songs he has memorized from *Mary Poppins,* watching him paint a bird feeder to be hung in the backyard, I can barely conceive that this book was begun several months before his birth. Since the genesis of *The Inheritance* in January 1992, I have depended on the assistance and indulgence of scores of people. One of the pleasures of completion is having the opportunity to thank them in print, for posterity.

This book could not have been reported and written without the cooperation of three remarkable families, families that prove that history wells up from below. Tim Carey, Leslie Maeby, and Frank Trotta not only granted me their time, thoughts, memories, and memorabilia, but introduced me to their parents and aunts and uncles. Those relatives— Mary Jane Brenc, Lorraine Burigo, Corinne Bush, Edith Carey, Richard Garrett, Jack and Vilma Maeby, Carole Ann Robbins, Frank Trotta Sr., and Marie Witold—made the past live for me. They recounted their own experiences and also those of the deceased grandparents and great-grandparents who animate these pages. I appreciate the patience of the spouses, children, and siblings in these three extended families, who bore my many intrusions with unfailing hospitality and good humor.

And in thanking the families, I must thank the man who led me to the State Street Gang, John Buckley.

This book required me to re-create not only lives but places and times, and so I depended greatly on several historians and archivists, who never tired of my presence and questions. Thomas Hollowak, a historian and archivist at the University of Baltimore, graciously shared his vast knowledge of Baltimore's Polonia and ensured that the appropriate portions of my manuscript were accurate in detail and nuance alike. Roberta Arminio of the Ossining Historical Society uncovered treasures in its collection and helped locate former residents who were vital to my research. The New Rochelle Public Library provided plentiful material from its vertical files.

Charles Robinson, Bob Medina, and Linda Amster afforded me use of *The New York Times*'s clipping files and photographs and let me peruse them unhurriedly. Arthur Browne and Michael Goodwin did the same at the *Daily News*. Milton Hoffman of the Gannett Suburban Newspapers shared both his personal files and extraordinary memory of Westchester County politics, and his colleague Frances Riley extracted essential photographs from the library.

Dan Dondero and Doug Lifrieri of Local 86 allowed me untrammeled access to the local's records. Marion Lee and Patricia Green of the United Association permitted me extensive use of the parent union's materials. Steven Horton opened the files of the New Rochelle Housing Authority, and proved invaluable in locating staff members and tenants from Frank Trotta Sr.'s years at the Hartley Houses. Roger Peterson, rightly nicknamed the Mayor of Crotonville, guided me through records of the neighborhood and its American Legion post. David Roepke of Ashland University shepherded me through the collected papers of F. Clifton White, a major source of insight into the modern conservative movement.

Many politicians, past and present, submitted to extensive interviews and excavated their own scrapbooks, photo albums, and home movies for my benefit. I want to particularly thank Thomas D'Alesandro Jr., James Buckley, Fred Field, Robert Keating, Lewis Lehrman, Cecil Moskowitz, Richard Ottinger, Joseph Pisani, and Edgar Silver. Stanley Church Jr. gave me great assistance in piecing together his father's political life, and Margaret Lavery did so in the case of her late husband, Hugh. Dick Behn supplied me with copies of many documents from the 1982 Lehrman campaign.

At various points during the development of this book, I was fortunate enough to enjoy the assistance of three exceptional researchers— Peter Edelman, Jude Hayes, and Jeff Jones. The finished book has been elevated by their exactitude and alacrity.

For favors too numerous to catalogue I also thank Ty Ahmad-Taylor, Ann Thacher Anderson, Helena Antoniades, Ann Costello, Russell Baker, Bob Boyle, Mike Brewster, David Bryson, Henry Carletti, Sean Carr, Maurice Carroll, Angela Carter, Chris Chivers, Stanley Ciesielski, Edith Cobos, Harry D'Agostino, Daniel DeFrancesco, Daphne Dennis, Jason DeParle, Frank DeRosa, Joe Doyle, George and Joy Dryfoos, Doris Dysinger, Dave Farage, Steve Firgau, Bob Freeman, Jim Fuerst, Angel Fuster, David Garth, Ari Goldman, George Gonzalez, LynNell Hancock, Phyllis Harris, Peg Hashem, Ned Hawkins, Bob Hering, Fred Hoffman, J.J. Hornblass, Ted Humes, John Jarosinski, Wendy Johnson, Lynn Keating, Tom Kelly, William Kennedy, Kathleen Kilmer, Linda Kulman, Pruda Lood, Frank Lynn, Judy Marriott, Mark Matthews, Wayne McCormack, James McManus, Chris McNickle, Edwin Meese III, Frank Mendelson, Nicolaus Mills, Betty Momrow, Andrea Montalbano, Mike Norman, John Northrip, Reverend Thomas O'Meara, W. Edward Orser, Annika Pergament, Bob Pruter, Michael Radutzky, Vinny Reda, Steve Ross, Mike Sager, Wendy Sager, Carl Saliba, Len Savino, John Scally, Mark Schoifet, Jack Schwartz, William Serrin, Dick Shepard, Jim Sleeper, Fraser Smith, David Spiegel, David Teich, Carol Van Rossem, Debbie Vargulick, Marsha Watson, Megan Williams, and John Wordock.

Two deans at the Columbia University Graduate School of Journalism, Steve Isaacs and Margo Amgott, arranged a one-semester leave for me that was absolutely integral to finishing the book. Without that sabbatical, I might still be writing now. The Freedom Forum Journalism Professors Publishing Program gave me a grant that supported vital research and travel.

I am fortunate to exist within a loose network of writers and editors who see each other as comrades, not competitors. Kevin Coyne and Alex Kotlowitz read the manuscript in its entirety, offering valuable criticism along the way, and fielded more anxious phone calls than anyone except a saint or a shrink should ever have to. The political scientist Gerald Pomper of Rutgers and the historian Alan Brinkley of Columbia vetted the manuscript for accuracy in their respective disciplines. Nick Lemann and Tom Watkins each brought a penetrating eye to particular chapters. When the time for intensive editing arrived, I relied greatly on Dick Blood, an old master, and James Kelleher, a young one.

At Simon & Schuster, Alice Mayhew championed this book from the beginning and demanded the very best work I could muster. Elizabeth Stein handled her share of the editing with talent, aplomb, and equanimity. I also want to thank Peter Anderson, Sarah Baker, Lydia Buechler, and Lisa Weisman.

There is no percentage high enough for the roles that my agent,

Barney Karpfinger, played in this book. He is my sounding board, first reader, confessor, and friend.

Two families buoyed me through the duration of this project. My wife, Cynthia, has made our home a safe harbor of support and diversion. After living through three books with me, she surely has earned a place in that particular region of heaven reserved for writers' spouses. My children, Aaron and Sarah, bring delight into every day. My father and stepmother, David and Phyllis Freedman, gave me sanctuary when it was needed, and uncomplainingly accepted my obsessive, preoccupied, downright antisocial self. My sister Carol rescued me several times from computer illiteracy, and my brother Ken gave me use of his radio studio to listen to various campaign tapes. But more than any of that, they provided love and comfort.

From the very outset of this project, I thought back often to the political arguments I joined decades ago in the households of two friends, Jim Lyons and Tim Mulligan. If as a liberal I have been able to inhabit the conservative experience—as it has been my ambition in *The Inheritance*—then I owe my open mind to these childhood companions. And it is one of the satisfactions of my present life to have Tim as both a neighbor and a reader.

Finally, I thank Deborah Kates. In finding her, I not only unlocked a part of the past, but felt for the first time that I might be able to solve the riddle of this book.

S.G.F.
March 8, 1996

Index

and blacks, 165, 287–88, 378–79
and Buckley's victory, 260
and Carey (Tim), 353, 354
childhood/youth of, 260, 265–67,
277-78, 281–85
and class issues, 277–78, 364
college years of, 285–88, 310–11
and Conservative Party, 260
early political activities of, 279–81
and elections of 1970, 261
and elections of 1972, 281–85
and "Honor America Day," 269–72,
284, 355, 379
law career of, 353, 354–56
as Lehrman lawyer, 369, 379
and Lehrman's 1982 campaign, 354,
355, 356–66, 378
marriage of, 311
moves to Greenwich, Connecticut, 379
and New York State Republican Party
platform, 336, 354, 355
and Nixon, 268, 273, 282–84, 290–91
and organized labor, 276, 277
Pisani as mentor for, 278–82, 284–85,
286, 287, 288, 353, 379
and Pisani's indictment/conviction,
363–73
and Reagan, 354–55
and religion, 373–78
and State Street Gang, 310–11, 353
and TAR Camp, 273, 274–76, 281–82,
338
and Vietnam War, 267–68, 269–72
and welfare system, 289–90, 380
and World War II stories, 265–67
Trotta, Frank, Sr., 198, 276, 288
and Buckley campaign, 260
and counterculture, 268
courtship/marriage of, 162
and Democratic politics, 165
and "Honor America Day," 270
janitorial job of, 165–66, 218, 220–25,
228
and Lehrman's 1982 campaign, 357,
364
and liberalism, 199
and race relations, 268
retirement of, 229
Trotta, Lorraine Burigo, 99, 110, 158, 199,
221, 223, 224, 272, 360, 379
birth of, 38
childhood/youth of, 100, 101, 106
and counterculture, 268
courtship/marriage of, 162
and Democratic politics, 162, 163, 165

income of, 288
and Nixon's resignation, 290
and organized labor, 276, 277
and orphans, 290
and public housing, 222
and race relations, 164–65
and religion, 376
as Republican, 260, 276
and Roosevelt's death, 113, 114–15
Silvio's relationship with, 148, 163, 164
telephone company job of, 164–65,
198
Trotta, Paul, 265–67, 272, 286, 359, 375,
379
Trotta, Susan Piening, 311, 356, 363, 365,
373, 377, 378
Truman, Harry S., 161–62, 205–6, 348,
423

Unions. See organized labor; specific
union
United Association of Journeymen
Plumbers and Steam Fitters
and Communism, 102–3, 159
conventions of, 147, 158
and discrimination, 203, 205, 206–8,
210, 217
founding of, 35
and government contracts, 160
insular quality to, 36
and New Deal, 105
as part of AFL, 102
and postwar years, 146
social/economic agenda of, 102, 230
on Truman, 161
See also apprenticeship system
United Auto Workers, 159, 206
Urban renewal, in Chicago, 182–86, 196

Van Riper, George, 330–32, 333, 341, 356,
401
Velella, Guy, 411, 412
Veterans
and education, 191, 329
effects of World War II on, 131, 132–33
and GI Bill, 191
housing for, 149–51, 191, 218
and Potter Club, 330
property-tax deduction for, 385
stories of, 265–67
See also specific organization
Veterans Administration (VA), 191, 192,
195
Veterans of Foreign Wars (VFW), 129,
219, 266, 269, 270